Database Systems

A Pragmatic Approach

■■■

Elvis C. Foster

Shripad Godbole

Apress®

ISBN-13 (pbk): 978-1-4842-0878-6

ISBN-13 (electronic): 978-1-4842-0877-9

Managing Director: Welmoed Spahr
Lead Editor: Jonathan Gennick
Editorial Board: Steve Anglin, Mark Beckner, Gary Cornell, Louise Corrigan, Jim DeWolf, Jonathan Gennick, Robert Hutchinson, Michelle Lowman, James Markham, Matthew Moodie, Jeff Olson, Jeffrey Pepper, Douglas Pundick, Ben Renow-Clarke, Gwenan Spearing, Matt Wade, Steve Weiss
Coordinating Editor: Jill Balzano
Compositor: SPi Global
Indexer: SPi Global
Artist: SPi Global
Cover Designer: Anna Ishchenko

Distributed to the book trade worldwide by Springer Science+Business Media New York, 233 Spring Street, 6th Floor, New York, NY 10013. Phone 1-800-SPRINGER, fax (201) 348-4505, e-mail orders-ny@springer-sbm.com, or visit www.springeronline.com. Apress Media, LLC is a California LLC and the sole member (owner) is Springer Science + Business Media Finance Inc (SSBM Finance Inc). SSBM Finance Inc is a **Delaware** corporation.

For information on translations, please e-mail rights@apress.com, or visit www.apress.com.

Apress and friends of ED books may be purchased in bulk for academic, corporate, or promotional use. eBook versions and licenses are also available for most titles. For more information, reference our Special Bulk Sales–eBook Licensing web page at www.apress.com/bulk-sales.

Any source code or other supplementary material referenced by the author in this text is available to readers at www.apress.com. For detailed information about how to locate your book's source code, go to www.apress.com/source-code/.

This book is dedicated to my late father, Claudius Foster, who taught me the discipline of being a responsible person. The book is also dedicated to my students — past, present, and future. You are the object of my inspiration and motivation; you are the reason for this book.

Contents at a Glance

Contents

About the Authors

 **Elvis C. Foster** is Associate Professor of Computer Science at Keene State College, New Hampshire. He holds a Bachelor of Science (BS.) in Computer Science and Electronics, as well as a Doctor of Philosophy (PhD) in Computer Science (specializing in strategic information systems and database systems) from University of the West Indies, Mona Jamaica. Dr. Foster has over 25 years of combined experience as a software engineer, database expert, information technology executive and consultant, and computer science educator. He has lectured at the higher education level in three different countries, including the United States, and has produced several outstanding computer science and information technology professionals, many of whom have excelled at graduate school as well as in the workplace.

Shripad V. Godbole is an independent database administrator/consultant with over 20 years of experience in diverse business environments, information infrastructure planning, diagnostics, and administration. His qualifications include Bachelor of Science (BS) in Physics, Bachelor of Computer Science (BCS), Master of Science (MS) in Physics with Specialization in Electronics — all from Poona University, Pune, India. He is also an Oracle Certified Professional Database Administrator (OCPDBA), and holds a Master of Business Administration (MBA) in Technology Management from University of Phoenix.

Preface

This book has been compiled with three target groups in mind: The book is best suited for undergraduate students who are pursuing a course in database systems. Graduate students who are pursuing an introductory course in the subject may also find it useful. Finally, practicing software engineers who need a quick reference on database design may find it useful.

The motivation that drove this work was a desire to provide a concise but comprehensive guide to the discipline of database design and management. Having worked in the information technology (IT) and software engineering industries for several years before making a career switch to academia, it has been my observation that many IT professionals and software engineers tend to pay little attention to their database design skills; this is often reflected in the proliferation of software applications with inadequately designed underlying databases. In this text, the discipline of database systems design and management is discussed within the context of a bigger picture — that of software engineering. The student is led to understand from the outset that a database is a critical component of a software system, and that proper database design and management is integral to the success of the software product. Additionally and simultaneously, the student is led to appreciate the huge value of a properly designed database to the success of a business enterprise.

The text draws from lectures notes that have been compiled and tested over several years with outstanding results. They draw on personal experiences gained in industry over the years, as well as the suggestions of various professionals and students. The chapters are organized in a manner that reflects my own approach in lecturing the course, but each chapter may be read on its own.

The text has been prepared specifically to meet three objectives: comprehensive coverage, brevity, and relevance. Comprehensive coverage and brevity often operate as competing goals. In order to achieve both, I have adopted a pragmatic approach that gets straight to the critical issues for each topic, and avoids unnecessary fluff, while using the question of relevance as the balancing force. Additionally, readers should find the following features quite convenient:

- Short paragraphs that express the salient aspects of the subject matter being discussed

- Bullet points or numbers to itemize important things to be remembered

- Diagrams and illustrations to enhance the reader's understanding

- Real-to-life examples

- Introduction of a number of original methodologies for database modeling and design

- Step-by-step, reader-friendly guidelines for solving generic database systems problems

- Each chapter begins with an overview and ends with a summary

- A chapter with sample examination questions (for the student) and case studies (for the student as well as the practitioner)

Organization of the Text

The text is organized in twenty-five (25) chapters, and an additional chapter consisting of sample examination questions and case studies. The chapters are placed into six divisions, with a seventh division for the appendices. The chapters and related divisions are as follows:

Part A: Preliminary Topics

Chapter 1, Introduction to Database Systems, introduces the database system (DBS) as an essential resource in the business organization. It also identifies the objectives and advantages of a DBS.

Chapter 2, The Database System Environment, discusses the environment of a database system. This includes the components, architecture, and personnel.

Part B: The Relational Database Model

Chapter 3, The Relational Model, discusses the fundamentals of the relational model for databases. It provides the foundation for subsequent chapters.

Chapter 4, Integrity Rules and Normalization, builds on chapter 3 to discuss the database normalization and other related topics.

Chapter 5, Database Modeling and Design, builds on chapters 3 and 4, and examines alternate methodologies for modeling and designing a database.

Chapter 6, Database Application Design, summarizes the process of application design and development for a database environment, within the larger context of software engineering.

Chapter 7, Relational Algebra, introduces relational algebra as the foundation for an understanding of databases languages such as Structured Query Language (SQL).

Chapter 8, Relational Calculus, introduces relational calculus as an alternate foundation that is equivalent to relational algebra.

Chapter 9, Relational System — a Closer Look, discusses established benchmarks for relational database management systems.

Part C: Structured Query Language

Chapter 10, Overview of SQL, introduces SQL as the universal database language.

Chapter 11, SQL Definition Statements, discusses the SQL statements that are used for creation and management of objects comprising the database.

Chapter 12, SQL Data Manipulation Statements, discusses SQL statements that facilitation the manipulation of data contained in the database.

Chapter 13, Logical Views and Security, discusses the importance of logical views, and how to create and use them. It also discusses database security, and the various SQL statements that can be used to enforce security constraints in the database.

Chapter 14, The System Catalog, discusses the system catalog as a vital resource of the database that can be used in its management.

Chapter 15, Some Limitations of SQL, discusses some limitations of SQL, and how they can be circumvented.

Part D: Some Commonly Used DBMS Suites

Chapters 16 – 20 provide an overview of some commonly used DBMs suites. This includes Oracle, DB2, Microsoft SQL Server, MySQL, and Delphi.

Part E: Advanced Topics

Chapter 21, Database Administration, provides an overview of database administration. This includes issues such as security, mmanagement, backup and recovery, tuning, among others.

Chapter 22, Distributed Database Systems, discusses the importance of distributed databases, and the challenges of maintaining them.

Chapter 23, Object Databases, discusses the importance of object databases, and the challenges of achieving them.

Chapter 24, Data Warehousing, provides an overview of data warehousing. This includes a discussion of the rationale for data warehousing, characteristic features of a data warehouse, architecture, and construction of a data warehouse.

Chapter 25, Web-Accessible Databases, discusses the relevance, architecture, supporting technologies, and implementation alternatives for Web-accessible databases.

Part F: Final Preparations

Chapter 26, Sample Exercises and Examination Questions is self-explanatory.

Part G: Appendices

Appendix 1, Review of Trees , gives you a chance to review information that you would have covered in your course in data structures. The same is true for appendix 2; Review of Hashing.

Finally, appendix 3, Review of Information Gathering Techniques, pulls some relevant information from the field of software engineering.

Text Usage

The text could be used as a one-semester or two-semester course in database systems, augmented with material from a specific database management system. However, it must be stated that it is highly unlikely that a one-semester course will cover all twenty-five chapters. The preferred scenario therefore is a two-semester course. Below are two suggested schedules for using the text; one assumes a one-semester course; the other assumes a two-semester course. The schedule for a one-semester course is a very aggressive one that assumes adequate preparation on the part of the participants. The schedule for a two-semester course gives the student more time to absorb the material, and also engage in a meaningful project .

One-Semester Schedule:	
Week	Topic
01	Chapters 01 & 02
02	Chapter 03
03	Chapter 04
04	Chapter 04
05	Chapters 05 & 06
06	Chapter 07
08	Chapter 08
08	Chapters 09 & 10
09	Chapter 11
10	Chapter 12
11	Chapter 12
12	Chapters 13 & 14
13	Chapters 15 & 16/17/18/19/20
14	Chapters 21 - 23
15	Chapters 24 & 25
16	Review

Two-Semester Schedule:	
Week	Topic
01	Chapters 01 & 02
02	Chapter 03
03	Chapter 04
04	Chapter 04
05	Chapters 05 & 06
06	Chapter 07
08	Chapter 08
08	Chapters 09 & 10
09	Chapter 11
10	Chapter 12
11	Chapter 12
12	Chapters 13 & 14
13	Chapters 15 & 16
14	Chapters 17 & 18
15	Chapters 19 & 20
16	Review
17	Chapters 21 & 22
18	Chapters 23 & 24
19	Chapter 25
20-21	Review
22-32	Course Project

Approach and Notations

As can be observed, I have employed a principle-then-example approach throughout the course. All principles and theories are first explained, and then clarified by examples. The reason for this approach is that I firmly believe one needs to have a firm grasp of database principles and theories in order to do well as a database designer or administrator. Database design is emphasized as a critical component of good software engineering, as well as the key to successful company databases.

Chapters 8 and 9 discuss relational algebra and relational calculus respectively, as the basis for modern database languages. Then chapters 11-15 cover the salient features of SQL, the universal database language. In these chapters, the BNF notation is extensively used, primarily because of its convenience and brevity, without sacrificing comprehensive coverage.

Feedback and Support

It is hoped that you will have as much fun using this book as I had preparing it. Additional support information can be obtained from the Web site http://www.elcfos.com or http://www.elcfos.net. Also, your comments will be appreciated.

Acknowledgments

My profound gratitude is owed to my wife, Jacqueline, and children Chris-Ann and Rhoden, for putting up with me during the periods of preparation of this text. Also, I must recognize several of my past and current students (from four different institutions and several different countries) who at various stages have encouraged me to publish my notes, and have helped to make it happen. In this regard, I would like to make special mention of Dionne Jackson, Kerron Hislop, Brigid Winter, Sheldon Kennedy, and Ruth Del Rosario.

Special appreciation is offered to my colleague Shripad Godbole, who has coauthored some of the chapters with me, particularly in divisions D and E. Being a practicing database administrator, Shripad has also served as a valuable resource in these areas. And through Shripad, heartfelt gratitude is extended to his wife, Smita, who has given him unwavering support in everything he has done over the years, including his involvement in this project.

I offer a big thank you to Dr. Han Reichgelt at Southern Polytechnic State University, who in many ways has been my professional mentor. As on previous occasions, I have relied on him for critical evaluations and advice. Speaking of critical evaluations, the contribution of my relatively new friend and colleague, Dr. Jared Bruckner at Southern Adventist University was also significant.

The editorial and production teams at Xlibris Corporation deserve mention for their work in facilitating initial publication of the volume. An equally significant level of gratitude is extended to the editorial team at Apress Publishing for recognizing the work's value and for investing the time and effort in the project. Thanks to everyone involved.

Finally, I should also make mention of reviewers Jared Bruckner, Marlon Moncrieffe, Jacob Mangal, Abrams O'Buyonge, and Han Reichgelt, each a practicing software engineer, information technology consult, or computer science professor who has taken time to review the manuscript and provide useful feedback. Thanks, gentlemen.

—Elvis C. Foster, PhD
Keene State College
Keene, New Hampshire, USA

PART A

■ ■ ■

Preliminary Topics

This preliminary division of the course is designed to cover some fundamentals. The objectives are

- to define and provide a rationale for database systems;

- to identify the many objectives, advantages, and desirable features of a database system;

- to discuss the salient features of a database system environment.

The division consists of two chapters:

- Chapter 1 — Introduction to Database Systems

- Chapter 2 — The Database System Environment

CHAPTER 1

■ ■ ■

Introduction to Database Systems

Welcome and congratulations on your entry to this course in database systems. The fact that you are in this course means that you have covered several fundamental topics in programming, data structures, user interface, and software engineering. Now you want to learn about databases — their significance, the underlying theoretical principles that govern them, how they are constructed, and their management. You are at the right place. This chapter addresses the first issue: the significance of database systems.

Topics covered include the following:

- Definition and Rationale
- Objectives of a Database System
- Advantages of a Database System
- Approaches to Database Design
- Desirable Features of a Database System
- Database Development Life Cycle
- Summary and Concluding Remarks

1.1 Definitions and Rationale

A *database system* (DBS) is a computerized record keeping system with the overall purpose of maintaining information and making it available whenever required. The database typically stores related data in a computer system.

A *database management system* (DBMS) is a set of programs that allow for the management of a database. Starting in chapter 2 and extending to subsequent chapters, we will cover several of the critical functions of a DBMS. Some of the more obvious ones are the following:

- Data definition (relation, dependencies, integrity constraints, views, etc.)

- Data manipulation (adding, updating, deleting, retrieving, reorganizing, and aggregating data)

- Data security and integrity checks

- Programming language support

Components of a DBS include:

- Hardware and operating system

- DBMS

- Database

- Related software systems and/or applications

- End users

End users communicate with the software systems/applications, which in turn, communicate (through the programming interface) with the DBMS. The DBMS communicates with the operating system (which in turn communicates with the hardware) to store data in and/or extract data from the database. Figure 1-1 illustrates.

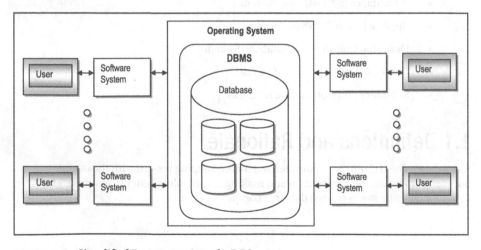

Figure 1-1. *Simplified Representation of a DBS*

Databases are essential to software engineering; many software systems have underlying databases that are constantly accessed, though in a manner that is transparent to the end user. Figure 1-2 provides some examples. Companies that compete in the marketplace need databases to store and manage their mission critical and other essential data.

Software Category	Database Need
Operating Systems	A sophisticated internal database is needed to keep track of various resources of the computer system including external memory locations, internal memory locations, free space management, system files, user files, etc. These resources are accessed and manipulated by active jobs. A job is created when a user logs on to the system, and is related to the user account. This job can in turn create other jobs, thus creating a job hierarchy. When you consider that in a multi-user environment, there may be several users and hundreds to thousands of jobs, as well as other resources, you should appreciate that underlying an operating system is a very complex database that drives the system.
Compilers	Like an operating system, a compiler has to manage and access a complex dynamic database consisting of syntactic components of a program as it is converted from source code to object code.
Information Systems	Information systems all rely on and manipulate internal databases, in order to provide mission critical information for organizations. All categories of information systems are included. Commmon categories include (but are not confined to) decision support systems (DSS), executive information systems (EIS), management information systems (MIS), Web information systems (WIS), enterprise resource planning systems (ERPS), and strategic information systems (SIS).
Expert Systems	At the core of an expert system is a knowledge base containing cognitive data which is accessed and used by an inference engine, to draw conclusions based on input fed to the system.
CAD, CAM and CIM Systems	A computer-aided design (CAD), computer-aided manufacturing (CAM), or computer-integrated manufacturing (CIM) system typically relies on a centralized database (repository) that stores data that is essential to the successful operation of the system.
Desktop Applications	All desktop applications (including hypermedia systems and graphics software) rely on resource databases that provide the facilities that are made available to the user. For example, when you choose to insert a bullet or some other enhancement in a MS Word document, you select this feature from a database containing these features.
CASE and RAD Tools	Like desktop applications, computer-aided software engineering (CASE) tools and rapid application development (RAD) tools rely on complex resource databases to service the user requests and provide the features used.
DBMS Suites	Like CASE & RAD tools, a DBMS also relies on a complex resource databases to service the user requests and provide the features used. Additionally, a DBMS maintains a very sophisticated meta database (called a data dictionary or system catalog) for each user database that is created and managed via the DBMS.

Figure 1-2. *Illustrations of the Importance of Database*

In this course you will learn how to design, implement and manage databases. In so doing, you will be exposed to various database technologies and methodologies that are common in the software engineering industry.

1.2 Objectives of a Database System

There are several primary and secondary objectives of a database system that should concern the computer science (CS) professional. Whether you are planning to design, construct, develop and implement a DBS, or you are simply shopping around for a DBMS, these objectives help you to develop an early appreciation for the field; they should also provide useful insight into where the course is heading. As you will soon see, these objectives are lofty, and it is by no means easy to achieve them all.

The primary objectives of a database system include the following:

- Security and protection — prevention of unauthorized users; protection from inter-process interference

- Reliability — assurance of stable, predictable performance

- Facilitation of multiple users

- Flexibility — the ability to obtain data and effect action via various methods

- Ease of data access and data change

- Accuracy and consistency

- Clarity — standardization of data to avoid ambiguity

- Ability to service unanticipated requests

- Protection of intellectual Investment

- Minimization of data proliferation — new application needs may be met with existing data rather than creating new files and programs

- Availability — data is available to users whenever it is required

Among the significant secondary objectives of a database system are the following:

- Physical data independence — storage hardware and storage techniques are insulated from application programs

- Logical data independence — data items can be added or subtracted or the overall logical structure modified without existing programs being affected

- Control of redundancy

- Integrity controls — range checks and other controls must prevent invalid data from entering the system

- Clear data definition — a data dictionary is usually kept

- Suitably friendly user interface

- Tunability — easy reorganizing the database to improve performance without changing the application programs

- Automatic reorganization of migration to improve performance

Clarification on Data Independence

Data independence is an important concept that needs further clarification: Data independence is the immunity of application programs to changes in structure and access strategy of data. It is necessary for the following reasons:

- Different applications and users will need to have different logical views (interpretation) of data.

- The tuning of the system should not affect the application programs.

Physical data independence implies that the user's view is independent of physical file organization, machine or storage medium. Logical data independence implies that each user (or application program) can have his/her (its) own logical view and does not need a global view of the database.

1.3 Advantages of a Database System

A database system brings a number of advantages to its end users as well as the company that owns it. Some of the advantages are mentioned below:

- Redundancy can be reduced.

- Inconsistencies can be avoided.

- Data can be shared.

- Standards can be enforced.

- Security restrictions can be applied.

- Integrity can be maintained.

- Conflicting requirements can be balanced.

- Improved performance due to speed of processing, reduction in paperwork, etc.

- Maintenance and retrieval of data are very easy — no complicated application program needed.

- Is not solely dependent on the high level language (HLL) programming for use.

- Logical views of data stored can be easily created.

- Record structures can change without any adverse effect on data retrieval (due to data independence).

1.4 Approaches to Database Design

Analysis of the management of data via computerized systems reveals five approaches that have been pursued over the past forty years:

- Instant small system — uses one file

- File processing systems — involve many files

- Other non-relational systems e.g. hierarchical, inverted, and network approaches

- Relational databases (the focus of this course) — pioneered by prominent individuals such as Edgar Codd, Ronald Fagin, Christopher Date, among others

- Object databases — a contemporary approach (also discussed later in the course)

Since the 1970s, relational databases have dominated the field of database systems. With the advancement of object databases (notably since the 1990s), relational databases continue to maintain dominance. Later in the course, you will understand why this dominance is likely to continue. For now, we assert that relational databases will be around for a long time in the foreseeable future, and they will be complemented (rather than challenged) by object databases.

1.5 Desirable Features of a DBS

Contemporary database systems must live up to de facto standards set by the software engineering industry. Roughly speaking, a well-designed database system must exhibit the following features (more specific standards will be discussed later in the course):

- Provide most (at least 70%) of the advantages mentioned earlier

- Meet most (at least 70%) of the objectives mentioned earlier

- Provide for easy communication with other systems

- Be platform independent

- Have a friendly user interface

- Be thoroughly documented

1.6 Database Development Life Cycle

You are no doubt familiar with the software development life cycle (SDLC). For the purpose of review, it is presented in Figure 1-3.

SDLC Phase	Related Deliverable(s)
Investigation & Analysis	Initial System Requirements; Requirements Specification
Design (Modeling)	Design Specification
Development (Construction)	Actual Software; Product Documentation
Implementation	
Management	Enhanced Software; Revised Documentation

Figure 1-3. *Software Development Life Cycle*

As mentioned earlier (section 1.1), databases do not exist in a vacuum, but are usually part of a software system. A *database development life cycle* (DDLC) may therefore be perceived from two perspectives:

- It may be viewed as being identical and concurrent with the SDLC. At each phase in the SDLC, consideration is given to the database as an integral part of the software product.

- If we consider that in many cases, the database has to be constructed and implemented, and managed as a separate resource that various software systems can tap into, then we may construct a similar but different life cycle for the database as illustrated in Figure 1-4.

DDLC Phase	Related Deliverable(s)
Database Investigation & Analysis	Initial Database Requirements
Database Modeling	Database Model
Database Designing	Database Design Specification
Database Development	Actual Database
Implementation	Actual Database in Use
Management	Enhanced Database; Revised Database Design Specification

Figure 1-4. *Database Development Life Cycle*

Note:

1. Applying basic investigation skills that you would have acquired in your software engineering course covers the database investigation and analysis phase. This course assumes that you have acquired those skills. The course therefore concentrates on the other phases.

2. With experience, the database modeling and database designing phases can be merged into one phase. This will be further clarified in chapters 3 through 5.

3. Once the database is in implementation phase, management of it becomes an ongoing experience, until the database becomes irrelevant to the organization.

1.7 Summary and Concluding Remarks

Let us summarize what we have covered in this chapter:

- A database system is a computerized record keeping system with the overall purpose of maintaining information and making it available on demand.

- The DBMS is the software that facilitates creation and administration of the database.

- The DBS is made up of the hardware, the operating system, the DBMS, the actual database, the application programs and the end users.

- There are several primary and secondary objectives of a DBS, which are of importance to the CS professional.

- A DBS brings a number of significant advantages to the business environment.

- There are five approaches to constructing a DBS. Three of them are traditional and are no longer used. The two contemporary approaches are the relational approach and the object-oriented approach. For various reasons, the relational approach is fundamental to a course in database systems.

- In striving to acquire a DBS, it is advisable to aspire for a minimum or 70% of the objectives and advantages. Additionally, one should strive for platform independence, user-friendliness, and thorough documentation.

- The database development life cycle outlines the main activities in the useful life of a DBS.

Interested? We have just begun to touch the surface. There is a lot more to cover. Most successful software systems are characterized by carefully designed databases. In fact, it is safe to say that the efficacy of the software system is a function of its underlying database. So stay tuned: the next chapter provides more clarification on the database environment.

1.8 Review Questions

1. What is a database system?

2. Why are database systems important?

3. What is a database management system (DBMS)?

4. What are the objectives (primary and secondary) of a DBS?

5. What is data independence, and how important is it?

6. What are the advantages of a DBS?

7. What are the possible approaches to acquiring a DBS?

8. How do database systems relate to software engineering?

9. Compare the software development life cycle to the database development life cycle.

1.9 References and/or Recommended Readings

[Connolly, 2002] Connolly, Thomas and Carolyn Begg. *Database Systems: A Practical Approach to Design, Implementation and Management* 3rd ed. New York, NY: Addison-Wesley, 2002. See chapter 1.

[Date, 2004] Date, Christopher J. *Introduction to Database Systems* 8th ed. Menlo Park, CA: Addison-Wesley, 2004. See chapter 1.

[Elmasri, 2007] Elmasri, Ramez and Shamkant B. Navathe. *Fundamentals of Database Systems* 5th ed. Reading, MA: Addison-Wesley, 2007. See chapter 1.

[Garcia-Molina, 2002] Garcia-Molina, Hector, Jeffrey Ullman and Jennifer Widom. *Database Systems: The Complete Book*. Upper Saddle River, NJ: Prentice Hall, 2002. See chapter 1.

[Hoffer, 2007] Hoffer, Jeffrey A., Mary B. Prescott and Fred R. McFadden. *Modern Database Management* 8th ed. Upper Saddle River, NJ: Prentice Hall, 2007. See chapters 1&2.

[Lewis, 2002] Lewis. Phillip M., Arthur Bernstein and Michael Kifer. *Databases and Transaction Processing: An Application Oriented Approach*. New York, NY: Addison-Wesley, 2002. See chapter 1.

[Martin, 1995] Martin, James, and Joe Leben. *Client/Server Databases: Enterprise Computing*. Upper Saddle River, NJ: Prentice Hall, 1995. See chapter 1.

[Pratt, 2002] Pratt, Phillip J. and Joseph J. Adamski. *Concepts of Database Management* 4th ed. Boston, Massachusetts: Course Technology, 2002. See chapter 1.

[Riccardi, 2003] Riccardi, Greg. *Database Management With Web Site Development Applications*. Boston, MA: Addison-Wesley, 2003. See chapter 1.

[Rob, 2007] Rob, Peter and Carlos Coronel. *Database Systems: Design, Implementation & Management* 7th ed. Boston, MA: Course Technology, 2007. See chapter 1.

[Ullman, 1997] Ullman, Jeffrey D., and Jennifer Widom. *A First Course in Database Systems*. Upper Saddle River, New Jersey: Prentice Hall, 1997. See chapter 1.

CHAPTER 2

■ ■ ■

The Database System Environment

This chapter discusses the environment of a database system. Topics covered include:

- Levels of Architecture
- Inter-level Mappings
- Database Administrator
- Database Management System
- Components of the DBMS Suite
- Front-end and Back-end Perspectives
- Database System Architecture
- Summary and Concluding Remarks

2.1 Levels of Architecture

In [Date, 2004], Christopher Date describes three levels of architecture of a database system, namely, the *external level*, the *conceptual level*, and the *internal level*. These levels are illustrated in Figure 2-1; we will briefly discuss each.

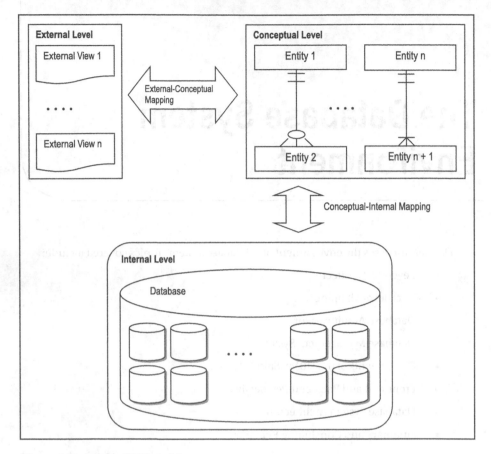

Figure 2-1. *Levels of DBS Architecture*

2.1.1 External Level

The *external level* is concerned with individual user views. It therefore varies according to users' perspectives. The external level is defined by the *external schema*.

Typically, the database is accessed through its external schema. The application programmer uses both the *host language* and the *data sublanguage* (DSL) to create a user interface that end users use to access the system:

- The DSL is the language that is concerned specifically with database objects and operations. To illustrate, SQL (*structured query language*) is the industry's standard DSL. Other examples of data sub-languages are QUEL and KQL (*knowledge query language*). These languages will be further discussed later in the course.

- The host language is that which supports the DSL in addition to other non-database facilities such as manipulation of variables, computations and Boolean logic. Host languages are typically high level languages (HLL); examples include COBOL, C, C++, Java, Pascal, RPG-400, etc.

Typically, the sublanguage consists of a *data definition language* (DDL), a *data manipulation language* (DML), and a *data control language* (DCL). These components are not necessarily distinct entities, but are typically part of a single coherent product.

The above-mentioned facilities allow users to define assorted logical views of data in the database. In summary, the external schema is the user interpretation of the database, but facilitated by the DSL.

2.1.2 Conceptual Level

The *conceptual level* is an abstract representation of the entire information content of the database; it also referred to as the logical or community user view. It is defined by means of the *conceptual schema*, which includes definition of each of the various types of conceptual records.

The conceptual schema includes defining the structure of the database, security constraints, operational constraints and integrity checks. It represents a closer picture of how data will be actually stored and managed, and is the level that most technical user will relate.

The conceptual schema must adhere to the data independence requirement. Also, it must be comprehensive since it represents the realization of the entire database design.

2.1.3 Internal Level

Also called the *storage view*, the *internal level* is the low level representation of the database. It is one level above the physical level, which deals with pages, cylinders and tracks on the storage device.

The internal level is defined by the *internal schema*, which addresses issues such as record types, indexes, field representation, physical storage sequence of records, data access, etc., and written in the internal DDL.

2.2 Inter-level Mappings

Continuing from the previous section, the literature also describes two levels of mappings that connect the three schemas (again, see [Date, 2004]). Figure 2-1 illustrates the different schemas and their interrelationships with respect to the DBMS. From the figure, observe that there are two levels of mapping — the *external-conceptual* mapping and the *conceptual-internal* mapping:

- The conceptual-internal mapping specifies how conceptual records are represented at the internal level. If changes are made at the internal level, this mapping must be updated. Traditionally, the *database administrator* (DBA) maintains this mapping in order to preserve data independence (the DBA is discussed in the next section). In contemporary systems, the DBMS automatically updates and maintains this mapping, transparent to the user.

- The external-conceptual mapping specifies how external views are linked to the conceptual level. In effect, this is achieved by application programs and logical views via the host language and the DSL.

It must be borne in mind that these levels are abstractions that facilitate understanding of the DBS environment. As an end user, you will most likely not visibly observe these levels of architecture. However, if as a software engineer, you find yourself on a software engineering team that is constructing or maintaining a DBMS (a huge undertaking), knowledge of these abstractions becomes critical.

2.3 The Database Administrator

The database administrator (DBA) has overall responsibility for the control of the system at the technical level. Some of the functions of the DBA include:

- Defining the conceptual schema (i.e. logical database design)

- Defining the internal schema (i.e. physical database design)

- Liaising with users and identifying / defining views to facilitate the external schema

- Defining security and integrity checks

- Defining backup and recovery procedures

- Monitoring performance and responding to changing requirements

In many organizations, the tendency is to include these functions in the job description of the software engineer. This is quite rational and prudent, since good software engineering includes good database design. However, large corporations that rely on company database(s) on an on-going basis, usually employ the services of one or more DBAs. Because of the importance of having reliable databases, DBAs are among the highest paid information technology (IT) professionals.

2.4 The Database Management System

The database management system (DBMS) is the software that facilitates management of the database. When a user issues a request via some DSL (for example SQL), it is the DBMS that interprets the request, executes the appropriate instructions and responds to the user.

Functions of the DBMS include the following:

- Data definition (relation, dependencies, integrity constraints, views, etc.)

- Data manipulation (adding, updating, deleting, retrieving, reorganizing, and aggregating data)

- Data security and integrity checks

- Management of data access (including query optimization), data recovery and concurrency

- Maintenance of a user-accessible system catalog (data dictionary)

- Support of miscellaneous non-database functions (e.g. utilities such as copy)

- Programming language support

- Transaction management (either all updates are made or none is made)

- Backup and recovery services

- Communication support (allow the DBMS to integrate with underlying communications software)

- Support for interoperability including open database connectivity (ODBC), Java database connectivity (JDBC), and other related issues

Optimum efficiency and performance are the hallmarks of a good DBMS. To illustrate the critical role of the DBMS, consider the steps involved when an application program accesses the database:

1. **Program-A** issues a request to the DBMS (expressed in terms of sub-schema language);

2. DBMS looks at **Program-A** sub-schema, schema and physical description (these information are stored in tables);

3. DBMS determines which files must be accessed, which records are needed and how access is done;

4. DBMS issues instruction(s) (reads or writes) to the operating system;

5. Operating system causes data transfer between disk storage and main memory;

6. DBMS issues moves to transfer required fields;

7. DBMS returns control to **Program-A** (possibly with a completion code).

Figure 2-2 provides a graphic representation, but bear in mind that these steps are carried out automatically, in a manner that is transparent to the user.

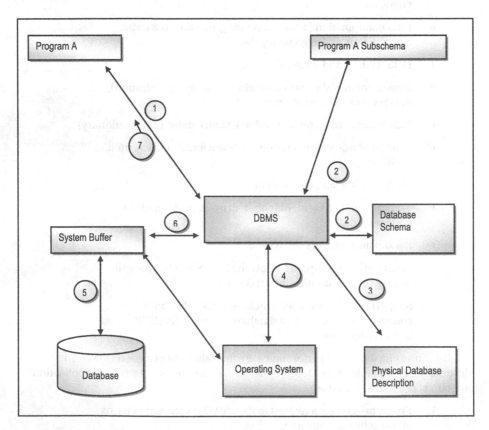

Figure 2-2. *Steps Involved When Application Programs Access a Database*

2.5 Components of DBMS Suite

The DBMS is actually a complex conglomeration of software components working together for a set of common objectives. For the purpose of illustration, we may represent the essential components of the DBMS as the following:

- DBMS Engine

- Data Definition Subsystem

- User Interface Subsystem

- Application Development Subsystem

- Data Administration Subsystem

- Data Dictionary Subsystem

- Data Communications Manager

- Utilities Subsystem

These functional components (illustrated in Figure 2-3) are not necessarily tangibly identifiable, but they exist to ensure the acceptable performance of the DBMS.

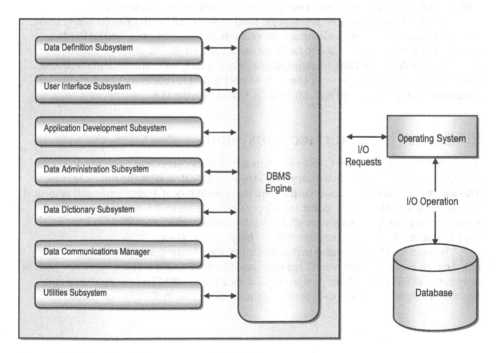

Figure 2-3. Functional Components of a DBMS

2.5.1 The DBMS Engine

The *DBMS engine* is the link between all other subsystems and the physical device (the computer) via the operating system. Some important functions are as follows:

- Provision of direct access to operating system utilities and programs (e.g. I/O requests, data compaction requests, communication requests etc.)

- Management of file access (and data management) via the operating system

- Management of data transfer between memory and the system buffer(s) in order to effect user requests

- Maintenance of overhead data and metadata stored in the data dictionary (system catalog)

2.5.2 Definition Tools Subsystem

The *data definition subsystem* (DDS or its equivalent) consists of tools and utilities for defining and changing the structure of the database. The structure includes relational tables, relationships, constraints, user profiles, overhead data structures, etc.

The DDL (data definition language) is used to define all database objects that make up the conceptual schema (relations, relationships, constraints, etc.). The DML (data manipulation language) is used to facilitate manipulation (insert, remove, update, find, query etc.) of data. The DML usually includes a query language. The DCL (data control language) is used to set up control environments for data management by the end user. As mentioned earlier, the DDL, DML and DCL comprise the DSL.

2.5.3 The User Interface Subsystem

The *user interface subsystem* (UIS or its equivalent) allows users and programs to access the database via an interactive query language such as SQL and/or the host language. The traditional interface is command based; however in recent times menus and graphical user interfaces (GUI) have become more prevalent. Of course, it is not uncommon for a product to provide the user with all three interfaces (for example Oracle). Other more sophisticated DBMS suites may use *natural language* interface.

The user interface may also include a DBMS-specific programming language (e.g. FoxPro, Scalable Application Language, and Oracle's PL/SQL). These languages pertain only to the DBMS in which they are used. Additionally, the DBMS may support multiple high level languages such as C++, Java, etc., thus making it more flexible and marketable.

As an example, suppose that a file, **Student** has fields {ID#, SName, FName, Status, DOB,...}for each record.
Two possible SQL queries could be:

SELECT ID#, SNAME, FNAME FROM STUDENT WHERE SNAME = "BELL";

SELECT ID#, SNAME, DOB FROM STUDENT WHERE DOB >= 19660101;

A more detailed study of SQL will be covered later in the course.

2.5.4 Application Development Subsystem

The *application development subsystem* (ADS or its equivalent) contains tools for
developing application components such as forms, reports, and menus. In some cases,
it may be merged with the user interface subsystem. Typically, this subsystem provides a
graphical user interface (GUI), which is superimposed on an underlying host language.
The suite may include an automatic code generator (as in Delphi and Team Developer),
or seamless access of the compiler of the host language (as in Oracle).

Other facilities that may be included such as:

- Report writer

- Project manager

- Menu builder

- Graphic data interpreter

2.5.5 Data Administration Subsystem

The *data administration subsystem* (DAS) consists of a collection of utilities that facilitate
effective management of the database. Included in this subsystem are facilities for backup
and recovery, database tuning, and storage management. It is typically used by DBAs as
well as software engineers.

2.5.6 Data Dictionary Subsystem

Also called the *system catalog* in many systems, the *data dictionary* (DD) contains
information on the database structure as well relationships among database objects. It is
automatically created and maintained by the DBMS.

The system catalog contains all metadata for the database. It can be queried using
the same commands used to manipulate source data; it is therefore of inestimable value
to the DBAs and software engineers. More will be said about the system catalog later in
the course.

2.5.7 Data Communications Manager

Traditionally, a separate system that is linked to the DBMS, the *data communications manager* (DCM) caries out functions such as:

- Handling communication to remote users in a distributed environment

- Handling messages to and from the DBMS

- Communication with other DBMS suites

Modern systems tend to have this subsystem as an integral part of the DBMS suite. In short, the data communications manager ensures that the database communicates effectively with all client requests in a client-server-based environment. Typically, the server-based portions of the DBMS will be running on machines designated as servers in the network. All other nodes are then deemed as client nodes that can request database services from a server. There may be several database servers in the network; also, a node may act as both a server and a client (provided the essential software components are in place).

2.5.8 Utilities Subsystem

Utilities are programs that perform various administrative tasks. The *utilities subsystem* consists of various utility programs that are applicable to the database environment. Examples of utilities are as follows:

- Load routines to create initial version of a database from non-database files

- Copy routines for duplicating information

- Reorganization routines to reorganize data in the database

- File deletion routine(s)

- Statistics routines to compute and store file statistics

- Backup and recovery utilities

- Other utilities (that might have been) developed by application programmers

2.6 The Front-end and Back-end Perspectives

A DBS can be perceived as a simple two-part structure:

- The Front-end consists of end users, applications and a programming interface.

- The Back-end consists of the actual DBMS and the database.

The front-end system may be on a different machine from the back-end system and the two connected by a communication network. For example, we may have a front-end system in Delphi or Java NetBeans, and a back-end system in Oracle, Sybase, MySQL, or DB2. Figure 2-4 illustrates.

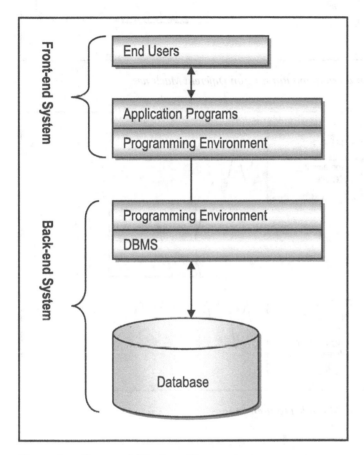

Figure 2-4. *Front-end / Back-end Perspective*

2.7 Database System Architecture

There may be added benefits of using different machines for the back-end and front-end system. Figures 2-5 – 2-7 show three possible configurations. Please note also that various network topologies are applicable to any computer network (network topology is outside of the scope of this course; however, it is assumed that you are familiar with such information).

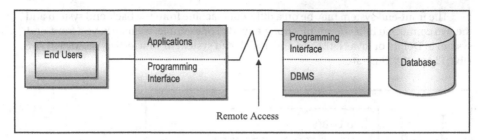

Figure 2-5. *Back-end and Front-end Running on Different Machines*

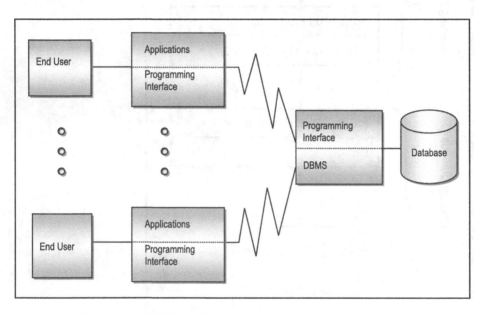

Figure 2-6. *One Back-end, Multiple Front-ends*

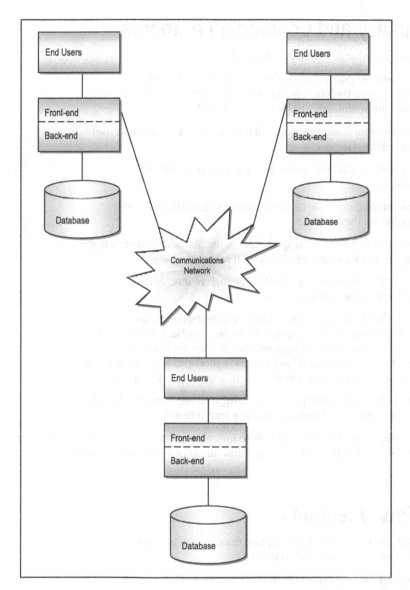

Figure 2-7. *Distributed System Where Each Machine has both Front-end and Back-end*

Discuss: What are some of the advantages of using distributive processing in a DBS environment?

2.8 Summary and Concluding Remarks

Here is a summary of what has been covered in this chapter:

- A database system can be construed as having three levels of architecture: the external, the conceptual and the internal. These levels are seamlessly interlinked by the DBMS.

- The external level constitutes all the external views that end users have of the database.

- The conceptual level relates to the logical structure of the database.

- The internal level relates to the physical structure of the files making up the database.

- The DBA is the official responsible for the planning, construction, Implementation and administration of the database.

- The DBMS is the software that facilitates creation and administration of the database.

- A database system can be construed as being comprised of a front-end system and a back-end system. The back-end system relates to the actual creation and administration of the database. The front-end system relates to the creation and administration of the user interface through which end users access the system.

- By applying the principle of separating front-end from back-end, we can conceive of various database architectures.

With this background, we are now ready to move ahead and learn more about the relational database model. You will learn the foundations of the model, and why it is so important.

2.9 Review Questions

1. With the use of a diagram, explain the different levels of architecture of a database system.

2. Explain the acronyms DSL, DML, DCL, and DDL. How are they all related?

3. What are the primary functions of the DBA?

4. What are the main functions of the DBMS?

5. With the aid of an appropriate diagram, explain how the DBMS ensures that requests from end-users are satisfactorily addressed.

6. Discuss the functional components of a DBMS. Use an appropriate diagram to illustrate.

7. Explain the concept of front-end and back-end systems, and show how they add flexibility to the implementation of distributed database systems.

2.10 References and/or Recommended Readings

[Connolly, 2002] Connolly, Thomas and Carolyn Begg. *Database Systems: A Practical Approach to Design, Implementation and Management* 3rd ed. New York, NY: Addison-Wesley, 2002. See chapter 2.

[Date, 2004] Date, Christopher J. *Introduction to Database Systems* 8h ed. Menlo Park, CA: Addison-Wesley, 2004. See chapter 2.

[Elmasri, 2007] Elmasri, Ramez and Shamkanf B. Navathe. *Fundamentals of Database Systems* 4th ed. Reading, MA: Addison-Wesley, 2004. See chapter 2.

[Garcia-Molina, 2002] Garcia-Molina, Hector, Jeffrey Ullman and Jennifer Widom. *Database Systems: The Complete Book.* Upper Saddle River, NJ: Prentice Hall, 2002. See chapter 1.

[Hoffer, 2007] Hoffer, Jeffrey A., Mary B. Prescott and Fred R. McFadden. *Modern Database Management* 8th ed. Upper Saddle River, NJ: Prentice Hall, 2007. See chapters 1&2.

[Martin, 1995] Martin, James, and Joe Leben. *Client/Server Databases: Enterprise Computing.* Upper Saddle River, NJ: Prentice Hall, 1995. See chapter 2.

[Rob, 2007] Rob, Peter and Carlos Coronel. *Database Systems: Design, Implementation & Management* 5th ed. Boston, MA: Course Technology, 2002. See chapter 1.

[Ullman, 1997] Ullman, Jeffrey D., and Jennifer Widom. *A First Course in Database Systems.* Upper Saddle River, NJ: Prentice Hall, 1997. See chapter 1.

PART B

■ ■ ■

The Relational Database Model

The next seven chapters will focus on the relational database model. As pointed out in chapter 1, there are other approaches to database design, but the relational model reigns supreme: it is superior to other traditional approaches; it remains a strong, viable alternative to or complement of (depending on your perspective) the more contemporary object-oriented model. Even if your choice is to construct an object database, a working knowledge of the relational model will still be required. For these and other reasons, mastery of the relational model is essential to good database administration and software engineering. The objectives of this division are

- to clearly define, describe and discuss the relational database model;

- to discuss how databases are planned, represented and implemented;

- to discuss the theory, rationale, and practical ramifications of normalization;

- to discuss important database integrity rules;

- to discuss relational algebra and relational calculus as the foundations to modern database languages;

- to discuss the standards to which database management systems ought to attain.

Chapters to be covered include:

- Chapter 3 — The Relational Model
- Chapter 4 — Integrity Rules & Normalization
- Chapter 5 — Database Modeling and Design
- Chapter 6 — Database User Interface Design
- Chapter 7 — Relational Algebra
- Chapter 8 — Relational Calculus
- Chapter 9 — Relational System — a Closer Look

CHAPTER 3

■ ■ ■

The Relational Model

This chapter introduces you to the fundamental principles and concepts upon which subsequent chapters will be built. Discussion advances under the following captions:

- Basic Concepts

- Domains

- Relations

- Relational Database System

- Identifying, Representing and Implementing Relationships

- Relation-Attributes List and Relationship List

- Non-relational Approaches

- Summary and Concluding Remarks

3.1 Basic Concepts

The relational model is by far the most widely used model for database design. The model owes its success to the fact that it is firmly founded on mathematical principles (set theory and linear algebra) which have been tested and proven; like the underlying principles, the model itself has been tested and proven oven the years. Before we can proceed, there are some fundamental concepts to be introduced (Figure 3-1):

Entity: An object, concept or thing about which data is stored. Examples include **PurchaseOrder, Person, Course, Department, Program, Student**. Entities are implemented as two-dimensional tables and ultimately files.

Attributes: Some qualities associated with the entity; e.g. **Order#, OrderDate** and **Item#** of entity **PurchaseOrder;** **Dept#** & **DeptName** of entity **Department.** Two synonymous terms for attributes are *elements* and *properties* ; they correspond to columns of a table and are ultimately implemented as fields of a record.

Entity Set: A set of related entities.

Relationship: An inherent mapping involving two or more entities. Relationships are represented in *relations.*

Relation: A two-dimensional (tabular) representation of entities and relationships. A binary relation contains two attributes; an *n*-ary relation contains n attributes. A binary relationship involves an association between two entities; an n-ary relationship involves an association among n entities. For a more formal definition, see section 3.3.

Tuples: Correspond to rows of the table, or records of a file.

Primary Key: An attribute or combination of attributes for which values uniquely identify tuples in the relation. The primary key is chosen from a set of *candidate keys.*

Candidate Keys: There may be more than one potential keys of a relation. Each is called a candidate key.

Alternate Key: A candidate key that is not the primary key.

Foreign Key: An attribute (or combination of attributes) that is primary key in another relation.

Domain: A pool of all legal values from which actual attribute values are drawn.

Cardinality: Number of tuples in a relation. The cardinality varies with time.

Degree: Number of attributes in a relation; also called the *arity.* Degree is also used to describe the number of entities implied by a relationship.

Figure 3-1. Basic Concepts

Figure 3-2 provides a list of commonly used relational terms and their informal equivalents:

Formal Relational Term	Informal Equivalents
Entity	Object conceptualized as a table, implemented as a file
Relation	As for entity
Tuple	Conceptualized as a row, implemented as a record
Attribute	Conceptualized as a column, implemented as a field
Cardinality	Conceptualized as the number of rows
Degree	Conceptualized as the number of columns
Domain	Conceptualized as a pool of legal values

Figure 3-2. Relational Terms and their Informal Equivalents

Figure 3-3 illustrates how the terms are applied. Observe that the idea of *entity* and *relation* seem to be similar. This will be clarified later. For now, assume that similarity.

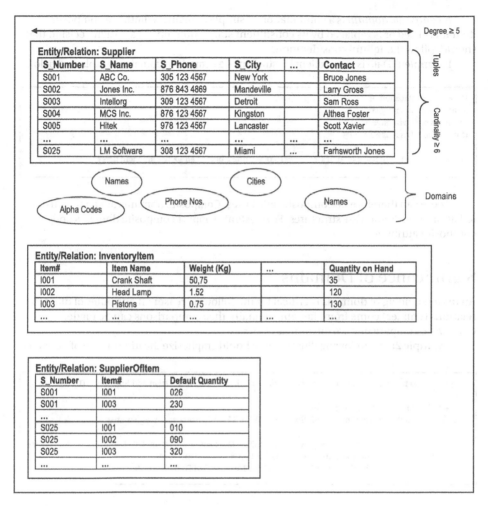

Figure 3-3. *Illustrating Basic Terms*

3.2 Domains

A domain is a named set of *scalar values* from which attribute values are drawn. Scalar values are non-decomposable (atomic) values.

Each attribute of a relation must be defined on an underlying domain. The attribute values must come from the underlying domain (as illustrated in Figure 3-3).

Domains are conceptual; they may not be (and usually are not) actually stored in the database. Rather, the subsets of the domains containing actual attribute values are stored. Domains are analogous to data types in high level programming languages such as Pascal, C++, Java, etc.

33

A *composite domain* is a combination of simple domains. Whether a composite domain is used or is replaced by its constituent simple domains, is a design decision that should follow thoughtful consideration.

Example 1: Date is an excellent illustration of a composite domain, as explained below:

Date is a combination of
Year which has range 0 .. 9999
Month which has range 1 .. 12
Day which has range 1 .. 31

This domain therefore has a total of 12 * 31 * 10,000 values, but not all values are valid dates.

There can therefore be composite attributes. Composite domains are analogous to Pascal records and C++ structures. Few systems support composite domains and composite attributes.

Significance of Domains

An understanding of domains is critical for the following reason: If attributes of different relations (entities) come from the same domain, then comparisons can be made; otherwise, comparisons are meaningless.

Example 2: The following illustrations should emphasize the importance of domains:

// Referring to figure 3.3 and using SQL statements on relations **InventoryItem** and **SupplierOfItem**:

// The following SQL statement is valid:
SELECT * FROM SupplierOfItems SI, Supplier S WHERE SI.S_Number = S.S_Number;

/* The following SQL statement is not a valid SQL statement since attempt is being made to compare attributes (**Weight** and **DefaultQuantity**) defined on different domains:*/
SELECT * FROM SupplierOfItems SI, InventoryItem I WHERE SI.DefaultQuantitty = I.Weight;

3.3 Relations

A relation R on a collection of domains D1, D2, ... Dn (not necessarily distinct) consists of two parts — a *heading* and a *body*.

The heading consists of a fixed set of attributes, or more precisely, attribute-domain pairs,

$$\{(A1:D1), (A2:D2), \ldots (An:Dn)\}$$

such that each attribute corresponds to exactly one domain and n is the degree of the relation. Another term used to describe the heading of a relation is the *predicate* of the relation.

The body consists of a time-varying set of tuples where each tuple consists of a set of attribute-value pairs

$$\{(A1{:}Vi1), (A2{:}Vi2), \ldots (An{:}Vin)\} \ (i = 1 \ldots m)$$

where m is the number of tuples *(cardinality)* in the set. The body of the relation is also sometimes referred to as the *proposition* of the relation. The proposition defines a set of tuples whereby for each row in the relation, the respective attributes take on legal values from their respective domains.

Observe that the definition of a relation appears to be similar to that of an entity. There are two subtle differences:

- The term *relation* as used, belongs to the field of relational systems. We talk about relations because we are discussing the relational model. Entities on the other hand, describe identifiable objects and/or situations.

- *Entity*, as defined does not account for relationships. Relation on the other hand, accounts for entities as well as relationships. Thus in the relational model, we represent entities as relations and (M:M) relationships (between entities) as relations. A binary relation for instance, has two attributes. If both attributes are foreign keys and they both constitute the primary key, this binary relation actually represents a *many-to-many relationship* between two referenced relations; otherwise it is (a relation that can be construed as) an entity. This point will become clear as we proceed.

The foregoing underscores the point that entities can be construed as special kinds of relations. In designing a database, the software engineer or database designer commences by identifying entities during the requirements specification. After further analysis, these entities are eventually implemented by normalized relations.

Note: A unary relation differs from a domain in the sense that former is dynamic and the latter static.

3.3.1 Properties of a Relation

Based on the relational model, all relations have the following properties:

- No duplicate tuples (records)

- Records are unordered

- Attributes are unordered

- Attribute values are atomic

The first and last properties are constraints that both end users and software engineers should be cognizant of, since they have to manage data contained in the database; they are also of interest to the database designer. The second and third properties on the surface are immaterial to end users as well as software engineers; they are usually enforced by the DBMS in a manner that is transparent to the end user. However, when the DBMS is written, concern has to be given to accessing of records. Further, DBMS suites are typically written to give the illusion that the attributes of a relation are ordered.

3.3.2 Kinds of Relations

A database will consist of various types of relations, some of them at different stages of the system. The common categories of relations are mentioned below:

1. **Base Relations** are named and permanently represented in the database. They make up the conceptual schema of the database; they form the foundation of the database.

2. **Views** (virtual relations) are derived from named (base) relations. A view stores the definition of the virtual relation (derived from base relations), but stores no physical data. It is simply a logical (conceptual/external) interpretation of data stored in base relations. SQL views and System i logical files are good examples of views.

3. **Snapshots** are named, derived relations. They differ from logical views in that they are represented in terms of definition as well as physically stored data. From the perspective of the end user, a snapshot relation is typically (but not necessarily) read-only. To illustrate, consider two systems — System-A and System-B — which both need to access a database table, Table-X. Suppose that System-A has update rights to Table-X, but System-B does not. Table-X is therefore stored in System-A's database; a duplicate version for read-only purposes, is stored in System-B, and is periodically updated (without user interference) from System-A.

4. **Query Results:** Queries are typically entered at a command prompt (they may be also embedded in high level language programs or stored in special query files). Results may be directed to screen, printer, or a named relation. An important principle to note is that a query when executed always results in a new relation. This principle will be elucidated later in the course.

5. **Intermediate Results:** The DBMS may create an intermediate relation to assist in furnishing a final answer to a complex query request. This will also be elucidated later in the course.

6. **Temporary Relations** are named relations that are destroyed at some point in time.

3.4 Relational Database System

A *relational database system* (RDBS) is a collection of time-varying *normalized relations*, managed through an appropriate user interface, and with desirable constraints and features that enhance the effective, efficient management of the database. These desirable features and constraints will be discussed (see chapter 9) as we progress through the course. The term *normalized relations* will be fully clarified in chapter 4; for now, just consider it to mean that the relations are designed to promote efficiency and accessibility.

The relations are conceptualized as tables and ultimately implemented as files. Each relation contains one and only one record type. Each relation has a primary key (chosen from a set of candidate keys). In many cases, the primary key is obvious and can be identified intuitively. In situations where this is not the case, the database designer, based on principles to be discussed in the next chapter, typically takes decision about the primary key.

Each record type is made up of *atomic attributes*. This means that each attribute is defined on a single domain, and can only have a value from that domain. Moreover, when data is loaded into the database, each record from any given table has a unique primary key value.

Superimposed on the database is a user interface that facilitates access of the database by end users. The database and the user interface are designed to ensure that certain objectives are met (section 1.2) and established standards are conformed to.

Steps in Building a Relational Database System

In constructing a RDBS, the following steps may be pursued:

a. Identify entities

b. Identify relationships

c. Eliminate unnecessary relationships

d. Develop *entity-relationship diagram* (ERD), *object-relationship diagram* (ORD) or some equivalent model

e. Normalize the database

f. Revise E-R diagram, O-R diagram, or the equivalent model used

g. Design the user interface

h. Proceed to development phase

Note that these steps are to be pursued within the context of a software engineering project. Accordingly, this course assumes that the reader is familiar with steps a-d, and h. The rest of this chapter will review steps b-d, while providing some (additional) insights probably not covered in your (introductory) software engineering course. Chapters 4 and 5 will focus on steps e and f; step g is covered in chapter 6, and step h is covered in chapters 10–14.

3.5 Identifying, Representing, and Implementing Relationships

As mentioned earlier, a relationship is an inherent mapping involving two or more relations. In planning a relational database, it is very important to know how to identify and represent relationships. Of course, the ultimate objective is successful implementation of the model. Let us take some time to discuss these issues:

3.5.1 Identifying Relationships

To identify relationships, you have to know what a relationship is (review section 3.1) and what types of relationships there are. There are six types of relationships:

- One-to-one (1:1) Relationship

- One-to-many (1:M) Relationship

- Many-to-one (M:1) Relationship

- Many-to-many (M:M) Relationship

- Component Relationship

- Subtype Relationship

The first four types of relationships are referred to as *traditional* relationships because up until object model (for database design) gained preeminence, they were essentially the kinds of relationships that were facilitated by the relational model. Observe also, that the only difference between a 1:M relationship and an M:1 relation is a matter of perspective; thus, a 1:M relationship may also be described as an M:1 relationship (so that in practice, there are really three types of traditional relationships). Put another way:

> If R1, R2 are two relations and there is a 1:M relationship between R1 and R2, an alternate way of describing this situation is to say that there is an M:1 relationship between R2 and R1.

For traditional relationships, to determine the type of relationship between two relations (entities) R1 and R2, ask and determine the answer to the following questions:

- How many records of R1 can reference a single record of R2?

- How many records of R2 can reference a single record of R1?

To test for a component relationship between any two relations R1 and R2, ask and determine the answer to the following questions:

- Is (a record of) R1 composed of (a record of) R2?

- Is (a record of) R2 composed of (a record of) R1?

For a subtype relationship, the test is a bit more detailed; for relations R1 and R2, ask and determine the answer to the following questions:

- Is (a record of) R1 also a (a record of) R2?

- Is (a record of) R2 also a (a record of) R1?

Possible answers to these questions are always, sometimes, or never. The possibilities are shown below:

R1 always R2, R2 always R1	⇒	R1 and R2 are synonymous
R1 always R2, R2 sometimes R1	⇒	R1 is a subtype of R2
R1 always R2, R2 never R1	⇒	Makes no sense
R1 sometimes R2, R2 always R1	⇒	R2 is a sub-type of R1
R1 sometimes R2, R2 sometimes R1	⇒	Inconclusive
R1 sometimes R2, R2 never R1	⇒	Makes no sense
R1 never R2, R2 always R1	⇒	Makes no sense
R1 never R2, R2 sometimes R1	⇒	Makes no sense
R1 never R2, R2 never R1	⇒	No subtype relationship

3.5.2 Representing Relationships

Having identified the entities and relationships, the next logical question is, how do we represent them? Four approaches have been used: *database hierarchies, simple networks, complex networks,* the *entity-relationship model* and the *object-relationship model.* The first three approaches are traditional approaches that have made way for the more reputed latter two approaches. We will therefore start by discussing the latter two approaches.

The Entity-Relationship Model

The popular answer to this challenge of database representation is the *entity-relationship diagram* (ERD or E-R diagram). Figure 3-4a shows the symbols used in an ERD, while Figure 3-4b provides an illustration based on the Crows-Foot notation. In the diagram, the convention to show attributes of each entity has been relaxed, thus avoiding clutter. Note also that relationships are labeled as verbs so that in linking one entity to another, one can read an entity-verb-entity formulation. If the verb is on the right or above the relationship line, the convention is to read from top-to-bottom or left-to-right. If the verb is on the left or below the relationship line, the convention is to read from bottom-to-top or right-to-left.

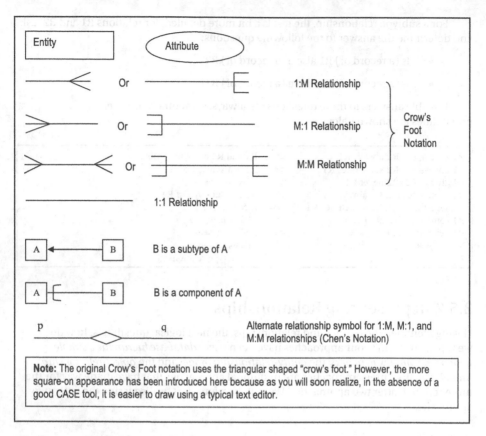

Figure 3-4a. Symbols Used in E-R Diagrams

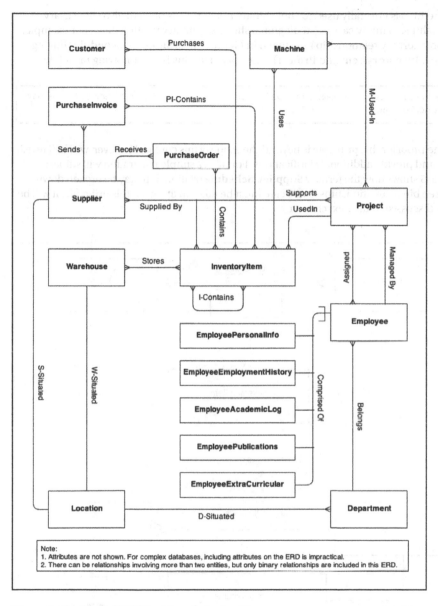

Figure 3-4b. *Partial ERD for Manufacturing Firm*

The ERD is normally used to show binary relationships but can also show n-ary relationships. In many cases, E-R diagrams show only binary relationships. For example, a possible ternary relationship not shown in Figure 3-4b is **Supplier-Schedule** (linking **Supplier**, **InventoryItem** and **Project**). The reason for this is the following principle:

> All relationships of degree greater than 2 can be decomposed to a set of binary relationships. This may or may not be required.

The proof for this principle is beyond the scope of this course. However, we shall revisit it later, and provide additional clarifications. For now, a simple illustration will suffice: Figure 3-5 shows how the ternary **Supplier-Schedule** relationship may be broken down into three binary relationships. Since care must be taken in applying this principle, it will be further discussed in the next chapter.

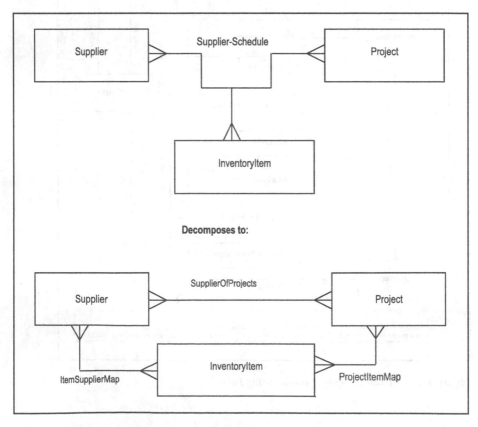

Figure 3-5. *Decomposing a Ternary Relationship*

The Object-Relationship Model

As you are aware, or will soon learn (from your software engineering course), there are, broadly speaking, two alternate paradigms for software construction: the functional approach (which is the traditional approach) and the object-oriented (OO) approach. In an object-oriented environment, the comparative methodology for the E-R diagram is the *object-relationship diagram* (ORD or O-R diagram). The concept of an ORD is similar to that of an ERD, and the diagrams are also similar, but there are a few exceptions:

- In the OO paradigm, the *object type* replaces the entity (type) of the relational model. Like the entity, an object type is a concept or thing about which data is stored. Additionally, the object type defines a set of operations, which will be applicable to all objects (instances) of that type.

- The symbol used to denote an object type is similar to an entity symbol, except that it has two extended areas — one for the attributes of the object type, and the other for its defined operations.

- The preferred diagramming convention is the UML (Unified Modeling Language) notation.

- Depending on the OO development tool, there might be additional notations regarding the cardinality (more precisely, multiplicity) of the relationships represented.

A full treatment of the OO approach is beyond the scope of this course. You are no doubt familiar with using UML diagrams in your OO programming courses. For a quick review of the fundamentals, please see references [Lee, 2002] and [Martin, 1993]. However, in the interest of comprehensive coverage, an overview of the approach is provided in chapters 5 and 23.

Database Tree

A *database tree* (hierarchy) is a traditional alternative, which used to be employed prior to the introduction or the E-R model; it was successfully employed in a system called RAMIS (the original acronym stands for "Random Access Management Information System"). A database tree (hierarchy) is a collection of entities and 1:M relationships arranged such that the following conditions hold:

- The root has no parent

- Each subsequent node has a single parent

Figure 3-6 illustrates a database hierarchy. Observe that it looks like a general tree (review your data structures). Except for the root (node A), each node has a parent node that it references. Note also that all the relationships are 1:M relationships (traditionally referred to as *parent-child relationships*).

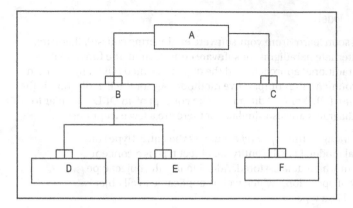

Figure 3-6. *Example of a Hierarchy (Tree)*

Database Networks

The database network approach is another traditional approach that is no longer employed. In the interest of historical context, a brief overview is provided here. A *simple database network* is a collection of entities and 1:M relationships arranged such that any member can have multiple parents, providing that the parents are different entities. Figure 3-7 illustrates the approach. It was successfully employed in a DBMS called the CODASYL system (the original CODASYL acronym stands for "Conference on Data Systems Languages").

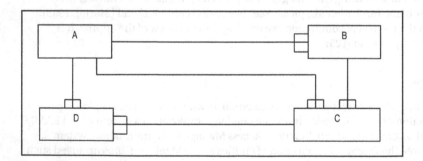

Figure 3-7. *A Simple Network*

A *complex database network* is a collection of entities and relationships, at least one of the relationships being an M:M relationship. Figure 3-8 illustrates. The complex network can be reduced to a simple network by replacing all M:M relationships with M:1 relationships. The technique for replacing M:M relationships will be discussed in the upcoming subsection.

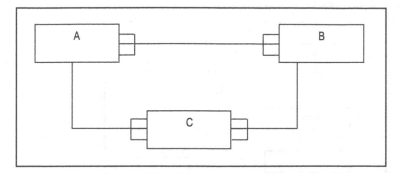

Figure 3-8. Complex Network

3.5.3 Multiplicity of Relationships

It is customary to indicate on the ERD (or ORD), the *multiplicity* (also called the *cardinality*) of each relationship. By this we mean, how many occurrences of one entity (or object type) can be associated with one occurrence of the other entity (or object type). This information is particularly useful when the system is being constructed. Moreover, violation of multiplicity constraints could put the integrity of the system is question, which of course is undesirable. Usually, the DBMS does not facilitate enforcement of multiplicity constraints at the database level. Rather, they are typically enforced at the application level by the software engineer.

Several notations for multiplicity have been proposed, but the Chen notation (first published in 1976, and reiterated in [Chen, 1994]) is particularly clear; it is paraphrased here: Place beside each entity (or object type), two numbers [x,y]. The first number (x) indicates the minimum participation, while the second (y) indicates the maximum participation.

An alternate notation is to use two additional symbols along with the Crow's Foot notation: an open circle to indicate a participation of zero, and a stroke (|) to indicate a participation of 1. The maximum participation is always indicated nearest to the entity (or object type) box.

For convenience, you could also use the Chen's notation for multiplicity, along with the Crow's Foot notation for representing the relationships. The Chen notation is preferred because of its clarity and the amount of information it conveys. Figure 3-9 provides an illustrative comparison of the two notations.

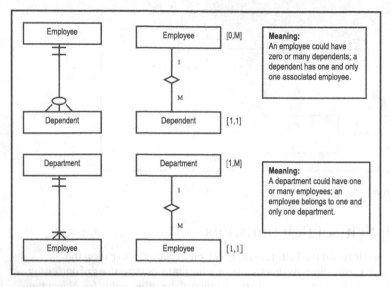

Figure 3-9. *Illustrating Multiplicity Notations*

3.5.4 Implementing Relationships

Assuming the E-R model, relationships can be implemented by following a set of guidelines as outlined below:

To implement a 1:M relationship, store the primary key of one as a foreign key of the other (foreign key must be on the "many side"). Figures 3.13 and 3.14 illustrate (there is a M:1 relationship between **Suppliers** and **Locations**; there are others that you should identify).

To implement an M:M relationship, introduce a third intersecting (1:M) relation. The new relation is usually keyed on all the foreign keys (or a *surrogate #*). Also, the original relations/entities form 1:M relationships with the intersecting relation (figure 3.10 illustrates).

To implement a subtype relationship, introduce a foreign key in the subtype, which is the primary key in the referenced super-type. Further, make the foreign key in the subtype, the primary key of that subtype. In the case of *multiple inheritance* (where a subtype has more than one super-types), make the introduced foreign keys in the subtype, candidate keys, one of which will be the primary key. Figures 3.11 and 3.12 illustrate this strategy.

To implement a component relationship, introduce in the component relation, a foreign key that is the primary key in the summary relation. This foreign key will form part of the primary key (or a candidate key) in the component relation. Figures 3.11 and 3.12 illustrate this strategy.

To implement a 1:1 relationship, introduce a foreign key in one relation (preferably the primary relation) such that the primary key of one is an attribute in the other. Then enforce a constraint that forbids multiple foreign keys referencing a single primary key. Alternately, treat the 1:1 relationship as a subtype relationship (but ignore enforcing inheritance).

A surrogate is an atomic attribute introduced either automatically the DBMS, or manually by the database designer. It is used to uniquely identify each tuple in the relation. This will be further clarified in chapter 5.

The foregoing strategies should underscore forcefully in your mind, the importance of foreign keys in database design. In fact, foreign keys are referred to as the "glue" that holds the database together. We shall revisit this concept in the next chapter.

In many textbooks and database environment, you will see and/or hear the term *parent-child relationship.* This is a rather lame term, borrowed from preexisting hierarchical database systems, to describe 1:1 and 1:M relationships. In a parent-child relationship, the *parent relation* is the referenced relation; the child relation is the *referencing relation.* Throughout this course, these terms are avoided because they are rather confusing, and do not accurately describe several scenarios involving 1:1 and/or 1:M relationships. Alternately, we will use no euphemism for 1:1 and 1:M relationships; instead of parent relation, we'll say the *referenced relation;* instead of child relation, we say *primary relation* or *referencing relation.*

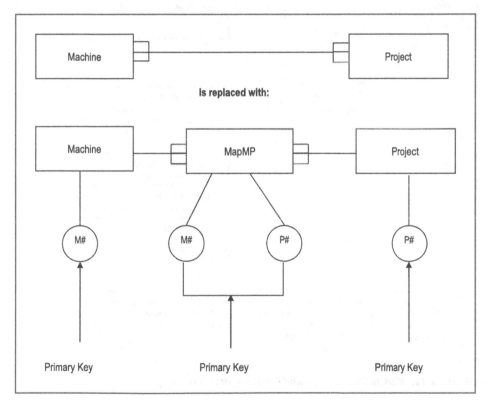

Figure 3-10. Implementing M:M Relationships

47

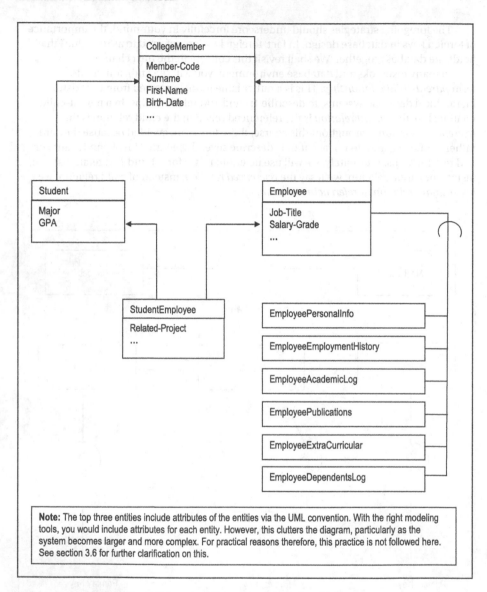

Figure 3-11. *Illustrating Subtype and Component Relationships*

Relation	Attributes
College Member	*MemberCode*, Surname, First-Name, BirthDate, ...
Student	*MemberCode*, Major, GPA, ...
Employee	*MemberCode*, JobTitle, SalaryGrade, ...
StudentEmployee	*MemberCode*, Related-Project
EmployeePersonalInfo	*MemberCode*, Address, Telephone, ...
EmployeeEmploymentHistory	*MemberCode*, *JobSequence*, Organization, ...
EmployeeAcademicLog	*MemberCode*, *LogSequence*, Institution, Period-Attended, Award, ...
EmployeePublications	*MemberCode*, *PublCode*, Title, Book-Journal-Flag, ...
EmployeeExtraCurricular	*MemberCode*, *ActivityCode*, Activity-Description, ...
Note:	
1. Primary key attributes and foreign key attributes are in italics.	
2. This is not a comprehensive RAL. For several of the relations included, there are additional attributes to be added (indicated by the three periods in the attributes column).	

Figure 3-12. Illustrating the Implementation of Subtype and Component Relationships

3.6 The Relation-Attributes List and Relationship List

In large, complex information systems projects, it is often impractical to attempt to develop and maintain ERDs, unless they are automatically generated and maintained by computer-aided software engineering (CASE) tools (more on these in chapter 5). Even when maintained by CASE tools, an ERD for such a project could become large, spanning several pages. Reading and interpretation then becomes difficult.

To circumvent the above challenges, a *Relation-Attribute List* (RAL) and a *Relationship List* (RL) may be constructed and maintained. The former maintains information on all relations of the system and the latter maintains information on all relationships implemented in the system. Figures 3-13 and 3-14 illustrate partial RAL and RL for the database model of Figure3-4b. As you examine these figures, please note the following:

- In practice, the format of the RL shown in Figure 3-14b is used as the final list over the format shown in Figure 3-14a (the format used in Figure 3-14a can be deduced by simply identifying all possible relationships among entities; hence, it may contain optional relationships and is therefore useful as a first draft).

- The revised RL of Figure 3-14b has been stripped of all M:M relationships (review section 3.5.4 on treating M:M relationships).

- The relations **PurchaseInvSummary** and **PurchaseInvDetail** of Figure 3-13, are used to replace the M:M relationship between **PurchaseInvoice** and **InventoryItem** in Figure 3-4b. Similarly, the relations **PurchaseOrdSummary** and **PurchaseOrdDetail** are used to replace the M:M relationship between **PurchaseOrder** and **InventoryItem** in Figure 3-4b.

- In constructing the RAL and RL, it is sometimes useful to use the RL to refine the RAL and vice versa. In particular, once you have identified all the (mandatory) relationships, you may use this along with the principles outlined in section 3.5.4 to refine the RAL.

- Remember, the model of Figure 3-4b, RAL of Figure 3-13, and the RL of Figure 3-14 do not represent a comprehensive coverage of the database requirements of a manufacturing firm; neither are they intended to be. Rather, they serve as useful illustrations.

Relation	Attributes
Customer	*Cust#*, Cust-Name, Address,... Reference Person, ...
Supplier	*Supp#*, SupplName, Address, *SupplLoc#*, ...
Machine	*Mach#*, Mach-Description, ...
Project	*Proj#*, ProjName, *ProjManagerEmp#*, ...
Warehouse	*Whouse#*, WhouseName, WhouseSize, *WhouseLoc#*, ...
InventoryItem	*Item#*, ItemName, ...
Location	*Loc#*, LocationName, DistanceFromHQ, ...
Department	*Dept#*, DeptName, *DeptLoc#*, ...
Employee	*Emp#*, EmpName, *EmpProj#*, *EmpDept#*, DOB,...
PurchaseOrdSummary	*OrderRef*, Order#, OrderDate, *OrderSupp#*, OrderStatus, ...
PurchaseOrdDetail	*PODOrderRef*, *OrderItem#*, OrderQuantity, OrderUnitPrice
PurchaseInvSummary	*PurchaseRef*, Invoice#, *InvSupp#*, *InvOrderRef*, InvDate, InvAmount, InvStatus, ...
PurchaseInvDetail	*PIDPurchaseRef*, *PIDItem#*, PIDItemQuantity, PIDItemUnitPrice
SaleInvSummary	*SaleRef*, SIInvoice#, SaleDate, *SaleCust#*, InvoiceStatus, SaleAmount, ...
SaleInvDetail	*SIDSaleRef*, *SaleItem#*, Quantity, UnitPrice
MachineUsage	*MUMach#*, *MUItem#*
MachProjects	*MPMach#*, *MPProj#*
ProjSupp	*PSSupp#*, *PSProj#*
ItemProj	*IPItem#*, *IPProj#*
SupplItems	*SISupp#*, *SIItem#*
Stock	*SWhouse#*, *SItem#*
ItemStruct	*ISThisItem#*, *ISCompItem#*
EmployeePersonalInfo	*EPIEmp#*, MaritalStatus, Address, Telephone, Email, ...
EmployeeEmploymentHistory	*EHEmp#*, *EHJobSequence*, Organization, Title, ...
EmployeeAcademicLog	*ALEmp#*, *ALLogSequence*, Institution, PeriodAttended, Award, ...
EmployeePublications	*EPEmp#*, *PublCode*, Title, BookJournalFlag, ...
EmployeeExtraCurricular	*EXEmp#*, *EXActivityCode*, ActivityDescription, ...
...	

Note:
1. *Primary key attributes and foreign key attributes are in italics.*
2. This is not a comprehensive RAL. For several of the relations included, there are additional attributes to be added (indicated by the three periods in the attributes column). Also, additional relations would be required in order to have a comprehensive model (indicated by the three periods in the previous row).
3. For each relation, an effort is made to keep attribute names unique (to the entire database), even if the attribute is a foreign key. For instance, in the relation **Employee**, the attribute **EmpDept#** is a foreign key that references **Dept#** in the relation **Department**. This convention applies for all foreign keys.
4. The attributes **OrderRef** (in **PurchaseOrdSummary** relation), **PurchaseRef** (in **PurchaseInvSummary** relation) and **SaleRef** (in **SaleInvSummary** relation) are examples of surrogates. Surrogates will be more thoroughly discussed in chapter 5.

Figure 3-13. *Partial Relation-Attributes List for a Manufacturing Firm's Database*

Relationship Name	Participating Relations	Type	Comment
SuppliedBy	Supplier, InventoryItem	M:M	Mandatory
Purchases	Customer, InventoryItem	M:M	Mandatory
Uses	Machine, InventoryItem	M:M	Mandatory
Used-In	InventoryItem, Project	M:M	Mandatory
M-Used-In	Machine, Project	M:M	Mandatory
Stores	Warehouse, InventoryItem	M:M	Mandatory
Contains	InventoryItem, InventoryItem	M:M	Mandatory
Assigned	Employee, Project	M:1	Mandatory
Belongs	Employee, Department	M:1	Mandatory
D-Situated	Location, Department	1:M	Mandatory
W-Situated	Warehouse, Location	1:1	Mandatory
S-Situated	Supplier, Location	1:1	Mandatory
Sends	Supplier, PurchaseInvoice	M:M	Mandatory
I-Contains	PurchaseInvoice, InventoryItem	M:M	Mandatory
RequestedOn	PurchaseOrder, InventoryItem	M:M	Mandatory
Receives	Supplier, PurchaseOrder	1:M	Mandatory
Supports	Supplier, Project	M:M	Mandatory
SupplierSchedule	Supplier, InventoryItem, Project	M:M	Optional
ComposedOf	Employee, EmployeePersonalInfo, EmployeeEmploymentHistory, EmployeeAcademicLog, EmployeePublications, EmployeeExtraCurricular	Comp	Mandatory

Figure 3-14a. Relationships List for a Manufacturing Firm's Database

Named Relation	Referenced Relations	Type	Comment
SaleInvSummary	Customer	M:1	Implements relationship Purchases
SaleInvDetail	SaleInvSummary	M:1	Implements relationship Purchases
	InventoryItem	M:1	Implements relationship Purchases
PurchaseInvSummary	Supplier	M:1	Implements relationships Sends and I-Contains
PurchaeInvDetail	PurchaseInvSummary	M:1	Implements relationship I-Contains
	InventoryItem	M:1	Implements relationship I-Contains
MachineUsage	Machine	M:1	Implements relationship Uses
	InventoryItem	M:1	Implements relationship Uses
MachProjects	Machine	M:1	Implements relationship M-Used-In
	Project	M:1	Implements relationship M-Used-In
PurchaseOrdSummary	Supplier	M:1	Implements relationships Receives and RequestedOn
PurchaseOrdDetail	PurchaseOrdSummary	M:1	Implements relationship RequestedOn
	InventoryItem	M:1	Implements relationship RequestedOn
Supplier	Location	1:1	Implements relationship S-Situated
SuppItems	Supplier	M:1	Implements relationship SuppliedBy
	InventoryItem	M:1	Implements relationship SuppliedBy
ProjSupp	Supplier	M:1	Implements relationship Supports
	Project	M:1	Implements relationship Supports
ItemProj	Project	M:1	Implements relationship UsedIn
	InventoryItem	M:1	Implements relationship UsedIn
Stock	Warehouse	M:1	Implements relationship Stores
	InventoryItem	M:1	Implements relationship Stores
ItemStruct	InventoryItem	M:1	Implements relationship Contains
	InventoryItem	M:1	Implements relationship Contains
Employee	Project	M:1	Implements relationship Assigned
	Department	M:1	Implements relationship Belongs
Warehouse	Location	1:1	Implements relationship W-Situated
Department	Location	1:1	Implements relationship D-Situated
EmployeePersonalInfo	Employee	M:1	Implements relationship ComposedOf
EmployeeEmploymentHistory	Employee	M:1	Implements relationship ComposedOf
EmployeeAcademicLog	Employee	M:1	Implements relationship ComposedOf
EmployeePublications	Employee	M:1	Implements relationship ComposedOf
EmployeeExtraCurricular	Employee	M:1	Implements relationship ComposedOf

Figure 3-14b. *Refined Relationships List for a Manufacturing Firm's Database*

3.7 Non-Relational Approaches

Prior to development of the relational model, the following approaches used to be employed:

- Inverted List Approach: Exemplified by DATACOM/DB

- Hierarchical Approach: Exemplified by Information Management System (IMS) database and the Random Access Management Information System (RAMIS)

- Network Approach: Exemplified by Conference on Data Systems Languages (CODASYL) initiative and Integrated Database Management System (IDMS) initiative

The strengths of the relational approach when compared to these approaches are its sound mathematical base, its flexibility, robustness, and simplicity.

In recent times, the *object oriented* (OO) model has been challenging the relational model on performance and efficiency for certain scenarios. Nonetheless, we expect that the two technologies will continue to peaceably coexist; huge investments have been made in relational database systems, and it is not likely that these will be abandoned. What is more likely to happen is that systems will be built based on relational databases, with object oriented user interfaces superimposed.

3.8 Summary and Concluding Remarks

Let us summarize what we have covered in this very important chapter:

- The relational database model is based on a number of fundamental concepts relating to the following: entity, entity set, relation, relationship, tuple, candidate key, primary key, alternate key, foreign key, domain, cardinality, degree.

- A domain is a named set of scalar values from which attribute values are drawn.

- A relation consists of a heading and a body. The heading consists of atomic attributes defined on specific domains. The body consists of a set of attribute-values pairs, where each attribute has a value drawn from its domain.

- In a database system, you are likely to find any combination of the following types of relations: base relations, logical views, snapshots, query results, intermediate results, and temporary relations.

- A relational database system (RDBS) is a collection of time-varying normalized relations, managed through an appropriate user interface, and with desirable constraints and features that enhance the effective, efficient management of the database.

- A relationship is an inherent mapping involving two or more relations. There are six types of relationships: one-to-one (1:1) relationship, one-to-many (1:M) relationship, many-to-one (M:1) relationship, many-to-many (M:M) relationship, component relationship, and subtype relationship.

- An E-R diagram (ERD) is a graphical representation of a database model. It is important to know how to represent relations/entities and relationships on the ERD.

- It is important to know how to implement the various types of relationships in the actual database design.

- The relation-attributes list (RAL) and relationship list (RL) are two useful alternatives to the E-R diagram, especially for large, complex systems.

- Database approaches that preexisted the relational approach include the inverted-list approach, the hierarchical approach and the network approach.

- A contemporary alternative to the relational approach is the object-oriented approach. However, given the efficacy of both approaches, it is more likely that they will complement each other in the future, rather than compete against each other.

Take the time to go over this chapter more than once if you need to, and make sure that you are comfortable with the concepts covered. In the upcoming chapter, we will build on the information covered in this chapter, as we discuss integrity rules and normalization. These two topics form the foundation for the rest of the course.

3.9 Review Questions

1. Clarify the following terms:

   - Entity

   - Attributes

   - Entity set

   - Relation

   - Relationship

   - Tuples

   - Primary key

   - Candidate key

   - Foreign key

   - Domain

- Cardinality

- Multiplicity

- Degree

Develop an illustrative data model to explain how these concepts are related.

2. Give the formal definition of a relation. Explain the different kinds of relations that may be found in a database.

3. Outline the steps to be observed in constructing a relational database system.

4. What are the types of relationships that may exist among information entities? For each, explain how it is identified, and how it is implemented.

5. Think about a problem that requires a small database system (requiring six to twelve entities or object types). Do the following:

    - Identity all required entities (object types).

    - Identify relationships among the entities (object types).

    - Develop an ERD or ORD.

    - Propose a relation-attributes list (RAL) and a relationship list (RL) to represent your model.

3.10 References and/or Recommended Readings

[Bruegge, 2002] Bruegge, Bernard and Allen H. Dutdt. *Object-Oriented Software Engineering: Conquering Complex and Changing Systems*. Upper Saddle River, NJ: Prentice Hall, 2002.

[Chen, 1994] Chen, Peter. "The Entity-Relationship Model – Toward a Unified View of Data," In *Readings in Database Systems* 2nd ed., pages 741-754. San Francisco, CA: Morgan Kaufmann, 1994.

[Chen, 2007] Chen, Peter. http://bit.csc.lsu.edu/~chen/display.html

[Connolly, 2002] Connolly, Thomas and Carolyn Begg. *Database Systems: A Practical Approach to Design, Implementation and Management* 3rd ed. New York: Addison-Wesley, 2002. See chapters 3 and 11.

[Date, 2004] Date, Christopher J. *Introduction to Database Systems* 8th ed. Menlo Park, California: Addison-Wesley, 2004. See chapters 3 and 6.

[Edward, 1992] Edward, David. *Information Modeling: Specification and Implementation*. Eaglewood Cliffs, NJ: Prentice Hall, 1992. See chapters 2-4.

[Elmasri, 2007] Elmasri, Ramez and Shamkanf B. Navathe. *Fundamentals of Database Systems* 5th ed. Reading, Massachusetts: Addison-Wesley, 2007. See chapters 3 and 7.

[Foster, 2010] Foster, Elvis C. *Software Engineering — a Methodical Approach*. Bloomington, IN: Xlibris Publishing, 2010. See chapter 10.

[Garcia-Molina, 2002] Garcia-Molina, Hector, Jeffrey Ullman and Jennifer Widom. *Database Systems: The Complete Book*. Upper Saddle River, New Jersey: Prentice Hall, 2002. See chapters 2 and 3.

[Hoffer, 2007] Hoffer, Jeffrey A., Mary B. Prescott and Fred R. McFadden. *Modern Database Management* 8th ed. Upper Saddle River, New Jersey: Prentice Hall, 2007. See chapters 3 and 4.

[Kifer, 2005] Kifer, Michael, Arthur Bernstein and Philip M. Lewis. *Database Systems: An Application-Oriented Approach* 2nd ed. New York: Addison-Wesley, 2005. See chapters 3 and 4.

[Kroenke, 2004] Kroenke, David M. *Database Processing: Fundamentals, Design and Implementation* 9th ed. Upper Saddle River, New Jersey: Prentice Hall, 2004. See chapters 2 and 3.

[Lee, 2002] Lee, Richard C. and William M. Tepfenhart. *Practical Object-Oriented Development With UML and Java*. Upper Saddle River, NJ: Prentice Hall, 2002.

[Lewis, 2002] Lewis. Phillip M., Arthur Bernstein and Michael Kifer. *Databases and Transaction Processing: An Application Oriented Approach*. New York: Addison-Wesley, 2002. See chapters 4 and 5.

[Martin, 1993] Martin, James and James Odell. *Principles of Object-Oriented Analysis and Design*. Upper Saddle River, New Jersey: Prentice Hall, 1993. See chapters 6 and 7, and appendix A.

[Martin, 1995] Martin, James. *Client/Server Databases: Enterprise Computing*. Upper Saddle River, New Jersey: Prentice Hall, 1995. See chapter 3.

[Riccardi, 2003] Riccardi, Greg. *Database Management With Web Site Development Applications*. Boston, Massachusetts: Addison-Wesley, 2003. See chapters 3 and 4.

[Rob, 2007] Rob, Peter and Carlos Coronel. *Database Systems: Design, Implementation & Management* 7th ed. Boston, Massachusetts: Course Technology, 2007. See chapters 2 and 3.

[Silberschatz, 2006] Silberschatz, Abraham, Henry F. Korth and S. Sudarshan. *Database Systems Concepts* 5th ed. New York, New York: McGraw-Hill, 2006. See chapters 2 and 6.

[Ullman, 1997] Ullman, Jeffrey D., and Jennifer Widom. *A First Course in Database Systems*. Upper Saddle River, New Jersey: Prentice Hall, 1997. See chapter 2.

■ ■ ■

CHAPTER 4

Integrity Rules and Normalization

In order to design high quality databases, you need to be cognizant of the fundamental integrity and normalization rules. We will discuss these rules in this chapter. Sub-topics to be discussed include:

- Fundamental Integrity Rules
- Foreign Key Concept
- Rationale for Normalization
- Functional Dependence and Non-loss Decomposition
- First Normal Form
- Second Normal Form
- Third Normal Form
- Boyce/Codd Normal Form
- Fourth Normal Form
- Fifth Normal Form
- Other Normal Forms
- Summary and Concluding Remarks

4.1 Fundamental Integrity Rules

Two fundamental integrity rules that the database designer must be cognizant of are the *entity integrity rule* and the *referential integrity rule*.

Entity Integrity Rule: The entity integrity rule states that no component of the primary key in a base relation is allowed to accept nulls. Put another way, in a relational model, we never record information about something that we cannot identify. Three points are worth noting here:

- The rule applies to base relations.

- The rule applies to primary key, not alternate keys.

- The primary key must be wholly non-null.

Referential Integrity Rule: The referential integrity rule states that the database must not contain unmatched foreign key values. By unmatched foreign key value, we mean a non-null foreign key value for which there is no match in the referenced (target) relation. Put another way, if B references A then A must exist. The following points should be noted:

- The rule requires that foreign keys must match primary keys, not alternate keys.

- Foreign key and referential integrity are defined in terms of each other. It is not possible to explain one without mentioning the other.

4.2 Foreign Key Concept

The concept of a foreign key was introduced in the previous chapter. Let us revisit this concept, by introducing a more formal definition:

Attribute FK of base relation R2 is a foreign key if and only if (denoted iff from this point) it satisfies the following conditions:
a. Each value of FK is either wholly null or wholly non-null.
b. There exists a base relation, R1 with primary key PK such that each non-null value of FK is identical to the value of PK in some tuple of R1.

We will use the notation R1 → R2 to mean, the relation R1 references the relation R2. In this case, R1 is the referencing (primary) relation and R2 is the referenced relation. Since R1 is the referencing relation, it contains a foreign key. We will also use the notion R1{A, B, C, ...} to mean, the relation R1 contains attributes A, B, C, and so on. Where specific examples are given, the relation-name will be highlighted or placed in upper case; attribute-names of specific examples will not be highlighted when stated with the related relation; however, they will be highlighted when reference is made to them from the body of the text.

Based on the definition of a foreign key, the following consequential points should be noted:

1.   The foreign key and the referenced primary key must be defined on the same domain. However, the attribute-names can be different (some implementations of SQL may require that they be identical).

2.   The foreign key need not be a component of the primary key for the host (holding) relation (in which case nulls may be accepted, but only with the understanding that they will be subsequently updated).

3.   If relations Rn, R(n-1), R(n-2) .... R1 are such that Rn → R(n-1) → R(n-2) → .... R2 → R1 then the chain Rn to R1 forms a *referential path*.

4.   A relation can be both referenced and referencing. Consider the referential path R3 → R2 → R1. In this case, R2 is both a referenced and a referencing relation.

5.   We can have a self-referencing relation. Consider for example, the relation **Employee**{Emp#, EmpName .... MgrEmployee#} with primary key [Emp#]where attribute **MgrEmp#** is a foreign key defined on the relation **Employee**. In this case we have a self-referencing relation.

6.   More generally, a referential cycle exists when there is a referential path from Rn to itself: Rn → R(n-1) → .... R1 → Rn

7.   Foreign-to-primary-key matches are said to be the "glue" that holds the database together. As you will see, relations are joined based on foreign keys.

Deletion of Referenced Tuples

Now that we have established the importance of foreign keys, we need to address a question: How will we treat deletion of referenced tuples? Three alternatives exist.

- *Restrict* deletion to tuples that are not referenced.

- *Cascade* deletion to all referencing tuples in referencing relations.

- Allow the deletion but *nullify* all referencing foreign keys in referencing relations.

The third approach is particularly irresponsible, as it could quite quickly put the integrity of the database in question, by introducing *orphan records*. Traditionally, DBMS suites implement the restriction strategy (and for good reasons). The cascading strategy has been surfacing in contemporary systems, as an optional feature. It must be used with much care, as it is potentially dangerous when used without discretion.

4.3 Rationale for Normalization

Normalization is the process of ensuring that the database (conceptual schema) is
defined in such a manner as to ensure efficiency and ease of data access. Normalization
ensures the following:

- Data integrity

- Control of redundancy

- Logical data independence

- Avoidance of modification anomalies

The following problems can be experienced from having un-normalized files
in a system:

- Data redundancy that leads to the modification anomalies

- Modification anomalies which include:

  ✓ Insertion anomaly: Data cannot be inserted when it is
    desirable; one has to wait on some future data, due to
    organization of the data structure

  ✓ Deletion anomaly: Deletion of some undesirable aspect(s)
    of data necessarily means deletion of some other desirable
    aspect(s) of data

  ✓ Update anomaly: Update of some aspect(s) of data
    necessarily means update of other aspect(s) of data

- Inefficient file manipulation; lack of ease of data access

- Inhibition to the achievement of logical data independence

- Compromise on the integrity of data

- Pressure on programming effort to make up for the poor design

Figure 4-1 indicates the six most commonly used *normal forms*. The hierarchy is
such that a relation in a given normal form is automatically in all normal forms prior to it.
Thus a relation in the second normal form (2NF) is automatically in the first normal form
(1NF); a relation in the third normal form (3NF) is in 2NF and so on. Edgar Frank Codd
defined the first three normal forms in the early 1970s; the Boyce-Codd normal form
(BCNF) was subsequently deduced from his work. The fourth and fifth normal forms
(4NF and 5NF) were subsequently defined by Ronald Fagin in the late 1970s.

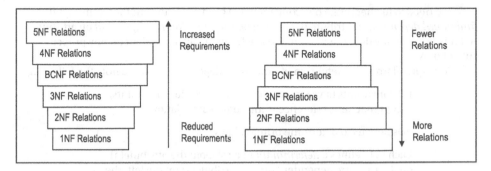

***Figure 4-1.** Normal Forms*

The *normalization procedure* involves decomposing relations into other relations of repeatedly higher normal forms. The process is reversible. Moreover, normalization must be conducted in a manner that ensures that there is no loss of information.

4.4 Functional Dependence and Non-loss Decomposition

Before discussion of the normal forms, we need to define and clarify two fundamental concepts: *functional dependence* and *non-loss decomposition*.

4.4.1 Functional Dependence

Given a relation, R{A, B, C, ...}, then attribute B is *functionally dependent* on attribute A, written A → B (read as "A determines B") if and only if (denoted *iff* from this point onwards) each value of A in R has precisely one B-value in R at any point in time. Attributes A and B may or may not be composite.

An alternate way to describe functional dependence (FD) is as follows: Given a value of attribute A, one can deduce a value for attribute B since any two tuples which agree on A must necessarily agree on B.

Example 1:

In relation **Employee** {Emp#, S-Name, F-Name, Address, ...}, the following FD holds.
Emp# → S-Name, F-Name, Address

From definition of primary key, all attributes of a relation are functionally dependent on the primary key. This is precisely what is required; in fact, an attribute (or group of attributes) qualifies as a candidate key iff all other attributes of the entity are dependent on it.

We need to further refine our concept of FD by introducing another term — *full functional dependence*: Attribute B is said to be *fully functionally dependent* on attribute A if it is functionally dependent on A and not functionally dependent on any proper subset of A.

As a spinoff from the definition of functional dependence, please note the following:

1. FD constraints have similarities with referential constraints, except that here, reference is internal to the relation.

2. FDs help us to determine primary keys.

3. Each FD defines a *determinant* in a relation: the attribute(s) on the right are dependent on the attribute(s) on the left; the attribute(s) on the left constitute(s) a determinant.

4.4.2 Non-loss Decomposition

Suppose we have a relation **R0** as follows: **R0**{Suppl#, SuplName, Item#, ItemName, Quantity, SuplStatus, Location}

Functional dependencies of **R0** are illustrated in Figure 4-2; they may also be listed as follows:

- [Suppl# , Item#] → {Quantity, SuplName, SuplStatus, Location, ItemName}

- Suppl# → {SuplName, SuplStatus, Location}

- Item# → ItemName

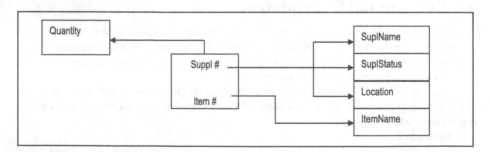

Figure 4-2. *FD Diagram for Relation R0*

Storing **R0** this way causes duplication. The reason is that **R0** is not sufficiently normalized. As an alternate, we could have the following:

   R1{Supl#, SuplNam, Location, SuplStatus}

   R2{Item#, ItemName}

   R3{Supl#, Item#, Quantity}

R1, **R2**, and **R3** constitute (an example of) a *non-loss decomposition* (NLD) of **R0**.

Here is a formal definition of an NLD:

> If R is a relation and P1, P2, ... Pn are projections on R such that
> P1 JOIN P2 JOIN ..... JOIN Pn = R,
> then P1, P2, ... Pn constitutes a non-loss decomposition of R.

Notice that we have glided into two new terms, *projection* and *join*. These will be formerly treated later in the course. Suffice it now to say that a projection on a relation is an extraction (into a new relation) of some attributes of the relation; a join requires at least two relations and may be construed as the opposite of a projection: If you can project R into P1 and P2, then you may be able to join P1 and P2 to yield R.

Given this definition, we need to address the following questions:

1. How do we find non-loss decompositions?

2. When should we replace a relation by a non-loss decomposition?

3. What are the advantages?

Heath's theorem (of [Heath, 1971]) addresses questions (1) and (2). The answer to the third question is stated in section 4.3 above. Heath's theorem is stated below:

> If we have a relation R{A, B, C, ...} and if A→B and B→ C, then projections P1{A, B} and P2{B, C} constitute a non-loss decomposition of R.

Example 2: Proof of Heath's Theorem:

> We wish to show that R0 {A, B, C} = P1 {A, B} JOIN P2 {B, C}.
>
> Let P1 {A, B} and P2 {B, C} be projections of R0 {A, B, C}
> Assume further that A,B,C are single attributes.
>
> Suppose that (a, b, c) is a tuple in R0.
> Then (a, b) is in P1 and (b, c) is in P2.
> So (a, b, c) is in P1 JOIN P2 .... (1)
>
> Suppose that (a, b, c) is in P1 JOIN P2.
> Then (a, b, c1) is in R0 for some value c1
> and (a1, b, c) is in R0 for some value a1.
> But B → C therefore b → c so that c1 must be c.
> Therefore (a, b, c) is in R0 .... (2)
>
> We have shown any tuple (a,b,c) that is in R0 is also in P1 JOIN P2, and that any tuple (a,b,c) that is in P1 JOIN P2 is also in R0. Therefore R0 = P1 JOIN P2.

Corollary of Heath's Theorem

An important corollary from Heath's theorem is as follows:

> If P1, P2, ... Pn is a non-loss decomposition of R and relations P1, P2, ... Pn all share a candidate key, then there is no reduction in data duplication.

Example 3: The following example illustrates the importance of the above-mentioned corollary:

> Suppose that a relation **Student**{SID, SName, Grade, Dept} is decomposed into S1{SID, SName} and S2{SID, Grade, Dept}.
>
> Assume further that **SID** is the primary key (or at least a candidate key) of **Student**. Note that **SID** also occurs in S1 and S2. It should be obvious that there is no point in proceeding with this decomposition as it simply compounds the duplication problem (**SID** would now be stored in two relations rather than one, to no avail).
>
> Also, decomposition of **Student** into S3{SID, SName} and S4{Grade, Dept} makes no sense.

Conclusion

Based on Heath's theorem and its corollary, we can assert with confidence, the following advice:

- Decompose only when there is a non-loss decomposition such that the resulting relations do not share a candidate key.

- Do not decompose if each resulting relation does not have a primary key.

4.5 The First Normal Form

> A relation R is in the first normal form (1NF) iff it is a flat file i.e. it has no repeating groups, no duplicate records, no null values in the primary key.
>
> Put another way, a relation is in 1NF iff all its underlying simple domains (hence attributes) are atomic, i.e. for every tuple in the relation, each attribute can have only one type of value.

By definition, all relations are in 1NF. This is by no means coincidental, but by design: we defined a relation to consist of atomic attributes, and subject to the entity integrity constraint and the referential integrity constraint. However, as you will soon see, having relations in 1NF only is often not good enough.

Example 4:

> Many accounting software systems on the market will have a file defined as follows:
> EndOfMonth{Acct#, Dept, Bal1, Bal2, ... Bal13}
>
> **Note:**
> 1. Bal1 ... Bal13 are defined on the same domain and therefore constitute a vast amount of space wasting.
> 2. The only time that Bal1 ... Bal13 are all non-null is after Bal13 is known (calculated).
> 3. At the end of each accounting period, this file must be *cleared* and *re-initialized* for the next accounting period.
>
> **Exercise:** How can these problems be solved?

Problems with Relations in 1NF Only

Relation **R0** of the previous section is in 1NF only. However it is undesirable to store it as is due to a number of problems. In the interest of clarity, the relation is restated here:

　　R0{Supl#, SuplName, Item#, ItemName, Quantity, SuplStatus, Location}

Functional dependencies of **R0** as illustrated in Figure 4-2 are as follows:

- FD1: [Supl#, Item#] → {Quantity, SuplName, SuplStatus, Location, ItemName}

- FD2: Supl# → {SuplName, SuplStatus, Location}

- FD3: Item# → ItemName

The following data anomalies exist with **R0** (and most relations in 1NF only):

- **Replication of data:** Every time we record a supplier - item pair, we also have to record supplier name and item name.

- **Insertion anomaly**: We cannot insert a new item until it is supplied; neither can we insert a new supplier until that supplier supplies some item.

- **Deletion anomaly**: We cannot delete an item or a supplier without destroying an entire shipment, as well as information about a supplier's location.

- **Update anomaly:** If we desire to update a supplier's location or item name, we have to update several records, in fact, an entire shipment, due to the duplication problem.

　　Insertion, deletion update anomalies constitute *modification anomalies,* caused by duplication of data due to improper database design.

4.6 The Second Normal Form

> A relation is in the second normal form (2NF) iff it is in 1NF and every *non-key attribute* is fully functionally dependent on the primary key.

By non-key attribute, we mean that the attribute is not part of the primary key. Relation R0 (of the previous section), though in 1NF, is not in 2NF, due to FD2 and FD3. Using Heath's theorem, we may decompose relation R0 as follows (note that the abbreviation PK is used to denote the primary key):

R1{Supl#, Sname, Location, SuplStatus} PK[Suppl#]

R2{Item#, Itemname} PK[Item#]

R3{Supl#, Item#, Qty} PK[Supl#, Item#]

We then check to ensure that the resulting relations are in 2NF (and they are).

So based on the definition of 2NF, and on the authority of Heath's theorem, we would replace **R0** with **R1**, **R2**, and **R3**. Please note the consequences of our treatment of **R0** so far:

1. The problems with relations in 1NF only have been addressed.

2. By decomposing, we have introduced foreign keys in relation R3.

3. JOINing is the opposite of PROJecting. We can rebuild relation R0 by simply JOINing R3 with R1 and R3 with R2, on the respective foreign keys.

4. From the definition of 2NF, two observations should be obvious: Firstly, if you have a relation with a single attribute as the primary key, it is automatically in 2NF. Secondly, if you have a relation with n attributes and $n-1$ of them form the primary key, the relation is also in 2NF.

Problems with Relations in 2NF Only

In this example, relations **R2** and **R3** are in 2NF (in fact they are in 3NF*), but *w*e still have potential problems with **R1**: What if we have a situation where there may be several suppliers from a given location? Or what if we want to keep track of locations of interest? In either case, we would have modification anomalies as described below:

- Insertion anomaly: We cannot record information about a location until we have at least one supplier from that location.

- Deletion anomaly: We cannot delete a particular location without also deleting supplier(s) from that location.

- Update anomaly: If we wish to update information on a location, we have to update all supplier records from that location.

These problems can be addressed if we take the necessary steps to bring R1 into the third normal form (3NF). But first, we must define what 3NF is.

4.7 The Third Normal Form

A relation is in the third normal form (3NF) iff it is in 2NF and no non-key attribute is fully functionally dependent on other non-key attribute(s).

Put another way, a relation is in 3NF iff non-key attributes are *mutually independent* and fully functionally dependent on the primary key. (Two or more attributes are mutually independent if none of them is functionally dependent on any combination of the other.)

Put another way, a relation is in 3NF iff it is in 2NF and every non-key attribute is *non-transitively* dependent on the primary key. (Non-transitivity implies mutual independence.)

Transitive dependence refers to dependence among non-key attributes. In particular, if A → B and B → C, then C is transitively dependent on A (i.e. A→ C transitively).

In the previous section, relation R1 is problematic because it is not in 3NF. If it is desirable to store additional information about the locations as indicated in the previous section, then we must be smart enough to discern that location is to be treated as an entity with attributes such as location code, location name (and perhaps others). Using Heath's theorem, we may therefore decompose R1 as follows:

> **R4**{Supl#, Sname, LocationCode} PK[Supl#]

> **R5**{LocationCode, LocationName} PK[LocationCode]

We now check to ensure that the relations are in 3NF (and they are). Again, please take careful notice of the consequences of our actions to this point:

1. The problems with relations in 2NF only have been addressed.

2. Again, by decomposing, we have introduced a foreign key in relation **R4**.

3. We can rebuild relation **R1** by simply JOINing **R4** with **R5** on the foreign key.

4. From the definition of 3NF, it should be obvious that if you have a relation with one candidate key and *n* mutually independent non-key attributes, or only one non-key attribute, it is in 3NF.

Problems with Relations in 3NF Only

Relations **R2**, **R3**, **R4**, and **R5** above are all in 3NF. However, it has been found that 3NF-only relations suffer from certain inadequacies. It is well known that 3NF does not deal satisfactorily with cases where the following circumstances hold:

- There are multiple composite candidate keys in a relation.

- The candidate keys overlap (i.e. have at least one attribute in common).

67

For these situations, the Boyce-Codd normal form (BCNF) provides the perfect solution. As you shall soon see, the BCNF is really a refinement of 3NF. In fact, where the above-mentioned conditions do not hold, BCNF reduces to 3NF.

4.8 The Boyce-Codd Normal Form

Simply, Boyce-Codd normal form (BCNF) requirement states:

> A relation is in BCNF iff every *determinant* in the relation is a candidate key.

A determinant is an attribute (or group of attributes) on which some other attribute(s) is (are) fully functionally dependent. Examination of **R2**, **R3**, **R4**, and **R5** above will quickly reveal that they are in BCNF (hence 3NF). We therefore need to find a different example that illustrates the importance of BCNF.

Consider the situation where it is desirous to keep track of animals in various zoos, and the assigned keepers for these animals. Let us tentatively construct the relation **R6** as shown below:

> **R6**{Zoo, Animal, Keeper}

Assume further that that a keeper works at one and only one zoo. We can therefore identify the following FDs:

- [Zoo, Animal] → Keeper

- Keeper → Zoo

Given the above, we conclude that [Zoo, Animal] is the primary key. Observe that **R6** is in 3NF but not in BCNF, since **Keeper** is not a candidate key but is clearly a determinant. Using Heath's theorem, we may decompose **R6** as follows:

> **R7**{Animal, Keeper} PK[Animal]

> **R8**{Keeper, Zoo} PK[Keeper]

As on previous occasions, let us examine the consequences of our action:

1. By achieving BCNF, we benefit from further reduction in data duplication, and modification anomalies.

2. A further advantage is that we can now store *dangling records*. In our example, a keeper can be assigned to a zoo even before he/she is assigned an animal.

3. One possible drawback with BCNF is that more relations have to be accessed (joined) in order to obtain useful information. Again referring to the example, **R7** must be joined with **R8** in order to derive Zoo-Animal pairs.

Observe: The principle of BCNF is very simple but profound. By being guided by it, you can actually bypass obtaining 1NF, 2NF and 3NF relations, and move directly into a set of BCNF relations. Adopting this approach will significantly simplify the analysis process. Moreover, in most practical situations, you will not be required to normalize beyond BCNF. This approach will be further clarified in the next chapter.

4.9 The Fourth Normal Form

The fourth normal form (4NF) relates to the situation where mutually independent, but related attributes form a relation and the inefficient arrangement causes duplication and hence modification anomalies. Consider the database file, **CTT-Schedule**, representing course-teacher-text combinations in an educational institution. Assume the following:

    a.   A course can be taught by several teachers.

    b.   A course can require any number of texts.

    c.   Teachers and texts are independent of each other i.e. the same texts are used irrespective of who teaches the course.

    d.   A teacher can teach several courses.

Figure 4-3 provides some sample data for the purpose of illustration.

Course	Teacher	Text
Calculus I	Prof A	Text 1
Calculus I	Prof B	Text1
Calculus II	Prof B	Text 2
Calculus II	Prof B	Text 3
Calculus II	Prof C	Text 2
Calculus II	Prof C	Text 3
...	...	...

Figure 4-3. CTT-Schedule File

Note that the theory so far, does not provide a method of treating such a situation, except flattening the structure (by making each attribute part of the primary key) as shown below:

        R9{Course, Teacher, Text} PK[Course, Teacher, Text]

Since **R9** is keyed on all its attributes, it is in BCNF. Yet, two potential problems are data redundancy and modification anomalies (the former leading to the latter). In our example, in order to record that Calculus II is taught by both Professor B and Professor C, four records are required. In fact, if a course is taught by p professors and requires n texts, the number of records required to represent this situation is p*n. This is extraordinary, and could prove to be very demanding on storage space.

Relation **R9**, though in BCNF, is not in 4NF, because it has a peculiar dependency, called a *multi-valued dependency* (MVD). In order to state the 4NF, we must first define MVD.

4.9.1 Multi-valued Dependency

A multi-valued dependency (MVD) is defined as follows:

> Given a relation R(A, B, C), the MVD A -» B (read "A multi-determines B") holds iff every B-value matching a given (A-value, C-value) pair in R depends only on the A-value and is independent of the C-value.
>
> Further, given R(A B C), A -» B holds iff A -» C also holds. MVDs always go together in pairs like this. We may therefore write A -» B/C.

Please note the following points arising from the definition of an MVD:

1. For MVD, at least three attributes must exist.

2. FDs are MVDs but MVDs are not necessarily FDs.

3. A -» B reads "A multi-determines B" or "B is multi-dependent on A."

Let us get back to **R9**: **Course -» Text/Teacher**. Note that **Course** is the pivot of the MVD. **Course -» Teacher** since **Teacher** depends on Course, independent of Text. **Course -» Text** since **Text** depends on **Course**, independent of **Teacher**.

4.9.2 Fagin's Theorem

Fagin's theorem (named after Ronald Fagin who proposed it) may be stated as follows:

> Relation R{A, B, C} can be non-loss decomposed into projections R1{A, B} and R2{A, C} iff the MVDs A -» B/C both hold.

Note that like Heath's theorem, which prescribes how to treat FDs, Fagin's theorem states exactly how to treat MVDs. With this background, we can proceed to defining the 4NF:

> A relation is in 4NF iff whenever there exists an MVD, say A -» B, then all attributes of R are also functionally dependent on A.
>
> Put another way, R{A, B, C...} is in 4NF iff every MVD satisfied by R is implied by the candidate key of R.
>
> Put another way, R{A, B, C...} is in 4NF iff the only dependencies are of the form [candidate key] → [other non-key attribute(s)].
>
> Put another way, R{A, B, C ...} is in 4NF iff it is in BCNF and there are no MVD's (that are not FDs).

In the current example, **R9** is not in 4NF. This is so because although it is in BCNF, an MVD exists. Using Fagin's theorem, we may decompose it as follows:

> **R10**{Course, Text} PK[Course, Text]

> **R11**{Course, Teacher} PK[Course, Teacher]

Note: Fagin's theorem prescribes a method of decomposing a relation containing an MVD that is slightlydifferent from the decomposition of an FD as prescribed by Heath's theorem: Figure 4-4 clarifies this.

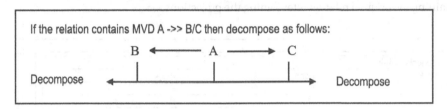

Figure 4-4. *Treating MVDs*

4.10 The Fifth Normal Form

So far we have been treating relations that are decomposable into two other relations. In fact, there are relations which cannot be so decomposed, but can be decomposed into n other relations where n > 2. They are said to be *n-decomposable* relations (n > 2). The fifth normal form (5NF) is also commonly referred to as the *projection-join normal form* (PJNF) because it relates to these (*n* > 2) projections (of a relation not in 5NF) into decompositions that can be rejoined to yield the original relation.

Recall the **SupplierSchedule** relationship (linking suppliers, inventory items and projects) mentioned in section 3.5; it is represented here as outlined below:

> **SupplierSchedule**{Suppl#, Item#, Proj#} PK[Suppl#, Item#, Proj#]

The relation represents a M:M relationship involving **Suppliers**, **Items**, and **Projects**. Observe the following features about the relation:

1. **SupplierSchedule** is keyed on all attributes and therefore by definition, is in BCNF. By inspection, it is also in 4NF.

2. It is not possible to decompose this relation into two other relations.

3. If there are *S* suppliers, N items and J projects, then theoretically, there may be up to S*N*J records. Not all of these may be valid.

4. If we consider S suppliers, each supplying N items to J projects, then it does not take much imagination to see that a fair amount of duplication will take place, despite the fact that the relation is in 4NF.

Let us examine a possible decomposition of **SupplierSchedule** as shown in Figure 4-5. If we employ the first two decompositions only, this will not result in a situation that will guarantee us the original **SupplierSchedule**. In fact, if we were to join these two decompositions (**SI** and **IP**), we would obtain a false representation of the original relation. The third projection (**PS**) is absolutely necessary, if we are to have any guarantee of obtaining the original relation after joining the projections.

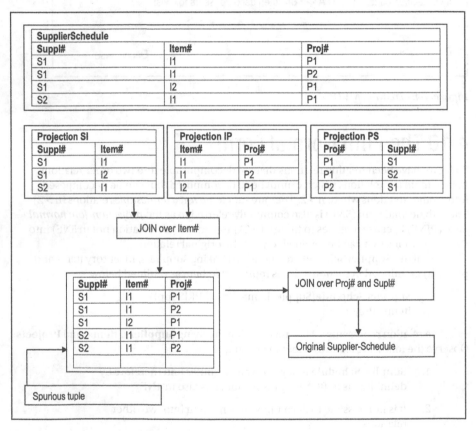

Figure 4-5. *Illustrating Possible Decompositions of Supplier-Schedule*

Note: The first join produces **SupplierSchedule** plus additional *spurious* tuples. The effect of the second join is to eliminate the spurious tuples. To put it into perspective, **SupplierSchedule** is subject to a (time independent) *3-decomposable (3D) constraint*, namely:

If	(s, i) is in SI
and	(i, p) is in IP
and	(p, s) is in PS
then	(s, i, p) is in **SupplierSchedule**

This is an example of a *join dependency (JD) constraint.*

4.10.1 Definition of Join Dependency

A join dependency (JD) constraint may be defined as follows:

> Relation R satisfies the JD P1, P2, ... Pn iff R = P1 JOIN P2 JOIN ... JOIN Pn where the attributes of P1 ... Pn are subsets of the attributes of R.

Relations that are in 4NF, but not in 5NF (such as **SupplierSchedule**) suffer from duplication, which in turn leads to modification anomalies. These problems are directly related to the presence of the JD constraint(s) in such relations. Fagin's theorem for 5NF relations provides the solution.

4.10.2 Fagin's Theorem

Fagin's theorem for the fifth normal form (5NF) states:

> A relation R is in 5NF (also called PJNF) iff every JD in R is a consequence of the candidate keys of R.
>
> In layman's terms if a relation R is in 4NF and it is n-decomposable into P1, P2 .. Pn, such that
> R = P1 JOIN P2 ... JOIN Pn where n > 2,
> such relation is not in 5NF. It may therefore be decomposed to achieve 5NF relations.
>
> Put another way, a relation R is in 5NF iff it is in 4NF and it is not decomposable, except the decompositions are based on a candidate key of R, and the minimum number of projections is 3.

Now examine relation **SupplierSchedule. SupplierSchedule** is not in 5NF because it has a JD (i.e. the JD constraint) that is not a consequence of its candidate key. In other words, **SupplierSchedule** can be decomposed, but this is not implied by its candidate key [Supl#, Item#, Proj#].

Note: For most practical purposes, you only have to worry about 5NF if you are try-ing to implement an M:M relationship involving more than two relations. Once in 5NF, further decompositions would share candidate keys and are therefore to no avail (recall corollary of Heath's theorem). Notwithstanding this, other normal forms have been proposed, as will be discussed in the upcoming section.

4.11 Other Normal Forms

The field of Database Systems is potentially a contemptuous one. Indeed, there are accounts of former friends or colleagues becoming foes over database quibbles (in Figure 4-7 of section 4.12, the current author relates a personal experience he had as a young software engineer on a project of national importance). Various individuals have proposed several database theorems and methodologies, but they have not all gained universal acceptance as have the normal forms of the previous sections. Two additional normal forms that have been, and will no doubt continue to be the subject of debate are the *domain-key normal form* (DKNF) and the *sixth normal form* (6NF). Without picking sides of the debate on these two normal forms, this section will summarize each.

4.11.1 The Domain-Key Normal Form

The domain-key normal form (DKNF) was proposed by Ronald Fagin in 1981. Unlike the other normal forms which all relate to FDs, MVDs and JDs, this normal form is defined in terms of domains and keys (hence its name). In his paper, Fagin showed that a relation DKNF has no modification anomalies, and that a relation without modification anomalies must be in DKNF. He therefore argued that a relation in DKNF needed no further normalization (at least, not for the purpose of reducing modification anomalies). The definition of DKNF is as follows:

> A relation is in DKNF if every constraint on the relation is a logical consequence of the definition of its keys and domains.

This definition contains three important terms that need clarification:

- A constraint is used to mean any rule relating to static values of attributes. Constraints therefore include integrity rules, editing rules, foreign keys, intra-relation references, FDs and MVDs, but exclude time-dependent constraints, cardinality constraints and constraints relating to changes in data values.

- A key is a unique identifier of a row (as defined in Chapter 3).

- A domain is a pool of legal attribute values (as defined in Chapter 3).

The implication of the DKNF is clear: If we have a relation that contains constraint(s) that is (are) not a logical consequence of its (candidate) key and domains, then that relation is not in DKNF, and should therefore be further normalized. The DKNF as proposed by Fagin, therefore represents an ideal situation to strive for.

Unfortunately, a number of problems arise from consideration of DKNF:

- Any constraint that restricts the cardinality of a relation (i.e. the number of tuples in the relation) will render it in violation of DKNF. (It was perhaps for this reason that Fagin excluded from his definition of constraints, time-dependent constraints or constraints relating to data values.) However, there are many relations for which such constraints are required.

- There is no known algorithm for converting a relation to DKNF. The conversion is intuitive and for this reason described as artistic rather than scientific.

- Not all relations can be reduced to DKNF (relations with cardinality constraints fall in this category).

- It is not precisely clear as to when a relation can be reduced to DKNF.

For these reasons, the DKNF has been compared by Date (see [Date, 2006]) to a "straw man... of some considerable theoretical interest but not yet of much practical ditto."

4.11.2 The Sixth Normal Form

A sixth normal form (6NF) has been proposed by C. J. Date in [Date, 2003], after several years of exploitation, expounding, and research in the field of database systems. It relates to so-called *temporal databases*. Date wrote a whole book on the subject; a summary of the essence is presented in this sub-section. Date defines a temporal database as a database that contains historical data as well as, or instead of current data. Temporal databases are often read-only databases, or update-once databases, but they could be used otherwise. In this sense, a temporal database may be considered as a precursor to a data warehouse (discussed in Chapter 24).

For the purpose of illustration, assume that we are in a college or university setting and desire to store the relation **Course** as defined below:

Course {CourseNo, CourseName, CourseCred}

Suppose further that we desire to show different courses at the time they existed in the database. To make our analysis more realistic, let us also make the following additional assumptions:

- The primary key is **CourseNo**; for any given course, the attribute **CourseNo** cannot be changed.

- For any given course, the attribute **CourseName** may be changed any point in time.

- For any given course, the attribute **CourseCred** may be changed any point in time.

We may be tempted to introduce a timestamp on each tuple, and therefore modify the definition of **Course** as follows:

Course {CourseNo, CourseName, CourseCred, EffectiveDate}

Figure 4-6 provides some sample data for the **Course** relation. By introducing the attribute **EffectiveDate**, we have actually introduced a new set of concerns as summarized below:

1. If we assume that the FD CourseNo → {CourseName, CourseCred, EffectiveDate} is (still) in vogue, then **Course** is in 5NF. However, in this case, if the **CourseName** or **CourseCred** of a given **Course** tuple changes at a given effective date, there is no way of showing what it was before, unless we create a new course and assign a new **CourseNo**. In either case, this clearly, is undesirable.

2. Suppose we assume the FDs CourseNo → CourseName and [CourseNo, EffectiveDate] → CourseCred.Then, the relation is not in 2NF, and therefore needs to be decomposed into two decompositions:

   CourseDef {CourseNo, CourseName} and

   CourseTimeStamp {CourseNo, EffectiveDate, CourseCred}

   Both of these relations would now be in 5NF. However, if we now desire to change the **CourseName** of a course for a given effective date, we cannot represent this in the current schema.

3. We could introduce a surrogate (say **CourseRef**) into relation **Course**, and key on the surrogate, while ignoring the FDs stated in (1) and (2) above. In this case, **Course** would be in violation of 3NF, and if we attempt to decompose, we would revert to the situation in case (2) above.

CourseNo	CourseName	CourseCred	EffectiveDate
CS120	Introduction to Computer Science	3	1990
CS120	Introduction to Computer Science	4	2005
CS140	Computer Programming I	3	1990
CS140	Computer Programming I	4	2005
CS145	Computer Programming II	3	1990
CS145	Computer Programming II	4	2005
CS130	Pascal Programming	3	1990
...			

Figure 4-6. *Sample Data for the Course Relation*

The reason for these problems can be explained as follows: The relation **Course** as described, defines the following predicate:

- Each course is to be accounted for (we say **Course** is under contract).

- Each course has a **CourseName** which is under contract.

- Each course has a **CourseCred** which is under contract.

The predicate involves three distinct propositions. We are attempting to use the timestamp attribute (**EffectiveDate**) to represent more than one proposition about the attribute values. This, according to Date, is undesirable and violates the sixth normal form. We now state Date's theorem for the sixth normal form (6NF):

A relation R is in 6NF iff it satisfies no non-trivial JDs at all. (A JD is trivial iff at least one of its projections is over all of the attributes of the relation.)

Put another way, a relation R is in 6NF iff the only JDs that it satisfies are trivial ones.

Note: 6NF as defined, essentially refines 5NF. It is therefore obvious from the definition that a relation in 6NF is necessarily in 5NF also.

Let us now revisit the **Course** relation: With the introduction of the timestamp attribute (**EffectiveDate**), and given the requirements of the relation, there is a non-trivial JD that leads to the following projections:

CourseInTime {CourseNo, EffectiveDate} PK [CourseNo, EffectiveDate]

CourseNameInTime {CourseNo, CourseName, EffectiveDate} PK [CourseNo, EffectiveDate]

CourseCredInTime {CourseNo, CourseCred, EffectiveDate} PK [CourseNo, EffectiveDate]

Observe that the projection **CourseInTime** is strictly speaking, redundant, since it can be obtained by a projection from either **CourseNameInTime** or **CourseCredInTime**. However, in the interest of clarity and completeness, it has been included.

This work by C. J. Date represents a significant contribution to the field of database systems, and will no doubt be a topical point of discussion in the future.

4.12 Summary and Concluding Remarks

This concludes one of the most important topics in your database systems course. Take some time to go over the concepts. Figure 4-7 should help you to remember the salient points.

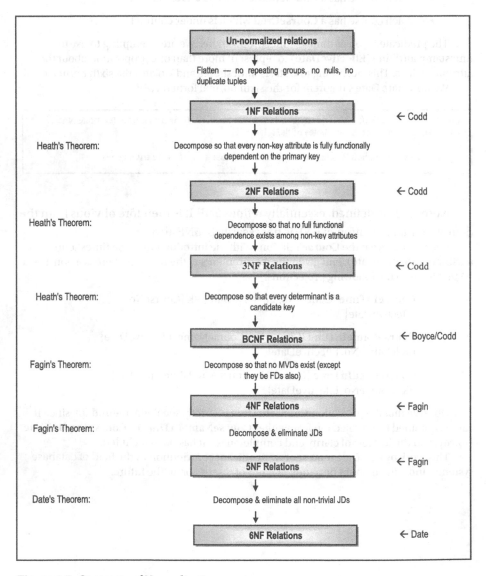

Figure 4-7. Summary of Normalization

Traditionally, it has been widely accepted that for most databases, attainment of 3NF is acceptable. This course recommends a minimum attainment of BCNF. Recall that as stated earlier (in section 4.8), BCNF is really a refinement of 3NF, and the normalization process can bypass 2NF and 3NF, and go straight to BCNF. In rare circumstances, it may be required to proceed to 5NF or 6NF, which is the ultimate.

Normalization is a technique that must be mastered by database designers. It improves with practice and experience, and ultimately becomes almost intuitive. As your mastery of normalization improves, you will find that there is a corresponding improvement in your ability to design and/or propose database systems for various software systems. However, be aware that the converse is also true: failure to master fundamental principles of database design will significantly impair one's ability to design quality software systems. Notwithstanding this, be careful not to be antagonistic about your views, as informed as they may be. In this regard, Figure 4-8 summarizes a practical experience of the author.

Between 1987 and 1990, I was part of the software engineering team that investigated, designed, developed and implemented two huge strategic information systems (though I did not know the correct term at the time) for the Central Bank of Jamaica — an Economic Management System (EMS) and a Bank Inspection System (BIS). Both projects were immensely successful. I have warm memories of them, but I relate two not-so-warm experiences as a word of caution to young database systems enthusiasts:

- I soon found a niche for myself and distinguished myself as a database design expert. However, I often ran into confrontations with my then supervisor (who subsequently became my consulting partner on a number of other major projects) for finding faults with the database design proposed by the project team. Looking back, I was brash and tactless, and often created enemies by my rash comments.
- On one occasion, my brash, tactless approach almost shattered the relationship with my best friend, Ashley. We along with three others were hired by the central bank, and placed on the project, after a regional search. That was special. Ashley and I had distinguished ourselves as outstanding software engineers and database experts. For that reason, we were asked to design a sub-system together. We soon had conflicts over the design approach to be taken. Ashley had one idea; I had another idea, and the two of us would not agree. Realizing that our friendship was heading south over the conflict, I backed off and allowed Ashley's proposal to be accepted, but later tweaked its implementation when he was not paying attention. Looking back, we were both being silly: The most prudent proposal should have been a merge of the two ideas.

Figure 4-8. Database Quibbles almost got me in Trouble

4.13 Review Questions

1.   State the two fundamental integrity rules and explain their significance.

2.   What is a foreign key? Illustrate using an appropriate example. How should foreign keys be treated?

3.   Clarify the following: functional dependence; non-loss decomposition; Heath's theorem. Provide examples that will illustrate the significance of these terms.

4.   State the normal forms covered in this Chapter. For each normal form, state it, explain in your own words what it means, provide an example of a relation that conforms to it and one that does not.

4.14 References and/or Recommended Readings

[Codd, 1972] Codd, Edgar F. "Further Normalization of the Database Relational Model." *Database* Systems, Courant Computer Science Symposia Series 6. Eaglewood Cliffs, NJ: Prentice Hall, 1972.

[Codd, 1974] Codd. Edgar F. "Recent Investigations into Relational Data Base Systems." Proc. IFIP Congress, Stockholm, Sweden, 1974.

[Connolly, 2002] Connolly, Thomas and Carolyn Begg. Database Systems: A Practical Approach to Design, Implementation and Management 3rd ed. New York: Addison-Wesley, 2002. See Chapter 13.

[Date, 2003] Date, Christopher J., Hugh Darwen and Nikos A. Lorentzos. Temporal Databases and the Relational Model. San Francisco, CA: Morgan-Kaufmann, 2003.

[Date, 2004] Date, Christopher J. *Introduction to Database Systems* 8th ed. Menlo Park, California: Addison-Wesley, 2004. See Chapters 11-13, 23.

[Date, 2006] Date, Christopher J. *Database Debunking*. http://www.dbdebunk.com/page/page/621935.htm (accessed June 2006)

[Elmasri, 2007] Elmasri, Ramez and Shamkant B. Navathe. *Fundamentals of Database Systems* 5th ed. Reading, MA: Addison-Wesley, 2007. See Chapters 10 and 11.

[Fagin, 1977] Fagin, Ronald. "Multi-valued Dependencies and a New Normal Form for Relational Databases." *ACM TODS 2, No. 3*, September 1977.

[Fagin, 1979] Fagin, Ronald. "Normal Forms and Relational Database Operations." *Proc. 1979 ACM SIGMOD International Conference on Management of Data*. Boston, MA, May-June 1979.

[Fagin, 1981] Fagin, Ronald. "A Normal Form for Relational Databases that is Based on Domains and Keys." *ACM TODS 6, No. 3*, September 1981.

[Garcia-Molina, 2002] Garcia-Molina, Hector, Jeffrey Ullman and Jennifer Widom. *Database Systems: The Complete Book*. Upper Saddle River, NJ: Prentice Hall, 2002. See Chapter 3.

[Heath, 1971] Heath. I. J. "Unacceptable File Operations in a Relational Database." *Proc. 1971 ACM SIGFIDET Workshop on Data Description, Access, and Control*. San Diego, CA., November 1971.

[Hoffer, 2007] Hoffer, Jeffrey A., Mary B. Prescott and Fred R. McFadden. *Modern Database Management* 6th ed. Upper Saddle River, NJ: Prentice Hall, 2002. See Chapters 5.

[Kifer, 2005] Kifer, Michael, Arthur Bernstein and Philip M. Lewis. Database Systems: An Application-Oriented Approach 2nd ed. New York, NY: Addison-Wesley, 2005. See Chapter 6.

[Kroenke, 2005] Kroenke, David M. *Database Processing: Fundamentals, Design and Implementation 9th ed.* Upper Saddle River, NJ: Prentice Hall, 2004. See Chapter 4.

[Lewis, 2002] Lewis. Phillip M., Arthur Bernstein and Michael Kifer. *Databases and Transaction* Processing: An Application Oriented Approach. New York, NY: Addison-Wesley, 2002. See Chapter 8.

[Martin, 1995] Martin, James, and Joe Leben. Client/Server Databases: Enterprise Computing. Upper Saddle River, NJ: Prentice Hall, 1995. See Chapters 10, 13, 14.

[Ozsu, 1991] Ozsu, M. Tamer, and Patrick Valduriez. Principles of Distributed Database Systems. Eaglewood Cliffs, NJ: Prentice Hall, 1991. See Chapter 2.

[Pratt, 2002] Pratt, Phillip J. and Joseph J. Adamski. Concepts of Database Management 4th ed. Boston, Massachusetts: Course Technology, 2002. See Chapter 5.

[Riccardi, 2002] Riccardi, Greg. Database Management With Web Site Development Applications. Boston, MA: Addison-Wesley, 2003. See Chapter 7.

[Rob, 2007] Rob, Peter and Carlos Coronel. *Database Systems: Design, Implementation & Management* 7th ed. Boston, MA: Course Technology, 2007. See Chapter 5.

[Ullman, 1997] Ullman, Jeffrey D., and Jennifer Widom. *A First Course in Database Systems*. Upper Saddle River, NJ: Prentice Hall, 1997. See Chapter 3.

■ ■ ■

Database Modeling and Design

Some database systems textbooks make much ado about having separate chapters for database modeling and database design. In this course, we will not, and the reason will become clear shortly. All discussions in chapters 3 and 4 contribute to database modeling and design. In particular, ERDs and normalization are paramount to a logical database model and design. In this chapter, we will clarify the roles of database modeling and database design, and then take a more detailed look at some approaches in these areas. The chapter proceeds under the following captions:

- Database Model and Database Design

- The E-R Model Revisited

- Database Design With the E-R Model

- The Extended Relational Model

- Database Design With the Extended Relational Model

- The UML Model

- Database Design With the UML Model

- Innovation: The Object/Entity Specification Grid

- Database Design Using Normalization Theory

- Database Model and Design Tools

- Summary and Concluding Remarks

5.1 Database Model and Database Design

Database modeling and database design are closely related; in fact, the former leads to the latter. However, it is incorrect to assume that the path from database modeling to database design is an irreversible one. To the contrary, changes in your database model will affect your database design and vice versa. This course therefore purports that you can work on your database model and your database design in parallel, and with experience, you can merge both into one phase. For the purpose of discussion, let us look at each phase.

5.1.1 Database Model

The database model is the blueprint for the database design. Database modeling is therefore the preparation of that blueprint. In database modeling, we construct a representation of the database that will be useful towards the design and construction of the database. Various approaches to database modeling have been proposed by different authors; the prominent ones are:

- The Entity-Relationship (E-R) Model

- The Object-Relationship (O-R) Model

- The Extended Relational Model

The E-R and O-R models were introduced in chapter 3 (sections 3.5.1 and 3.5.2). Chapter 3 also introduced the Relation-Attributes List (RAL) and the Relationship List (RL section 3.6) as an alternative to the E-R model in situations where E-R modeling is impractical. We will revisit the E-R model later in this chapter, and then introduce the extended relational model.

5.1.2 Database Design

The database design is the (final) specification that will be used to construct the actual database. Database designing is therefore the preparation of this specification. In preparing the database specification, the database model is used as input. As such, the guidelines given in chapter 3 (section 3.5.4) on implementing relationships are applicable. Five approaches to database design that will be discussed later in this chapter are:

- Database Design via the E-R Model

- Database Design via the Extended Relational Model

- Database Design via the UML Model

- Database Design via the Entity/Object Specification Grid

- Database Design via Normalization Theory

5.2 The E-R Model Revisited

Recall that in chapter 3, the similarity and differences between an entity and a relation were noted. If we assume the similarity, then the E-R model can be construed as merely a specific interpretation of the relational model.

In order to unify the informal E-R model with the formal relational model, Codd introduced a number of conventions specific to the E-R model. These are summarized in Figure 5-1 and illustrated in Figure 5-2. Note that the model displayed in the figure represents only a section of the (partial) database model introduced in chapter 3 (review Figure 3-4b). Figure 5-2a employs the Chen notation, while Figure 5-2b employs the Crow's Foot notation. In both cases, the attributes of entities have been omitted, except for primary key attributes (as mentioned in chapter 3 and emphasized later in this chapter, there are more creative ways to represent attributes). Figure 5-3 illustrates the representation of super-type and subtype relationships.

- A *weak entity* is one that cannot exist by itself. For instance, if employees have dependents then **Dependents** is a weak entity and **Employee** is a *regular entity*. On the E-R diagram, weak entities are represented by double lines.

- Relationships may be represented by either Chen's notation, or the Crow's Foot notation.

- If Chen's notation is used to represent relationships, then the following apply:
  - The double diamond indicates a relationship between weak and regular entity.
  - The name of the relationship is written inside the diamond.
  - A double relationship line represents *total participation;* a single relationship line represents *partial participation*. For instance, If all dependents must have a reference employee, participation is total on the part of dependents; however, all employees need not have dependents, so that participation is partial on the part of employees.

- *Entity Types* are used to distinguish entities. An entity can be a *subtype* of another entity that is a *super-type*. For instance, in an organization, the entity Programmer would be a subtype of the entity Employee, the super-type. All properties of a super-type apply to its subtype; the converse does not hold. Figure 5.3 illustrates how subtypes and super-types are represented.

- Implementation of relationships can be realized as discussed in chapter 3. Furthermore, the fundamental integrity rules (section 4.1) must also be upheld.

Figure 5-1. *E-R Model Conventions*

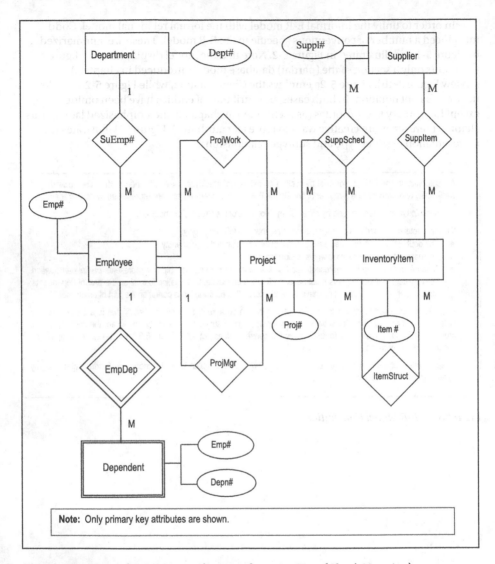

Figure 5-2a. *Partial E-R Diagram for Manufacturing Firm (Chen's Notation)*

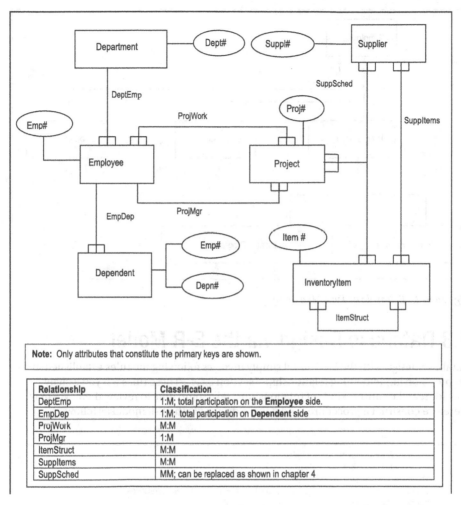

Note: Only attributes that constitute the primary keys are shown.

Relationship	Classification
DeptEmp	1:M; total participation on the **Employee** side.
EmpDep	1:M; total participation on **Dependent** side
ProjWork	M:M
ProjMgr	1:M
ItemStruct	M:M
SuppItems	M:M
SuppSched	MM; can be replaced as shown in chapter 4

Figure 5-2b. *Alternate Partial E-R Diagram for Manufacturing Firm (Crow's Feet Notation)*

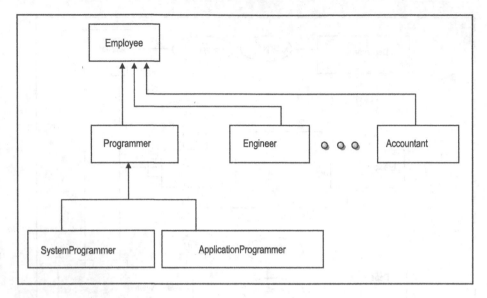

Figure 5-3. *Example of Type Hierarchy*

5.3 Database Design via the E-R Model

Database design with the E-R model simply involves following the rules established in chapter 3 on implementing relationships (section 3.5.4). These rules tell you exactly how to treat the various kinds of relationships; take some time to review them. We may therefore construct a procedure for database design via the E-R model as follows:

1. Identify all entities and their related attributes.
2. Classify the entities (weak versus strong).
3. Identify all relationships among the entities.
4. Classify the relationships (mandatory versus optional); decide on which optional relationships will be retained and which ones will be eliminated.
5. Construct an ERD or the equivalent (review chapter 3).
6. Refine the model.
7. Using the guidelines for implementing relationships (section 3.5.4), construct a final set of relations, clearly indicating for each relation, its attributes, candidate key(s), and primary key. The RAL and RL of chapter 3 (section 3.6) may be employed.
8. By consistently following this procedure, you will obtain a set of relations that will be normalized to at least the Boyce-Codd normal form (BCNF). You can then apply your normalization theory until you achieve the desired level of normalization.

Note: The illustrations given in chapter 3 (figures 3.4b, 3.13 and 3.14) are applicable here.

Figure 5-4. *Database Design Procedure Using the E-R Model*

5.4 The Extended Relational Model

Even with the conventions above, the E-R model was found lacking in its treatment of certain scenarios. Recognizing this, Codd and Date introduced an alternate *extended relational model* (which for convenience will be abbreviated as the XR model), the essence of which is described here (for more details, see [Date, 1990] and [Date, 2004]).

The XR model makes no distinction between entities and relations; an entity is a special kind of relation. Structural and integrity aspects are more extensive and precisely defined than those of the E-R model. The XR model introduces its own special operators apart from those of the basic relational model. Additionally, entities (and relationships) are represented as a set of E-relations and P-relations.

The model includes a formal catalog structure by which relationships can be made known to the system, thus facilitating the enforcement of integrity constraints implied by such relationships.

As you will see later in the course, it turns out that the XR model forms the basis of how the system catalog is handled in most contemporary DBMS suites. We shall therefore spend a few moments to look at the main features of the model.

5.4.1 Entity Classifications

Under the XR model, the following entity classifications hold:

- Kernel entities

- Characteristic entities

- Designative entities

- Associative entities

- Sub-type/super-type entities

Kernel Entities: *Kernel entities* are those entities that have independent existence. They are what the database is really about. For example, in an inventory system, kernel entities might be **Purchase Order**, **Receipts of Goods** (Invoice), **Inventory Item**, **Department** and **Issuance of Goods** (to various departments). Referring to the example used in the previous section, kernel entities would be **Suppliers**, **InventoryItems**, **Projects, Employees**, and **Departments**.

Characteristic Entities: *Characteristic entities* describe other entities. For instance (referring to Figure 5-2b), **Dependent** is a characteristic of **Employee**. Characteristics are existence-dependent on the entity they describe.

Designative Entities: An entity, regardless of its classification, can have a property (attribute) whosefunction is to *designate* (reference) some other entity, thus implementing a 1:M relationship. For instance (referring to Figure 5-2b), **Employee** is *designative* of **Department**, and **Project** is designative of **Employee** (due to relationship **ProjMgr**). Put another way, a designation is the implementation of an M:1 relationship. The designating entity is the entity on the "many-side" of a 1:M relationship. **Note** that a characteristic entity is necessarily designative since it designates the entity on which it is existence-dependent. Note however, that a designative entity is not necessarily characteristic. Entities **Project, Employee**, and **Dependent** amplify these points (see Figure 5-2).

89

Associative Entities: *Associative entities* represent M:M relationships among two or more entities. For example, from Figure 5-2b, the relationships **ProjWork**, **SuppSched**, **SuppItems**, and **ItemStruct** would be implemented as associative entities. In a college database with kernel entities **Program** and **Course** (among others of course), and a M:M relationship between them, the associative entity representing the relationship could be **ProgramStructure**, which would include foreign keys referencing **Program** and **Course** respectively. Note that the associative entity is the intersecting relation in the implementation of a M:M relationship (review chapter 3, section 3.5.4).

Subtype/Super-type Entities: If we have two entities E1 and E2, such that a record of E1 is always a record of E2, and a record of E2 is sometimes a record of E1, then E1 is said to be a subtype of E2. The existence of a subtype implies the existence of a super-type: To say that E1 is a subtype of E2, is equivalent to saying that E2 is the super-type of E1. For illustration, review Figure 5-3.

5.4.2 Surrogates

Recall that the concept of a surrogate was first introduced in chapter 3 (section 3.5.4). In understanding the X-R model, the role of surrogates is very important; we therefore revisit the concept here. Surrogates are system controlled primary keys, defined to avoid identification of records (tuples) by user-controlled primary keys. They are also often used to replace composite primary keys. Two consequences of surrogates arise (both of which can be relaxed with a slight deviation from the XR model which does not enforce surrogates, *E-relations* and *P-relations* as mandatory):

- Primary and foreign keys can be made to always be non-composite.

- Foreign keys always reference corresponding E-relations (more on this shortly).

Surrogates provide two significant benefits:

- In some traditional DBMS suites, composite primary keys are not allowed; surrogates are therefore imperative.

- Even if allowed by the DBMS, composite primary keys are sometimes cumbersome; surrogates are useful replacements in these circumstances.

To demonstrate the usefulness of surrogates in simplifying database model and ultimate design (with respect to avoiding cumbersome composite primary keys), let us suppose that we want to track purchase orders and their related invoices. The related entities that we would need to track are **Supplier**, **InventoryItem**, **PurchaseOrder** and **PurchaseInvoice**. These are not all included in Figure 5-2; however they are represented in figure 3-4b of chapter 3 (please review). By following through on the E-R model, or by applying normalization principles of chapter 4, we may construct a tentative set of normalized relations as illustrated in Figure 5-5a. Notice how potentially cumbersome the composite keys would be, particularly on relations **PurchaseOrdDetail** and **PurchaseInvDetail**. However, by introducing surrogates as illustrated in Figure 5-5b, we minimize the need to use complex composite keys.

Supplier {Suppl#, SuppName, Address, E-mail, ContactPerson, Telephone, ...}
PK [Supplier#]

InventoryItem {Item#, ItemName, QuantityOnHand, LastPrice, AveragePrice, ...}
PK [Item#]

PurchaseOrdSummary {Order#, OrderDate, *OrderSupp#*, OrderStatus, OrderEstimate, ...}
PK [Order#, OrderDate, OrderSupp#] /* Assuming order numbers may be repeated after a cycle of several years */

PurchaseOrdDetail {POD*Order#*, *PODOrderDate*, POD*OrderSupp#*, *PODItem#*, OrderQuantity, ...}
PK [PODOrder#, PODOrderDate, PODOrderSupp#, PODItem#]

PurchaseInvSummary {Invoice#, *InvOrder#*, *InvOrderDate*, *InvSupp#*, InvDate, InvAmount, InvStatus, InvDiscount, InvTax, InvAmountDue, ...}
PK [Invoice#, InvoiceDate, InvOrder#, InvOrderDate, InvSupp#]

PurchaseInvDetail {PIDInvoice#, PIDInvoiceDate, PIDInvOrder#, PIDInvOrderDate, PIDInvSupp#, PIDItem#, PIDItemQuantity, PIDItemUnitPrice}
PK [PIDInvoice#, PIDInvoiceDate, PIDInvOrder#, PIDInvOrderDate, PIDInvSupp#, PIDItem#]

Note: Foreign keys are *italicized*.

Figure 5-5a. *Model to Track Purchase Orders and Invoices (without Surrogates)*

Supplier {Suppl#, Supp-Name, Address, E-mail, Contact-Person, Telephone, etc.)
PK [Supplier#]

InventoryItem {Item#, Item-Name, Quantity-On-Hand, Last-Price, Average-Price, etc.}
PK [Item#]

PurchaseOrdSummary {OrderRef, Order#, OrderDate, OrderSupp#, OrderStatus, OrderEstimate, ...}
PK [OrderRef] /* OrderRef is a surrogate. Alternately, we may define Order# to be non-repeatable */

PurchaseOrdDetail {*PODOrderRef*, *PODItem#*,, OrderQuantity}
PK [PODOrderRef, PODItem#] /* or introduce a surrogate, **PODCode**, and make it the PK */

PurchaseInvSummary {PurchaseRef, Invoice#, *InvOrderRef*, InvDate, InvAmount, InvStatus, InvDiscount, InvTax, InvAmountDue, ...}
PK [PurchaseRef] /* PurchaseRef is a surrogate */

PurchaseInvDetail {PIDPurchaseRef, PIDItem#, PIDItemQuantity, PIDItemPrice}
PK [PIDPurchaseRef, PIDItem#] /* or introduce a surrogate, **PIDCode**, and make it the PK */

Note: Foreign keys are *italicized*.

Figure 5-5b. *Alternate Model to Track Purchase Orders and Invoices (with Surrogates)*

5.4.3 E-Relations and P-Relations

The original XR model specification prescribes the use of *E-relations* and *P-relations*. The database would contain one *E-relation* for each entity type — a unary relation that lists surrogates for all tuples of that entity (type). To illustrate, let us revisit the manufacturing firm's partial database (Figure 5-2) of previous discussions: Suppose for a moment that the **Supplier** relation contains two tuples, the **InventoryItem** relation contains three tuples, and the **Department** relation contains three tuples. A possible internal representation of the E-relations for this scenario is illustrated in Figure 5-6a. An "E" is inserted in front of the original relation name (for example **E-Supplier**) to denote the fact that this is an E-relation being represented. The percent sign (%) next to the attributes (for example **Suppl%**) are used to denote the fact that these attributes are really surrogates.

In addition to the E-relations concerned with tuples, a special binary E-relation would be required to link so-called E-relations to the original relations. We will call this the *host E-relation*. It is illustrated in Figure 5-6b. This would allow users to relate to the database using relation names that they are familiar with; translation would be transparent to them.

Properties (attributes) for a given entity type are represented by a set of *P-relations*. The P-relation stores all property characteristics and values of all tuples listed in the corresponding E-relation. Properties can be grouped together in a single n-ary relation, or each property can be represented by P-relation, or there can be a convenient number of P-relations used; the choice depends on the designer. In the interest of simplicity, let us assume the third approach; let us assume further, that there is a P-relation for each E-relation. A convenient possible representation for the E-relations of Figure 5-6a is illustrated in Figure 5-6c. A "P" is inserted in front of the original relation name (for example **P-Supplier**) to denote the fact that this is a P-relation being represented. Notice also that each P-relation contains a foreign key that ensures that each tuple is referenced back to its correspondent in the associated E-relation.

Carrying on with the assumption that there is a P-relation for each E-relation: In addition to the basic P-relations, a special P-relation would be required to store the characteristics of each property (to be) defined in the database. Let us call this the *host P-relation*. It is represented in Figure 5-6d. By including this relation, we allow users the flexibility of adding new properties to a relation, modifying existing properties in a relation, or deleting pre-existent properties from a relation. These changes are referred to as *structural changes* to a relation; they will be amplified later in the course (chapter 11).

E-Supplier: Suppl%	E-InventoryItem: Item%	E-Department: Dept%
SE1	IE1	DE1
SE2	IE2	DE2
	IE3	DE3

Figure 5-6a. *Illustrating E-relations*

E-Host:	
Relation	**E-relation**
Department	E-Department
InventoryItem	E-InventoryItem
Supplier	E-Supplier

Figure 5-6b. *Illustrating the Host E-relation*

P-Supplier:			
Suppl%	**Suppl#**	**SuppName**	**Address**
SE1	S1	Smithsonian	11 Sydney Way …
SE2	S2	Bruce Jones Inc.	14 Maple Street …

P-InventoryItem:			
Item%	**Item#**	**ItemName**	
IE1	I1	HP 500 Printer	
IE2	I2	Epson 1070 Printer	
IE3	I3	Xerox Laser Printer	

P-Department:			
Dept%	**Dept#**	**DeptName**	
DE1	D1	Design	
DE2	D2	Research	
DE3	D3	Synthesis	

Figure 5-6c. *Illustrating The P-relations*

P-Host:			
Property	**E-relation**	**Type**	**Length**
Dept#	E-Department	Number	04
DeptName	E-Department	Character	40
…			
Item#	E-InventoryItem	Character	08
DeptName	E-InventoryItem	Character	30
…			
Suppl#	E-Supplier	Character	08
SupplName	E-Supplier	Character	40
Address	E-Supplier	Character	45
…			

Figure 5-6d. *Illustrating the Host P-relation*

93

As you will later see (in chapter 14), it is application of this methodology that assists in the implementation of sophisticated system catalogs that characterize contemporary DBMS suites. However, with this knowledge, you can actually model and design databases to mirror E-relations and P-relations as described. One obvious advantage is that if you used one P-relation instead of one for each E-relation, then in accessing the database for actual data, you would be accessing fewer relations (in fact just one relation) than if you had used another approach (such as the E-R model). The flip side to this advantage is that this relation would be extremely large for a medium sized or large database; this could potentially offset at least some of the efficiency gained from just having to access one relation for data values.

5.4.4 Integrity Rules

With this set-up, accessing and manipulating data in the database is accomplished by the DBMS through the E and P relations. For this reason, additional integrity rules must be imposed. The complete list of integrity rules follows:

1. Entity integrity rule (review section 4.1)

2. Referential rule (review section 4.1)

3. XR Model Entity Integrity: E-relations accept insertions and deletions but no updates (surrogates don't change)

4. Property Integrity: A property cannot exist in the database unless the tuple (entity) it describes exists

5. Characteristic Integrity: A characteristic entity (tuple) cannot exist unless the entity (tuple) it describes exists

6. Association Integrity: An association entity (tuple) cannot exist unless each participating entity (tuple) also exists

7. Designation Integrity: A designative entity (tuple) cannot exist unless the entity (tuple) it designates also exists

8. Subtype Integrity: A subtype entity (tuple) cannot exist except there be a corresponding super-type entity (tuple)

The following rules apply to subtypes and super-types:

1. All characteristics of a super-type are automatically characteristics of the corresponding subtype(s), but the converse does not hold.

2. All associations in which a super-type participates are automatically associations in which the corresponding subtype(s) participate, but the converse does not hold.

3. All properties of a given super-type apply to the corresponding subtype(s), but the converse does not hold.

4. A subtype of a kernel is still a kernel; a subtype of a characteristic is still a characteristic; a subtype of an association is still an association.

Exercise

> Model and design a database using the E-R model. Repeat the exercise using the X-R model. Implement both databases and compare their performance.

5.5 Database Design via the XR Model

The following approach, developed by Date and outlined in [Date, 1990], employs the basic XR method, but relaxes the requirement that surrogates, E-relations and P-relations are mandatory. The (partial)database model represented in Figure 5-2 will be used for the purpose of illustration.

Before proceeding, we now introduce a notation that has become necessary: The notation R.A will be used to mean attribute A in relation (or entity) R. For instance, **Department.Dept#** denotes attribute **Dept#** in the relation **Department**. The database design approach involves seven steps as summarized in Figure 5-7 and clarified in the upcoming subsections.

1. Determine kernel entities.
2. Determine characteristic entities.
3. Determine Designative entities.
4. Determine associations.
5. Determine subtypes and super-types.
6. Determine component entities.
7. Determine properties of each entity.
8. Construct a relation-attribute list (RAL) for each relation.
9. By consistently following this procedure, you will obtain a set of relations that will be normalized to at least the Boyce-Codd normal form (BCNF). You can then apply your normalization theory until you achieve the desired level of normalization.

Figure 5-7. *Database Design Procedure Using the XR Model*

5.5.1 Determining the Kernel Entities

The first step involves determining the kernel entities. As mentioned, earlier, kernels are the core relations. In the example, the kernels are **Department, Employee, Supplier, Project**, and **InventoryItem**. Each kernel translates to a base relation. The primary key of each could be the user controlled ones, or surrogates may be introduced.

5.5.2 Determining the Characteristic Entities

The second step involves determining and properly structuring the characteristic entities. As mentioned above, a characteristic entity is existence-dependent on the entity it describes. One characteristic exists in the example, namely **Dependent**. Characteristics also translate to base relations. The foreign key in **Dependent** would be **DepnEmp#**, which would reference **Employee.Emp#**. Notice that we did not use the attribute name **Emp#** as the foreign key in **Dependent**, but **DepnEmp#**. This decision is based on the following principle:

> It is good design practice to define each attribute so that it is unique to the database (even if the attribute is a foreign key).

It should be noted that not all DBMS products support this principle (some require that a foreign key must have the same name as the attribute it references). You should therefore check to ascertain whether the product you are using supports it (Oracle and DB2 both do). Two strong arguments can be given in defense of this principle:

- Simply, it makes good sense and leads to a cleaner, more elegant database design.

- It avoids confusion when queries involving the joining of multiple relations are constructed and executed on the database. This will become clearer in division C (particularly chapter 12) of the text.

Moving on to data integrity, we would require the following integrity constraints on the **Dependent** relation:

- Null FKs not allowed

- Deletion is cascaded from the referenced to the referencing records

- Update cascaded from the referenced to the referencing records

Two alternatives exist for choice of primary key:

a. The foreign key combined with the attribute that distinguishes different characteristics within the target entity (e.g. [**Emp#**, **DepnName**]);

b. Introduce a surrogate (e.g. **DepnRef**). The surrogate could be defined in such as way as to allow you to key solely on it; or it could be defined to allow you to key on the foreign key, combined with it (e.g. [**Emp#**, **DepnRef**]).

5.5.3 Determining the Designative Entities

This third step involves identifying and properly structuring the designative entities. As mentioned earlier, a designation is a 1:M or 1:1 relationship between two entities. In the example, designations are **ProjMgr**, **DeptEmp**, and **EmpDep**. However, **EmpDep** is a characteristic (that has already been identified above).

From the theory established in chapter 3 (section 3.5.4), a designation is implemented by the introduction of a foreign key in the relation for the designating entity. Following this principle, we would introduce foreign key, **EmpDept#** in relation **Employee** (where **EmpDept#** references **Department.Dept#**), and foreign key, **ProjManagerEmp#** in relation **Project** (where **ProjManagerEmp#** references **Employee.Emp#**).

Integrity constraints for designations would typically be:

- Null FKs allowed in the designating entity if the participation is partial

- Null FKs not allowed in the designating entity if the participation is full

- Deletion of referenced records restricted

- Update of referenced records restricted (although for some practical purposes, update could be cascaded)

Typically, the foreign key in a designative entity is a non-key attribute. Consequently, there are normally no keying issues. However, there could be exceptions to this observation (for instance in the case where an intersecting relation is introduced to implement a M:M relationship).

5.5.4 Determining the Associations

Step 4 involves identification and implementation of all associations. As mentioned earlier, associations are the implementation of M:M relationships. They translate to base relations. In the example, associations are **ProjWork**, **SuppItems**, **ItemStruct**, and **SuppSched**. Again relying on the theory established in chapter 3 (section 3.5.4) on the implementation of M:M relationships, we would introduce four base relations for the four associations — **ProjWork**, **SuppItems**, **ItemStruct**, and **SuppSched**. However, as established in chapter 4 (section 4.10), **SuppSched** should be replaced with three relations, namely **SuppItems**{Suppl#, Item#}, **ItemProj**{Item#, Proj#}, and **ProjSupp**{Proj#, Suppl#}. Additionally, and in keeping with the principle of having unique attribute names for the entire database, we will change the foreign key attribute names to names that are unique but easily traceable to the attributes they reference.

Integrity constraints for associations would typically be:

- Null FKs not allowed

- Deletion of referenced records restricted

- Update of referenced records restricted

Two alternatives exist for choice of primary key:

a.   Key on the aggregation of the foreign keys.

b.   Introduce a surrogate and key on it.

5.5.5 Determining Entity Subtypes and Super-types

The fifth step relates to identifying and properly implementing subtype-super-type relationships among the entities. Care should be taken here, in not introducing subtype-super-type relationships where traditional relationships would suffice (review section 3.5). Each entity type translates to a base relation. Each base relation will contain attributes corresponding to properties of the entities that apply within the type hierarchy. Again being guided by principles established in chapter 3 (section 3.5.4), each subtype will share the primary key of its super-type. Further, the primary key of a subtype is also the foreign key of the said subtype. The illustrations provided in chapter 3 (Figures 3-11 and 3.12) are also applicable here.

No subtype-super-type relationship appears in the model of Figure 5-2. However, in Figure 5-3, there are a few: **Programmer**, **Engineer** and **Accountant** are subtypes of **Employee**; **SystemProgrammer** and **ApplicationProgrammer** are subtypes of **Programmer**. Note also that in a subtype, except for the primary key (which is also a foreign key), no additional attributes of the super-type need to be repeated, since they are inherited. However, additional attributes may be specified (in the subtype). For example (still referring to Figure 5-3), the **Programmer** entity may contain the attribute **ProgLanguage** to store the programmer's main programming language; this would not apply to **Employee**.

For subtypes, integrity constraints on foreign (primary) keys may be:

- Nulls not allowed

- Deletion of referenced records restricted (in super-type)

- Deletion of referencing records allowed (in subtype but not in super-type)

- Update cascaded from the super-type

5.5.6 Determining Component Entities

Component entities were not discussed in Date's original work on the database design via the XR model. However, in the interest of comprehensive coverage, this sub-section has been added. As mentioned in the previous sub-section, care should be taken in not introducing component relationships where traditional relationships would suffice (review section 3.5). Each entity type translates to a base relation. Each base relation will contain attributes corresponding to properties of the entities that apply within the type hierarchy. Again being guided by principles established in chapter 3 (section 3.5.4), each component will include a foreign key, which is the primary key in the summary relation.

Further, this foreign key will form part of the primary key (or a candidate key) in the component relation. For examples, please refer to figures 3-11 and 3.12 of chapter 3.

For components, integrity constraints on foreign (primary) keys may be:

- Null FKs not allowed

- Deletion of referenced records restricted (in summary)

- Deletion of referencing records allowed (in component but not in summary)

- Update cascaded from the summary

5.5.7 Determining the Properties

The final step in this (modified) XR approach is to carefully determine the properties in each relation (entity). This is actually easy, but in order to avoid mistakes, you must be diligent:

- Except for associations, in your initial system investigation (which would be part of the required software engineering or systems analysis), you would have identified the basic properties for each identified entity. That is your starting point.

- Next, go through steps 1-3, 5, and 6 above, and observe the guidelines for dealing with characteristics, designations, subtypes and components. These steps tell you when and where to introduce foreign keys.

- Next, observe step 4 above for treating associations.

By following this procedure, you will be able to confidently determine the properties for each relation in the database; in fact, you will end up with a list that is identical or very similar to the one provided in Figure 5-5 above. This finalized list is illustrated in Figure 5-8. As you examine the figure, please note the following:

1. All primary key and foreign key attributes are italicized.

2. The principle of having each attribute with a unique attribute name (including foreign keys) has been followed.

3. The database specification is presented via a Relation-Attributes List (RAL) — a technique introduced in chapter 3 (section 3.6).

Relation	Properties (Attributes)	Comment
Kernels:		
Department	*Dept#*	The primary key
	DeptName	
	...	
Employee	*Emp#*	The primary key
	EmpName	
	EmpDept#	References **Department.Dept#**
	...	
Supplier	*Suppl#*	The primary key
	SupplName	
	...	
Project	*Proj#*	The primary key
	ProjName	
	ProjManagerEmp#	References **Employee.Emp#**
	...	
InventoryItem	*Item#*	The primary key
	ItemName	
	...	
Characteristics:		
Dependent	*DepnRef*	Surrogate and primary key
	DepnName	
	DepnEmp#	References **Employee.Emp#**
	...	
Associations:		
SuppItems	*SISuppl#*	References **Supplier.Suppl#**
	SIItem#	References **InventoryItem.Item#**
	SIRef	Surrogate and primary key
ItemProj	*IPItem#*	References **InventoryItem.Item#**
	IPProj#	References **Project.Proj#**
	IPRef	Surrogate and primary key
ProjSupp	*PSProj#*	References **Project.Proj#**
	PSSuppl#	References **Supplier.Suppl#**
	PSRef	Surrogate and primary key
ProjWork	*PWEmp#*	References **Employee.Emp#**
	PWProj#	References **Project.Proj#**
	PWRef	Surrogate and primary key
ItemStruct	*ISThisItem#*	References **InventoryItem.Item#**
	ISComplItem#	References **InventoryItem.Item#**
	ISRef	Surrogate and primary key
Note: Primary key attributes and foreign keys are *italicized*.		

Figure 5-8. Partial Database Specification for Section of Manufacturing Firm's Database

With this additional information, you can now revisit the database specification of chapter 3 (Figures 3-4b, 3-13 and 3-14) and revise it accordingly (left as an exercise for you). In so doing, please observe that while the ERD of Figure 5-2 is similar to that of Figure 3-4b, they are not identical; they highlight different aspects of a manufacturing environment, with various areas of overlap. By examining both figures, you should come away with a better sense of what a database model and specification for such an environment would likely entail. The key is to apply sound information gathering techniques (as learned in your software engineering course and summarized in appendix 3), coupled with your database knowledge.

5.6 The UML Model

An alternate methodology for database modeling is the *Unified Modeling Language* (UML) notation. UML was developed by three contemporary software engineering paragons — Grady Booch, James Rumbaugh and Ivar Jacobson. These three professionals founded Rational Software during the 1990s, and among several other outstanding achievements, developed UML for the expressed purpose of being a universal modeling language. Although UML was developed, primarily for *object-oriented software engineering* (OOSE), it is quite suitable for database modeling. Figure 5-9 provides a description of the main symbols used in UML. Note that with UML comes a slight change in the database jargon ("entity" is replaced with "object type"), consistent with the fact that UML is primarily for OOSE.

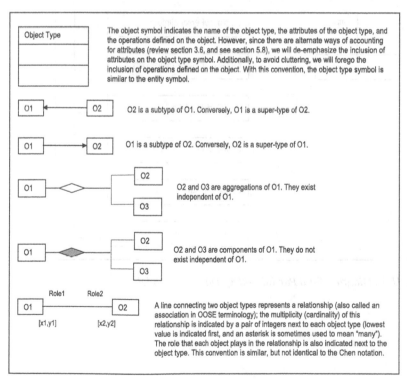

Figure 5-9. Symbols Used in UML Notation for Database Modeling

Note that the UML notation makes a distinction between a component relationship and an aggregation relationship. In the case of the component relationship, the constituent object types are existence dependent on a main object type. In the case of an aggregation relationship, the constituent object types are existence independent of the aggregation object type. Figure 5-10 illustrates the UML diagram for the (partial) college database model that was introduced in chapter 3 (Figure 3-11). Notice that except for the **StudentEmployee** object type, which has been omitted, the information represented is essentially similar to what was represented in Figure 3-11. The only difference here is that the appropriate UML symbols have been used.

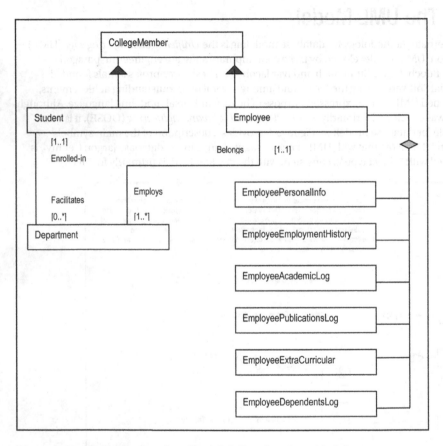

Figure 5-10. *UML Diagram for a Partial College Database Model*

Let us examine another example: Suppose that you were hired at a large marketing company that needs to keep track of its sales of various products and product lines over time. Suppose further that the company operates out of various offices strategically located across the country and/or around the world. How would you construct a database conceptual schema that would allow the company to effectively track its sales? One way to solve this problem is to employ what is called a *star schema* — a central relation (or object type) is connected to two or more relations (or object types) by forming a M:1 relationship with each. Figure 5-11 illustrates such a schema for the marketing company. The central relation (often referred to as the *fact table*) is **SalesSummary**. The surrounding relations (often referred to as *dimensional tables*) are **Location**, **TimePeriod**, **ProductLine**, and **Product**. Each forms a 1:M relationship with **SaleSummary,** the central relation. Notice that consistent with the theory, **SalesSummary** has a foreign key that references each of the referenced relations (object types). Finally, observe also that in this illustration, the attributes for each relation (object type) have been included in the diagram.

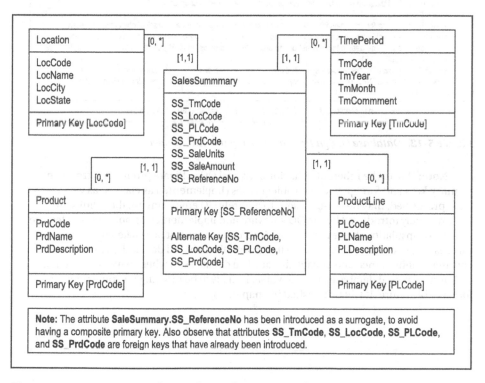

Figure 5-11. *UML Diagram for Tracking Sales Summary for a Large Marketing Company*

5.7 Database Design via the UML Model

Database design with the UML model is somewhat similar to database design with the E-R model. The points of divergence relate to the differences in notation between the two approaches as well as the semantic jargon used. The rules that prescribe bow to treat various types of relationships (section 3.5.4) are still applicable. However, in order to be consistent with object-oriented (OO) terminology, you would replace the term relation (or entity) with the term object type. With this in mind, we may construct a procedure for database design via the UML model as follows:

---

1. Identify all object types and their related attributes.
2. Identify all relationships among the object types.
3. Classify the relationships (mandatory versus optional); decide on which optional relationships will be retained and which ones will be eliminated.
4. Construct an O-R diagram using UML notation or the equivalent (review chapter 3).
5. Refine the model.
6. Using the guidelines for implementing relationships (section 3.5.4), construct a final set of object types, clearly indicating for each object type, its attributes, candidate key(s), and primary key. I you do not have the appropriate database modeling and design tools, construct an object-type-attributes list (OAL) similar to the RAL of chapter 3, and a RL (review section 3.6).
7. By consistently following this procedure, you will obtain a set of object types that will be normalized to at least the Boyce-Codd normal form (BCNF). You can then apply your normalization theory until you achieve the desired level of normalization

Note: The illustrations given in chapter 3 (figures 3.4b, 3.11, 3.12, 3.13, and 3.14) are applicable here.

Figure 5-12. *Database Design Procedure Using the UML Model*

Note: Due to the inherent behavior of typical OO software products, introducing primary keys and foreign keys into object types (implemented as classes) as we have prescribed, may be unnecessary. In a purely OO environment, these links are automatically introduced by the OO software and implemented as pointers — a feature called encapsulation; however, they are internal and cannot be tracked by the user. For this reason, many OO pundits argue that normalization and data independence run counter to inheritance and encapsulation. The debate as to when to use an OO database versus a relational database and vice versa, is likely to be ongoing for some time into the foreseeable future. It will be revisited in chapter 23.

5.8 Innovation: The Object/Entity Specification Grid

This section introduces an innovative approach to database design specification that has been successfully used by the author on a number of major projects. The approach may be construed as an extension of the UML model, but is applicable to any database model.

As mentioned in chapter 3 (section 3.6), for large complex projects (involving huge databases with tens of entities or object types), unless a CASE or RAD tool which automatically generates the ORD or ERD is readily available, manually drawing and maintaining this important aspect of the project becomes virtually futile. Even with a CASE tool, perusing several pages of O-R (E-R) diagram may not be much fun. In such cases, an *object/entity specification grid* (O/ESG) is particularly useful. In a relational database environment, the term *entity specification grid* (ESG) is recommended; in an object-oriented environment, the term *object specification grid* (OSG) is recommended.

The O/ESG presents the specification for each object type (or entity) as it will be implemented in a database consisting of normalized relations. The conventions used for the O/ESG are shown in Figure 5-13; a summary of these conventions follows:

- Each object type (or entity) is identified by a reference code, a descriptive name, and an implementation name (indicated in square brackets).

- For each object type (or entity), the attributes (data elements) to be stored are identified.

- Each attribute is specified by its descriptive name, the implementation name indicated in square brackets, a physical description of the attribute (as described below), and whether the attribute is a foreign key.

- For physical description, the following letters will be used to denote the type of data that will be stored in that attribute, followed by a number which indicates the maximum length of the field: (A) alphanumeric, (N) numeric, or (M) memo. This is specified within square braces. For instance, the notation [Dept#] [N4] denotes a numeric attribute of maximum length 4 bytes. In the case of an attribute that stores a memo (M), no length is indicated because a memo field can store as much information as needed. If a real number value is being stored with a decimal value, two numbers will be used: the first number will indicate the length for the whole number part and the second number will indicate the field length of the decimal part (e.g. [N(9,2)]).

- An attribute that is a foreign key is identified by a comment specifying what object type (or entity) is being referenced. The comment appears in curly braces.

- For each object type (or entity) a comment describing the data to be stored is provided.

- An itemized specification of indexes to be defined (starting with the primary key) is provided for each object type (or entity).

- Each operation to be defined on an object type (or entity) will be given a descriptive name and an implementation name, indicated in square brackets.

Reference Number – Descriptive Name [Implementation Name]
Attributes: /* Itemized specification of all attributes of this object type (or entity) */
Comments: /* A brief description of the storage purpose of this object type (or entity) */
Indexes: /* Itemized specification of anticipated indexes, starting with the primary key */
Valid Operations: /* Itemized list of operations to be defined on this object type (or entity) */

Figure 5-13. *O/ESG Conventions*

Figure 5-14 provides an illustration of O/ESG for four of the object types (or entities) that would comprise the manufacturing firm's database of earlier discussion (review Figure 5-7). In actuality, there would be one for each object type (or entity) comprising the system.

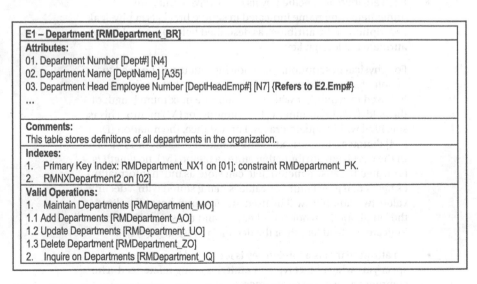

Figure 5-14. *Partial O/ESG for Manufacturing Environment*

E2 – Employee [RMEmployee_BR]
Attributes:
01. Employee Identification Number [Emp#] [N7]
02. Employee Last Name [EmpLName] [A20]
03. Employee First Name [EmpFName] [A20]
04. Employee Middle Initials [EmpMInitl] [A4]
05. Employee Date of Birth [EmpDOB] [N8]
06. Employee's Department [EmpDept#] [N4] {**Refers to E1.Dept#**}
07. Employee Gender [EmpGender] [A1]
08. Employee Marital Status [EmpMStatus] [A1]
09. Employee Social Security Number [EmpSSN] [N10]
10. Employee Home Telephone Number [EmpHomeTel] [A14]
11. Employee Work Telephone Number [EmpWorkTel] [A10]
...
Comments:
This table stores standard information about all employees in the organization.
Indexes:
1. Primary Key Index: RMEmployee_NX1 on [01]; constraint RMEmployee_PK.
2. RMEmployee_NX2 on [02, 03, 04]
3. RMEmployee_NX3 on [09]
4. RMEmployee_NX4 on [10] or [11]
Valid Operations:
1. Manage Employees [RMEmployee_MO]
1.1 Add Employees [RMEmployee_AO]
1.2 Update Employees [RMEmployee_UO]
1.3 Delete Employees [RMEmployee_ZO]
2. Inquire on Employees [RMEmployee_IO]
3. Report on Employees [RMEmployee_RO]

E3 – Supplier [RMSupplier_BR]
Attributes:
01. Supplier Number [Suppl#] [N4]
02. Supplier Name [SupplName] [A35]
03. Supplier Contact Name [SupplContact] [A35]
04. Supplier Telephone Numbers [SupplPhone] [A30]
05. Supplier E-mail Address [SuppEmail] [A30]
...
Comments:
This table stores definitions of all employee classifications.
Indexes:
1. Primary Key Index: RMSupplier_NX1 on [01]; constraint RMSupplier_PK.
2. RMSupplier_NX2 on [02]
3. RMSupplier_NX3 on [04]
Valid Operations:
1. Manage Suppliers[RMSupplier_MO]
1.1 Add Suppliers [RMSupplier_AO]
1.2 Update Suppliers [RMSupplier_UO]
1.3 Delete Suppliers [RMSupplier_ZO]
2. Inquire on Suppliers [RMSupplier_IO]
3. Report on Suppliers [RMSupplier_RO]

Figure 5-14. *Partial O/ESG for Manufacturing Environment* (*continued*)

E4 – Project [RMProject_BR]
Attributes:
01. Project Number [Proj#] [N4]
02. Project Name [ProjName] [A15]
03. Project Summary [ProjSumm] [M]
04. Project's Manager [ProjManagerEmp#] [N7] {**References E2.Emp#**}
...
Comments:
This table stores definitions of all company projects.
Indexes:
1. Primary Key Index: RMProject_NX1 on [01]; constraint RMProject_PK.
2. RMProject_NX2 on [02]
Valid Operations:
1. Manage Projects [RMProject_MO]
1.1 Add Projects [RMProject_AO]
1.2 Update Projects [RMProject_UO]
1.3 Delete Projects [RMProject_ZO]
2. Inquire on Projects [RMProject_IO]
3. Report on Projects [RMProject_RO]

Figure 5-14. *Partial O/ESG for Manufacturing Environment* (*continued*)

5.9 Database Design via Normalization Theory

Although this is seldom done, you can actually use the normalization theory as discussed in chapter 4 to design the basic conceptual schema (involving the structure of the base relations) of a relational database. In practice, normalization is used as a check-and-balance mechanism to acceptability of a database's conceptual schema. As such, normalization can (and should) be applied to each of the database design approaches discussed.

This section looks at two sample database design problems, and shows how the normalization theory can be used to solve them. We will advance the discussion by using two problem scenarios that will hopefully identify with.

5.9.1 Example: Mountaineering Problem

Suppose that we wish to record information about the activities of mountaineers in a relational database. Let us make the assumption that a climber can only begin one climb per day. Figure 5-15 illustrates an initial set attributes (with suggested implementation names in square brackets) for the database.

Begin Date	[BDATE]
End Date	[EDATE]
Climber Name	[CNAME]
Climber Address	[CADDR]
Name of Mountain	[MNAME]
Height of Mountain	[MHGHT]
Country of Mountain	[CTRYNM]
District of Mountain	[DIST]

Figure 5-15. Attributes for the Mountaineering Problem

How may we obtain an appropriate conceptual schema for the mountaineering problem? We may approach this problem in one of two ways:

- *The Pragmatic Approach*: Identify related attributes that form data entities, normalize these entities, then identify and rationalize relationships among the entities.

- *The Classical (theoretical) Approach*: Start out by creating one large 1NF relation involving all attributes, progressively decompose into relations of higher normal forms until the given requirements are met.

In the interest of illustrating application of the theory of normalization, we shall pursue the second approach. However, please bear in mind that in most real life situations, you will be advised to employ the pragmatic approach. Several of the cases in chapter 26 (for instance, assignments 1 and 2) provide an excellent opportunity for you to do this.

Step 1 — Create a large 1NF Relation

We introduce three new attributes: **Climber Identification** [CID#], **Mountain Identification** [MTN#], and **Country Code** [CTRYCD]; store all attributes as relation **M** as shown in Figure 5-16. The figure also states the observed functional dependencies.

```
Relation M:
Primary Key              [BDATE & CID#]
Begin Date               [BDATE]
End Date                 [EDATE]
Climber Identification   [CID#]
Climber Name             [CNAME]
Climber Address          [CADDR]
Mountain Identification  [MTN#]
Name of Mountain         [MNAME]
Height of Mountain       [MHGHT]
Country Code             [CTRYCD]
Country of Mountain      [CTRYNM]
District of Mountain     [DIST]


Functional Dependencies:
FD1: [BDATE, CID#] → EDATE, CNAME, CADDR, MTN#, MNAME, MHGHT, CTRYCD, CTRYNM,
     DIST
FD2: CID# → CNAME, CADDR
FD3: CTRYCD → CTRYNM
FD4: MTN# → MNAME, MHGHT, DIST, CTRYCD, CTRYNM
```

Figure 5-16. *Revised Initial 1NF Relation for the Mountaineering Problem*

Step 2 — Obtain 2NF Relations

The second step is to obtain a set of 2NFrelations. Because of this FD2, the relation can be non-loss decomposed via Heath's theorem to obtain:

Relation **M1**: {CID#, CNAME, CADDR} PK [CID#]

Relation **M2**: {BDA.TE, CID#, EDATE, MTN#, MNAME, MHGHT, CTRYCD, CTRYNM, DIST} PK [CID#, BDATE]

Step 3 — Obtain 3NF Relations

Next, we seek to obtain 3NF relations. Based on FD3 and FD4, relation **M2** is not in 3NF. Again applying Heath's theorem for non-loss decomposition, we obtain the following relations:

Relation **M3**: {CTRYCD, CTRYNM} PK [CTRYCD]

Relation **M4**: {MTN#, MNAME, MHGHT, CTRYCD, DIST} PK [MTN#]

Relation **M5**: {BDATE, CID#, MTN#, EDATE} PK [CID#, BDATE]

Step 4 — Obtain BCNF (and higher order) Relations

Next, we seek to obtain relations of higher order normal forms. Observe that relations **M1**, **M3**, **M4**, and **M5** are in BCNF, 4NF and 5NF.

Note: We could have forgone steps 1-3 and gone straight for BCNF relations by simply observing the FDs shown in Figure 5-16, and decomposing via Heath's theorem. As your confidence in database design grows, you will (hopefully) be able to do this.

5.9.2 Determining Candidate Keys and then Normalizing

In many cases, the database designer may be faced with the problem where basic knowledge of data to be stored is available, but it is not immediately clear how this partial knowledge will translate into a set of normalized relations. For instance, you may be able to identify an entity (or set of entities), but are not sure what the primary key(s) to this (these) entity (entities) will be. With experience, you will be able to resolve these challenges intuitively. However, what do you do in the absence of that invaluable experience? The relational model provides a theoretical approach for dealing with this problem, as explained in the following example.

Suppose that it is desirable to record the information about the performances of students in certain courses in an educational institution environment. Assume further, that a set of functional dependencies have been identified, but it is not sure what the final set of normalized relations will be and how they will be keyed. Figure 5-17 illustrates a summary of the information (assumed to be) known in the case. As usual, we start off by assuming that the relation shown (**StudPerfDraft**) is in 1NF.

Relation StudPerfDraft:

Course	[C]
Teacher	[T]
Hour	[H]
Room	[R]
Student	[S]
Grade	[G]

Functional Dependencies:
FD1:[H, R] → C
FD2: [H, T] → R
FD3: [C, S] → G
FD4: [H, S] → R
FD5: C → T

Figure 5-17. *Initial 1NF Relation for the Student Performance Problem*

Step 1 — Determine the Candidate Key

Having assumed that **StudPerfDraft** is in 1NF, our next step is to determine a candidate key of the relation. We do this by chasing the explicit and implicit dependencies. Any FD that ends up determining all attributes (directly or indirectly) constitutes a candidate key. The technique is referred to as *computing closures.*

> The closure of an FD, denoted FD⁺, is the set of all implied dependencies.

We shall examine each explicit FD in turn and determine all the attributes that it determines (explicitly or implicitly), bearing in mind that any attribute or combination of attributes that is a determinant, necessarily determines itself. Hence, we conclude the following:

- HR →CHR → CTHR
- HT→ HTR → HTRC
- CS → CSG → CSGT
- HS → HSR→ CHSR → CHSRG → CHSRGT
- C → CT

From this exercise, observe that [H,S] is the only candidate key; it is therefore the primary key (PK).

Step 2 — Obtain 2NF Relations

The next step is to obtain 2NF relations. We may rewrite the initial relation as follows:
StudPerfDraft {H, S, C, T, R, G} with PK [H,S]

Observe that **StudPerfDraft** is in 2NF.

Step 3 — Obtain 3NF Relations

Step 3 is to obtain 3NF relations. **StudPerfDraft** is not in 3NF due to FD5 (C →T). To resolve this, decompose via Heath's Theorem to obtain:
   R1 {H, S, C, R, G} with PK [H,S] and **R2** {C ,T} with PK [C].

Step 4 — Obtain BCNF Relations

Our fourth step is to obtain a set of BCNF relations. Observe that **R2** is in BCNF but **R1** is not, due to FD3 ([C,S] → G). To resolve this, decompose via Heath's theorem to obtain:
   R3 {C, S,G} with PK [C,S] and **R4** {H, S, C, R} with PK [H,S].
   R3 is now in BCNF but **R4** is not, due to FD1 ([H,R] → C). Decompose via Heath's theorem to obtain:
   R5 {H, R, C} with PK [H,R] and **R6** {H, S, R} with PK [H,S].
   We now have **R2**, **R3**, **R5**, and **R6** all in BCNF. Additionally, note that all the FDs have been resolved, except for FD2 ([H,T] → R). This may be resolved by introducing the relation **R7** as follows:
   R7 {H, T, R} with PK [H, T].

Step 5 - Obtain Higher Order Normalized Relations

There are no MVDs or JDs, therefore relations **R2**, **R3**, **R5**, **R6** and **R7** are in 4NF and 5NF.
Note:

1.   This is a rather trivial example; a college database is a much
     more complex system than the representation presented
     here. Moreover, questions may be raised as to the veracity
     of some of the FDs stated (for instance FD5). However, the
     representation succeeds in providing the application of the
     normalization theory, and that was the sole intent.

2.   Relation **R6** fulfills FD4 ([H,S] → R), and **R7** fulfills FD2
     ([H, T] → R). Strictly speaking, **R7** may be considered
     redundant, since we can determine what teacher is in a room
     at a given time by accessing **R5** and **R2**.

5.10 Database Model and Design Tools

At this point you must be wondering, how in the world are you supposed to model and
design a complex database, and keep track of all the entities and relationships? The good
news is, there are various tools that are readily available, so there's no need to panic. The
standard general purpose word processors (such as MS Office, Word Perfect, Open Office,
etc.) are all fortified with graphics capabilities so that if you spend a little time with any
of these products, you will figure out how to design fairly impressive database model/
design diagrams. Better yet, there is a wide range of CASE tools and/or modeling tools
that you can use. Figure 5-18 provides an alphabetic list of some of the commonly used
products. While some of the products in the list are quite impressive, the list is by no
means comprehensive, so you do not have to be constrained by it. Some of the products
are available free of charge; for others, the parent company offers free evaluation copies.

Product	Parent Company	Comment
ConceptDraw	CS Odessa	Supports UML diagrams, GUI designs, flowcharts, ERD, and project planning charts.
DataArchitect	theKompany.com	Supports logical and physical data modeling. Interfaces with ODBC and DBMSs such as MySQL, PostgreSQL, DB2, MS SQL Server, Gupta SQLBase, and Oracle. Runs on Linux, Windows, Mac OS X, HP-UX, and Sparc Solaris platforms.
Database Design Tool (DDT)	Open Source	A basic tool that allows database modeling that can import or export SQL.
Database Design Studio	Chilli Source	Allows modeling via ERD, data structure diagrams, and data definition language (DDL) scripts. Three products are marketed: DDS-Pro is ideal for large databases; DDD-Lite is recommended for small and medium-sized databases; SQL-Console is a GUI-based tool that connects with any database that supports ODBC.
DBDesigner 4 and MySQL Workbench	fabFORCE.net	This original product was developed for the MySQL database. The replacement version, MySQL Workspace is targeted for any database environment, and is currently available for the Windows and Linux platforms.
DeZign	Datanamic	Facilitates easy development of ERDs and generation of corresponding SQL code. Supports DBMSs including Oracle, MS SQL Server, MySQL, IBM DB2, Firebird, InterBase, MS Access, PostgreSQL, Paradox, dBase, Pervasive, Informix, Clipper, Foxpro, Sybase, SQLite, ElevateDB, NexusDB, DBISAM.
Enterprise Architect	Sparx Systems	Facilitates UML diagrams that support the entire software development life cycle (SDLC). Includes support of business modeling, systems engineering, and enterprise architecture. Supports reverse engineering as well.
ER Creator	Model Creator Software	Allows for the creation of ERDs, and the generation of SQL and the generation of corresponding DDL scripts. Also facilitates reverse engineering from databases that support ODBC.
ER Diagrammer	Embarcadero	Similar to ER Creator

Figure 5-18. Some Commonly Used Database Planning Tools

Product	Parent Company	Comment
ERWin Data Modeler	Computer Associates	Facilitates creation and maintenance o data structures for databases, data warehouses, and enterprise data resources. Runs on the Windows platform. Compatible with heterogeneous DBMSs
MagicDraw	No Magic	A relatively new product that has just been introduced to the market. Appears to be similar to Enterprise Architect.
Oracle Designer	Oracle	Supports design for Oracle databases.
Oracle JDeveloper	Oracle	Supports UML diagramming.
Power Designer	Sybase	Supports UML, business process modeling, and data modeling. Integrates with development tools such as .NET, Power Builder (a Sybase Product), Java, and Eclipse. Also integrates with the major DBMSs.
SmartDraw	SmartDraw	A graphics software that facilitates modeling in the related disciplines of business enterprise planning, software engineering, database modeling, and information engineering (IE). Provides over 100 different templates (based on different methodologies) that you can choose from. Supported methodologies include UML, Chen Notation, IE Notation, etc.
TogetherSoft	Borland	Provides UML-based visual modeling for various aspects of the software development life cycle (SDLC). Allows generation of DDL scripts from the data model. Also supports forward and reverse engineering for Java and C++ code.
Toolkit for Conceptual Modeling (TCM)	University of Twente, Holland	Includes various resources for traditional software engineering methodologies as well as object-oriented methodologies based on the UML standards.
Visio	Microsoft	Facilitates modeling in support of business enterprise planning, software engineering, and database management.
Visual Thought	CERN	Similar to Visio but is free
xCase	Resolution Software	A database modeling tool that supports all aspects of the database development life cycle (DDLC): it supports ERD design, documentation, SQL code generation, logical and physical migration across multiple DBMS platforms, and data analysis.

Figure 5-18. *Some Commonly Used Database Planning Tools (continued)*

5.11 Summary and Concluding Remarks

It is now time to summarize what we have covered in this chapter:

- A database model is a blueprint for subsequent database design. It is a representation of the database. We have looked at three database models: the E-R model, the XR model and the UML model.

- Database design involves preparation of a database specification, which will be used to construct the database. We have discussed database design via the E-R model, the XR model, the UML model, the O/ESG, and normalization theory.

- The E-R model is the oldest model for relational databases that has been discussed. It involves the use of certain predefined symbols to construct a graphical representation of the database.

- Database design via the E-R model involves following eight steps that lead to a normalized database specification.

- The XR model is an alternate model that compensates for the weaknesses in the E-R model. It involves grouping information entities into different predefined categories that will assist in the design phase.

- Database design via the XR model involves following nine steps that lead to a normalized database specification.

- The UML model is similar to the E-R model. However, it requires taking an object-oriented approach, and employs different notations from the E-R model.

- Database design via the UML model involves following seven steps that lead to a normalized database specification.

- The O/ESG methodology describes an efficient way of developing a comprehensive, normalized database specification.

- Database design via normalization theory describes a rudimentary approach to database design that relies on mastery of the principles of normalization.

You are now armed with all the requisite knowledge needed to design quality databases. However, you will likely find that a review of this and the previous two chapters, along with practice, may be necessary until you have gained mastery and confidence with the concepts, principles and methodologies. The next chapter discusses the design of the user interface for a database system.

5.12 Review Questions

1. Describe in your own words (with appropriate illustrations) the approach to database design based on the following (in each case, describe approach, then outline the advantages and disadvantages from your perspective):

   - The E-R Model

   - The X-R Model

   - The UML Model

   - The O/ESG Methodology

   - Normalization Theory

2. The following are three software systems for which a database is to be designed:

   - An Inventory Management System

   - A Lab Scheduling System for users of a computer lab

   - A Bookshop Manager System for an educational institution

   For each system, develop a database specification based on at least three of the five approaches above. Compare the database specifications derived. Compare the methodologies. Which one(s) are you most comfortable with and why?

3. How important are surrogates in the design of a database? By considering an appropriate example, demonstrate how surrogates may be used in database design.

4. Compare the UML database model with the E-R model. What are the similarities? What are the differences? You may use appropriate illustrations in your response.

5.13 References and/or Recommended Readings

[Connolly, 2002] Connolly, Thomas and Carolyn Begg. *Database Systems: A Practical Approach to Design, Implementation and Management* 3rd ed. New York, NY: Addison-Wesley, 2002. See chapters 13-15.

[Date, 1986] Date, Christopher J. *Relational Database: Selected Writings*. Reading, MA: Addison-Wesley, 1986.

[Date, 1990] Date, Christopher J. *Introduction to Database Systems* 5h ed. Menlo Park, CA: Addison-Wesley, 1990. See chapter 22.

[Date, 2004] Date, Christopher J. *Introduction to Database Systems* 8h ed. Menlo Park, CA: Addison-Wesley, 2004. See chapters 12-14.

[Elmasri, 2007] Elmasri, Ramez and Shamkant B. Navathe. *Fundamentals of Database Systems* 5th ed. Reading, MA: Addison-Wesley, 2007. See chapters 7, 10 and 11.

[Garcia-Molina, 2002] Garcia-Molina, Hector, Jeffrey Ullman and Jennifer Widom. *Database Systems: The Complete Book*. Upper Saddle River, NJ: Prentice Hall, 2002. See chapter 3.

[Hoffer, 2007] Hoffer, Jeffrey A., Mary B. Prescott and Fred R. McFadden. *Modern Database Management* 8th ed. Upper Saddle River, NJ: Prentice Hall, 2007. See chapters 5.

[Jensen, 1992] Jensen, C. S. and L. Mark. "Queries on Change in Extended Relational Model." *IEEE Transactions on Knowledge and Data Engineering Vol. 4 Issue 2*, April 1992. pp. 192-200.

[Kifer, 2005] Kifer, Michael, Arthur Bernstein and Philip M. Lewis. Database Systems: An Application-Oriented Approach 2nd ed. New York: Addison-Wesley, 2005. See chapter 4.

[Kroenke, 2006] Kroenke, David M. *Database Processing: Fundamentals, Design and Implementation 10h ed.* Upper Saddle River, NJ: Prentice Hall, 2006. See chapters 3-6.

[Lee, 2002] Lee, Richard C. and William M. Tepfenhart. *Practical Object-Oriented Development With* UML and Java. Upper Saddle River, NJ: Prentice Hall, 2002. See chapter 8.

[Lewis, 2002] Lewis, Phillip M., Arthur Bernstein and Michael Kifer. *Databases and Transaction Processing: An Application Oriented Approach.* New York, NY: Addison-Wesley, 2002. See chapter 8.

[Martin, 1993] Martin, James and James Odell. *Principles of Object Oriented Analysis and Design.* Eaglewood Cliffs, NJ: Pretence Hall, 1993. See chapters 6 and 7.

[Pratt, 2002] Pratt, Phillip J. and Joseph J. Adamski. *Concepts of Database Management* 4th ed. Boston, MA: Course Technology, 2002. See chapters 5 and 6.

[Rob, 2007] Rob, Peter and Carlos Coronel. *Database Systems: Design, Implementation & Management* 7th ed. Boston, MA: Course Technology, 2007. See chapters 4, 6 and 9.

[Rumbaugh, 1991] Rumbaugh, James, et. al. *Object Oriented Modeling And Design.* Eaglewood Cliffs, NJ: Pretence Hall, 1991. See chapter 4.

[Ullman, 1997] Ullman, Jeffrey D., and Jennifer Widom. *A First Course in Database Systems.* Upper Saddle River, NJ: Prentice Hall, 1997. See chapter 3.

CHAPTER 6

■ ■ ■

Database User Interface Design

This chapter covers the essentials of good database user interface design. A properly designed database system typically includes a user interface that facilitates end users accessing the system. The chapter presumes that you are familiar with basic software engineering principles as well as user interface design principles as covered in your undergraduate degree. The chapter is therefore a summary that includes:

- Introduction
- Deciding on the User Interface
- Steps in the User Interface Design
- User Interface Development and Implementation
- Summary and Concluding Remarks

6.1 Introduction

At this stage we have settled on all relations (and attributes). Remember, we implement relations, tuples and attributes as files, records and fields.

Designing the user interface to facilitate user access is the next step. The user interface should facilitate at least the following basic functions: data insertion, data update, data deletion, and information retrieval (query and print). This is important, as it is not acceptable to give end users direct, unfettered access to the database; were this to be done, the integrity of the system would be compromised in very short order. What is more desirable is to provide the end users with a user friendly, controlled environment that gives users all the privileges and functionalities that they need and nothing more.

The user interface will consist of menus from which user operations can be accessed. Depending on the software development tool used, it will be constructed from various building blocks, and there will be various categories of user interface objects (review your software engineering notes).

The system must also facilitate various user (external) views through logical interpretation of objects. This must be developed using the DBMS and/or whatever software development tool is being used. Note that if the O/ESG methodology (discussed in section 5.8) is employed, you will be well on your way with the user interface specification.

Example: By the way of illustration, let us revisit the O/ESG for the partial database specification of the manufacturing firm, discussed in the previous chapter (section 5.8). Figure 6-1 shows a repeat of the O/ESG for the **Employee** entity. According to the figure (adopting the conventions from section 5.8), this entity could be implemented as a relational table named RMEmployee_BR. The user interface should anticipate and support various logical views on this relational table. Following are some examples:

- Employees arranged by Name

- Employees arranged by Telephone Numbers

- Employees arranged by Departments

- Employees arranged by Social Security Number

E2 – Employee [RMEmployee_BR]
Attributes:
01. Employee Identification Number [Emp#] {N7}
02. Employee Last Name [EmpLName] {A20}
03. Employee First Name [EmpFName] {A20}
04. Employee Middle Initials [EmpMInitl] {A4}
05. Employee Date of Birth [EmpDOB] N8
06. Employee's Department [EmpDept#] {N4} **Refers to E1.Dept#**
07. Employee Gender [EmpGender] {A1}
08. Employee Marital Status [EmpMStatus] {A1}
09. Employee Social Security Number [EmpSSN] {N10}
10. Employee Home Telephone Number [EmpHomeTel] {A14}
11. Employee Work Telephone Number [EmpWorkTel] {A10}
...
Comments:
This table stores standard information about all employees in the organization.
Indexes:
1.   Primary Key Index: RMEmployee_NX1 on [01]; constraint RMEmployee_PK.
2.   RMEmployee_NX2 on [02, 03, 04]
3.   RMEmployee_NX3 on [09]
4.   RMEmployee_NX4 on [10] or [11]
Valid Operations:
1.   Manage Employees [RMEmployee_MO]
1.1 Add Employees [RMEmployee_AO]
1.2 Update Employees [RMEmployee_UO]
1.3 Delete Employees [RMEmployee_ZO]
2.   Inquire on Employees [RMEmployee_IO]
3.   Report on Employees [RMEmployee_RO]

Figure 6-1. *Excerpt from the Partial O/ESG for Manufacturing Environment*

6.2 Deciding on User Interface

User interfaces can be put into three broad categories — m*enu-driven interface, command interface* and *graphical user* interface (GUI). Figure 6-2 compares the approaches in terms of relative complexity of design (COD), response time (RT), and ease of use (EOU).

Command entry interfaces are the oldest type; they typify traditional operating systems, compilers and other software development tools. Up until the mid-1990s, menu driven interfaces were the most frequently used, dominating the arena of business information and application system. Since the late 1980s, graphical interfaces have become very popular, and clearly dominate user interfaces of the current era. Of course, the approaches can be combined.

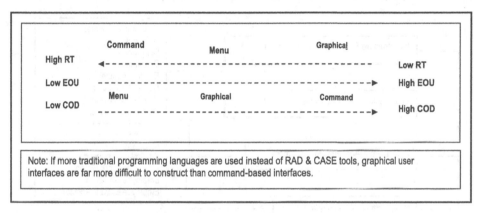

Figure 6-2. Comparison of User Interface Categories

6.3 Steps in User Interface Design

How you design the user interface will depend to a large extent on the type of user interface your software requires, It will also depend on the intended users of the software (experts, knowledgeable intermittent, or novices).

6.3.1 Menu or Graphical User Interface

If the user interface is to be menu driven or graphical, the following steps are recommended (assuming object-oriented design):

1. Put system objects (structures and operations) into logical groups. At the highest level, the menu will contain options pointing to summarized logical groups.

2. For each summarized logical group, determine the component sub-groups where applicable, until all logical groups have been identified.

3. Let each logical group represent a component menu.

4. For each menu, determine options using an object-oriented strategy to structure the menu hierarchy (object first, operation last).

5. Design the menus to link the various options. Develop a menu hierarchy tree or a *user interface topology chart* (UITC).

6. Program the implementation.

Figure 6-3 illustrates a partial user interface topology chart (UITC) for a college/ university administrative information system (CUAIS). The UITC displays the main user interface structure for the system; it is fully discussed in [Foster, 2010]; however, it is intuitive enough for you to understand it. The CUAIS project is also described in [Foster, 2010]; like the UITC, a full discussion is not necessary here.

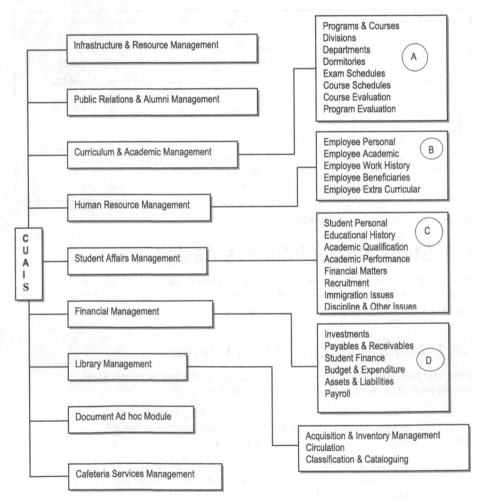

Figure 6-3. *Partial UITC for a CUAIS Project*

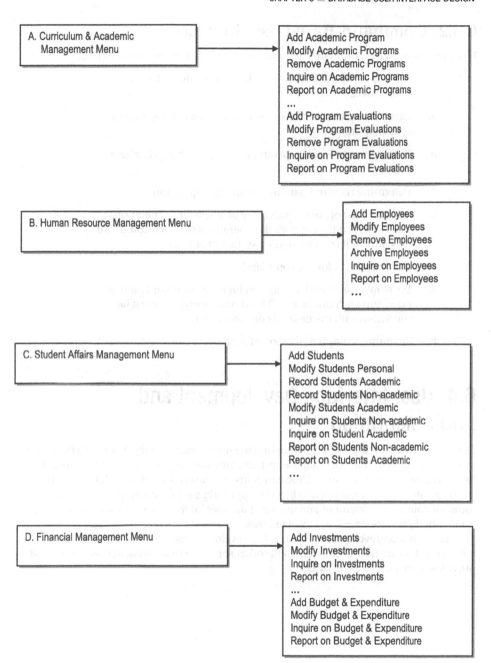

A. Curriculum & Academic Management Menu

Add Academic Program
Modify Academic Programs
Remove Academic Programs
Inquire on Academic Programs
Report on Academic Programs
...
Add Program Evaluations
Modify Program Evaluations
Remove Program Evaluations
Inquire on Program Evaluations
Report on Program Evaluations

B. Human Resource Management Menu

Add Employees
Modify Employees
Remove Employees
Archive Employees
Inquire on Employees
Report on Employees
...

C. Student Affairs Management Menu

Add Students
Modify Students Personal
Record Students Academic
Record Students Non-academic
Modify Students Academic
Inquire on Students Non-academic
Inquire on Student Academic
Report on Students Non-academic
Report on Students Academic
...

D. Financial Management Menu

Add Investments
Modify Investments
Inquire on Investments
Report on Investments
...
Add Budget & Expenditure
Modify Budget & Expenditure
Inquire on Budget & Expenditure
Report on Budget & Expenditure

Figure 6-3. Partial UITC for a CUAIS Project (continued)

6.3.2 Command-Based User Interface

If the user interface is command-driven, the following steps are recommended:

1. Develop an *operations-set* i.e. a list of operations that will be required.

2. Categorize the operations — user operations as opposed to system operations.

3. Develop a mapping of operations with underlying database objects.

4. Determine required parameters for each operation.

5. Develop a list of commands (may be identical to operations set). If this is different from the operations set, each command must link to its corresponding system operations.

6. Define a syntax for the command.

7. Develop a user interface support for each command (and by extension each operation). This interface support must be consistent with the defined command syntax.

8. Program the implementation of each operation.

6.4 User Interface Development and Implementation

Designing, constructing and implementing the user interface really belongs to the realm of software engineering, not database systems. However, as you are aware (and as has been emphasized in this course), the two fields are closely related. In order to construct the user interface, you will need to have an appropriate set of software development tools. Of course, development and testing of the user interface must proceed according to established software development standards.

The software development tool used to develop the user interface will depend to a large extent on the user requirements (another software engineering matter). Figure 6-4 provides some possible scenarios.

Scenario	Solution Alternative
1. It is desirable to have front-end and back-end based on the same DBMS.	Use a DBMS suite that provides facilities for both front-end and back-end systems. Oracle, DB2 and Informix are excellent examples.
2. Front-end and back-end can be based on different software development tools.	The alternative of an object-oriented RAD tool, superimposed on a relational or object database has become the norm. Products such as DB2, Oracle, Informix, Sybase and MS SQL Server are good candidates for back-end systems. DB2, Oracle, and Informix are regarded as universal databases, supporting both relational and object databases. With respect to the front-end system, your choice of development tool will depend on whether or not web access is critical.
3. Front-end must support web access.	Products such as Cold Fusion, Poet Software, Delphi, WebSphere, etc. are very popular.
4. Front-end need not support World Wide Web (WWW) access.	Earlier versions of Delphi, C++ Builder, Visual Basic, etc. will suffice.
5. A purely object oriented environment is desired.	The product Rational Rose comes readily to mind.

Figure 6-4. *Possible Scenarios for User Interface*

It must be emphasized that user interface design and development can and often occur independent of database design and development. This is one of the potent results of data independence (review sections 1.2 and 2.9): the user interface applications are immune to structural and/or physical changes in the database. In fact, as mentioned in section 2.9, the user interface (which is part of the front-end system) may reside on a different machine (with a different operating system) from the actual database (which is part of the back-end system). So in addition to data independence, we can have *platform independence*.

Two prominent protocols that facilitate platform independence between database and user interface are *open database connectivity* (ODBC) and *Java database connectivity* (JDBC).

Open Database Connectivity: ODBC is an open standard *application programming interface* (API) for accessing a database. A software product that desires to access an external database must include in its suite, an ODBC driver for that database. The ODBC driver converts the database objects into a generic format that is understood by the software. The target DBMS must also support ODBC. This facilitates communication and transfer of data among heterogeneous databases, irrespective of the platform that they reside on. Microsoft is a strong proponent of ODBC; in fact, the ODBC software is typically bundled with the Windows operating system (under Control Panel Ȥ Administrative Tools). ODBC is also supported by other leading operating systems (Unix, Linux, Windows, System i, etc.).

Java Database Connectivity: JDBC is a Sun Microsystems product that allows Java programs to access heterogeneous databases, irrespective of their platforms. This API is included in J2SE and J2EE releases. JDBC cooperates with the ODBC protocol; as such, a program running JDBC can reach ODBC-accessible databases.

ODBC and JDBC may be considered as subsets of the wider set of protocols described as Common Object Request Broker Architecture (CORBA). CORBA will be further discussed in chapter 22 (section 22.6). For the purpose of illustration, Figure 6-5 provides a summary of the steps you would take in order to configure an Oracle database server to be accessed from Delphi 7.0 (or some later version) through ODBC (assuming a Windows environment).

1. Install Oracle DBMS Server on the database server. This installation will automatically include installation of Oracle's ODBC driver.
2. Install Oracle DBMS Client on client machine(s). This typically includes components such as Oracle Net Manager, Network Transport, and Oracle ODBC Driver.
3. Install front-end system (e.g. Delphi) on client machine(s).
4. On each client machine:
   a. Configure the Network Client Access file (Oracle **C:\Oracle\ora10g\network\admin\tnsnames**) to include a service that connects to the database on the DB Server.
   b. Configure ODBC (via the Control Panel) to connect to the DB server through the client service established in 4a.
5. In your front-end system (Delphi), select **Database** from the main menu; then select from the list, the DB service name established in 4b, and log on the foreign DB server.
6. From this point, you can now create front-end (Delphi) datasets and data sources that connect to the foreign DB server through the (local) Service name established above.

Figure 6-5. *Accessing an Oracle Database from Delphi via ODBC*

6.5 Summary and Concluding Remarks

Here is a summary of what we have covered in this chapter:

- The user interface for a database system should provide the end users with a user friendly, controlled environment that gives users all the privileges and functionalities that they need and nothing more.

- In planning the user interface, you must first decide what type of interface will be provided. The interface may be command-based, menu-driven, or GUI-based.

- Next, you should design the user interface using established principles of user interface design.

- The final step is the development and implementation of the user interface. Features that the user interface will provide will influence the tools used in developing the user interface. For instance, if the database is to be accessible from the WWW, then the tools used must facilitate such capability.

So now you know how to design a database and a user interface for that database. Later in the course, you will learn Structured Query Language (SQL), the universal database language. In preparation for this, the next two chapters discuss the relational algebra and relational calculus respectively — two subjects areas that will enhance your appreciation of SQL.

6.6 Review Questions

1. What are the types of user interfaces which may be constructed for end users of a database system? How do they compare in terms of efficiency and convenience?

2. Outline the steps to be taken in the construction of a user interface for end users of a database system.

3. Referring to revision question 2 of the previous chapter, propose a user interface model for any (or all) of the following:

   - An Inventory Management System

   - A Lab Scheduling System for users of a computer lab

   - A Bookshop Manager System for an educational institution

4. Identify four different scenarios for development of a user interface for a database system. Recommend an appropriate software development tool for each scenario.

6.7 References and/or Recommend Readings

[Carroll, 2002] Carroll, John. *Human-Computer Interaction in the New Millennium.* Reading, MA: Addison-Wesley, 2002.

[Foster, 2010] Foster, Elvis. *Software Engineering — A Methodical Approach.* Bloomington, IN: Xlibris Publishing, 2010. See chapters 6, 11, and 12.

[Raskin, 2000] Raskin, Jef. *The Human Interface: New Directions for Designing Interactive Systems.* Reading, MA: Addison-Wesley, 2000.

[Shneiderman, 2005] Shneiderman, Ben. *Designing the User Interface: Strategies for Effective Human-Computer Interaction* 4th ed. Reading, MA: Addison-Wesley, 2005.

[Sommerville, 2001] Sommerville, Ian. *Software Engineering*, 6th ed. Reading, Massachusetts, Addison-Wesley, 2001. See chapter 15.

CHAPTER 7

■ ■ ■

Relational Algebra

One of the reasons for the success and longevity of the relational model is that it is firmly grounded on mathematical principles (of linear algebra and set theory), which are well known and well documented. The (normalized) relational tables are by design, organized in such a way as to promote and facilitate manipulation of data to yield meaningful information. As mentioned earlier in the course (chapter 2), data manipulation relates to the addition, update, deletion, retrieval, reorganization, and aggregation of data. It turns out that the first three aspects are far more straightforward than the latter three.

In this and the next chapter, the focus is on the latter three aspects of data manipulation — retrieval, reorganization and aggregation. The intent is to expose you to the underlying database theory that had to be developed in order to have DBMS suites that support these data manipulation requirements. As you will soon come to appreciate, mastery of SQL (which is mandatory, if you intend to do well in this field) or any database language is greatly enhanced by an understanding of the fundamental underlying theory. The ecture proceeds under the following sub-topics:

- Introduction
- Basic Operations of Relational Algebra
- Syntax of Relational Algebra
- Aliases, Renaming and the Relational Assignment
- Other Operations
- Summary and Concluding Remarks

7.1 Introduction

Relational algebra consists of a collection of operations on relations. Each operation produces new relation(s) from one or more already existing relation(s).

Through relational algebra, we can achieve the following objectives:

- Defining a scope for retrieval
- Defining a scope for update
- Defining virtual information

- Defining snapshot data for snapshot relations

- Defining access rights i.e. data for which authorization of some kind is to be granted

- Defining integrity constraints apart from those that are part of the relational model

Earlier in the course, it was mentioned that every DBMS has a data sublanguage (DSL). Typically, the DSL is based on relational algebra, relational calculus (to be discussed in the next chapter), or a combination of both. It is therefore imperative for you to have a good grasp of this topic.

The relational algebra is said to be prescriptive — you specify precisely how an activity is to be carried out. In so doing, there are certain operations that you will learn to use.

7.2 Basic Operations of Relational Algebra

There are eight basic relational algebra operations with which you need to become familiar; they are informally described below:

1. **Union (UNION):** The union of relations R1 and R2 builds a relation R3 consisting of tuples in either R1 or R2 inclusive. Corresponding attributes of R1 and R2 must be defined on the same domain.

2. **Difference (MINUS):** The difference of relation R1 and relation R2 is a new relation R3, with tuples appearing in R1, but not in R2. Corresponding attributes from R1 and R2 must be defined on the same domain.

3. **Restriction (RESTRICT):** A restriction extracts specified tuples from a specified relation R1, by imposing some condition on the relation. The resulting relation R2, has only the specified tuples. RESTRICT is replaced by the SELECT in modern systems, the latter usually being more powerful than the original.

4. **Product (PRODUCT):** The Cartesian product of two relations R1 and R2 is a third relation R3, consisting of the concatenation of every tuple in R1 with every tuple R2.

5. **Projection (PROJECT):** A projection extracts specified attributes from a specified relation R1 into a new relation R2.

6. **Join (JOIN):** The join of two relations R1 and R2 builds a new relation R3, such that the tuples from R1 and R2 satisfy some specified condition. However, in the unqualified form, it is generally used to mean *natural join*. A more generic form of the JOIN operation is discussed in section 7.3.5.

The *natural join* (implied by the notation R1 JOIN R2) assumes that there is an attribute or combination of attributes that is common to both R1 and R2 (same attribute name and characteristics). Let us denote the common attribute(s) in R1 and R2 as Z. The natural join creates a relation R3, where every tuple from R1 is concatenated with every tuple from R2, provided that R1.Z = R2.Z. Finally, a projection is performed on the result in the previous step to yield a single copy of each attribute (thus removing either R1.Z or R2.Z) in the final result.

7. **Intersection (INTERSECT):** The intersection builds a relation R3, from two specified relations R1 and R2, where R3 has tuple that exist in both R1 and R2. Corresponding attributes of R1 and R2 must be defined on the same domain.

8. **Division (DIVIDE BY):** Division takes a relation R1 of degree $m+n$ and a second relation R2 of degree n and produces a third relation R3 of degree m, where all the n attribute values appearing in R2 also appear in R1, concatenated with the other m attribute values.

7.2.1 Primary and Secondary Operations

The operations may be classified into *primary operations* and *secondary operations*: Primary operations include UNION, DIFFERENCE, SELECT, PROJECT, and PRODUCT. Secondary operations include JOIN, INTERSECT, and DIVIDE BY. Secondary operations are derivable from the primary operations.

7.2.2 Codd's Original Classification of Operations

Codd's original classifications placed the operations in two broad categories as follows: *Traditional operations* included UNION, INTERSECT, DIFFERENCE, and PRODUCT. *Special operations* included RESTRICT, PROJECT, JOIN, and DIVIDEBY.

7.2.3 Nested Operations

The output of each operation is another relation; likewise, the input to each operation is a set of one or more relations. We say that the relational operation is *closed on relational algebra*. Since each operation produces a new relation as output, we can nest operations so that the output of one forms the input to another. This will become clear in the ensuing examples.

7.3 Syntax of Relational Algebra

We shall use as frame of reference for this and the next few chapters, a section of a college database, as defined in Figure 7-1. Some sample data is provided in Figure 7-2.

Student {Stud#, Sname, Fname, Sex, Addr, Spgm#, Hall#, DoB ...}
       Primary Key [Stud#]
       Spgm# references **Program.Pgm#**
       Hall# references **Hall.Hall#**
Program {Pgm#, Pgmname ...}
       Primary Key [Pgm#]
Hall {Hall#, Hallname ...}
       Primary Key [Hall#]
Dept {Dept#, Dname, Dhead#, DDiv#}
       Primary Key [Dept#]
       Dhead# references **Staff.Staff#**
       DDiv# references **Division.Div#**
Staff {Staff#, Staffname ...}
       Primary Key [Staff#]
Course {Crs#, Crsname ...}
       Primary Key [Crs#]
Pgm_Struct {PSPgm#, PSCrs#, PSCrsSeqn)
       Primary Key [PsPgm#, PsCrs#]
       PSPgm# references **Program.Pgm#**
       PSCrs# references **Course.Crs#**
Division {Div#, Divname, Divhead# ...}
       Primary Key [Div#]
       Divhead# references **Staff.Staff#**

Note: In order to demonstrate how the natural join works, the recommended convention of keeping attribute names unique for the database (even if the attribute is a foreign key) has been deliberately relaxed **for Student.Hall#.**

Figure 7-1. *Cross Section of a College Database*

Student:

Stud#	Sname	Fname	Spgm#	Hall#	DoB
100	Foster	Bruce	BSC1	Chan	1978
105	Jones	Bruce	BSC2	Chan	1970
110	James	Enos	BSC1	Urv	1966
115	James	Yvonne	BSC1	Mars	1970
120	Douglas	Henry	BSC2	Urv	1970
125	Henry	Suzanne	BSC2	Urv	1968
130	Lambert	Cecille	BSC5	Mars	1978
...					

Program:

Pgm#	Pgmname		
BSC1	Bachelor of Science in MIS		
BSC2	Bachelor of Science in Computer Science		
BSC3	Bachelor of Science in Electronic Engineering		
BSC4	Bachelor of Science in Mathematics		
BSC5	Bachelor of Science in Computer Science & Mathematics		
BSC6	Bachelor of Science in Computer Science & Electronics		
BSC7	Bachelor of Science in Chemistry		
BSC8	Bachelor of Science in Physics		
...			

Dept:

Dept#	Dname	Dhead#	DDiv#
MTH	Department of Mathematics	S10	D01
CSC	Department of Computer Science	S15	D01
PHY	Department of Physics	S05	D01
MGT	Department of Management Studies	S20	D01
MSC	Department of Music	S30	D02
...			

Course:

Crs#	Crsname		
CS100	Introduction to Computer Science		
CS210	Data Structures		
CS220	Visual Programming		
CS330	Software Engineering		
CS360	Database Systems		
...			
M100	Calculus I		
M110	Mechanics		
M200	Calculus II		
M210	Linear Algebra		
...			

Figure 7-2. *Sample Data for a Cross-section of a College/University Database[Showing only attributes relevant to the examples discussed]*

Hall:

Hall#	Hallname	
Chan	Chancellor Hall	
Len	Lenheim Hall	
Mars	Mary Seacole Hall	
Urv	Urvine Hall	
...		

Staff:

Staff#	Staffname	
S05	Prof. Christine Farr	
S10	Dr. Paul Phillips	
S15	Dr. Scott Foster	
S20	Prof. Hans Gaur	
S25	Dr. Bruce Lambert	
S30	Dr. Carolyn Henry	
S35	Dr. Enid Armstrong	
S40	Dr. Calvin Golding	
...		

Pgm_Struct:

PSPgm#	PSCrs#	PSCrsSeqn	
BSC1	M100	01	
BSC1	M200	02	
BSC1	CS100	03	
BSC1	CS210	04	
BSC1	CS220	05	
...			
BSC2	CS100	01	
BSC2	CS210	02	
BSC2	CS220	03	
...			
BSC2	M100	16	
...			

Division:

Div#	DivName	Divhead#	
D01	Division of Pure & Applied Sciences	S25	
D02	Division of Arts & Humanities	S30	
D03	Division of Education & Psychology	S35	
...			

Figure 7-2. Sample Data for a Cross-section of a College/University Database[Showing only attributes relevant to the examples discussed] (continued)

In the interest of clarity, two commonly used notations have been adopted, both with slight modifications. They are the Ullman notation [Garcia-Molina, 2002] and the Date notation [Date, 2004]. Bear in mind however, that the syntactical implementation of relational algebra will vary from one product to another. What is important therefore, is that you understand the concepts discussed. The BNF (Backus-Naur Form) conventions shown in Figure 7-3 will be assumed. Additionally, several of the examples will contain clarifying comments that conform to how comments are made in the C-based programming languages (e.g. // this is a comment, /* and so is this */). Use of the BNF notation and C-based comments will continue through chapter 8 as well.

::=	This symbol means 'is defined as'
<...>	Required input supplied by the user are enclosed in angular brackets
[...]	Optional items are enclosed in square brackets
ItemA	ItemB	Choice: ItemA or ItemB may be chosen by the user
{...}	Repetition: Items enclosed within curly braces may be repeated zero to n times. The contemporary convention is to use the curly braces to indicate user choice; however, to avoid confusion, that convention will not be used; we will stick to the more traditional convention as specified.

Figure 7-3. *BNF Notations*

7.3.1 Select Statement

Based on the Ullman notation, the **SELECT** statement is of the form

SelectStatement ::=
SELECT <Condition> (<RelationalExpression>)

Condition ::=
[NOT] <Attribute1> **Theta** <Attribute2 | Literal> {AND | OR <Condition>}

RelationalExpression ::=
<RelationName> | <SelectStatement> | <ProjectStatement> | <ProductStatement> |
<ThetaJoinStatement> | <UnionStatement> | <IntersectStatement> | <MinusStatement> |
<DivisionStatement>

Note:

1. *Theta* represents a valid Boolean operator i.e. any of the following: =, >, <, <>, <=, >=

2. A *relational expression* is either a relation or an expression that results in the creation of a relation.

3. A *condition* is an expression that evaluates to true or false. Complex conditions may be built by using brackets and connectors AND, OR, NOT as in normal Boolean logic.

Example 1: To select all students enrolled in program B.Sc. in MIS, the following statement (based on the Ullman notation) would apply:

SELECT Spgm# = 'BSC1' (Student)

An alternate syntax of the **SELECT** statement as described in [Date, 2004] follows:

```
Select ::=
<RelationalExpression> [WHERE <Condition>]

Condition ::=
[NOT] <Attribute1> Theta <Attribute2 | Literal> {AND | OR <Condition>}

RelationalExpression ::=
<RelationName> | <SelectStatement> | <ProjectStatement> | <ProductStatement> |
<ThetaJoinStatement> | <UnionStatement> | <IntersectStatement> | <MinusStatement> |
<DivisionStatement>
```

As you will soon see, this syntax is much closer to the actual implementation in SQL.

Example1b: To select all students enrolled in program B.Sc. in MIS, the following statement (based on the Date notation) would apply:

```
Student WHERE Spgm# = 'BSC1'
```

7.3.2 Projection Statement

Based on the Ullman notation, the **PROJECT** statement is of the form

```
Project ::=
PROJ <Attribute> {,<Attribute>} (<RelationalExpression>)

Attribute ::=
<AttributeName> | <Relation.AttributeName>
```

Example 2a: The following are two projections on the relation **Student**

```
// To extract attributes Stud#, Spgm# only from relation Student:
PROJ Stud#, Spgm# (Student)

/* To extract attributes Stud#, Spgm# only from the selection of students enrolled in B.Sc. in MIS: */
PROJ Stud#, Spgm# (SELECT Spgm# = 'BSC1' (Student))

// Note: Do not mix the notations like this (Ullman-Date):
PROJ Stud#, Spgm# (Student WHERE Spgm# = 'BSC1')
```

Based on the Date notation, the alternate syntax of the **PROJECT** statement that is much closer to the SQL implementation is as follows:

```
Project ::=
<Attribute> {,<Attribute>} FROM <RelationalExpression>

Attribute ::=
<AttributeName> | <Relation.AttributeName>
```

Example 2b: With this syntax, the above two projections would be written as follows:

```
// To extract attributes Stud#, Spgm# only from relation Student:
Stud#, Spgm# FROM Student

/* To extract attributes Stud#, Spgm# only from the selection of students enrolled in B.Sc. in MIS: */
Stud#, Spgm# FROM Student WHERE Spgm# = 'BSC1'

// Note: Do not mix the notations like this (Date-Ullman):
Stud#, Spgm# FROM (SELECT Spgm# = 'BSC1' (Student))
```

7.3.3 Natural Join Statement

The Ullman notation and Date notation essentially agree on the format of the natural join. The natural **join** statement is of the form

```
JoinStatement ::=
<RelationalExpression> JOIN <RelationalExpression> {JOIN <RelationalExpression>}
```

Example 3: To join **Student** with **Hall** on the foreign key **Hall#**:

```
Student JOIN Hall
/* This statement produces a relation with each tuple of the relation Student concatenated with a given tuple
of the relation Hall. The concatenated tuples from each of the two input relations (Student and Hall) agree
on the attribute value of Hall#. The final result eliminates one of the two columns Student.Hall# and
Hall.Hall#, since their values are identical. */
```

Please note:

1. The natural join is realized by the join logical file in an IBM System i environment (supported by the operating system), as well as query and open query. However, generally, the RDBMS provides the facility to create complex logical views involving joins of several relations.

2. On modern systems, the designer is allowed to clearly define the foreign key constraint at (or subsequent to) the point of creation of the table **Student**. In more sophisticated environments (for example, DB2 and Oracle), the foreign key name could be different from the referenced attribute, so long as its characteristic features are the same (as mentioned in previous chapters, it is good design practice to use distinct attribute names in different relations). In such cases, an *equijoin* (to be clarified shortly) would normally take the place of a natural join.

3. The operating system or DBMs traverses both relations and joins on matching keys i.e. the foreign key in the first relation is used to reference the primary key in the second relation.

4. The natural join is associative. Moreover, in specifying it, it is not necessary to identify the participating attributes, since they would have been identified when the foreign key constraint is defined.

Example 4: To obtain a list showing **Sname** and **Hallname** combinations:

```
/* We first must link Sname from relation Student to Hallname from relation Hall, via a natural
join. Then project on the required attributes. The solution follows:  */

PROJ Sname, Hallname (Student JOIN Hall) /* Based on Ullman notation, or */

Sname, Hallname FROM Student JOIN Hall /* Based on Date notation */
```

7.3.4 Cartesian Product

Both the Ullman notation and the Date notation essentially agree on the format of the Cartesian (or cross) product. The **PRODUCT** statement is of the form

```
ProductStatement ::=
<RelationalExpression> TIMES <RelationalExpression>
```

The resulting virtual relation has all tuples of the first relation concatenated with all tuples of the second relation.

Example 5a: We desire to have a list showing combinations of department name and name of the related department head: Two solutions are possible. Firstly we can take a cartesian product of **Dept** and **Staff**, followed by a selection, followed by a projection. Secondly, we could take an equijoin, followed by a projection. The second solution is clarified in the next sub-section (example 5b).

Solution 1:
PROJ Dname, Staffname (SELECT Dhead# = Staff# (Dept TIMES Staff)) /* Based on Ullman notation */
/* or */
Dname, Staffname FROM (Dept TIMES Staff) WHERE Dhead# = Staff# /* Based on Date notation */

Solution 2: Specifies an equijoin, followed by a projection. See example 5b below.

Please note:

1. This example illustrates that a natural join is equivalent to a Cartesian product followed by a selection. Proof of this principle is not necessary for this course. However, the principle can be easily illustrated as in Figure 7-4.

Dept

Dept#	Dname	Dhead#
D1	Mathematics	S1
D2	Computer Science	S2
D3	Music	S3

Staff

Staff#	Staffname
S1	Bruce
S2	Henry
S3	Jacobson

Dept TIMES Staff

Dept#	Dname	Dhead#	Staff#	Staffname
D1	Mathematics	S1	S1	Bruce
D1	Mathematics	S1	S2	Henry
D1	Mathematics	S1	S3	Jacobson
D2	Computer Science	S2	S1	Bruce
D2	Computer Science	S2	S2	Henry
D2	Computer Science	S2	S3	Jacobson
D3	Music	S3	S1	Bruce
D3	Music	S3	S2	Henry
D3	Music	S3	S3	Jacobson

Dept TIMES Staff WHERE D-Head# = Staff# is equivalent to Dept JOIN (Dhead# = Staff#) Staff

Dept#	Dname	Dhead#	Staff#	Staffname
D1	Mathematics	S1	S1	Bruce
D2	Computer Science	S2	S2	Henry
D3	Music	S3	S3	Jacobson

Figure 7-4. Illustrating That a Join is Obtained by a Cross Product Followed by a Selection

2. If there is at least one pair of matching keys in both relations, a natural join (if matching attribute names are identical) or an equijoin (if matching attribute names have different names) is preferred to a cross product. The match must be between a foreign key (in the primary relation) and a primary key (in the referenced relation).

3. The Cartesian product, as defined in the relational model, is associative. However its mathematical counterpart (from which it is drawn) is not. The reason for this is partly due to the fact that in the definition of a relation, no emphasis is placed on the order of the attributes (review section 3.3.1).

7.3.5 Theta-Join

The *Theta-join* is presented in some texts as the general case of the **JOIN** operation. The BNF form for the theta-join based on Ullman's notation is as follows:

```
ThetaJoinStatement ::=
SELECT <Condition> (<RelationalExpression> TIMES <RelationalExpression>)
Condition ::=
[NOT] <Attribute1> Theta <Attribute2 | Literal> {AND | OR <Condition>}
```

The BNF form for the theta join based on Date's notation is as follows:

```
ThetaJoinStatement ::=
<RelationalExpression> TIMES <RelationalExpression> WHERE <Condition>
Condition ::=
[NOT] <Attribute1> Theta <Attribute2 | Literal> {AND | OR <Condition>}
```

An alternate notation for representing this has been described by [Russell, 2006], and is particularly clear; it is paraphrased below:

```
ThetaJoinStatement ::=
<RelationalExpression> JOIN (<Condition>) <RelationalExpression>
Condition ::=
[NOT] <Attribute1> Theta <Attribute2 | Literal> {AND | OR <Condition>}
```

Incidentally, this latter notation is really a simplification of the Ullman notation, and is fully reconcilable with either the Date or Ulman notation, bringing additional clarity to the specification of the theta-join. This is illustrated in example 5b. Moreover, as you will see in chapter 12, the ANSI version of the SQL join is comparable to this notation; we will therefore refer to it as the ANSI join notation.

Observe that both the Ullman notation and the Date notation convey the point that a join is really a cross product followed by a selection; the Russell notation implies it. In each of the three cases, the result is a set of tuples from the cross product of the first relation with the second relation that satisfy the given condition. Moreover, with this definition, we can bring further clarity to the equijoin and the natural join as follows:

- The equijoin is simply the specific case where **theta** (the operator) is the equal operation. It is applicable in situations where matching attributes do not have identical names; typically, one attribute (or combination of attributes) constitutes a foreign key in one relation, while the other attribute (or combination of attributes) constitutes a candidate key in the other relation.

- The natural join is a special case of the equijoin, where the attributes compared from both relations are not just defined on the same domain, but have the same name. Further, the natural join will eliminate one of the two (sets of) identical attributes from the final result.

Example 5b: Let us revisit the problem in example 5a — constructing a list showing combinations of department name and name of the related department head. This second solution involves an equijoin.

```
Solution 1:
// Based on Ullman notation:
PROJ Dname, Staffname (SELECT Dhead# = Staff#  (Dept TIMES Staff))

// Based on Date notation:
Dname, Staffname FROM (Dept TIMES Staff) WHERE Dhead# = Staff#

Solution 2:
// Based on the Ullman notation combined with the ANSI notation:
PROJ Dname, Staffname (Dept JOIN (Dhead# = Staff#) Staff))

// Based on the Date notation combined with the ANSI notation:
Dname, Staffname FROM Dept JOIN (Dhead# = Staff#) Staff
```

7.3.6 Union, Intersection, Difference Statements

The **UNION, INTERSECT and MINUS** statements are similarly represented in Ullman's notation as well as Date's notation. The respective syntax forms are as follows:

```
<RelationalExpression> UNION <RelationalExpression>

<RelationalExpression> INTERSECT <RelationalExpression>

<RelationalExpression> MINUS <RelationalExpression>
```

Note:

1. These are binary operations and in each case, both relations must have corresponding attributes that are defined on the same domain.

2. **Union** and **intersect** are associative, but **minus** is not.

7.3.7 Division Statement

The **DIVIDEBY** statement is of the form

R1 DIVIDEBY R2

In this format, relation R1 contains $[m + n]$ attributes and relation R2 has n attributes. The operation of division is as follows:

- Every attribute of R2 must be an attribute of R1.

- The resulting relation will have remaining attributes of R1.

- A tuple occurs in R1 DIVIDEBY R2 if it occurs in R1, concatenated with every tuple in R2.

Example 6: Figure 7-5 provides two illustrations that should help you gain insight into the division operation. The first demonstrates how the division operation works; the second demonstrates that the division operation is the opposite of the Cartesian product operation.

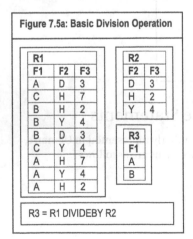
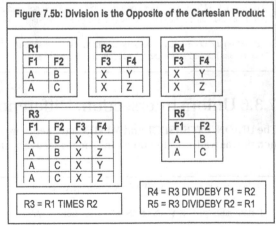

Figure 7-5. *Illustrating the Division Operation*

A formal definition of division is as follows:

> A relation R1 of degree (m+n), divided by a relation R2 of degree n, gives a relation R3 of degree m. Consider the m attributes as X and the n attributes as Y. Then R1 consists of pairs (x,y), and R2 consists of y where x ∈ X and y ∈ Y. So R1(x,y) DIVIDEBY R2(y) = R3(x) where (x,y) appears in R1 for all values of y in R2.

This definition has been recently refined in (the latest editions of) Date's classic text on database system [Date, 2004]. If you need additional information on the subject matter, Date's text is recommended. However, since mastery of this is scarcely applicable (if at all) at this level (in any event, division is a secondary operation), no further discussion will take place.

7.4 Aliases, Renaming and the Relational Assignment

In addition to the basic operations, three additional (advanced) operations defined on relations are

- Alias Operation
- Rename Operation
- Assignment Operation

7.4.1 The Alias Operation

Aliasing is giving an alternate name to a relation. The format is:

> <Relation> ALIASES <RelationalExpression>

Example 7:

> Department ALIASES Dept

Aliasing is used when it is desirable to refer to different tuples in the same relation, or when it is desirable to use a more convenient relation name in an application. Later in the course, as you learn SQL (in an Oracle environment), you will see that aliases are implemented as *synonyms* in Oracle.

Example 8: Suppose that we need to find all students who share birthdays with at least one other student. The solution is obtained by taking the cross product of **Student** and itself, and then searching for matches on **DoB**:

// **Solution based on Ullman Notation:**

Stud2 ALIASES Student

SELECT (Student.Stud# <> Stud2.Stud#) AND (Student.DoB = Stud2.DoB) (Student TIMES Stud2)

// **Solution based on Date Notation:**

Stud2 ALIASES Student

Student TIMES Stud2 WHERE Student.Stud# <> Stud2.Stud# AND Student.DoB = Stud2.DoB

7.4.2 The Assignment Operation

The assignment operator is a colon followed by an equal sign (:=), and is used to have the system remember the results of other operation(s), which may be required for later use. The format of the assignment is:

<Relation>: = <RelationalExpression>

The example in the upcoming subsection illustrates how relational assignments are done.

7.4.3 The Rename Operation

The **RENAME** operation renames specified attributes of a specified relation R1, into a new relation R2. We have established that it is desirable to have unique attribute names in each relation. Further, in the case of nested operations, it is a good habit to have an unambiguous way of referring to attributes of the results of an inner expression, from an outer expression. The **RENAME** operation is ideal for these situations. The format of the **RENAME** operation (based on Date's notation) is:

<RelationalExpression> RENAME <Attribute> AS <Attribute>
{, <Attribute> AS <Attribute>}

As with selection, brackets may be used to avoid ambiguity. Ullman's notation has been omitted here; though slightly different in syntax, its result is similar.

Examples 9: The following examples illustrate the use of renaming and relational assignment:

Student RENAME Hall# AS StudHall#

Pgm_Struct RENAME PSPgm# AS Program#, PSCrs# AS Course#

/* Referring to the previous example (Example 8), the solution could be as follows: */

// **Solution based on Ullman Notation:**

Stud2 ALIASES Student

Stud3: = Stud2 RENAME Stud# AS Stud#2, DoB AS DoB2

SELECT (Stud# <> Stud#2) AND (DoB = DoB2) (Student TIMES Stud3)

// **Solution based on Date Notation:**

Stud2 ALIASES Student

Stud3: = Stud2 RENAME Stud# AS Stud#2, DoB AS DoB2

Student TIMES Stud3 WHERE Stud# <> Stud#2 AND DoB = DoB2

7.5 Other Operators

Other operations to facilitate computation usually exist. A brief summary of some of the common additional operators is provided here (based on Date's notation). These will be further clarified, once the student is exposed to a DSL such as SQL (which we will discuss later in the course).

Extend: The **EXTEND** operator takes a relation as input, and returns a replica of it with one additional column (attribute), as defined by the user. The BNF notation for the syntax is

---

EXTEND <RelationalExpression> ADD <ScalarExpression> AS <NewAttribute>
[WHERE <Condition>]

Example 10: List courses in program "BSC1", with an additional descriptive column

---

EXTEND Pgm_Struct ADD 'Bachelor of Science in MIS' AS MyPgm
WHERE PSPgm# = 'BSC1'

Aggregate: The *aggregate operations* are used to summarize (aggregate) the values of a column of a relation. The standard operators are COUNT, COUNTD, SUM, SUMD, AVGD, MAX, MIN. COUNT, SUM and AVG return numeric values; MAX and MIN return alphanumeric or numeric values, depending on the column in question. COUNTD, SUMD, and AVGD avoid duplicate values for that column. Each operator is specified with a column (attribute) as follows:

```
<AggregateOperator> (<Attribute>)
```

Note: The aggregate operations are typically used in a scenario where data is grouped.

Grouping: By grouping data from a relation, we can derive summarized information for the purpose of analysis. Grouping and aggregation usually go together. For the purpose of discussion, let us assume that the relational algebra syntax for defining a group is as follows:

```
<RelationalExpression> GROUPBY <AttributeList>
```

where <Attribute List> is simply a list of attributes, with the comma as the separator. Grouping is normally embedded as part of some larger relational algebra expression. With the above notation, we can extract summary information from relations as in the following example.

Example 11: Produce a list showing the academic program and corresponding number of courses for each program:

```
// Solution based on Ullman Notation:
PROJ PSPgm#, COUNT (Nbr) ((EXTEND Pgm_Struct ADD (1)AS Nbr)
 GROUPBY PSPgm#)

// Solution based on Date Notation:
PSPgm#, COUNT (Nbr) FROM ((EXTEND Pgm_Struct ADD (1)AS Nbr)
 GROUPBY PSPgm#)
```

7.6 Summary and Concluding Remarks

Let us summarize what we have covered in this chapter:

- The relational algebra is said to be prescriptive — you specify precisely how an activity is to be carried out.

- The eight basic operations of relational algebra are UNION, MINUS, RESTRICT, PRODUCT, PROJECT, JOIN, INTERSECT and DIVIDE BY. Each operation follows a specific syntax.

- In addition to the basic operations, other relational operations include ALIASES, RENAME, EXTEND and GROUP BY.

The next chapter discusses relational calculus as an equivalent alternative to relational algebra.

7.7 Review Questions

1. Why is relational algebra important?

2. Briefly describe the basic operations of relational algebra.

3. Using the college database described in this chapter, practice writing relational algebra statements that will yield certain desirable results.

4. The following is an abridged specification of tables comprising a music database:

Musicians {MNO, MNAME, DOB, MCOUNTRY}   Primary key [MNO]

Compositions {CNO, TITLE, MNO, CDATE}   Primary key [CNO]

Ensembles {ENO, ENAME, ECOUNTRY, MNO-MGR}   Primary key [ENO]

Performances {PNO, PDATE, CNO, CITY, PCOUNTRY, ENO}   Candidate keys [PDATE, ENO], [PNO]

EnsembleMembers {ENO, MNO, INSTRUMENT}   Primary key [ENO, MNO]

Write relational algebra statements to realize the following:

a. Registered musicians from CUB or CAN (where "CUB" and "CAN" are abbreviated codes for Cuba and Canada respectively).

b. Give the ENO of every ensemble that includes a VIOLIN or GUITAR player.

c. Give the ENO of every ensemble that includes a VIOLIN player but not a GUITAR player.

    d.   List all compositions (CNO and TITLE) by DAVID FOSTER.

    e.   List all performances (PNO, CNO, MNO, & PCOUNTRY) of compositions that have been performed in the country of origin.

7.8 References and/or Recommended Readings

[Connolly, 2002] Connolly, Thomas and Carolyn Begg. *Database Systems: A Practical Approach to Design, Implementation and Management* 3rd ed. New York, NY: Addison-Wesley, 2002. See Chapter 4.

[Date, 2004] Date, Christopher J. *Introduction to Database Systems* 8h ed. Menlo Park, CA: Addison-Wesley, 2004. See Chapter 7.

[Elmasri, 2007] Elmasri, Ramez and Shamkant B. Navathe. *Fundamentals of Database Systems* 5th ed. Reading, MA: Addison-Wesley, 2007. See Chapter 6.

[Garcia-Molina, 2002] Garcia-Molina, Hector, Jeffrey Ullman and Jennifer Widom. *Database Systems: The Complete Book*. Upper Saddle River, NJ: Prentice Hall, 2002. See Chapter 5.

[Kifer, 2005] Kifer, Michael, Arthur Bernstein and Philip M. Lewis. Database Systems: An Application-Oriented Approach 2nd ed. New York, NY: Addison-Wesley, 2005. See Chapter 5.

[Martin, 1995] Martin, James, and Joe Leben. *Client/Server Databases: Enterprise Computing*. Upper Saddle River, NJ: Prentice Hall, 1995. See Chapter 11.

[Russell, 2006] Russell, Gordon. *Database eLearning*. http://www.grussell.org/ (accessed July 2006).

[Ullman, 1997] Ullman, Jeffrey D., and Jennifer Widom. *A First Course in Database Systems*. Upper Saddle River, NJ: Prentice Hall, 1997. See Chapter 4.

CHAPTER 8

■ ■ ■

Relational Calculus

This chapter discusses relational calculus as an alternate way of manipulating relations in a database. The partial college database, introduced in the previous chapter (Figures 7-1 and 7-2) will be used as a frame or reference. It must be constantly borne in mind that relational algebra and relational calculus are mutual equivalents; most DBMS suites will implement one or the other, or aspects of both, depending on what is convenient to the developers. The chapter proceeds under the following subtopics:

- Introduction

- Calculus Notations and Illustrations

- Quantifiers, Free and Bound Variables

- Substitution Rule and Standardization Rules

- Query Optimization

- Domain Related Calculus

- Summary and Concluding Remarks

8.1 Introduction

In relational calculus, we simply specify what is required, not how to obtain the required relation(s). Relational algebra, on the other hand, provides a collection of explicit operations in SELECT, JOIN, PROJECT etc., which can be used to tell the system how to derive desired relation(s).

Example 1: Suppose that we are interested in obtaining a list of program names and associated course names for the Bachelor of Science in MIS.

The stepwise relational algebra solution can be described as follows:
a. Take the equijoin of relation **Pgm_Struct**, **Program**, and **Course**
b. Select tuples with Pgm# = 'BSC1'
c. Take a projection on attributes Pgmname and Crsname

The relational calculus formulation can be described as follows:
Get Pgmname and Crsname from **Pgm_Struct**, **Program**, **Course** such that there exists a program structure tuple (PSP. PCS) in Pgm_Struct, a program P in **Program**, and course(s) C in **Course**, where PSP = P, PSC = C and PSP = 'BSC1'

In relational calculus, the user describes what is required; the system is left to decide how to service the user's request. Relational calculus is therefore said to be descriptive, while relational algebra is said to be prescriptive. As you shall see, this distinction is only superficial. More fundamentally, relational calculus and relational algebra are mutual equivalents: any algebra formation has a calculus equivalent and vice versa. Relational calculus is derived from a branch of mathematics called predicate calculus. It uses the idea of *tuple variable* (range variable). A tuple variable refers to a row of a relation at any given time. The relation is called the range. The Ingres language QUEL is similar to the original relational calculus language ALPHA, introduced by Codd.

Referencing an attribute is done by the following notation:

<TupleVariable.AttributeName> | <AttributeName>

Example 2a:

Let PS be a tuple of relation **Pgm_Struct**.
Then PS.PSPgm# refers to the value of the attribute PSPgm# in relation **Pgm_Struct** for some tuple PS.

Tuple variables may be implicit or explicit in SQL, as illustrated below:
Example 2b:

SELECT Pgm_Struct.PSPgm# FROM Pgm_Struct WHERE Pgm_Struct.PSPgm# = 'BSC1';
// is equivalent to
SELECT PS.PSPgm# FROM Pgm_Struct PS WHERE PS.PSPgm# = 'BSC1';

Tuple variables may also be implicit or explicit in QUEL, as illustrated below:
Example 2c:

RANGE OF PS is Pgm_Struct
RETRIEVE (PS.PSPgm#) WHERE PS.PSPgm# = 'BSC1'
// is equivalent to
RETRIEVE (Pgm_Struct.PSPgm#) WHERE Pgm_Struct.PSPgm# = 'BSC1'

Relational calculus of this sort is sometimes referred to as tuple calculus. An alternate domain calculus, based on domains, has been developed by Lacroix and Pirotte [Lacroix, 1977]. Query by example (QBE) is a language developed on this (domain calculus). This course focuses on the former, and not the latter.

8.2 Calculus Notations and Illustrations

As in the previous chapter, the BNF notation for expressing syntactical components of a language will be employed. In the examples that will follow to the end of the chapter, the semicolon is used to punctuate the calculus statements in the interest of clarity. However, bear in mind that the original QUEL language did not require such punctuations. The salient syntactical components of relational calculus are as follows:

1. **Relational Operators** include =, <, >, <=, >=, =>, <> while *connectives* include AND, NOT, OR

RelationalOperator ::= = | < | <= | > | >= | => | <>
Connective ::= AND | OR | NOT

---

2. **Comparisons** are done variable-with-variable, attribute-with-literal or attribute-with-attribute, separated by operators.

Comparison::= <CompFormat1> | <CompFormat2> | <CompFormat3>

CompFormat1 ::= <Variable> <Operator> <Variable>
CompFormat2 ::= <Attribute> <Operator> <Attribute>
CompFormat3 ::= <Attribute> <Operator> <Literal> | <ScalarExpression>

Attribute ::= <TupleVariable.AttributeName> | <AttributeName>

Note: A comparison evaluates to true or false (similar to a relational algebra condition). The implication operator (=>) works as follows: P => Q means if condition P holds, then so does condition Q. Two alternate interpretation are as follows:

- If P is true, so is Q; otherwise P is false.

- Either Q is true or P is false, i.e. P => Q means Q or P'.

3. **De Morgan's Law** for logical expressions is applicable:

(P AND Q AND R ...)' = P' OR Q' OR R' ...
(P OR Q OR R ...)' = P' AND Q' AND R' ...

---

4. **Boolean Expressions** can be derived by combination of comparisons using connectors AND, OR, NOT:

> **BooleanExpression::=** [NOT] <Comparison> {<Connector> <BooleanExpression>}
> **Connector::=** AND | OR

Note: Boolean expressions may be bracketed in the interest of clarity. This is necessary in situations where there are nested expressions.

5. **Range Definition** is as follows:

> **RangeDefinition::=** RANGE OF <TupleVariable> IS <Relation> | (<RelationalExpression>)

6. **Relational Expression:** A tuple calculus relational expression is of the following form:

> **RelationalExpression ::=** <TargetList> [WHERE <WFF>];
> **TargetList ::=** [<Attribute> =] <Attribute> [AS <Attribute>] | <TupleVariable> {,<TargetList>}

Note:

- Where the tuple variable alone is specified, all attributes associated with the variable are implied (remember that a tuple variable is defined on a relation which has attributes).

- The relational expression defines a projection on attributes in the target list from the Cartesian product of all referenced relations (from the target list). The WFF (*well formed formula*) dictates a selection from the Cartesian product.

7. **Well-Formed Formula** (WFF): A well-formed formula (WFF) is of the following form:

> **WFF ::=** <Comparison> | NOT <WFF> | <Comparison> AND <WFF> |
> <Comparison> OR <WFF> | If <Comparison> Then <WFF> |
> EXISTS <Variable> (<WFF>) | FORALL <Variable> (<WFF>)

Example 3: List all students, (names and ID#) who share surname with other students.

```
Solution using QUEL:

RANGE OF Y IS Student;
RANGE OF X IS Student;
RETRIEVE (X.Sname, X.Stud#) WHERE (X.Stud# <> Y.Stud#) AND (X.Sname = Y.Sname);
```

Note: The QUEL verb RETRIEVE describes retrieval. The pure calculus follows the RETRIEVE verb. Also note that the original QUEL did not use a semicolon to punctuate statements. It is done here simply to improve readability.

Example 4a: List all programs (showing Pgm#) that include the course M100.

```
RANGE of PS is Pgm_Struct;
(PS. PSPgm#) WHERE PS.PSCrs# = 'M100';
```

Example 4b: List all programs (showing Pgm# and PgmName) that include the course M100.

```
RANGE OF PS is Pgm_Struct;
RANGE OF P IS Program;
(PS. PSPgm#, P.PgmName) WHERE (PS.PSPgm# = P.Pgm# AND PS.PSCrs# = 'M100');
```

Example 5: List all program codes and related course codes.

```
RANGE OF PS IS Pgm_Struct;
(PS.PSPgm#, PS.PSCrs#);
```

Example 6: List all program names and related course names.

```
RANGE OF PS IS Pgm_Struct;
RANGE OF P IS Program;
RANGE OF C IS Course;
(P.Pgmname, C.Crsname) WHERE (EXISTS PS (PS.PSPgm# = P.Pgm# AND PS.PSCrs# = C.Crs#));
```

Example 7: We could rewrite the solution to example 4 as follows:

```
RANGE OF PS IS Pgm_Struct;
M100PGM = PS.PSPgm# WHERE PS.PSCrs# = 'M100';
```

8.3 Quantifiers, Free and Bound Variables

Carrying on, we need to introduce two quantifiers, and clarify what is meant by *free* and *bound* variables. The mathematical notations will be introduced, followed by the relational calculus notations. The mathematical notations are indicated in Figure 8-1:

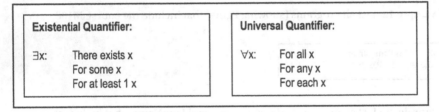

Existential Quantifier:

∃x: There exists x
      For some x
      For at least 1 x

Universal Quantifier:

∀x: For all x
      For any x
      For each x

Figure 8-1. *Quantifiers*

Additionally, if P(x) is a condition in tuple variable x, then

- (∃x) (P(x)) means ∃x satisfying P(x)

- (∀x) (P(x)) means all variables in range of x satisfies the condition P(x)

As expressed in the previous section, the relational calculus notations for the universal and existential quantifiers as follows:

```
FORALL <Tuple-Variable> <WFF>
EXISTS <Tuple-Variable> <WFF>
```

8.3.1 Well-Formed Formula

Based on the notation given in the previous section, a WFF may be clarified as follows:

a.   A simple comparison (condition) is a WFF

b.   If F is a WFF, so are NOT (F) and (F)

c.   If F1, F2 are WFF then so are (F1 AND F2), (F1 OR F2) and (If F1 THEN F2)

    d.   If the tuple variable x occurs *freely* in a WFF F then ∃x (F) and
        ∀x (F) are WFFs

    e.   Nothing else

In layman's terms, a WFF is a simple or complex comparison involving attributes and scalar values. As can be confirmed from the forgoing sections and examples, WFFs are necessary for constructing appropriate data retrieval statements from the database.

8.3.2 Free and Bound Variables

A tuple variable is bounded if it occurs with either an existential or universal quantifier. Consider the scenario below:

∀p (p.grade = 'Good')   is equivalent to   ∀q(q.grade = 'Good')

This is an example of a bound occurrence of tuple variable *p*. The condition on *p* is either true or false, even if a particular value of *p* is not substituted. Note also that *p* can be replaced by *q*. Now consider the following:

p.grade = 'Good'   is not equivalent to   q.grade = 'Good'

This is an example of a free occurrence of variable *p*. The variable occurs in a simple condition (comparison) — when a particular value of *p* is substituted we can have a difference. Note that *p* cannot be replaced by *q*.

The following are some rules for free and bound variables:

    a.   All occurrences of variables in a simple condition (comparison) are free.

    b.   Any free/bound occurrence in WFF F is also free/bound in NOT F, (F).

    c.   Any free/bound occurrence in WFF F1, F2 is free/bound in (F1) AND (F2) as well as (F1) OR (F2).

    d.   Every free occurrence of x in F is bound in ∃x (F) or ∀x (F); the occurrence of other variables are not affected.

    e.   A tuple variable cannot be both free and bound in the same statement.

So to paraphrase and summarize, a tuple variable is bound in an expression if it is associated with a quantifier; once bound, it remains in this state for the expression. Here is another illustration:

EXISTS P (PS.Pgm# = P.Pgm#)

In this expression, P is bound and PS is free.

Example 8: The example below should further clarify the correct usage of bound and free variables.

RANGE OF P is Program; RANGE OF PS IS Pgm_Struct;
PS.PSPgm#, P.Pgmname WHERE (PS.PSPgm# = P.Pgm#) AND EXISTS PS (PS.PSCrs# = 'M100');

/* This is unacceptable because PS is used to mean two different things (both bound and free). The statements
   should be replaced by the following: */

RANGE OF P is Program; RANGE OF PS IS Pgm_Struct; RANGE OF PS2 IS Pgm_Struct;
PS.PSPgm#, P.Pgmname WHERE (PS.PSPgm# = P.Pgm#) AND EXISTS PS2 (PS2.PSCrs# = 'M100') AND
(PS2.PSPgm# = PS.PSPgm#);

Example 9: List surname of students with DoB after 1975 (assuming the date format of YYYYMMDD).

RANGE OF S IS Student;
S.Sname WHERE S.DoB > 19751231;

Example 10: Find programs (names) that do not include course M100.

RANGE OF PS IS Pgm_Struct;
RANGE OF P IS Program;
P.Pgmname WHERE EXISTS PS (PS.PSCrs# <> 'M100' AND PS.PSPgm# = P.Pgm#);

Example 11: List courses (code and name) that occur in all disciplines programs).

RANGE OF C IS Course;
RANGE OF P IS Program;
RANGE OF PS IS Pgm_Struct;
RANGE OF PS2 IS Pgm_Struct;

C.Crs#, C.Crsname WHERE FORALL P EXISTS PS
((PS.PSPgm# = P.Pgm#) AND EXISTS PS2 ((PS2.PSCrs# = PS.PSCrs#) AND (PS2.PSPgm# <> PS.PSPgm#))
    AND (PS.PSCrs# = C.Crs#));

Example 12: Give the name of all programs with course M100.

```
RANGE OF P IS Program;
RANGE OF PS IS Pgm_Struct;
P.Pgmname WHERE EXISTS PS (PS.PSPgm# = P.Pgm# AND PS.PSCrs# = 'M100');
```

Example 13: Give the names of department heads that are not division heads.

```
RANGE OF S IS Staff;
RANGE OF D IS Dept;
RANGE OF DV IS Division;
S.Staffname WHERE EXISTS D EXISTS DV (D.Dhead# = S.Staff# AND D.DDiv# = DV.Div#
AND D.Dhead# <> DV.Divhead#);
```

8.4 Substitution Rule and Standardization Rules

It is sometimes necessary to introduce "dummy" (apparently redundant) tuple variables, in conformance with an old rule that forbids retrieval of a quantified (bounded) variable(s). Further, for many data sub-languages (including SQL), if x and y are tuple variables and W is a WFF involving x and y, then

```
x.attribute WHERE (∃y) (W(x,y)) is equivalent to x.attribute WHERE W(x,y)
```

This rule often simplifies the database query statement by avoiding the use of the existential quantifier, and will become clear when we discuss SQL later in the course.

Additionally, due to the limitation of some DBMS suites in their support of relational calculus notations, it is often useful to apply certain substitution and standardization rules. These are mentioned below (Figure 8-2):

Substitution Rule for Quantifier:

If x is free in WFF F Then
$\forall x\, (F(x)) \equiv \forall y\, (F(y))$ and
$\exists x\, (F(x)) \equiv \exists y\, (F(y))$

Standardization Rules WFFs:

Let x, y be tuple variables and let A,B be WFFs

1. $(A)'' \equiv A$
2. $(x=y)' <=> x <> y$
3a. $(A\ or\ B)' <=> A'\ AND\ B'$
3b. $(A\ AND\ B)' <=> A'\ OR\ B'$
4a. $(\forall x\,(A))' <=> \exists x\,(A)'$
4b. $(\exists x\,(A))' <=> \forall x\,(A)'$
4c. $\forall x\,(A) <=> (\exists x)'\,(A)'$
5. If A then B $<=> (A)'\ or\ B$
6. If x does not occur in A, Then A AND $\forall x\,(B) <=> \forall x\,(A\ AND\ B)$
7. If x does not occur in B. Then $(\exists x\,(A)\ or\ B\,) <=> \exists x\,(A\ OR\ B)$

Figure 8-2. Substitution and Standardization Rules

8.5 Query Optimization

We have stated that every relational calculus expression has a relational algebra equivalent and vice versa. Query optimization involves the transformation from calculus to algebra to optimized algebra. The rules for conversion are outlined in Figure 8-3:

---

1. Take the Cartesian product of all relations used
2. Select the required tuples
3. Project on desired attributes
4. Optimize by
   - taking selection (restriction) first (before product);
   - replacing cross product(s) with natural join(s) or equijoin(s) where possible;
   - taking the projection on the result.
5. Apply quantifiers from right to left as follows:
   - For the quantifier "EXIST RX" (where RX is a tuple variable that ranges some relation R), project the current intermediate result to eliminate all attributes of R.
   - For the quantifier "FORALL RX" (where RX is a tuple variable that ranges some relation R), divide the current intermediate result by the (possibly restricted) relation associated with RX.

Figure 8-3. Query Optimization Rules

Example 14: Replace the calculus specification in example 12 with an algebra specification.

The non-optimized algebra solution follows:

// Rule 1:
R1:= Pgm_Struct TIMES Program;

// Rule 2 (via Ullmman Notation):
R2:= SELECT (PSCrs# = 'M100' AND (PSpgm# = Pgm#) (R1));
// Rule 2 (via Date Notation):
R2 :- R1 WHERE PSCrs# = 'M100' AND PSpgm# = Pgm#;

// Rule 3 (via Ullman Notation):
R3:= PROJ Pgmname (R2);
// Rule 3 (via Date Notation):
R3:= Pgmname FROM R2;

The optimized algebra solution follows:

// Based on Ullman notation and Russell notation combined:
PROJ Pgmname (SELECT Crs# = 'M100'(Pgm_Struct) JOIN (PSPgm# = Pgm#) Program);

// Based on Date notation and Russell notation combined:
Pgmname FROM ((Pgm_Struct WHERE PSCrs# = 'M100') JOIN (PSPgm# = Pgm#) Program);

// Based on Date notation :
Pgmname FROM (Pgm_Struct WHERE PSCrs# = 'M100') TIMES Program) WHERE PSPgm# = Pgm#;

The two solutions are illustrated in Figure 8-4. Note that existential quantifiers are ignored in the translation process as long as the quantified variables are not implicated as part of retrieved attribute-list (hence the rule towards the beginning of the previous section). Also recall that existential qualifiers can effectively replace universal quantifiers.

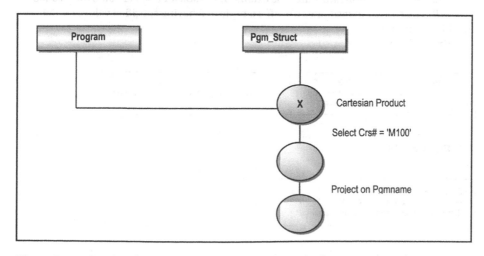

Figure 8-4a. *Graphical Representation of Non-optimized Solution to Example 12*

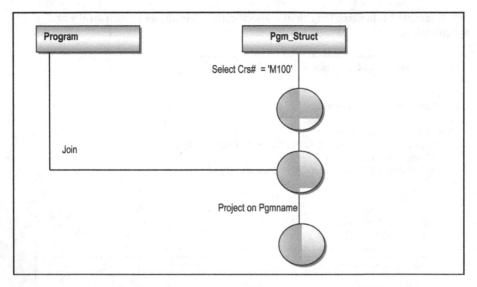

Figure 8-4b. *Graphical Representation of Optimized Solution to Example 12*

8.6 Domain Oriented Relational Calculus

Domain related relational calculus involves the manipulation of *domain variables* instead of tuple variables (these must be defined similar to tuple variables). It supports an additional form of comparison called the membership condition. A member condition takes the form

R(A:V {,A:V}) where

R is a relation, A is an attribute, V is a domain variable or a scalar value (also called a *literal*). The condition evaluates true iff ∃ a tuple in R having specified values for the specified attribute.

Example 15:

Pgm_Struct (PSPgm#: 'BSC1', PSCrs#: 'M100')
is a membership condition that evaluates true if ∃ a tuple in relation **Pgm_Struct** satisfying the condition
PSPgm# = 'BSC1' and PSCrs# = 'M100'.

Example 16:

Pgm_Struct (PSPgm# : Ref_Pgm)
evaluates to true if ∃ a tuple in **Pgm_Struct** satisfying the condition PSPgm# = Ref_Pgm
where **Ref_Pgm** is some domain variable.

Query-by-Example (QBE) is an attractive implementation of domain calculus by Microsoft Access. The user simply completes a table on the screen in order to make a query request. Further discussion of domain calculus is omitted from this course. Suffice it to say that domain calculus has its advantages in more complicated comparisons and is particularly useful when one is willing to concentrate on domain variables rather then tuple variables.

8.7 Summary and Concluding Remarks

It's now time to summarize what we have covered in this chapter:

- Relational calculus is said to be descriptive, meaning, you describe precisely the activity required. The chapter concentrated on tuple calculus, i.e., calculus related to the manipulation of tuple variables.

- There are a number of standard relational calculus notations that allow you to succinctly describe data to be retrieved from relational tables. Retrieval statements essentially involve manipulating tuple variables using well-formed formulas (WFFs). A WFF is essentially a simple or complex condition.

- WFFs often involve the use of free and bound variables. The rules for these must be strictly followed.

- Query optimization is the process of obtaining the most efficient relational algebra equivalent for a relational calculus statement. In so doing, the basic rules for query optimization must be observed.

- Domain oriented calculus is calculus related to the manipulation of domain variables. It is an alternative to tuple calculus.

The language QUEL very closely resembled the relational calculus. The more contemporary SQL represents exhibits both relational calculus and relational algebra features.

8.8 Review Questions

1. Why is relational calculus important? Explain why relational algebra is said to be prescriptive, and relational calculus is said to be descriptive. Provide an example to illustrate.

2. Describe the salient components of relational calculus.

3. Using the college database described in this chapter, practice writing relational calculus statements that will yield certain desirable results.

4. Explain the concept and process of query optimization. Use an appropriate example to illustrate.

8.9 References and/or Recommended Readings

[Codd, 1971] Codd, Edgar F. "A Data Base Sub-language Founded on the Relational Calculus." *Proc. 1971 ACM SIGFIDET Workshop on Data Description, Access and Control.* San Diego, CA, November 1971.

[Codd, 1972] Codd, Edgar F. "Relational Completeness of Database Sub-languages." *In Data Base Systems: Courant Computer Science Symposia Series 6.* Eaglewood Cliffs, NJ: Prentice Hall, 1972.

[Connolly, 2002] Connolly, Thomas and Carolyn Begg. *Database Systems: A Practical Approach to Design, Implementation and Management* 3rd ed. New York, NY: Addison-Wesley, 2002. See Chapter 4.

[Date, 2004] Date, Christopher J. *Introduction to Database Systems* 8h ed. Menlo Park, CA: Addison-Wesley, 2004. See Chapter 8.

[Elmasri, 2007] Elmasri, Ramez and Shamkant B. Navathe. *Fundamentals of Database Systems* 5th ed. Reading, MA: Addison-Wesley, 2007. See Chapter 6.

[Kuhns, 1967] Kuhns, J.L. "Answering Questions by Computer: A Logical Study." *Report RM-5428-PR.* Santa Monica, CA: Rand Corporation, 1967.

[Lacroix, 1977] Lacroix M. and A. Pirotte. "Domain-Oriented Relational Languages." *Proc. 3rd International Conference on very Large Data Bases.* October 1977.

[Ullman, 1997] Ullman, Jeffrey D., and Jennifer Widom. *A First Course in Database Systems.* Upper Saddle River, New Jersey: Prentice Hall, 1997. See Chapter 4.

■ ■ ■

CHAPTER 9

Relational System — a Closer Look

We have covered much ground in our study of database systems. We have also established the importance of the relational model and its significant contribution to the field of database systems. We now pause to conduct a more enlightened discussion of this contribution and its effect on the field. This rather short chapter proceeds under the following subtopics:

- The Relational Model Summarized

- Ramifications of the Relational Model

- Summary and Concluding Remarks

9.1 The Relational Model Summarized

Figure 9-1 summarizes the salient features of the relational model that have been established so far.

---

1. Data structure supporting the following:
   - Domains
   - Normalized relations
   - Attributes (including candidate/primary keys) which comprise the structure of the normalized relations
   - Rows (tuples) of time dependent data for each relation

2. Data integrity rules which include:
   - Entity integrity rule
   - Referential integrity rule

3. Data manipulation features which include support of the following:
   - Relational algebra and/or relational calculus
   - Relational assignment
   - Entry, maintenance and deletion of data

4. Desirable features as discussed in chapters 1 and 2

Figure 9-1. *Salient Features of Relational Model*

The above features define the minimum requirements of a relational system. Other desirable features of a database system discussed in chapters 1 and 2 are still important. As it has turned out, meeting those standards was (and is) not easy. For years, they have eluded, and continue elude software engineering firms aspiring to construct and market DBMS suites. As you will soon see, the standards bar has been raised even higher for contemporary products.

9.2 Ramifications of the Relational Model

The relational model has very far-reaching implications, and makes very stringent demands on the software engineering industry, to deliver DBMS products that meet a minimum set of standards. Let us briefly look at some of these ramifications.

9.2.1 Codd's Early Benchmark

In 1982, Edgar F. Codd (referred to by many as the father of database systems), in a paper entitled "Relational Database: A Practical Foundation for Productivity" (see [Codd, 1982]), proposed that a system could be regarded as relational if it supported at least, the following:

- Relational databases

- The operations RESTRICT, PROJECT and (natural) JOIN, without requiring any prior definition of access paths to support these operations

Codd further asserted the following:

- The operations may be supported explicitly or implicitly.

- The system must internally optimize user requests for desirable performance.

Based on those minimum requirements, DBMS suites were classified in one of four categories: tabular, minimally relational, relationally complete, and fully relational. These classifications are clarified in Figure 9-2.

Category	Requirement
Tabular	The system supports tabular data structure only, but not set-level operations.
Minimally Relational	The system is tabular and supports the operations RESTRICT, PROJECT, and JOIN.
Relationally Complete	The system is tabular and supports all of the operations of relational algebra.
Fully Relational	The system supports all aspects of the model including domains and integrity rules.

Figure 9-2. Categorization of DBMS Suites

Not many products were able to survive the rigors of that benchmark. Interestingly, three of the products that survived the test are still doing well in the industry today; they are Oracle, DB2 and INGRES.

9.2.2 Revised Definition of a Relational System

In 1985, Codd, in a paper captioned *"Is Your DBMS Really Relational?"* (see [Codd, 1985]), revised the definition of a relational system. Christopher Date later made some important recommendations about the revised model. The revised model with its recommendations is presented here (Figure 9-3).

1. Structural features include:
   - Relations including base relations, views, queries, and snapshots
   - Attributes which comprise the structure of the normalized relations
   - Domains
   - Primary keys
   - Foreign keys
   - Queries
   - User defined data types
   - Rows (tuples) of time dependent data for each relation

2. Integrity features including:
   - Entity integrity rule
   - Referential integrity rule
   - Primary key inheritance rules
   - Type inheritance and conversion rules (user defined)
   - User-defined integrity rules
   - Ensure closure and uniqueness of attributes

3. Manipulation features including:
   - Entry, maintenance and deletion of data
   - Theta-select
   - Projection on certain attributes, while omitting others
   - Theta-join and natural join
   - Outer join (discussed in chapter 12)
   - Divide
   - Union
   - Intersection
   - Difference
   - Relational assignment
   - Rename
   - Extend
   - Summarize

4. Desirable features including those mentioned in chapters 1 and 2

Figure 9-3. *Codd's Revised Definition of a Relational System*

Additionally, Codd proposed 12 rules for determining how relational a DBMS product is. With these 12 rules added to the redefined model, a DBMS is considered to be fully relational if it satisfies all structural, integrity and manipulative features, and fulfills the 12 rules. Christopher Date subsequently proposed a *zero-rule* that essentially summarized Codd's 12 rules. The zero-rule and Codd's 12 rules are presented here.

Date's Zero-Rule

According to [Date, 1990], a system qualifies as a **relational**, **database,** and **management** system (highlights are deliberate) iff it uses its **relational** facilities exclusively to **manage** its **database**.

This is a loaded statement that will become clearer as you progress through the course. For instance, after studying chapters 12 – 14, you will have a better appreciation of what it means to use the relation facilities of a database to manage the said database. Moreover, it is not sufficient to take a system that is fundamentally not relational, add an interface that facilitates PROJECT, JOIN, SELECT (only), and then claim that the system is relational. Instead, everything must be relational — the view mechanism, the catalog, the structure, the integrity features, and the operations supported.

Codd's Twelve Rules

Rule 1: The Information Rule: All information in the database must be represented as relational tables, subject to established integrity constraints, structural and manipulation features (mentioned earlier).

Rule 2: The Guaranteed Access Rule: All data stored in the database must be logically addressable by specifying the relation, the related attribute(s), and the primary-key-value.

Rule 3: Systematic Treatment of Null Values: The DBMS is required to have a consistent way of representing and treating so-called "missing information" that is different from regular data values, and independent of the data types supported.

Rule 4: The Active Online Catalog Rule: The system should host a comprehensive relational catalog that is accessible to authorized users via the regular query language. Chapter 14 will provide more clarification on the importance of the system catalog.

Rule 5: Comprehensive Data Sub-Language: The system must support at least one relational language that meets the following criteria:

a.   has a linear syntax;

b.   can be used both interactively and within application programs;

c.   provides adequate support of DDL, DML, and DCL operations.

This requirement is adequately fulfilled in SQL, the universal standard database language that will be covered in chapters 10 – 14.

Rule 6: The View Updating Rule: All views that are theoretically updateable must be updateable by the system (this will be clarified in chapter 13).

Rule 7: High-level Insert, Update, and Deletion: The system must support set-wise DML operations such as INSERT, UPDATE, and DELETE operations. Chapter 11 will demonstrate that SQL fulfills this requirement.

Rule 8: Physical Data Independence: The system should isolate all application programs (and end user accesses) from the physical structure of the database. Changes in one should not affect the other.

Rule 9: Logical Data Independence: The system should isolate all application programs (and end user accesses) from the logical structure of the database. Changes in one should not affect the other.

Rule 10: Integrity Independence: Integrity constraints must be specified separately from application programs and stored in the system catalog. It must be possible to change such constraints as required, without effect on the applications that access the database.

Rule 11: Distribution Independence: Existing applications should continue to operate successfully when distributed versions of the DBMS are first introduced or upgraded.

Rule 12: Nun-subversion: If the system provides a low-level (record-at-a-time) interface, then it should not be possible to use this interface to undermine or bypass relational security or integrity constraints of the system.

9.2.3 Far Reaching Consequences

These constraints set a very high standard for relational DBMS (RDBMS) suites to attain. In fact, for a considerable period of time, the industry did not see a product that irrefutably met all of these requirements. On the other hand, many proposed products have fallen by the wayside, due to failure to come close enough to the established standards. With incremental improvements to products such as (but not only) DB2, Oracle, Informix, and Sybase over several years, the industry can now boast of products meeting these standards (but not without room for improvement). Chapters 16 – 20 take a look at some of these products.

Is the benchmark too high for RDBMS products? Not at all. It defines an ideal that software engineering firms can strive to attain. It also establishes a firm mathematical basis for the relational model. In this regard, the work of Codd, Date, Fagin, and others cannot be over applauded. To a certain extent, the standards have protected the consuming public from rogue companies that might have tried to exploit us by marketing inferior database products under false claim of them being relational. We have seen many such attempts, but for the most part, they have not gone very far.

In the next two divisions of the text, you will discover a rather interesting phenomenon: Many of the standards described in the revised benchmark for a RDBMS have been implemented in SQL, the universal database language, and leading DBMS products such as DB2, Oracle, Sybase, Informix, MS SQL Server, and MySQL. This is comforting information.

9.3 Summary and Concluding Remarks

Here is a summary of what has been covered in this chapter:

- The benchmarks for a relational database system may be defined in terms of the data structure requirements, the data integrity requirements, and the data manipulation requirements.

- Over the years, the database systems industry has embraced Codd's benchmarks (first introduced in 1982 and subsequently revised in 1985) as the standards for relational DBMS suites. The revised standards also include Codd's twelve rules and Date's zero-rule.

- Even though these standards are more than two decades old, they still remain binding on the industry. In fact, many of the smaller DBMS products still struggle to meet them.

Although Codd died in 2003, his legacy will no doubt continue to live and guide the field of database systems well into the foreseeable future. Date, a colleague of Codd, continues to be a renowned author and consultant in the field. So thankfully, we are in good hands.

9.4 Review Questions

1. Describe in your own words, what is meant by a relational DBMS.

2. Conduct a critical evaluation and comparative analysis of three leading DBMS products that you are familiar with. Use Codd's revised definition of a relational database system as your benchmark.

3. Conduct a critical evaluation of E.F. Codd's contribution to the field of database systems.

9.5 References

[Codd, 1982] Codd, Edgar F. "Relational Database: A Practical Foundation for Productivity," *Communications of the ACM*, Vol. 25, Issue 2, February 1982. pp. 109-117.

[Codd, 1985] Codd, Edgar F. "Is Your DBMS Really Relational?" and "Does Your DBMS Run By the Rules?" *ComputerWorld*, October 14 and October 21, 1985.

[Date, 1990] Date, Christopher J. *Introduction to Database Systems* Vol. I 5th ed. Menlo Park, California: Addison-Wesley, 1990. See Chapter 15.

PART C

■ ■ ■

The Structured Query Language

The next six chapters will focus on the Structured Query Language (SQL). This language has become the universal standard database language. It is therefore imperative that as a student of computer science, or a practicing IT professional, you are not just familiar, but have a working knowledge of the language. The objectives of this division are:

- to provide a solid overview of SQL as a database language;
- to help you gain a good working knowledge of the main SQL data definition statements;
- to help you gain a good working knowledge of the main SQL data manipulation statements;
- to help you gain insights and a good working knowledge of logical views and system database security;
- to discuss and illustrate the importance and usefulness of the system catalog;
- to discuss some limitations of SQL.

Chapters to be covered include:

- Chapter 10 — Overview of SQL
- Chapter 11 — SQL Definition Statements
- Chapter 12 — SQL Data Manipulation Statements
- Chapter 13 — Logical Views & Security
- Chapter 14 — The System Catalog
- Chapter 15 — Some Limitations of SQL

CHAPTER 10

■ ■ ■

Overview of SQL

The Structured Query Language (SQL) has become the universal language of choice
for DBMS products. A study of this language is therefore imperative for the student of
computer science or computer information systems. This and the next few chapters will
help you acquire a working knowledge of the language, as implemented in the Oracle
environment (Oracle 10G or 11G). One fact you need to be immediately cognizant of is
that there are different implementations of SQL. However, the implementations usually
have more in common than differences; therefore once you have mastered the language
in one DBMS environment, adjusting to another environment is a trivial matter.
The chapter proceeds under the following subheadings:

- Important Facts

- Advantages of SQL

- Summary and Concluding Remarks

10.1 Important Facts

Structure Query Language (SQL) is an example of a DSL — consisting of DDL, DCL, and
DML as defined in chapter 2. First developed by IBM in the 1970s, SQL is the universal
language of databases.

SQL may be described as an interactive query language as well as a database
programming language. Commands can be entered directly at the command prompt,
or embedded in application programs, written in some other language. Examples of
languages that support embedded SQL include COBOL, BASIC, RPG IV, Java, Oracle
PLSQL, Pascal, C++, Visual Basic, FoxPro, etc. The latest set of standards for SQL that is
available for public access is SQL-2007. SQL-2007 is an enhancement of SQL-2003 to
allow for better compatibility with the Extensible Markup Language (XML), and other
refinements. In this text, we essentially concentrate on core SQL statements; these
statements are also consistent with SQL-2003. The standards are updated roughly every
four years. For more information, please see the references listed in section 10.5.

SQL is a non-procedural (descriptive) language that closely mirrors the relational
calculus as discussed in chapter 8; there are also features that mirror the relational
algebra of chapter 7. Although the language was originally introduced by IBM, no
organization has a monopoly on it. Different implementations of SQL have their own
idiosyncrasies and flavors. Some of the major DBMS suites are Oracle, DB2, Informix,
Sybase, Ingres, Delphi, MS SQL Server, and MySQL.

10.1.1 Commonly Used DDL Statements

Figure 10-1 provides a list of commonly used DDL statements of SQL. You will observe that the statements are self-explanatory. This makes learning of the language very easy, particularly when compared to more cryptic traditional programming languages. Another feature that you will notice about SQL is that it is symmetrical and follows very consistent standards (language experts favor the term *orthogonal* to describe this feature). Thus, for most database objects, you can create the object, alter (i.e. modify) it, or drop (i.e. remove) it from the system. And the main database objects that you will be working with are tables, indexes, constraints and views; in the case of Oracle, there are also databases, tablespaces, sequences and synonyms. Of course, there are other database objects that will be covered later in the course.

Generic DDL Statements:	
Statement	**Explanation**
Create-Table	Creates a database table. The table may be a relational table, an object table, or an XML table; the default is relational.
Alter-Table	Alters the physical and/or logical structure of a table.
Drop-Table	Removes a table from the system catalog. The table and all its data are deleted. Most DBMS products will forbid you to delete a table that contains referenced tuples.
Create-Index	Creates an index on a table. There are different types of indexes, but the default is B-tree.
Alter-Index	Modifies the structure of an index.
Drop-Index	Removes an index from the system catalog.
Create-Constraint	Creates a constraint on a database table. As you will later see, there are different types of constraints.
Alter-Constraint:	Modifies the terms of a constraint.
Drop-Constraint	Removes a constraint from the system catalog.
Create-View	Creates a logical view of data contained in physical database tables. Remember, a view is a virtual relation.
Alter-View	Allows modifications to a logical view.
Drop-View	Removes a logical view from the system catalog.

Oracle Specific Statements:	
Statement	**Explanation**
Create-Database	Creates a database. An Oracle database is a complex object which in turn consists of tablespaces, which in turn consists of datafiles and other related physical objects.
Alter-Database	Modifies the database.
Drop-Database	Removes the database from the system catalog.
Create-Tablespace:	Creates a tablespace. A tablespace is a logical container within a database. It can contain several datafiles that contain the actual database objects.
Alter-Tablespace	Modifies a tablespace
Drop-Tablespace	Removes a tablespace from the system catalog.
Create-Sequence	Creates a sequence. A sequence is a special database object which is used to storing unique numbers. Sequences are useful in coding attributes of certain database records.
Alter-Sequence	Modifies a sequence.
Drop-Sequence	Removes a sequence from the system catalog.
Create-Synonym	Creates an alias of a database object.
Drop-Synonym	Removes a synonym from the system catalog. Note that synonyms cannot be altered, since they are logical objects.

Figure 10-1. Commonly Used DDL Statements of SQL

10.1.2 Commonly Used DML and DCL Statements

The commonly used DML and DCL statements of SQL are indicated in Figure 10-2. The DML statements are often referred to as SUDI (select, update, delete and insert) statements. The DCL statements fall into three categories: those that affect how DML operations take place (mainly COMMIT and ROLLBACK); those that relate to system privileges; and those that affect the environmental settings of the end user.

DML Statements:	
Statement	Explanation
Select	Retrieves data from database tables in a manner that is consistent with user specifications.
Update	Updates data contained in physical database tables.
Delete	Removes data from physical database tables.
Insert	Inserts data into physical database tables.
DCL Statements:	
Statement	Explanation
Commit:	Forces system buffer to write data database tables on disk.
Rollback	Undoes earlier commit by reinstating the database table to its state prior to the last update.
System Privilege Statements	A set of statements that govern database security.
Environment Setting Statements	A set of statements that govern environmental settings of database users.

Figure 10-2. *Commonly Used DML & DCL Statements of SQL*

10.1.3 Syntax Convention

In the next four chapters (chapters 11 – 14), the core DDL DML and DCL statements of SQL will be discussed. The convention that will be employed for each statement is to present the full (or close-to-full) syntax in BNF format, then discuss the most common abridged format(s) of the statement; all the examples provided will be based on abridged formats of the statements discussed. In most cases, it is unlikely that you will need to use the full syntax of a statement; however, the full syntax is given to provide you with an accurate perspective of the possibilities, and in the interest of completeness.

10.2 Advantages of SQL

SQL brings a number of significant advantages to the software engineering industry. Some of these advantages are as follows:

> **Rapid Software Development:** SQL enhances rapid development of business application systems by its powerful and easy-to-learn statements. In fact, most RAD tools, DBMS suites, and CASE tools support the language.

Higher software Quality: SQL brings higher software quality to the software engineering arena. By using more powerful SQL statements, than would be possible in traditional high level languages, the software engineer is likely to produce shorter code with fewer errors. The descriptive nature of the language is useful in this regard.

Higher Productivity: SQL brings higher productivity to businesses by providing superior database management features than possible in systems developed with traditional high-level languages alone. These superior database management features include the following:

- Faster access to data

- Larger files

- Set-at-a-time access instead of record-by-record access

- Powerful data aggregation facilities to provide meaningful end-user information

- Facilitation of logical views to provide meaningful end-user information

- Facilities for the enforcement of data integrity constraints, independent of application programs

- Facilities for logically reorganizing data to provide useful information to end users

- Facilities for the enforcement of database security constraints

Data Independence: SQL helps DBMS suites to meet the objective of data independence, with its associated benefits (review chapter 1).

Standardization: SQL facilitates standardization among competing software development tools, since they all are forced to support the language.

10.3 Summary and Concluding Remarks

Let us summarize what we have covered in this chapter:

- SQL is the universe database language. It consists of various statements for creating and administering a database. These statements can be classified as DDL statements, DML statement, and DCL statements.

- SQL can be used at the command prompt, or embedded in other high-level language programs.

- SQL brings a number of significant advantages to the software engineering industry.

SQL is not without a fair amount of limitations. In order to fully understand the limitations, you need to have a working knowledge of the language first. With this in mind, a discussion of these limitations is left for chapter 15.

The next chapter discusses the main DDL statements of SQL. As you will see, they are easy to learn and use.

10.4 Review Questions

1. What are the most common DDL statements of SQL? Briefly explain the purpose of each.

2. What are the main DML statements of SQL? Briefly explain the purpose of each.

3. Explain the three categories of DCL statements in SQL.

4. Identify some of the advantages of SQL.

10.5 Recommended Readings

[Eisenberg, 2000] Eisenberg, Andrew and Jim Melton. "SQL Standardization: The Next Step." *SIGMOD Record* Vol.29, no.1, March 2000. pp. 63 – 67.

[Kulkarni, 2003] Kulkarni, Krishna. *Overview of SQL:2003*. San Jose, CA: Silicon Valley Laboratory, IBM Corp., 2003. http://www.wiscorp.com/SQL2003Features.pdf (accessed August 2008).

[WISC, 2008] Whitemarsh Information Systems Corp. *SQL.* http://www.wiscorp.com/SQLStandards.html (accessed August 2008).

CHAPTER 11

■ ■ ■

SQL Data Definition Statements

The main SQL definition statements in an Oracle 10G environment are shown in Figure 11-1. These statements relate to the six basic types of database objects in Oracle — tables, indexes, views, constraints, synonyms, and sequences. Other more advanced types of database objects include databases, table-spaces, data-files, users, user profiles, functions, and procedures.

Create-Table	Create-Index	Create-Constraint	Create-View
Alter-Table	Alter-Index	Alter-Constraint	Alter-View
Drop-Table	Drop-Index	Drop-Constraint	Drop-View
Create-Database	Create-Tablespace	Create-Sequence	Create-Synonym
Alter-Database	Alter-Tablespace	Alter-Sequence	Drop-Synonym
Drop-Database	Drop-Tablespace	Drop-Sequence	

Figure 11-1. Commonly Used SQL Definition Statements

This chapter will focus on tables, synonyms, sequences and indexes; a discussion of the more advanced objects will follow in subsequent chapters. The chapter will proceed under the following subtopics:

- Overview of Oracle's SQL Environment

- Database Creation

- Database Management

- Tablespace Creation

- Tablespace Management

- Table Creation Statement

- Dropping or Modifying a Table

- Working With Indexes

177

- Creating and Managing Sequences

- Altering and Dropping Sequences

- Creating and Managing Synonyms

- Summary and Concluding Remarks

11.1 Overview of Oracle's SQL Environment

The most basic working environment provided in Oracle is the Oracle SQL *Plus environment. It is a command entry interface, and gives the new SQL user an excellent opportunity to learn the language. This default editor is a line editor: you are allowed to enter your SQL command on a line-by-line basis, terminated by a semicolon or forward slash (/). Some line editing commands and file editing commands are included in Figure 11-2.

SQL *Plus File Editing Commands	
Command	Purpose
SAVE <Filename>	Save the file specified
GET <Filename>	Read the file specified
START <Filename>	Get and execute the file specified
EDIT <Filename>	Read the file specified for update
SPOOL <Filename>	Write SQL statements to a file
EDIT	Edits the last SQL statement in **Notepad** environment

SQL *Plus Line Editing Commands	
Command	Purpose
I <Text>	Input text
L	List
L <n>	List line n
<n> <Text>	Edit line n

Figure 11-2. *Oracle SQL *Plus Editing Commands*

Alternately, you can use **Notepad** or any other text editor to key in your SQL statements, save it as a text file, then read it into the SQL *Plus environment via the GET or START command for text (**.txt**) files, or the @ command for SQL (**.sql**) files. In such case, the path and filename must be specified within single quotes.

In addition to SQL *Plus, Oracle provides other more user-friendly GUI-based components for learning and using SQL. These include Oracle Enterprise Manager (OEM), Oracle SQL Developer (OSQLD), and Oracle iSQL *Plus. You may read more about these components in Chapters 16 and 25. Finally, Oracle implements its own host language, called PL/SQL. It is a simple language with a predominantly Pascal-like syntax. Although coverage of the syntax of this language is beyond the scope of this course, a few examples will contain Pl/SQL code (particularly in Chapter 12). Because of the simplicity of the syntax, you should be able to read the code and understand it, so there is no need to panic.

Throughout the remainder of the course, a slight modification of the BNF notation will be used for specifying the syntax of SQL statements. The symbols used are shown in Figure 11-3. Additionally, from time to time, you will observe the inclusion of clarifying comments that conform to how comments are made in the C-based programming languages (e.g. // this is a comment, /* and so is this */). These comments serve to clarify the syntactic representations or examples that they appear in.

::=	This symbol means 'is defined as'
<...>	Required input supplied by the user are enclosed in angular brackets
[...]	Optional items are enclosed in square brackets
ItemA | ItemB	Choice: ItemA or ItemB may be chosen by the user
ItemA /* Or */ ItemB	Choice: ItemA or ItemB may be chosen by the user. This option is used when the syntactic elements are complex to the point where using a single slash (as in the preceding case) would not provide the clarification needed.
{...}	Repetition: Items enclosed within curly braces may be repeated zero to n times. The contemporary convention is to use the curly braces to indicate user choice; however, to avoid confusion, that convention will not be used; we will stick to the more traditional convention as specified.

Figure 11-3. BNF Notation Symbols

11.2 Database Creation

In the Oracle environment, database creation is quite involved, requiring you to be aware of several intricate details about the Oracle DBMS itself. A database may be created in one of three ways: manually, using the Database Configuration Assistant (DBCA), or during installation of the Oracle Database server software. In each case, the **Create-Database** statement is employed (manually or automatically). However, there are certain procedures and intricate details which have to be carefully observed. In the interest of getting you started, these intricacies will be de-emphasized for now. Below (Figure 11-4) is the syntax of the **Create-Database** statement, followed by a simple example.

```
Create-Database ::=
CREATE DATABASE <Database-Name>
[USER SYS IDENTIFIED BY <Password> ]
[USER SYSTEM IDENTIFIED BY <Password>]
[CONTROLFILE REUSE]
[LOGFILE [GROUP <n> (File-spec {,File-spec})
        { GROUP <n> (File-spec {,File-spec})}]
[MAXLOGFILES <n>] [MAXLOGMEMBERS <n>] [MAXLOGHISTORY <n>]
[MAXDATAFILES <n>] [MAXINSTANCES <n>]
[ARCHIVELOG|NOARCHIVELOG] [FORCE LOGGING]
[CHARACTER SET <Charset>] [NATIONAL CHARACTER SET <Charset>]
[DATAFILE File-spec [Auto-extend Clause] {, File-spec [Auto-extend Clause]}]
[EXTENT MANAGEMENT LOCAL]
[Default-temporary-tablespace-Clause]
[Undo-tablespace-Clause]
[Set-Time-Zone-Clause]

Auto_Extend-Clause ::=
AUTOEXTEND ON|OFF NEXT <n> K|M MAXSIZE <n>|UNLIMITED K|M

Default-temporary-tablespace-Clause ::=
DEFAULT TEMPORARY TABLESPACE <TablespaceName>
[TEMPFILE File-spec
[EXTENT MANAGEMENT LOCAL]
[UNIFORM SIZE <n> K|M]
```

Figure 11-4. Syntax of the Create-Database Statement

```
Undo-tablespace-Clause ::=
UNDO TABLESPACE <TablespaceName> DATAFILE File-spec

Set-Time-Zone-Clause ::=
SET TIME_ZONE = '<Time-Zone-Spec>'

File-spec ::= '<PathtoFile>' SIZE <Integer> K|M [REUSE]

Note:
1.    File-Spec is a path to a physical operating system file that you specify, based on your environment and database standards.
2.    If you specify locally managed TBS (EXTENT MANAGEMENT LOCAL), you must specify the default temporary TBS.
3.    IF you specify locally managed TBS and the Datafile-Clause, you must specify the default temporary TBS and a datafile for
      that TBS.
4.    If you specify locally managed TBS but do not specify the Datafile-Clause, you can omit the default temporary TBS  Clause.
      Oracle will create a temporary TBS called TEMP with a 10M datafile.
5.    The default temporary TBS size is (uniform) 1M.
6.    The default log-file size (if you do not specify the Log-File-Clause, Oracle creates two log-files) is 100M.
7.    Time zone is specified as a number of hours and minutes ahead of (+) the standard GMT, or by using a predetermined time-
      zone name (as obtained from the view v$TIMEZONE_NAMES).

Example:

CREATE DATABASE SampleDB
  CONTROLFILE REUSE
  LOGFILE
    GROUP 1 ('C:\Oracle\Oradata\SampleDB\Log0101.log', 'D:\Oracle\Oradata\SampleDB\Log0101.log') SIZE 50K,
    GROUP 2 ('C:\Oracle\Oradata\SampleDB\Log0201.log', 'D:\Oracle\Oradata\SampleDB\Log0202.log') SIZE  50K
  MAXLOGFILES 5
  MAXLOGHISTORY 100
  MAXDATAFILES 10
  MAXINSTANCES 2
  ARCHIVELOG
  CHARACTER SET AL32UTF8
  NATIONAL CHARACTER SET AL16UTF16
  DATAFILE
    'C:\Oracle\Oradata\SampleDB\System0101.dbf' AUTOEXTEND ON,
    'D:\Oracle\Oradata\SampleDB\System0201.dbf ' AUTOEXTEND ON
  NEXT 10M MAXSIZE UNLIMITED
  DEFAULT TEMPORARY TABLESPACE Temp_TBS
  UNDO TABLESPACE Undo_TBS
  SET TIME_ZONE = '+02:00';
```

Figure 11-4. *Syntax of the Create-Database Statement (continued)*

Observation: In some systems, database creation is as simple as creating a directory (library or folder depending on the operating system used). Unfortunately, this is not the case in Oracle. For more details on this matter, see the Oracle Product Documentation [Oracle, 2008].

11.3 Database Management

Once the database has been created, it must be populated with database objects. Database objects include tablespaces (specific to Oracle), tables, indexes, views, synonyms, procedures, triggers, packages, sequences, users, roles, etc. As a good DBA and/or software engineer, you will also need to carry out performance tuning on your database.

This may involve reorganizing database tables and indexes, deleting unnecessary indexes or moving other objects. You will also be required to periodically perform backup and recovery procedures, or make alterations to the database itself. These issues will be more thoroughly discussed in Chapter 21. However, to enhance your overall appreciation, the syntax for the **Alter-Database** statement is provided (Figure 11-5). This statement is used extensively to effect structural as well as status changes to the database.

```
Alter-Database ::=
Alter Database [<DatabaseName>]
Startup-Clauses | Recovery-Clauses | Datafile-Clauses | Logfile-Clauses | Controlfile-Clauses |
Standby-Database-Clauses | Default-Settings-Clauses | Conversion-Clauses |
Redo-Thread-Clauses | Security-Clause;

Startup-Clauses::= Startup1 | Startup2 | Startup3
Startup1 ::= MOUNT [STANDBY | CLONE DATABASE]
Startup2 ::= OPEN READ ONLY
Startup3 ::= OPEN READ WRITE [RESETLOGS | NORESETLOGS] [MIGRATE]

Recovery-Clauses ::= General-Recovery-Clause | Managed-Standby-Recovery | END BACKUP

General-Recovery-Clause ::=
RECOVER [AUTOMATIC [FROM '<PathtoFile>']]
Full-Database-Recovery-Clause | Partial-Database-Recovery-Clause | LOGFILE '<PathtoFile >'
TestCorruption | RecoveryOption1 | RecoveryOption2

TestCorruption ::= [TEST] | [ALLOW <n> CORRUPTION] | [NOPARALLEL] | [PARALLEL <n>]
RecoveryOption1 ::= RECOVER [AUTOMATIC [FROM '<PathtoFile >']] CANCEL
RecoveryOption2 ::= RECOVER [AUTOMATIC [FROM '<PathtoFile >']] CONTINUE [DEFAULT]

Full-Database-Recovery-Clause ::= Standby1 | Standby2 | Standby3 | Standby4
Standby1 ::= [STANDBY] DATABASE UNTIL CANCEL
Standby2 ::= [STANDBY] DATABASE UNTIL TIME <Timestamp>
Standby3 ::= [STANDBY] DATABASE UNTIL CHANGE <n>]
Standby4 ::= [STANDBY] DATABASE USING BACKUP CONTROLFILE

Partial-Database-Recovery-Clause ::= PartialR1 | PartialR2 | PartialR3 | PartialR4
PartialR1 ::= TABLESPACE <Tablespace> {, <Tablespace>}
PartialR2 ::= DATAFILE '<PathtoFile>' | <File-Number> {, '<PathtoFile >' | <File-Number>}
PartialR3 ::= STANDBY TABLESPACE <Tablespace> {, <Tablespace>}
                UNTIL [CONSISTENT WITH] CONTROLFILE
PartialR4 ::= STANDBY DATAFILE '<PathtoFile >' | <File-Number> {, '<PathtoFile >' | <File-Number>}
                UNTIL [CONSISTENT WITH] CONTROLFILE

Managed-Standby-Recovery-Clause ::=
RECOVER MANAGED STANDBY DATABASE Recover-Clause | Cancel-Clause | Finish-Clause
```

***Figure 11-5.** Syntax for Alter-Database Statement*

```
Recover-Clause ::= RClause1 | RClause2 | RClause3 | RClause4 | RClause5 | RClause6 | RClause7 | RClause8 |
                   RClause9 | RClause10 | RClause11 | RClause12 | RClause13 | RClause14
RClause1 ::= DISCONNECT [FROM SESSION]
RClause2 ::= TIMEOUT <n>
RClause3 ::= NOTIMEOUT
RClause4 ::= NODELAY
RClause5 ::= DEFAULT DELAY
RClause6::= DELAY <n>
RClause7::= NEXT <n>
RClause8::= EXPIRE <n>
RClause9 ::= NO EXPIRE
RClause10 ::= NOPARALLEL
RClause11::= PARALLEL <n>
RClause12 ::= THROUGH [THREAD <n>] SEQUENCE <n>
RClause13 ::= THROUGH ALL ARCHIVELOG
RClause14::= THROUGH ALL | LAST | NEXT SWITCHOVER


Cancel-Clause ::=
CANCEL [IMMEDIATE] [WAIT | NOWAIT]


Finish-Clause ::=
DISCONNECT [FROM SESSION] [NOPARALLEL] | [PARALLEL <n>]
FINISH [SKIP [STANDBY LOGFILE]][WAIT | NOWAIT]


Datafile-Clause ::= DFSpec1 | DFSpec2 | DFSpec3 | DFSpec4 | DFSpec5 | DFSpec6 | DFSpec7 | DFSpec8 | DFSpec9 |
                    DFSpec10
DFSpec1 :: = CREATE DATAFILE <File-Number> | '<File-Name>' {,<File-Number> | '<File-Name>'}
              [AS NEW] | [AS  <File-spec> {, <File-spec>}]
DFSpec2 :: = DATAFILE <File-Number> | '<File-Name>' {, <File-Number> | '<File Name>'} ONLINE
DFSpec3 :: = DATAFILE <File-Number> | '<File-Name>' {, <File-Number> | '<File Name>'} OFFILINE  [DROP]
DFSpec4 :: = DATAFILE <File-Number> | '<File-Name>' {, <File-Number> | '<File Name>'} RESIZE <n> [K|M]
DFSpec5 :: = DATAFILE <File-Number> | '<File-Name>' {, <File-Number> |  '<File Name>'} Autoextend-Clause
DFSpec6 :: = DATAFILE <File-Number> | '<File-Name>' {, <File-Number> |  '<File Name>'}  END BACKUP
DFSpec7 :: = TEMPFILE <File-Number> | '<File-Name>' {, <File-Number> |  '<File Name>'}
              ONLINE | OFFLINE |  Autoextend_Clause
DFSpec8 :: =TEMPFILE <File-Number> | '<File-Name>' {, <File-Number> |  '<File Name>'} DROP [INCLUDING DATAFILES]
DFSpec9 :: = TEMPFILE <File-Number> | '<File-Name>' {, <File-Number> |  '<File Name>'} RESIZE <nr> [K|M]
DFSpec10 :: = RENAME FILE '<PathtoFile>' {, '<PathtoFile>' } TO '<PathtoFile>' {, '<PathtoFile>' }


Autoextend-Clause ::= AutoOnOption | AutoOffOption
AutoOnOption ::= AUTOEXTEND OFF
AutoOffOption ::= AUTOEXTEND ON [NEXT <nr> [K|M] [Maxsize-Clause]]
```

Figure 11-5. Syntax for Alter-Database Statement (continued)

```
Maxsize-Clause ::= FixedSize | VariableSize
VariableSize ::= MAXSIZE UNLIMITED
FixedSize ::= MAXSIZE <nr> [K|M]


Logfile-Clauses ::= LogClause1 | LogClause2 | LogClause3 | LogClause4 | LogClause5 | LogClause6 | LogClause7 |
                    LogClause8 | LogClausen9 | LogClause10
LogClause1 ::=  ARCHIVELOG | NOARCHIVELOG
LogClause2::=  [NO] FORCE LOGGING
LogClause3::=  ADD [STANDBY] LOGFILE [THREAD <n>] [GROUP <n>] Logfile-Spec {, [GROUP <n>] Logfile-Spec}
LogClause4::=  DROP [STANDBY] LOGFILE Logfile-Spec
LogClause5::=  ADD [STANDBY] LOGFILE MEMBER '<PathtoFile>' [REUSE]
                    {, '<PathtoFile>' [REUSE]} TO Logfile-Spec {, Logfile-Spec}
LogClause6::=  DROP [STANDBY] LOGFILE MEMBER '<PathtoFile>' {, '<PathtoFile>'}
LogClause7::=  ADD SUPPLEMENTAL LOG DATA [(PRIMARY KEY | UNIQUE INDEX
                    {, PRIMARY KEY | UNIQUE INDEX}) COLUMNS]
LogClause8::=  DROP SUPPLEMENTAL LOG DATA
LogOClause9::=  RENAME FILE '<PathtoFile>' {, '<PathtoFile>'} TO '<PathtoFile>' {, '<PathtoFile>'}
LogClause10::=  CLEAR [UNARCHIVED] LOGFILE Logfile-Spec {, Logfile-Spec} [UNRECOVERABLE DATAFILE]


Logfile-Spec ::= LogOption1 | LogOption2 | LogOption3
LogOption1 ::= GROUP <n>
LogOption2 ::= ( '<PathtoFile>' {, '<PathtoFile>'})
LogOption3 ::= '<PathtoFile>'


Controlfile-Clauses ::= CFOption1 | CFOption1 | CFOption3
CFOption1 ::=  CREATE STANDBY CONTROLFILE AS '<PathtoFile>' [REUSE]
CFOption2 ::=  BACKUP CONTROLFILE TO Tracefile-Clause
CFOption3 ::=  BACKUP CONTROLFILE TO  '<PathtoFile>' [REUSE]


Tracefile-Clause ::=
TRACE [AS '<PathtoFile> [REUSE] [RESETLOGS | NORESETLOGS]]


Standby-Database-Clauses ::= SClause1 | SClause2 | SClause3 | SClause4 | SClause5 | SClause6 | SClause7 |
                    SClause8 | SClause9
SClause1 ::= ACTIVATE [PHYSICAL | LOGICAL] STANDBY DATABASE [SKIP [STANDBY LOGFILE]]
SClause2::= SET STANDBY DATABASE TO MAXIMIZE PROTECTION | AVAILABILITY | PERFORMANCE
SClause3 ::= REGISTER [OR REPLACE] [PHYSICAL | LOGICAL] LOGFILE Logfile-Spec {, Logfile-Spec}
SClause4 ::= START LOGICAL STANDBY APPLY [[NEW PRIMARY <DBLINK>] | [INITIAL <Scan-value>]]
SClause5 ::= STOP | ABORT LOGICAL STANDBY APPLY
SClause6 ::= NOPARALLEL
SClause7 ::= PARALLEL <n>
SClause8 ::= COMMIT TO SWITCHOVER TO PHYSICAL | LOGICAL PRIMARY | STANDBY
SClause9::= [WITH | WITHOUT SESSION SHUTDOWN] [WAIT | NOWAIT]


Default-Settings-Clauses ::= DSClause1 | DSClause2 | DSClause3 | DSClause4
DSClause1 ::= [NATIONAL] CHARACTER SET <Charset>
DSClause2 ::= Set-Time-Zone-Clause
DSClause3 ::= DEFAULT TEMPORARY TABLESPACE <TablespaceName>
DSClause4 ::= RENAME GLOBAL_NAME TO <Database-Name>.<Domain>
```

Figure 11-5. *Syntax for Alter-Database Statement (continued)*

```
Set-Time-Zone-Clause ::=
SET TIME_ZONE = '± <HH:MM>' | <Time-Zone-Region>

Conversion-Clauses ::=
CONVERT | ResetOption
ResetOption ::= RESET COMPATIBILITY


Redo-Thread-Clauses ::= EnableThread | DisableThread
EnableThread ::= ENABLE [PUBLIC] THREAD <n>
DisableThread ::= DISABLE THREAD <n>

Security-Clause ::=
GUARD ALL | STANDBY | NONE

Examples:

ALTER DATABASE SampleDB MOUNT;

ALTER DATABASE SampleDB READ ONLY;

ALTER DATABASE SampleDB BACKUP CONTROLFILE TO TRACE AS 'C:\Oracle\EFDB06\SampleTrace';
```

Figure 11-5. *Syntax for Alter-Database Statement (continued)*

There is also a **Drop-Database** statement that allows you to delete the database. In order to use it you must have administrator privilege. Also, be aware that not all component files are removed from the operating system when this command is issued. As an alternative, you can use the DBCA to delete a database.

11.4 Tablespace Creation

In the Oracle environment, another database object that must be created as part of the database preparation is a tablespace. A tablespace is the holding area for all database objects (actually, the objects are stored in datafile(s) contained within the tablespace). A database must have at least one tablespace, but typically has several. The following are tablespaces which are typically found in a database:

- System tablespace (prefixed SYSTEM): This is a default tablespace used for system resources.

- Temporary tablespace (prefixed TEMP): Used for intermediate results such as internal sorts for user queries.

- Tools tablespace (prefixed TOOLS): Used for Oracle administrative tools.

- Index tablespace (prefixed INDX): For storing and maintaining indexes.

- Undo tablespace (prefixed UNDOTBS): For automatic logs due to data changes (this is particularly useful for data rollbacks and/or data recoveries after a catastrophe).

- Users tablespace (prefixed USER): For storing user created tables.

A full discussion of Oracle tablespaces is beyond the scope of this course. However, in the interest of a credible introduction, Figure 11-6 provides the syntax of the **Create-Tablespace** statement, along with an example.

```
Create-Tablespace::=
CREATE [TEMPORARY | UNDO] TABLESPACE <TablespaceName>
[DATAFILE File-spec {, File-spec}
[MINIMUM EXTENT <n> [K|M]] /*NA If locally managed */
[BLOCKSIZE <n> [K]]
[LOGGING | NOLOGGING]
[FORCE LOGGING]
[ONLINE | OFFLINE]
[AutoExtend-Clause]
[[DEFAULT] STORAGE [COMPRESS | NOCOMPRESS] Storage-Spec] /*NA  if TEMPORARY above */
[PERMANENT | TEMPORARY] /*NA if TEMPORARY above; default is PERMANENT;  */
                        /*TEMPORARY NA for locally managed TBS */
[Extent-Management-Clause]
[SEGMENT SPACE MANAGEMENT MANUAL | AUTO];   /* MANUAL is the default; AUTO recommended */

AutoExtend-Clause ::= AutoOn | AutoOff
AutoOn ::=  AUTOEXTEND OFF
AutoOff ::=  AUTOEXTEND ON NEXT <n> K|M MAXSIZE UNLIMITED | <n> [K|M]

Extent-Management-Clause ::= DictionaryOption | LocalOption1 | LocalOption2
DictionaryOption ::= EXTENT MANAGEMENT DICTIONARY
LocalOption1 ::= EXTENT MANAGEMENT LOCAL AUTOALLOCATE
LocalOption2 ::= EXTENT MANAGAEMENT LOCAL UNIFORM [SIZE <n> [K|M]]

File-spec ::=
'<PathtoFile>' SIZE <Integer> K|M [REUSE]

Storage-Spec ::=
INITIAL <n> [K|M] NEXT <n> [K|M]
PCTINCREASE <n> MINEXTENTS <n>
MAXEXTENTS <In> | UNLIMITED
FREELISTS <n> FREELIST GROUPS <n>
OPTIMAL <n> [K|M]
[PCTUSED <n>] [PCTFREE <n>]
[INITRANS <n>] [MAXFRANS <n>]
[BUFFER_POOL KEEP | RECYCLE | DEFAULT]

Example:

CREATE TABLESPACE SampleTBS
DATAFILE 'C:\Oracle\Oradata\SampleDB\SampleTBS.dbf' SIZE 500M
AUTOEXTEND ON NEXT 1M
MAXSIZE UNLIMITED
EXTENT MANAGEMENT LOCAL UNIFORM SIZE 100K
SEGMENT SPACE MANAGEMENT AUTO;

Note: Locally managed TBS is depicted by the clause EXTENT MANAGEMENT LOCAL.  This is default in
Oracle 10G and can therefore be omitted.
```

Figure 11-6. *Syntax for Create-Tablespace Statement*

11.5 Tablespace Management

Once the tablespace has been created and populated with database objects, it will need to be managed. This is normally done via the **Alter-Tablespace** command. Through this command, you can effect structural as well as status changes to the tablespace. As with the **Create-Tablespace** command, a full discussion of is beyond the scope of this course. However, in the interest of credibility, its syntax, as well as an example is provided in Figure 11-7. Of course, you can also delete a tablespace via the **Drop-Tablespace** statement. Figure 11-8 provides the syntax along with an example. Finally, through a component called Oracle Enterprise Manager (OEM), you can manage tablespaces (and most other database objects) in a GUI environment.

```
Alter-Tablespace::=
ALTER TABLESPACE <TablespaceName>
[ADD DATAFILE | TEMPFILE File-spec {, File-spec}]
[RENAME DATAFILE '<PathtoFile>' {, '<PathtoFile >' } TO '<PathtoFile >' {, '<PathtoFile >'}]
[DATAFILE | TEMPFILE ONLINE | OFFLINE]
[DEFAULT STORAGE [COMPRESS | NOCOMPRESS] Storage-Spec]
[MINIMUM EXTENT <n> [K|M]]
[Online-Offline-Clause]
[COALESCE]
[BEGIN | END BACKUP]
[READ ONLY | WRITE]
[PERMANENT | TEMPORARY]
[LOGGING | NOLOGGING]
[[NO] FORCE LOGGING];

Storage-Spec ::=  /* As defined in Create-Tablespace */

File-spec ::=  /* As defined in Create-Tablespace */

Online-Offline-Clause ::= ONLINE | Offline-Spec
Offline-Spec ::=  OFFLINE [NORMAL | TEMPORARY | IMMEDIATE]

Example:

ALTER TABLESPACE SampleTBS
OFFLINE NOLOGGING;
```

Figure 11-7. *Syntax for Alter-Tablespace Statement*

```
Drop-Tablespace ::=
DROP TABLESPACE <Tablespace> [INCLUDING CONTENTS [AND DATAFLES]] [CASCADE
CONSTRAINTS];

Example:
DROP TABLESPACE SampleTBS INCLUDING CONTENTS AND DATAFILES;
```

Figure 11-8. *Syntax for Drop-Tablespace Statement*

11.6 Table Creation Statement

Once the database and tablespaces have been configured, the next logical step is to create database objects which (in Oracle's case) will be stored in the tablespace(s). The first type of database objects to be created is the relational and/or object tables; this is done via the **Create-Table** statement. The **Create-Table** statement is one of the most multi-faceted statements in SQL (next to the **Select** statement). The complete syntax is shown in Figure 11-9, while an abridged version of the statement is provided in Figure 11-10.

Create-Table::=
Create-Relational-Table | Create-Object-Table | Create-XML-Table

Create-Relational-Table ::=
CREATE [GLOBAL TEMPORARY] TABLE [<Schema>·] <TableName> [(Relational-Properties)]
[ON COMMIT DELETE | PRESERVE ROWS]
[Physical-Properties Table-Properties] [Storage-clause];

Relational-Properties ::=
Column-Definition {, Column-Definition}
[Constraint-Definition {, Constraint-Definition}]

Column-Definition ::=
<Column-Name> Data-Type-Spec [DEFAULT <Expression>]
[Inline-Constraint | Inline-Ref-Constraint]

// Data-Type-Spec refers to any valid type specification as outlined in figure 11.11

Constraint-Definition ::=
Inline-Constraint | Out-of-line-Constraint | Inline-Ref-Constraint | Out-of-Line-Ref-Constraint

Out-of-line-Constraint ::= Out-Constraint-Unique | Out-Constraint-Primary | Out-Constraint-Foreign | Out-Constraint-Check
Out-Constraint-Unique ::= [CONSTRAINT <Constraint-Name>] UNIQUE (<Column> {,<Column>}) [Constraint-State]
Out-Constraint-Primary ::=
[CONSTRAINT <Constraint-Name>] PRIMARY KEY (<Column>[ASC/DESC]{, <Column>[ASC/DESC]}) [Constraint-State]
Out-Constraint-Foreign ::=
[CONSTRAINT<Constraint-Name>] FOREIGN KEY (<Column> {,<Column>}) Reference-Clause [Constraint-State]
Out-Constraint-Check ::= [CONSTRAINT<Constraint-Name>] Check-Spec [Constraint-State]

Check-Spec ::= CFormat1 | CFormat2 | CFormat3
CFormat1 ::= Check (<Column> BETWEEN <Value1> AND <Value2>)
CFormat2 :::= CHECK (<Column> operator <Value>)
CFormat3 :::= CHECK (<Column> IN <Value> {,<Value>})

Inline-Constraint ::= In-Constraint-Null | In-Constraint-Unique | In-Constraint-Primary | In-Constraint-Foreign |
                                      In-Constraint-Check
In-Constraint-Null ::= [CONSTRAINT <Constraint-Name> [NOT] NULL [Constraint-State]
In-Constraint-Unique ::= [CONSTRAINT <Constraint-Name> UNIQUE [Constraint-State]
In-Constraint-Primary ::= [CONSTRAINT <Constraint-Name> PRIMARY KEY [Constraint-State]
In-Constraint-Foreign ::= [CONSTRAINT <Constraint-Name> Reference-Clause [Constraint-State]
In-Constraint-Check ::= [CONSTRAINT <Constraint-Name> Check-Spec [Constraint-State]

Figure 11-9. *The Create-Table Statement*

Reference-Clause ::=
REFERENCES [<Schema>·] <ObjectName> [(<column>)]
[ON DELETE CASCADE] | [ON DELETE SET NULL]

Constraint-State ::= Exception-Clause | Using-Index-Clause | CState1 | CState2 | CState3 | CState4 | CState5
CState1 ::= [NOT] DEFERRABLE
CState2 ::= INITIALLY IMMEDIATE | DEFERRED
CState3 ::= ENABLE | DISABLE
CState4 ::= VALIDATE | NOVALIDATE
CState5 ::= REPLY | NO REPLY

Inline-Ref-Constraint ::= IROption1 | IROption2 | IROption3
IROption1 ::= SCOPE IS [<Schema>·] <Scope-Table>
IROption2 ::= WITH ROWID
IROption3 ::= [CONSTRAINT <Constraint-Name>] Reference-Clause [Constraint-State]

Out-of-Line-Ref-Constraint ::= OROption1 | OROption2 | OROption3
OROption1 ::= SCOPE FOR (<Ref-Column> | Ref-Attribute>) IS [<Schema·>] <Scope-Table>
OROption2 ::= REF (<Ref-Column> | <Ref-Attribute>) WITH ROWID
OROption3 ::= [CONSTRAINT <Constraint-Name>] FOREIGN KEY (<Ref-Column> | <Ref-Attribute>)
            Reference-Clause [Constraint-State]

Using-Index-Clause ::= UIOption1 | UIOption2 | UIOption3 | UIOption4 | UIOption5 | UIOption6 | UIOption7 | UIOption8
UIOption1 ::= USING INDEX <Index Name>
UIOption2 ::= USING INDEX (Create-Index)
UIOption3 ::= USING INDEX PCTFREE | INITRANS | MAXTRANS <Integer>
UIOption4 ::= USING INDEX Storage-Clause
UIOption5 ::= USING INDEX TABLESPACE <Tablespace>
UIOption6 ::= USING INDEX SORT | NOSORT
UIOption7 ::= USING INDEX LOGGING | NOLOGGING
UIOption8 ::= USING INDEX LOCAL | Global-Partition-Index

Global-Partition-Index ::=
GLOBAL PARTITION BY RANGE (<Column> {,<Column>})
(Index-Partitioning-Clause)

Index-Partitioning-Clause ::=
PARTITION [<Partition>] VALUES LESS THAN (<Value> {,<Value>})
[Segment-Attributes- Clause]

Segment-Attributes-Clause ::=
[TABLESPACE <Tablespace>]
[Physical-Attributes-Clause] [LOGGING | NOLOGGING]

Figure 11-9. *The Create-Table Statement (continued)*

Physical–Attributes-Clause ::=
[PCTFREE <n>] [PCTUSED <n>] [INITRANS <n>] [MAXTRANS <n>]
[Storage–Clause]

Exception-Clause ::=
EXCEPTIONS INTO [<Schema·>] <Table>

Physical-Properties ::= PPOption1 | PPOption2 | PPOption3 | PPOption4 | PPOption5
PPOption1 ::= Segment- Attributes-Clause [COMPRESS | NOCOMPRESS]
PPOption2 ::= ORGANIZATION HEAP [Segment –Attributes-Clause] [COMPRESS | NOCOMPRESS}
PPOption3 ::= ORGANIZATION INDEX [Segment-Attributes-Clause] IOT-Clause
PPOption4 ::= ORGANIZATION EXTERNAL External-Table-Clause
PPOption5 ::= CLUSTER <Cluster-Name> (<Column> {,<Column>})

External-Table-Clause ::=
([TYPE Access-Driver-Type] External-Data-Properties)
[RESET LIMIT <Integer>|UNLIMITED]

External-Data-Properties ::=
DEFAULT DIRECTORY <Directory>
[ACCESS PARAMETERS (<Opaque-Format-Spec>)] | [ACCESS PARAMETERS USING CLOB <Sub-query>]
LOCATION ([<Directory>:} '<Path-to-File>' {,[<Directory>:] '<Path-to-File >'})

Note: Opaque-format-space allows you to specify access parameters and their values.

Table-Properties ::=
[Column-Properties] [Table-Partitioning-Clause] [CACHE | NOCACHE]
[Parallel-Clause] [ROWDEPENDENCIES | NOROWDEPENDENCIES]
[MONITORING | NOMONITORING]
[Enable-Disable-Clause {Enable-Disable-Clause}] [Row-Moment-Clause]
[AS <Sub-query>]

Column-Properties::= CPOption1 | CPOption2
CPOption1 ::= Object-Type-Col-Properties | Nested-Table-Col-Properties | XML-Type-Col-Properties
CPOption2 ::= Varrey-Col-Properties | LOB-Storage-Clause [LOB-Partition–Storage]

Paralled-Clause::= NOPARALLEL | Parallel-Option
Parallel-Option ::= PARALLEL [<Integer>]
// **Note:** Default is NOPARALLEL.

Row-Movement-Clause::=
ENABLE | DISABLE ROW MOVEMENT

Table-Partitioning-Clause ::=
Range-Partition | Hash-Partition | List-Partition | Composite-Partition

Figure 11-9. *The Create-Table Statement (continued)*

Enable-Disable-Clause::= EDOption1 | EDOption2 | EDOption3
EDOption1 ::= ENABLE | DISABLE [VALIDATE | NOVALIDATE] UNIQUE (<Column >{, <Column>)
        [Using- Index-Clause] [Exception-Clause] [CASCADE] [KEEP | DROP INDEX]
  EDOption2 ::= ENABLE | DISABLE [VOLATE | NOVOLATILE] PRIMARY KEY
        [Using-Index-Clause] [Exception- Clause] [CASCADE] [KEEP | DROP INDEX]
  EDOption3 ::= ENABLE | DISABLE [VOLATILE | NOVOLATILE] CONSTRAINT <Constraint-Name>
        [Using-Index-Clause] [Exception-Clause] [CASCADE] [KEEP DROP | INDEX]

Using-Index-Clause :: = UIOption9 | UIOption10 | UIOption11
UIOption9 ::= USING INDEX [<Schema>.] <IndexName>
UIOption10 ::= USING INDEX (Create-Index)
UIOption11 ::= USING INDEX Index-Alternatives {Index-Alternatives}

Note: Create Index is defined in the Create-Index statement.

Index-Alternatives ::= LOCAL | Global-Partitioned-Index | IAOption1 | IAOption2 | IAOption3 | IAOption4 | IAOption5 |
                IAOption6 | IAOption7 |
IAOption1 ::= PCTFREE <Integer>
IAOption2 ::= INITRANS <Integer>
IAOption3 ::= MAXTRANS <Integer>
IAOption4 ::= TABLESPACE <Tablespace>
IAOption5 ::= Storage-Clause
IAOption6 ::= SORT | NSORT
IAOption7 ::= LOGGING | NOLOGGING   /* Default is LOGGING */

Storage-Clause :: =
STORAGE (INITIAL <n> [K|M] NEXT <n> [K|M]
PCTINCREASE <n> MINEXTENTS <n>
MAXEXTENTS <In> | UNLIMITED
FREELISTS <n> FREELIST GROUPS <n>
OPTIMAL <n> [K|M]
[PCTUSED <n>] [PCTFREE <n>]
[INITRANS <n>] [MAXFRANS <n>]
[BUFFER_POOL KEEP | RECYCLE | DEFAULT])

Range-Partition::=
PARTITION BY RANGE (<Column>{, <Column>})
(PARTITION [<Partition-Name>] Range-Values-Clause Table-Partition-Desc
{, PARTITION[<Partition-Name>] Range-Values-Clause Table-Partition-Desc})

Range-Values-Clause::=
VALUES LESS THAN (<Value>|MAXVALUE {, <Value>|MAXVALUE})

Figure 11-9. *The Create-Table Statement (continued)*

Table-Partition-Desc ::=
[Segment-Attributes-Clause]
[[COMPRESS[<Integer>]] | NOCOMPRESS]
[OVERFLOW [Segment-Attributes-Clause]]
[LOB-Storage-Clause | Varray-Col-Properties]
[Partition-Level-Subpartition]

Lob-Storage-Clause::= LOB-Option1 | LOB-Option2
LOB-Option1 ::= LOB (<LOB-Item>{, <LOB-Item>}) STORE AS (LOB-Parameters) | <LOB-Segment-Name >
LOB-Option2 ::= LOB (<LOB-Item>{, <LOB-Item>}) STORE AS <LOB- Segment-Name> (LOB-Parameters)

LOB-Parameters ::=
TABLESPACE <Tablespace>
[ENABLE | DISABLE STORAGE IN ROW]
[Storage-Clause]
[CHUNK <Integer>] [PCTVERSION <Integer>] [RETENTION]
[FREEPOOLS <Integer>][CACHE [READS] [LOGGING | NOLOGGING]]
[NOCACHE]

LOB-Partition-Storage ::=
PARTITION <Partition-Name> LOB-Storage-Clause | Varray-Col-Properties
[(SUBPARTITION <Subpartition-Name> LOB- Storage -Clause | Varrey-Col- Properties
{LOB- Storage -Clause |Varray-Col-Properties })]

Partition-Level-Subpartition ::= PLOption1 | PLOption2
PLOption1 ::= SUBPARTITIONS <Hash-Subpartition-Quantity>
                [STORE IN (<Tablespace> {, <Tablespace> })]
PLOption2 ::= (Subpartition-Spec {, Subpartition-Spec })

Subpartition- Spec ::=
SUBPARTITION [<Subpartition-Name>]
[List-Values-Clause] [Partitioning- Storage -Clause]

Partitioning- Storage-Clause ::= PSOption1 | PSOption2 | PSOption3 | PSOption4 | PSOption5
PSOption1 ::= [TABLESPACE<Tablespace]
PSOption2 ::= [OVERFLOW [TABLESPACE <Tablespace>])
PSOption3 ::= [LOB (<LOB-Item> STORE AS (TABLESPACE <Tablespace>)]
PSOption4 ::= [VARRAY <Varray-Item> STORE AS LOB <LOB-Segment-Name>]
PSOption5 ::= [LOB (<LOB-Item>) STORE AS <LOB-Segment-Name> [(TABLESPACE<Tablespace>)]]

List-Values-Clause ::= LVOption1 | LVOption2
LVOption1 ::= VALUES (DEFAULT | NULL)
LVOption2 ::= VALUES (<Value> {, <Value>})

Figure 11-9. *The Create-Table Statement (continued)*

Hash-Partition ::=
PARTITION BY HASH (<Column> {, <Column>})
Individual- Hash-Partitions / Hash- Partitions-By- Quantity

Individual-Hash-Partitions::=
(PARTITION [<Partition-Name> Partitioning-Storage-Clause]
{,PARTITION [<Partition-Name> Partitioning-Storage-Clause}])

Hash-Partitions-by-Quantity::=
PARTITIONS <Integer> [STORE IN (<Tablespace> {, <Tablespace>})]
[OVERFLOW STORE IN (<Tablespace>{, <Tablespace>})]

List-Partition ::=
PARTITION BY LIST (<Column>)
(PARTITION [<Partition-Name>] List-Values-Clause Table-Partition-Descr
{ , PARTITION [<Partition-Name>] List Values-Clause Table-Partition Descr})

Composite-Partition ::=
PARTITION BY RANGE (<Column>{,<Column>})
Subpartition-by-List | Subpartition-by-Hash
(PARTITION [<Partition-Name>] Range-Values-Clause Table-Partition-Descr
{, PARTITION [<Partition-Name>] Range Values Clause Table-Partition-Descr})

Subpartition-by-Hash::= SHOption1 | SHOption2
SHOption1 ::= SUBPARTITION BY HASH (<Column> {,<Column>}) Subpartition-Template
SHOption2 ::= SUBPARTITION BY HASH(<Column>{,<Column>})
       SUBPARTITIONS <Integer> [STORE IN (<Tablespace> {, <Tablespace>})])

Subpartition-Template ::= STOption1 | STOption2 | STOption3 | STOption4
STOption1 ::= SUBPARTITION TEMPLATE Hash-Subpartition-by-Quantity
STOption2 ::= SUBPARTITION TEMPLATE Individual-Hash-Subparts {, Individual-Hash-Subparts}
STOption3 ::= SUBPARTITION TEMPLATE (List-Subpartition-Desc {, List-Subpartition-Desc})
STOption4 ::= SUBPARTITION TEMPLATE Range-Subpartition-Desc {, Range-Subpartition-Desc}

Hash-Subpartition-by-Quantity ::= PARTITIONS <Integer> [STORE IN (<Tablespace> {, <Tablespace>})]
Individual-Hash-Subparts ::= SUBPARTITION [Subpartition] Partitioning-Storage-Clause
List-Subpartition-Desc ::= SUBPARTITION [Subpartition] Partitioning-Storage-Clause
Range-Subpartition-Desc ::= SUBPARTITION [Subpartition] List-Values-Clause [Partitioning-Storage-Clause]

Subpartition-by-List ::=
SUBPARTITION BY LIST (<Column>)[Subpartition-Template]

Range-Values-Clause ::=
VALUES LESS THAN (<Value>|MAXVALUE {,<Value>|MAXVALUE})

Figure 11-9. The Create-Table Statement (continued)

```
IOT-Clause ::=  IOTOption1 | IOTOption2 | IOTOption3 | IOTOption4
IOTOption1 ::=  Mapping-Table-Clause [Index-Org-Overflow-Clause]
IOTOption2 ::=  PCTHRESHOLD <Integer> [Index-Org-Overflow- Clause]
IOTOption3 ::=  COMPRESS [<Integer>] [Index Org-Overflow- Clause]
IOTOption4 ::=  NOCOMPRESS [Index-Org-Overflow- Clause]


Mapping-Table-Clause ::=  NOMAPPING | MappingOption
MappingOption  ::= MAPPING TABLE


Index-Org-Overflow-Clause ::=
[INCLUDING <Column>] OVERFLOW [Segment-Attributes-Clause]


Object-Type-Col-Properties ::=
COLUMN <Column> Substitutable-Column-Clause


Substitutable-Column-Clause ::=  SCOption1 | SCOption2
SCOption1 ::=  [ELEMENT] IS OF [TYPE] (ONLY <Type>)
SCOption2 ::=  [NOT] SUBSTITUTABLE AT ALL LEVELS


Nested-Table-Col-Properties ::=
NESTED TABLE <Nested-Item >|COLUMN-VALUE [Substitutable-Column-Clause]
STORE AS <Storage-Table> [((Object-Properties) [Physical-Properties] [Column-Properties])]
[RETURN AS LOCATOR  | VALUE]
```

Note:
1. Object-properties are the same as table-properties for relational tables. However, instead of specifying column, you specify attributes of the object.
2. <Nested-item> represents the users supplied column-name (or top level attribute of the table's object type) whose type is nested table.
3. <Storage-Table>represents the user-supplied table where rows of the nested-item reside.

```
Varray-Col-Properties ::=  VPOption1 | VPOption2 | VPOption3
VPOption1  ::=  VARRAY <Varray-Item> Substitutable–Column-clause
VPOption2  ::=  VARRAY < Varray-Item> STORE AS LOB <LOB-Segment-Name>
VPOption3  ::=  VARRAY < Varray-Item> STORE AS [<LOB-Segment-Name>] (LOB-Parameters)
```

Note:
1. <LOB-Segment-Name> represents the user-supplied name for the LOB data segment. It assumes one LOB-item only.
2. <Varray-Item> represents the user-supplied name of variable array.

```
XML-Type-Col-Properties ::=
XMLTYPE [COLUMN] <Column>[XML-Type-Storage] [XML-Schema-Spec]
```

Figure 11-9. *The Create-Table Statement (continued)*

```
XML-Type-Storage ::= XTOption1 | XTOption2 | XTOption3
XTOption1 ::= STORE AS OBLJECT RELATIONAL
XTOption2 ::= STORE AS CLOB [LOB-Parameters]
XTOption3 ::= STORE AS CLOB [<LOB-Segment-Name> [(LOB-Parameters)]]


XML-Schema-Spec ::= XSOption1 | XSOption2
XSOption1 ::= [XMLSCHEMA <XML-Schema-URL>] ELEMENT <Element>
XSOption2 ::= [XMLSCHEMA <XML-Schema-URL>] ELEMENT <XML-Schema-URL> # <Element>
```

Note:
1. <XML-Schema-URL>represents the user-supplied URL of a registered XML schema (URL schema must have been registered via package DBMS-XMLSCHEMA)
2. <Element> represents the user-supplied element name.

```
Create-Object-Table ::=
CREATE [GLOBAL TEMPORARY] TABLE [<SCHEMA>·]
<TableName> OF [<Schema>·] <Object-Type>
[Object-Table-Substitution]
[(Object-Properties)] [ON COMMIT DELETE | PRESERVE ROWS]
[OID-Clause] [OID-Index-Clause]
[Physical-Properties] [Table-Properties];


Object-Table-Substitution ::=
[NOT] SUBSTITUTABLE AT ALL LEVELS


Object-Properties ::= OPOption1 | OPOption2
OPOption1 ::= <Column> | <Attribute> [DEFAULT<Expression>]
                [Inline-Constraint {Inline-Constraint}] | [Inline-Ref-Constraint]
OPOption2 ::= Out-of-line Constraint | Out-of-line-Ref-Constraint | Supplemental-Logging-Props


Supplemental-Logging-Pops ::=
SUPPLEMENTAL LOG GROUP<Log-Group-Number>(<Column>{,<Column>}) [ALWAYS]


OID-Clause ::= OCOption1 | OCOption2
OCOption1 ::= OBJECT IDENTIFIER IS SYSTEM GENERATED
OCOption2 ::= OBJECT IDENTIFIER IS PRIMARY KEY


OID-Index-Clause ::= OIOption1 | OIOption2
OIOption1 ::= OIDINDEX [<IndexName>] (Physical-Attributes-Clause)
OIOption2 ::= OIDINDEX [<IndexName>] (TABLESPACE <Tablespace>)


Create- XML-Table ::=
CREATE TABLE [<Schema>·] <TableName> OF XMLTYPE
[XMLTYPE XML-Type-Storage] [XML-Schema-Spec]


XML-Schema-Spec ::=
[XMLSCHEMA <XML-Schema-URL>]
ELEMENT [<XML-Schema-URL> # ] <XML-Element>
```

Note: The XML-Element is specified as a string in double quotes.

Figure 11-9. *The Create-Table Statement (continued)*

```
Create-Table-Statement::=
CREATE TABLE [<Schema>.] <Base-table>
     (Column-Definition {,Column-Definition}
     [,Constraint-Definition {, Constraint-Definition}]);

Column-Definition ::=
<Column> <Data-type> [DEFAULT <ScalarExpression>][NOT NULL][UNIQUE]

Constraint-Definition ::=
[CONSTRAINT <Constraint-Name>] Primary-Key-Spec | Foreign-Key-Spec | NOT NULL | Check-Spec | Unique-Spec

Primary-Key-Spec ::=
PRIMARY KEY (<Column> [ASC/DESC] {,<Column> [ASC/DESC] })

Foreign-Key-Spec ::=
FOREIGN KEY (<Column>) REFERENCES [<Schema>.] <Base-table> [(<Column>)]
[ON DELETE CASCADE]

Check-Spec ::= CFormat1 | CFormat2 | CFormat3
CFormat1 ::= Check (<Column> BETWEEN <Value1> AND <Value2>)
CFormat2 :::= CHECK (<Column> operator <Value>)
CFormat3 :::= CHECK (<Column> IN <Value> {,<Value>})

Unique-Spec ::= UNIQUE <Column>
```

Figure 11-10. *Abridged Version of the Create-Table Statement*

The Data-Type-Spec defines a set of valid data types are indicated in Figure 11-11. This list is not exhaustive, but includes the more commonly used data types.

Data Type	Meaning
Scalar Data Types:	
CHAR (<Length> [BYTE|CHAR])	Character or string of specified length; default is BYTE; max length is 2000 bytes.
VARCHAR2 (<Length> [BYTE|CHAR])	Variable string of specified maximum possible length; default is CHAR; max length is 4000 bytes. Type VARCHAR is same as VARCHAR2, and is there for backward compatibility.
NCHAR (<Length>)	Similar to CHAR, but used for Unicode character set; default length is 1 character.
NVARCHAR2 (<Length>)	Similar to VARCHAR2, but used for Unicode character set.
LONG	Variable length character up to 2GB. CLOB or NCLOB preferred. Included for backward compatibility.
NUMBER(<Length> [<Decimal>])	Fixed and floating point (numeric) data; default is 38 digits; valid range is $-1 * 10^{-130}$ to $9.999 * 99^{125}$
DECIMAL(<Length>, <Decimal>)	Same as NUMBER((<Length>, <Decimal>).
INTEGER	Defaults to NUMBER(38).
SMALLINT	Same as INTEGER.
FLOAT [(<Length>)]	Similar NUMBER; default length is 38; maximum length or 126.
REAL	Defaults to NUMBER(63).
DOUBLE PRECISION	Same as NUMBER(38)
DATE	Date in the form century, year, month, day, hour, minute, second. Can be displayed in various formats. Range is January 1, 4712 BC to December 31, 9999 AD. Default time is 12:00 AM.
TIMESTAMP [(<Precision>)]	Similar to DATE, but with possibility of fractional seconds precision.
TIMESTAMP [(<Precision>)] [WITH TIME ZONE]	Similar to TIMESTAMP, but stores the time zone displacement. Displacement is the difference (in hours and minutes) between the local time and the Universal Time Coordinate (UTC), also known as the Greenwich Mean Time
RAW (<Length>)	Variable length unstructured data; maximum 2000 bytes. BLOB or BFILE preferred. Included for backward compatibility.
LONG RAW (<Length>)	Variable length unstructured data; maximum 2GB. BLOB or BFILE preferred. Included for backward compatibility.
BLOB	Binary Large Object; maximum 4GB of unstructured binary data.
CLOB	Character BLOB; maximum 4GB of unstructured character data.
NCLOB	Unicode Character BLOB; maximum 4GB of unstructured character data.
BFILE	Large external file, stored by the operating system; maximum file size of 4GB supported. Oracle stores a pointer to the file.
ROWID	Binary data representing a physical row address of a table's row. Occupies 10 bytes.
UROWID	Binary data representing any type of row address – physical, logical, or foreign. Can be up to 4000 bytes.
Collection Data Types:	
VARRAY	Variable array; elements are ordered and have a maximum limit.
TABLE	Nested table; elements are not ordered, and there is no limit on the possible number of elements.
Reference Data Type:	
REF	Reference (via a pointer) to data stored in another object table

Figure 11-11. *Valid Data Types*

Please note:

1. The semicolon (;) signals the end of the SQL statement and each clause is separated by a comma (,).

2. In some systems (e.g. DB2), primary keys must be declared NOT NULL.

3. Most DBMS suites provide a utility that allows the user to key data into the table, once it has been created. Earlier versions of Oracle do not. However, through Enterprise Manager, later versions (starting with Oracle 9i) do.

4. Data can be entered in the table via the SQL insert statement (which you will learn in Chapter 12) or an application program, written for that purpose.

5. The matter of missing values is of much concern to any creditable DBMS. In DB2 and Oracle, nulls are used to represent missing or irrelevant information. Note that null is not the same as zero or blank. If nulls are allowed for an attribute and no data is provided, the system provides a null value for that attribute.

6. In many modern DBMS, a GUI sits on top of SQL definition statements so user may not use them.

7. Some DBMS, (e.g. Oracle) provide the user with the flexibility of specifying which attribute of a referenced table is to be used in the foreign key characteristic.

8. The operator specified in the **Check-Clause** may be any valid Boolean operator as defined in Chapters 7 and 8. When the third form of the **Check-Clause** is used, the column specified must be one of the values specified.

9. Value, Value1 and Value2 in the **Check-Clause** represent literal values.

Example 1: To create base relations **Program**, **Course** and **Pgm-Struct** as described in Chapter 7.

```
CREATE TABLE Program
(Pgm# CHAR (5) NOT NULL,
Pgmname CHAR (30) NOT NULL,
CONSTRAINT ProgPK PRIMARY KEY (Pgm#));

CREATE TABLE Course
(Crs# CHAR (5) NOT NULL,
Crsname CHAR (30) NOT NULL,
CONSTRAINT CoursePK PRIMARY KEY (Crs#));

CREATE TABLE Pgm_Struct
(PSPgm# CHAR (5) NOT NULL,
PSCrs# CHAR (5) NOT NULL,
CONSTRAINT ProgStructPK     PRIMARY KEY (PSPgm# ,PSCrs#),
CONSTRAINT ProgStructFK1   FOREIGN KEY (PSPgm#) REFERENCES Program (Pgm#),
CONSTRAINT ProgStructFK2   FOREIGN KEY (PSCrs#) REFERENCES Course (Crs#));
```

Example 2: The following example illustrates how the **check** constraints can be specified during table creation.

```
CREATE TABLE Student
(Stud# NUMBER (7) NOT NULL,
Sname CHAR (15) NOT NULL,
Fname CHAR (15) NOT NULL,
Mname CHAR (15),
Sex CHAR (1) NOT NULL,
DoB NUMBER (8),
Spgm# CHAR (5),
CumGPA NUMBER (4,2),
CONSTRAINT StudentPK        PRIMARY KEY (Stud#),
CONSTRAINT StudentFK1       FOREIGN KEY (Spgm#) REFERENCES Program (Pgm#),
CONSTRAINT StudentCheck1    CHECK (Sex IN ('M', 'F')),
CONSTRAINT StudentCheck2    CHECK (DoB BETWEEN 19000101 AND 21991231),
CONSTRAINT StudentCheck3    CHECK (CumGPA >= 0));
```

Once your table has been created, you may view the structure of the table via the **Describe** statement, which has the following format:

```
DESCRIBE <BaseTable>;
```

Example 3: The following statement will cause the structure of the table **Student** to be listed on the screen.

```
DESCRIBE Student;
```

You can also create a table from an existing table by feeding the output of a **Select** statement as the input to a **Create-Table** statement. The format of the **Create-Table** statement for this is:

```
CREATE TABLE <TableName> [(<Column> {,<Column>}] AS <Sub-query>;
```

The sub-query component of the statement is specified by a **Select** statement. An example of this is provided below; this will be much clearer after you have been introduced to the **Select** statement (next chapter).

Example 4: The following statements create two snapshot relations: the first one stores Computer Science courses only; the second stores Computer Science and Information Systems majors only.

CREATE TABLE CSCourses AS SELECT * FROM Course WHERE Crs# LIKE 'CS%';

CREATE TABLE CSMajors (Stud#, Sname, Fname, Sex) AS SELECT * FROM Student WHERE (Spgm# = 'BSC1' OR Spgm# = 'BSC2');

11.7 Dropping or Modifying a Table

A table may be dropped (deleted from the system) via the **Drop-Table** statement. The syntax is:

Drop-Table ::= DROP TABLE [<Schema>.] <TableName> [CASCADE CONSTRAINTS];

To drop all referential integrity constraints that refer to primary and unique keys in the dropped table, specify the **Cascade-Constraints-Clause**. If you omit this clause, and such referential integrity constraints exist, Oracle will return an error and will not drop the table.

Example 5: The following statement removes table **CSCourses** from the system:

DROP TABLE CSCourses CASCADE CONSTRAINTS;

When a table is removed, all references to it are removed from the system catalog. Any attempt to access a non-existent table will result in an execution error.

The structure of a table can be modified via the **Alter-Table** statement. Figure 11-12 provides the detailed syntax for the **Alter-Table** statement, while Figure 11-13 shows an abridged version.

```
Alter-Table ::=
ALTER TABLE [<Schema>.] <Table-Name>
[Alter-Table-Props | Column-clauses | Constraint-Clauses | Alter-Table-Partitioning | Alter-External-Table-Clauses |
Move-Table-Clause]
[Enable-Disable-Clause] | [ENABLE | DISABLE TABLE LOCK] | [ENABLE | DISABLE ALL TRIGGERS];


Alter-Table-Props::=
Physical-Attributes-Clause | LOGGING | NOLOGGING | COMPRESS | NOCOMPRESS | Supplemental-log-Group-Clauses |
Allocate-Extent-Clause | Deallocate-Unused-Clause | CACHE  | NOCACHE | MONITORING | NOMONITORING |
Upgrade-Table-Clause | Record-Per-Block clause | Row-Movement-Clause | Parallel-Clause | Renew-Table-Spec
[Alter-IOT-Clauses]


Supplemental-Log-Group-Clauses::= SLClause1 | SLClause2
SLClause1 ::= ADD SUPPLEMENTAL LOG GROUP <LogGroup> (<Column> {,<Column>}) [ALWAYS]
SLClause2 ::=  DROP SUPPLEMTAL LOG GROUP <LogGroup>


Allocate-Extent-Clauses::=
ALLOCATE EXTENT [(Extent-Spec {Extent-Spec})]


Extent-Spec::= ESOption1 | ESOption2 | ESOption3
ESOption1 ::= Size <M> [K|M]
ESOption2 ::= DATAFILE '<PathtoFile>'
ESOption3::= INSTANCE <n>
```

Figure 11-12. *The Alter-Table Statement*

Deallocate-Unused-Clause::=
DEALLOCATE UNUSED [KEEP <n> [K|M]

Upgrade-Table-Clause::=
UPGRADE [[NOT] INCLUDING DATA] [Column-Properties]

Record Per-Block-Clause::=
MINIMIZE | NOMINIMIZE RECORD PER BLOCK

Rename-Table-Spec::=
RENAME TO <New-TableName>

Alter-IOT-Clauses::=
IOT-Clause | Alter-Overflow-Clause | Alter-Mapping-Table-Clause | COALESCE

// **IOT-Clause** is defined in Create-Table

Alter-Overflow-Clauses::= AOClause1 | AOClause2
AOClause1 ::= Add-Overflow-Clause
AOClause2 ::= OVERFLOW {Allocate-Extent-Clause} | Deallocate-Unused-Clause

Add-Overflow-Clause::=
ADD OVERFLOW [Segment-Attributes-Clause]
[(PARTITION [Segment-Attributes-Clause] {, PARTITION [Segment-Attributes-Clause]})]

// **Segment-Attributes-Clause** is defined in Create-Table

Alter-Mapping-Table-Clauses::= AMClause1 | AMClause2
MClause1 ::= MAPPING TABLE UPDATE BLOCK REFERENCES
MClause2 ::= MAPPING TABLE Allocate-Extent-Clause | Deallocate-unused-Clause

Column-Clauses::=
{Add-Column-Clause}| {Modify-Column-Clause} | {Drop-Column-Clause}|
Rename-Column-Clause | {Modify-Collection-Retrieval} |
{Modify-LOB-Storage-Clauses} | {Alter-Varray-Col_Props}

Add-Column-Clause::=
ADD (Column-Definition-{,Column-Definition})

// **Column-Definition** is defined in Create-Table

Modify-Column-Clause::=
MODIFY Modify-Col-Props | Modify-Col-Substitutable

Modify-Col-Props::=   /*Similar but not identical to Column Definition*/
(<Column> [Data-type-Spec] [DEFAULT <Expression>] {Inline-Constraint}
{, <Column> [Data-type-Spec] [DEFAULT <Expression>] {Inline-Constraint})

// **Inline-Constraints** defined in Create-Table

Modify-Col-Substitutable::=
COLUMN <Column> [NOT] SUBSTITUTABLE AT ALL LEVELS [FORCE]

Figure 11-12. *The Alter-Table Statement (continued)*

```
Drop-Column-Clause::= DCOption1 | DCOption2 | DCOption3 | DCOption4 | DCOption5 | DCOption6
DCOption1 ::= SET UNUSED COLUMN <Column> [[CASCADE CONSTRAINTS] | INVALIDATE]
DCOption2 ::= SET UNUSED (<Column> {,<Column>}) [[CASCADE CONSTRAINTS] | INVALIDATE]
               {[[CASCADE CONSTRAINTS] | INVALIDATE]}
DCOption3 ::= DROP COLUMN <Column> [[CASCADE CONSTRAINTS] | INVALIDATE] [CHECKPOINT <n>]
DCOption4 ::= DROP COLUMN (<Column> {,<Column>} [[CASCADE CONSTRAINTS] | INVALIDATE]
               {[[CASCADE CONSTRAINTS] | INVALIDATE]} [CHECKPOINT <n>]
DCOption5 ::= DROP UNUSED COLUMNS [CHECKPOINT <n>]
DCOption6 ::= DROP COLUMNS CONTINUE [CHECKPOINT <n>]


Rename-Column-Clause::=
RENAME COLUMN <Old-Column> TO <New-Column>


Modify-Collection-Retrieval::=
MODIFY NESTED TABLE <Collection-Item> RETURN AS LOCATOR | VALUE


Modify-LOB-Storage-Clause::=
MODIFY LOB (<LOB-Item>) (Modify-LOB-Parms)


Modify-LOB-Parms::= MLParm1 | MLParm2 | MLParm3 | MLParm4 | MLParm5 | MLParm6
MLParm1 ::= Storage-Clause | Allocate-Extent-Clause | Deallocate-Unused-Clause | RETENTION | CACHE
MLParm2 ::= PCTVERSION <n>
MLParm3 ::= FREEPOOLS  <n>
MLParm4 ::= REBUILD FREEPOOLS
MLParm5 ::= NOCACHE [LOGGING | NOLOGGING]
MLParm6 ::= CACHE READS [LOGGING / NOLOGGING]


Alter-Varray-Col-Props::=
MODIFY-VARRAY <Varray-Item> (Modify-LOB-Parms)


Constraints-Clauses ::= Drop-Constraint-Clause | ACClause1 | ACClause2 | ACClause3 | ACClause4 |
                ACClause5 | ACClause6
ACClause1 ::= ADD Out-of-Line-Constraint < Out-of-Line-Constraint >
ACClause2 ::= ADD Out-of-Line-Ref-Constraint
ACClause3 ::= MODIFY CONSTAINT <Constraint-Name> <Constraint-State>
ACClause4 ::= MODIFY PRIMARY KEY <Constraint-Name>
ACClause5 ::= MODIFY UNIQUE (<Column> {,<Column>}) <Constraint-State>
ACClause6 ::= RENAME CONSTRAINT <Old-Constraint> To <New-Constraint>

/*Constraint-State, Out-of-Line-Constraint, Out-of-Line-Ref-Constraints are as defined in Create-Table*/

Drop-Constraint-Clause::= DCOption1 | DCOption2 | DCOption3
DCOption1 ::= DROP PRIMARY KEY [CASCADE] [KEEP | DROP INDEX]
DCOption2 ::= DROP UNIQUE (<Column> {,<column>}) [CASCADE] [KEEP | DROP INDEX]
DCOption3 ::= DROP CONSTRAINT <Constraint> [CASCADE]
```

Figure 11-12. *The Alter-Table Statement (continued)*

Alter-Table-Partitioning::=
Modify-Table-Default-Attributes | Set-Subpartition-Template | Modify-Table-Partition | Modify-Table-Subpartition |
Move-Table-Partition | Move-Table-Subpartition | Add-Table-Partition | Coalesce-Table-Partition |
Drop-Table-Partition | Drop-Table-Subpartition | Rename-Partition-Subpart | Truncate-Partition-Subpart |
Split-Table-Partition | Split-Table-Subpartition | Merge-Table-Partitions | Exchange-Partition-Subpart |
Merge-Table-Subpartition

Modify-Table-Defaults-Attributes::=
MODIFY DEFAULT ATTRIBUTES [FOR PARTITION <Partition>]
[Segment-Attributes-Clause] [COMPRESS | NOCOMPRESS] [PTCTHRESHOLD <n>] [[COMPRESS <n>] |
NOCOMPRESS] [Alter-Overflow-Clause] [LOB {(<LOB-Item>) (<LOB-Parameters>)} {VARRAY <Varray> (<LOB-Parameters>)}]

// **Segment-Attributes-Clause** and **LOB-Parameters** are defined in Create-Table

Set-Subpartition-Template::= SSTOption1 | SSTOption2 | SSTOption3
SSTOption1 ::= SET SUBPARTITION TEMPLATE Hash-Subpartition-by-Quantity
SSTOption2 ::= SET SUBPARTITION TEMPLATE (Range-Subpartition-Desc {, Range-Subpartition-Desc })
SSTOption3 ::= SET SUBPARTITION TEMPLATE (List-Subpartition-Desc {, List-Subpartition-Desc })

/***Hash-Subpartition-by-Quantity, Range-Subpartition-Desc** , and **List-Subpartition-Desc** are defined in Create-Table */

Modify-Table-Partition::=
Modify-Range-Partition | Modify-Hash-Partition | Modify-List-Partition

Modify-Range-Partition::=
MODIFY PARTITION <Partition> Partition-Attributes | Add-Hash-Subpartition | Add-List-Subpartition |
Alter-Mapping-Table-Clause | Coalesce-Subpartition | Rebuild-Unusable

Coalesce-Subpartition::=
COALESCE SUBPARTION [Update-Global-Index-Clause] [Parallel-Clause]

// **Parallel-Clause** is defined in Create-Table

Update-Global-Index-Clause::=
UPDATE | INVALIDATE GLOBAL INDEXES

Rebuild-Unusable::=
[REBUILD] UNUSABLE LOCAL INDEXES

Partition-Attributes::=
[{Physical-Attributes-Clause | LOGGING | NOLOGGING | Allocate-Extent-Clause | Deallocate-Unused-Clause}]
[OVERFLOW {Physical-Attributes-Clause | LOGGIN |NOLOGGING | Allocate-Extent-Clause | Deallocate-Unused-Clause}]
[COMPRESS | NOCOMPRESS] [LOB-Varray-Option]

LOB-Varray-Option::= LOBOption1 | LOBOption2
LOBOption1 ::= {LOB <LOB-Item> Modify-LOB-Parms}
LOBOption2 ::= VARRAY <Varray> Modify-LOB-Parms

Figure 11-12. *The Alter-Table Statement (continued)*

Add-Hash-Subpartition::=
ADD Subpartition-Specs [Update-Global-Index-Clause] [Parallel-Clause]

// **Parallel-Clause** and **Subpartition**-Specs are defined in Create-Table

Add-List-Subpartition::=
ADD Subpartition-Specs

Alter-Mapping-Table-Clause::=
MAPPING TABLE Allocate-Extent-Clause | Deallocate-Unused-Clause | Update-Block-Refs

Update-Block-Refs::=
UPDATE BLOCK REFERENCES

Modify-Harsh-Partition::=
MODIFY PARTITION <Partition> Partition-Attributes | Rebuild-Unusable |
Alter-Mapping-Table-Clause

Modify-List-Partition::=
MODIFY PARTITION <Partition> Partition-Attributes | Rebuild-Unusable | Add-Drop-Values

Add-Drop-Values::=
ADD | DROP VALUES (<Partition-Value> {,<Partition-Value>})

Modify-Table-Subpartition::=
MODIFY SUBPARTITION <Subpartition> Modify-Hash-Subpartition | Modify-List-Subpartition

Modify-Hash-Subpartition::=
Rebuild-Unusable | {LOB-Varray-Option} | Allocate-Extent-Clause | Deallocate-Unused-Clause

Modify-List-Subpartition::=
Rebuild-Unusable | {LOB-Varray-Option} | Allocate-Extent-Clause | Deallocate-Unused-Clause | Add-Drop-Subvalues

Add-Drop-Subvalues::=
ADD | DROP VALUES (<Value> {<Value>})

Move-Table-Partition::=
MOVE PARTITION <Partition> [MAPPING TABLE] [Table-Partition-Description]
[Update-Global-Index-Clause] [Parallel-Clause]

Table-Partition-Description::=
[Segment-Attributes-Clause] | [[COMPRESS [<Integer>]] | NOCOMPRESS]
[OVERFLOW [Segment-Attribute-Clause]]
[{LOB-Storage-Clause | Varray-Col-Properties}] [Partition-Level-Subpartition]
[Partition-Level-Subpartition]

// Components not defined here are all defined in Create-Table

Figure 11-12. *The Alter-Table Statement (continued)*

Move-Table-Subpartition::=
MOVE Subpartition-Spec [Update-Global-Index-Clause] [Parallel-Clause]

Add-Table-Partition::=
ADD-Range-Partition-Clause | Add-Hash-Partition-Clause | Add-List-Partition-Clause

Add-Range-Partition-Clause::=
ADD PARTITION [<Partition>] Range-Value-Clause [Table-Partition-Description]

// **Range-Value-Clause** defined in Create-Table

Add-Hash-Partition-Clause::=
ADD PARTITION [<Partition>] Partitioning-Storage-Clause [Update-Global-Index-Clause] [Parallel-Clause]

// **Partitioning-Storage-Clause** and **Parallel-Clause** defined in Create-Table

Add-List-Partition-Clause::=
ADD PARTITION [<Partition>] List-Value-Clause [Table-Partition-Description]

Coalesce-Table-Partition::=
COALESCE PARTITION [Update-Global-Index-Clause] [Parallel-Clause]

Drop-Table-Partition::=
DROP PARTITION <Partition> Update-Global-Index-Clause [Parallel-Clause]

Drop-Table-Subpartition::=
DROP SUBPARTITION <Subpartition> [Update-Global-Index-Clause [Parallel-Clause]

Rename-Partition-Subpartition::=
RENAME PARTITION | SUBPARTITION <Oldname> TO <Newname>

Truncate-Partition-Subpartition::=
TRUNCATE PARTITION | SUBPARTITION <Partition | Subpartition>
[DROP | REUSE STORAGE] [Update-Global-Index-Clause [Parallel-Clause]]

Split-Table-Partition::=
SPLIT PARTITION <Partition> AT | VALUES (<Value> {,<Value>}) [INTO (Partition-spec, Partition-Spec)]
[Update-Global-Index-Clause] [Parallel-Clause]

Partition-Spec::=
PARTITION [<Partition>] [Table-Partition-Description]

Split-Table-Subpartition::=
SPLIT SUBPARTITION <Subpartition> VALUES (<Value> | NULL {,<Value> | NULL}] INTO
(Subpartition-Spec, Subpartition-Spec) [Update-Global-Index-Clause] [Parallel-Clause]

Merge-Table-Partitions::=
MERGE PARTITIONS <Partition-1> , < Partition-2> INTO Partition-Spec
[Update-Global-Index-Clause] [Parallel-Clause]

Figure 11-12. The Alter-Table Statement (continued)

Subpartition_Spec ::=
SUBPARTITION [<Subpartition>] [List-values-Clause] [Partitioning-Storage-Clause]

// **List-Values-Clause** and **Partitioning-Storage-Clause** are defined in Create-Table

Merge-Table-Subpartition::=
MERGE SUBPARTITIONS <Subpartition-1> , <Subpartition-2> [INTO Subpartition-Spec]
[Update-Global-Index-Clause] [Parallel-Clause]

Exchange-Partition-Subpartition::=
EXCHANGE Partition-Extended-Name | Subpartition-Extended-Name WITH TABLE <TableName>
[INCLUDING | EXCLUDING INDEXES] [WITH | WITHOUT VALIDATION]
[Exceptions-Clause] [Update-Index-Clauses] [Parallel-Clause]

Partition-Extended-Name ::= PNOption1 | PNOption2
PNOption1 ::= PARTITION <PartitionName>
PNOption2 ::= PARTITION FOR (<Partition-Key-Value> {, Partition-Key-Value>})

Subpartition-Extended-Name ::= SPNOption1 | SPNOption2
SPNOption1 ::= SUBPARTITION <SubpartitionName>
SPNOption2 ::= SUBPARTITION FOR (<Subpartition-Key-Value> {, Subpartition-Key-Value>})

Update-Index-Clauses ::= Update-Global-Index-Clause | Update-All-Indexes-Clause
Update-Global-Index-Clause ::= UPDATE | INVALIDATE GLOBAL INDEXES
Update-All-Index-Clause ::= UPDATE INDEXES [(<IndexName> {, <IndexName>})]

Exception-Clause::=
EXCEPTIONS INTO [<Scheme>.] <TableName>

Alter-External-Table-Clause::=
Add-Column-Clause | Modify-Column-Clause | Drop-Column-Clause | Parallel-Clause | External-Data-Properties |
    Reject-Spec {Alter-External-Table-Clause}

Reject-Spec::=
REJECT LIMIT <Integer> | UNLIMITED

// **Parallel-Clause** and **External-Data-Properties** are defined in Create-Table

Move-Table-Clause::=
MOVE [ONLINE] [Segment-Attributes-Clause] [COMPRESS | NOCOMPRESS]
[IOT-Clause] {LOB-Storage-Clause | Varray-Col-Properties} [Parallel-Clause]

Move-Table-Clause::= MTOption1 | MTOption2 | MTOption3
MTOption1 ::= ENABLE | DISABLE [VALIDATE | NOVALIDATE] UNIQUE (<Column> {,<Column>}
            [Unique-Index-Clause] [Exceptions-Clause] [CASCADE] [KEEP | DROP] INDEX
MTOption2 ::= ENABLE | DISABLE [VALIDATE | NOVALIDATE]
            PRIMARY KEY [Unique-Index-Clause] [Exceptions-Clause] [CASCADE] [KEEP | DROP] INDEX
MTOption3 ::= ENABLE | DISABLE [VALIDATE | NOVALIDATE] CONSTRAINT (<Constraint>
            [Unique-Index-Clause] [Exceptions-Clause] [CASCADE] [KEEP | DROP] INDEX

// Components not defined here have been defined earlier, or in Create-Table

Figure 11-12. *The Alter-Table Statement (continued)*

```
Alter-Table ::=
ALTER TABLE <TableName>
[ADD Column-Definition]
[MODIFY Column-Definition]
[ADD Constraint-Definition]
[DROP <Column> {,<Column>}]
[DROP PRIMARY KEY]
[DROP FOREIGN KEY (<Column> {,<Column>})]
[DROP/DISABLE/ENABLE  CONSTRAINT <Constraint-Name>];

// Column-Definition and Constraint-Definition are as defined in Create-Table (see figure 11.10)
```

Figure 11-13. Abridged Version of the Alter-Table Statement

Example 6: We could add an additional attribute for course-abbreviation to the **Course** table:

```
ALTER TABLE Course ADD Crsabbr CHAR (4);
```

Note:
1. The table now has three columns — **Crs#**, **Crsname**, **Crsabbr**.
2. Existing records in the table are all amended to have the additional attribute.
3. The records are not ALTERED at the time of the statement, but noted in the system catalog. At the next read of the table, the DBMS appends NULLed attribute values to the records. The next write to disk writes the expanded records if the additional null values have been updated to the non-null.
4. It is a good habit to assign default values to attributes appended subsequent to table creation and usage, provided that this is supported by the DBMS.

Example 7: The following statement appends an additional attribute (and foreign key) to the **Student** table.

```
ALTER TABLE Student ADD Hall# CHAR (4)
ADD FOREIGN KEY (Hall#) REFERENCES Hall (Hall#);
```

Oracle also allows you to rename a table (or any valid database object) via the **Rename** command. You can also remove all rows from a table via the **Truncate-Table** command. The abridged syntax for each command is as follows:

```
Rename-Statement ::= RENAME <Object-name> TO <Object-name>;

Truncate-table-Statement ::= TRUNCATE TABLE <TableName>;
```

207

Example 8: The following statements a) renames the **Hall** table to **Dormitory** and b) deletes all tuples of the **Student** table.

```
RENAME Hall TO Dormitory;

TRUNCATE TABLE Student;
```

11.8 Working with Indexes

An index is a database object that is used to speed up the retrieval of tuples from base relations. The index is independent of the table it indexes. It stores address pointers to tuples of the base relation. Once created, indexes are automatically maintained by the DBMS, and used to service certain user access requests as required. The software engineer's (or DBA's) only responsibility is to create them.

An index may be created whenever any of the following circumstances holds:

- A column or combination of columns is frequently used in system query conditions (e.g. join conditions).

- A column contains a wide range of values.

- A column contains a large number of null values.

- The table is large and most queries on it are expected to retrieve less than 2 % – 4% of the tuples.

- A column or combination of columns is frequently used in the **Order-By** clause of queries.

An index is not necessary when any of the following circumstances holds:

- The table is small.

- Most queries are expected to retrieve more than 2% - 4% of the tuples.

- The table is frequently updated (there are exceptions to this rule).

- Columns are not often used in database queries.

An experienced software engineer or DBA can reasonably determine what indexes are to be created in a database, as this could seriously affect the performance of the database. When queries are executed, the DBMS first checks to see whether there are indexes that will facilitate efficient access of the requested data. If it finds such indexes, it uses them; otherwise, it creates temporary indexes required to service the queries.

Figure 11-14 shows the full syntax of the **Create-Index** statement, an abridged version of which is provided in Figure 11-16. Figure 11-15 provides the full syntax for the **Alter-Index** statement.

Create-Index ::=
CREATE [UNIQUE | BITMAP] INDEX [<Schema>·] <IndexName>
ON Cluster-Index-Clause | Table-Index-Clause | Bitmap-Join-Index-Clause

Cluster-Index-Clause ::=
CLUSTER [<Schema>·] <Cluster> Index-Attributes

Index-Attributes ::=
[Physical-Attributes-Clause] [LOGGING | NOLOGGING] [ONLINE] [REVERSE]
[SORT | NOSORT] [Parallel-Clause] [Key-Compression] [Compute-Stat] [Tablespace-Spec]
{ Index-Attributes }

Key-Compression ::= NOCOMPRESS | Compress-Option
Compress-Option ::= COMPRESS <Integer>

Compute-Stat ::=
COMPUTE STATISTICS

Tablespace-Spec ::=
TABLESPACE <Tablespace> | DEFAULT

Figure 11-14. *The Create-Index Statement*

/* **Physical-Attributes-Clause** and **Parallel-Clause** are defined in Create-Table */

Table-Index-Clause ::=
[<Schema>·] <Table> [<Table-Alias>]
(Index-Expr [ASC/DESC] {,Index-Expr [ASC/DESC] })
[Global-Partitioned-Index | Local-Partitioned-Index] [Index-Attributes] [Domain-Index-Clause]

Index-Expr ::=
<Column> | <Column-Expression>

// Column expressions occur in function-based indexes

Global-Partitioned-Index ::=
GLOBAL PARTITION BY RANGE (<Column>{,<Column>})
(Index-Partitioning-Clause>

Index-Partitioning-Clause ::=
PARTITION [<Partition>] VALUES LESS THAN (<Value> {,<Value>})
[Segment-Attributes-Clause]

// **Segment-Attributes-Clause** defined in Create-Table

Local-Partitioned-Index ::=
LOCAL [On-Range-Partitioned-Table | On-List-Partitioned-Table | On-Hash-Partitioned-Table |
On-Comp-Partitioned-Table]

On-Range-Partitioned-Table ::=
(PARTITION [<Partition> [Segment-Attributes-Clause]]
{,PARTITION [<Partition> [Segment-Attributes-Clause]]})

// **On-List-Partition-Table** is as for On-Range-Partition-Table

On-Hash-Partitioned-Table ::= OHPOption1 | OHPOption2
OHPOption1 ::= STORE IN (<TableSpace> {,<TableSpace>})
OHPOption2 ::= On-Range-Partitioned-Table

On-Comp-Partitioned-Table ::=
STORE IN (<TableSpace> {,<TableSpace>})
(PARTITION [<Partition> {Segment-Attribute-Clause} [Index-Subpartition-Clause]]
{,PARTITION [<Partition> {Segment-Attributes-Clause}[Index-Subpartition-Cause]]})

Index-Subpartition-Clause ::= ISCOption1 | ISCOption2
ISCOption1 ::= STORE IN (<TableSpace>{,<TableSpace>})
ISCOption2 ::= (SUBPARTITION[<Subpartition>[TABLESPACE<Tablespace>]]
                {, SUBPARTITION[<Subpartition>[TABLESPACE<TableSpace>]]})

// **Segment-Attributes-Clause** is defined in Create-Table

Figure 11-14. *The Create-Index Statement (continued)*

```
Domain-Index-Clause ::=
INDEXTYPE IS <IndexType> [Parallel-Clause]
[PARAMETERS ('<ODCI-Parameters>')]


Bitmap-Join-Index-Clause ::=
[<Schema>·] <Table> ([[<Schema>·]<Table>·] | [<Table-Alias>·] <Column>[ASC/DESC]
{,[[<Schema>·]<Table>·] | [<Table-Alias>·]<Column>[ASC/DESC]]})
FROM [<Schema>·]<Table> [<Table-Alias>]
{,[<Schema>·]<Table> [<Table-Alias>]}
WHERE <Condition>[Local-Partitioned-Index] Index-Attributes
```

Figure 11-14. *The Create-Index Statement (continued)*

```
Alter-Index ::=
ALTER INDEX [<Schema>·]<Index>
{Deallocate-Unused-Clause | Allocate-Extent-Clause | Parallel-Clause |
Physical-Attributes-Clause | LOGGIN | NOLOGGING} | Rebuild-Clause | ENABLE | DISABLE | UNUSABLE |
COALESCE | Rename-Index | Index-Parms1 | Monitor-Usage | Updated-Block-Ref |
Alter-Index-Partitioning};


Index-Parms1 ::=
PARAMETERS ( '<ODCI-Parameters>' )


Rename-Index ::=
RENAME TO <NewIndexName>


Monitor-Usage ::=
MONITORING | NONMONITORING  USAGE


Update-Bloc-Ref ::=
UPDATE BLOCK REFERENCES


Alter-Index-Partitioning ::=
Modify-Index-Default-Attributes | Modify-Index-Partition | Rename-Index-Partition |
Drop-Index-Partition | Split-Index-Partition | Modify-Index-Subpartition


Modify-Index-Default-Attributes ::=
MODIFY DEFAULT ATTRIBUTES [FOR PARTITION <Partition>]
{Physical-Attributes-Clause | LOGGING | NOLOGGING | TableSpace-Spec}

// Physical-Attributes-Clause is defined in Create-Table

Modify-Index-Partition ::=
MODIFY PARTITION <Partition>
{Physical-Attributes-Clause | LOGGING | NOLOGGING | Allocate-Extent-Clause  | Deallocate-Unused-Clause}
Index-Parms2  | COALESCE | UNUSEABLE | Update-Block-Ref
```

Figure 11-15. *The Alter-Index Statement*

```
Index-Parms2 ::=
PARAMETERS ('<Alter-Partition-Parms>')

// Physical-Attributes-Clause is defined in Create-Table
// Allocate-Extent-Clause and Deallocate-Unused-Clause defined in Alter-Table

Rename-Index-Partition ::= RIPOption1 | RIPOption2
RIPOption1 ::= RENAME PARTITION <partition> TO <NewName>
RIPOption2 ::= RENAME SUBPARTITION <Subpartition> TO <NewName>

Drop-Index-Partition ::=
DROP PARTITION <Partition>

Split-Index-Partition ::=
SPLIT PARTITION <Partition> AT (<Value> {,<Value>})
[INTO (Index-Partition-Description, Index-Partition-Description)] [Parallel-Clause]

Index-Partition-Description ::=
PARTITION [<Partition> {[Segment-Attributes-Clause | Key-Compression]}]

// Segment-Attributes-Clause is defined in Create-Table

Modify-Index-Subpartition ::=
MODIFY SUBPARTITION <Subpartition> UNUSABLE | Allocate-Extent-Clause |
Deallocate-Unused-Clause

// Allocate-Extent-Clause and Deallocate-Unused-Clause are defined in Alter-Table
```

Figure 11-15. *The Alter-Index Statement (continued)*

```
Create-Index ::=
CREATE [UNIQUE] [BITMAP] INDEX <Index> ON <TableName> (<Column> [ASC/DESC]
{,<Column> [ASC/DESC]}) [CLUSTER];
```

Figure 11-16. *Abridged Version of the Create-Index Statement*

Note:

1. The default order is ASC(ending).

2. The (left-right) ordering of the columns in the index is significant in the usual major-minor convention.

3. The CLUSTER option specifies that this is a clustering index — index values are clustered.

4. The UNIQUE option specifies that no two rows in the indexed table will be allowed to have the same value for the index column(s).

5.   The default algorithm for Oracle indexes is B-tree; however the user has the option of creating a bit-map index. The bit-map is like a matrix representing row-IDs and columns. It is useful in situations where many column values are identical (for instance where the primary key is composite).

Finally, you can drop an index via the **Drop-Index** statement. The syntax for this statement is shown in Figure 11-17.

Drop-Index ::=
DROP INDEX [<Schema>.] <Index> [FORCE];

Figure 11-17. *The Drop-Index Statement*

Example 9: The following statements create indexes on the tables indicated:

CREATE INDEX PgmX ON Program (Pgmname);

CREATE INDEX CrsX ON Course (Crsname);

Example 10: The following statement drops the index **CrsX**:

DROP INDEX CrsX;

Note: When a table is dropped, all its related indexes are automatically dropped also.

11.9 Creating and Managing Sequences

A sequence is an Oracle database object that automatically generates unique numbers. It is typically used to create primary key values, particularly if the primary key is a single attribute. For composite primary keys, or other alphanumeric codes, the sequence could still be useful in generating a unique number, which is to be concatenated with some other data to comprise a code.

A sequence provides two significant advantages:

• Its use could lead to shorter application code.

• When sequence values are cached, processing efficiency is enhanced.

The syntax for the **Create-Sequence** statement is shown in Figure 11-18. As you can see, the statement is quite straightforward, and the clauses self-explanatory.

```
Create-Sequence ::=
CREATE SEQUENCE <SequenceName> [INCREMENT BY <Number>]
[START WITH <Number2>] [MAXVALUE <Number3> | NOMAXVALUE]
[MINVALUE <Number4> | NOMINVALUE] [CYCLE | NOCYCLE]
[CACHE <Number5> | NOCACHE];
```

Figure 11-18. *The Create-Sequence Statement*

The sequence is accessed via two pseudo columns CURRVAL and NEXTVAL. Typically, it is accessed via a **Select** statement to retrieve its current value, or via an **Insert** statement to insert data into a table (both statements will be discussed in the next chapter).

Example 11: The following examples illustrate how a sequence is created and used:

```
CREATE SEQUENCE DeptnoSeqn INCREMENT BY 05 START WITH 0 MAXVALUE 9095  NOCYCLE;
```

To use the sequence in inserting a row into the table, the following statement may be embedded into a PL/SQL program block:

```
INSERT INTO DEPT(Dept#, Dname) VALUES(DeptnoSeqn.NEXTVAL, &DeptName);
```

To view the current value, do a selection on DUAL (DUAL is the general purpose pseudo table used when a scalar value which is not stored in a specific database table is to be displayed):

```
SELECT DeptnoSeqn.CURRVAL FROM DUAL;
```

11.10 Altering and Dropping Sequences

The attributes of a sequence may be modified via the **Alter-Sequence** statement. Its syntax is similar to that of the **Create-Sequence** statement (see Figure 11-19): The following guidelines apply to sequence modification:

- Only the owner of a sequence (or a user with alter privilege to the sequence) can modify it.

- Only future sequence numbers are affected by the modification.

- To restart a sequence, it has to be deleted and then recreated.

```
Alter-Sequence ::=
ALTER SEQUENCE <SequenceName> [INCREMENT BY <Number>]
[START WITH <Number2>] [MAXVALUE <Number3> | NOMAXVALUE]
[MINVALUE <Number4> | NOMINVALUE] [CYCLE | NOCYCLE]
[CACHE <Number5> | NOCACHE];
```

Figure 11-19. The Alter-Sequence Statement

A sequence may be removed via the **Drop-Sequence** command, which has the following syntax:

```
DROP SEQUENCE <SequenceName>;
```

11.11 Creating and Managing Synonyms

A synonym is a virtual object (i.e. the alias of an object), used to fulfill any or both of the following purposes:

- Shortening the length of an object's name

- Referring to an object (typically a table) owned by another schema (user)

The **Create-Synonym** command has the following syntax:

```
CREATE [PUBLIC] SYNONYM <SynonymName> FOR <[Schema.]ObjectName];
```

Note: If the synonym is public (created with keyword PUBLIC), other users have access to it; otherwise, it is private to the user who created it. Synonym, as used here, corresponds to the term "alias", as used in Chapter 7.

Example 12: The following example creates a synonym called **ValidDate** for an object of the same name in another schema:

```
CREATE PUBLIC SYNONYM ValidDate FOR Jones.ValidDate;
```

Here, the object **ValidDate** (which could be any valid Oracle database object, including a function) resides in a schema called Jones, and synonym is created in the current schema.

The syntax for deleting a synonym is:

```
DROP SYNONYM <SynonymName>;
```

11.12 Summary and Concluding Remarks

It's time to summarize what was covered in this chapter:

- The Oracle SQL*Plus environment provides a line editor that allows you to enter, edit and execute SQL statements. However, you may use any text editor of your choice and import the SQL statement into the SQL*Plus environment. Other alter GUI-based environments are iSQL *Plus, Oracle Enterprise Manager (OEM), and Oracle SQL Developer (OSQLD).

- The **Create-Database** statement allows you to create an Oracle database. Alternately, you may use the Oracle DBCA.

- The **Alter-Database** statement allows you to change features of a database, and the **Drop-Database** statement allows you to delete the current database. Alternately, you may use the Oracle DBCA.

- The **Create-Tablespace** statement allows you to create a tablespace. The **Alter-Tablespace** statement allows you to change features of a tablespace, and the **Drop-Tablespace** statement allows you to delete a tablespace.

- The **Create-Table** statement allows you to create a table. The **Alter-Table** statement allows you to change features of a table, and the **Drop-Table** statement allows you to delete a table.

- The **Create-Index** statement allows you to create an index. The **Alter-Index** statement allows you to change features of an index, and the **Drop-Index** statement allows you to delete an index.

- The **Create-Sequence** statement allows you to create a sequence. The **Alter-Sequence** statement allows you to change features of a sequence, and the **Drop-Sequence** statement allows you to delete a sequence.

- The **Create-Synonym** statement allows you to create a synonym. The **Drop-Synonym** statement allows you to delete a synonym.

Each of the database objects discussed in this chapter can be created and fully managed using the OEM, OSQLD, or Oracle iSQL *Plus. However, in the interest of learning SQL, it is recommended that you stick with SQL *Plus. The upcoming chapter discusses the common DML and DCL statements of SQL.

11.13 Review Questions

1. What are the commonly used SQL definition statements?

2. Use the Oracle DBCA component to create a database. Practice writing SQL statements to create simple databases.

3. Practice writing SQL statements to modify different aspects of a database.

4. Write SQL statement to add a tablespace to your database. Create a second tablespace to hold the tables described in your sample college database.

5. Practice writing SQL statements to modify different aspects of a tablespace.

6. Write SQL statements to create the tables described in the sample college database described in Chapter 7 (Figure 7-1).

7. Write appropriate SQL statements to do the following:

   • Add a constraint to a table.

   • Modify a constraint.

   • Enable or disable a constraint.

8. Write SQL statements to define indexes on your database tables.

9. Practice writing SQL statements to modify or drop indexes.

10. By considering the **Student** table in your sample college database, write SQL statement to create a sequence for this table. Describe and demonstrate how this sequence could be used.

11. What is a synonym and how is it used in a database? Practice writing SQL statements to create and drop a synonym.

11.14 References and/or Recommended Readings

[Connolly, 2002] Connolly, Thomas and Carolyn Begg. *Database Systems: A Practical Approach to Design, Implementation and Management* 3rd ed. New York, NY: Addison-Wesley, 2002. See Chapter 6.

[Couchman, 1999] Couchman, Jason and Christopher Allen. *Oracle Certified Professional: Application Developer Guide*. New York, NY: Osborne/McGraw-Hill, 1999. See Chapters 3 and 4.

[Elmasri, 2007] Elmasri, Ramez and Shamkant B. Navathe. *Fundamentals of Database Systems* 5th ed. Reading, MA: Addison-Wesley, 2007. See Chapter 8.

[Martin, 1995] Martin, James, and Joe Leben. *Client/Server Databases: Enterprise Computing*. Upper Saddle River, NJ: Prentice Hall, 1995. See Chapters 15 and 19.

[Rob, 2007] Rob, Peter and Carlos Coronel. *Database Systems: Design, Implementation & Management* 7th ed. Boston, MA: Course Technology, 2007. See Chapter 7.

[Oracle, 2008] Oracle Corporation. *SQL Reference*. http://www.oracle.com/technology/index.html (accessed October 2008).

[Shah, 2002] Shah, Nilesh. *Database Systems Using Oracle: A Simplified Guide to SQL and PL/SQL*. Upper Saddle River, NJ: Prentice Hall, 2002. See Chapters 3 and 4.

[Ullman, 1997] Ullman, Jeffrey D., and Jennifer Widom. *A First Course in Database Systems*. Upper Saddle River, NJ: Prentice Hall, 1997. See Chapter 5.

CHAPTER 12

■ ■ ■

SQL Data Manipulation Statements

There are four core DML statements in SQL, namely INSERT, UPDATE, DELETE, and SELECT. These statements apply to base tables and views (views will be discussed in the next chapter). The chapter proceeds under the following subheadings:

- Insertion of Data
- Update Operations
- Deletion of Data
- Commit and Rollback Operations
- Basic Syntax for Queries
- Simple Queries
- Queries Involving Multiple Tables
- Queries Involving the Use of Functions
- Queries Using LIKE, BETWEEN and IN Operators
- Nested Queries
- Queries Involving Set Operators
- Queries With Runtime Variables
- Queries Involving SQL Plus Format Commands
- Embedded SQL
- Dynamic Queries
- Summary and Concluding Remarks

The chapter will continue to use examples based on the college database described in Chapter 7, so feel free to take some time to review this.

12.1 Insertion of Data

There are three general formats of the **Insert** statement; the abridged form of the syntax for each format is provided in Figure 12-1:

Note:

1. The first format is used when the attribute values to be inserted are explicitly provided with the statement (typically by an SQL user).

2. The second format is used when the attribute values to be inserted are implicitly provided from program variables (useful in embedded SQL). Oracle's host language is PL/SQL (a Pascal-like language). The optional ampersand (&) that precedes the program variable denotes an execution time variable; the user will be prompted to specify a value when the SQL statement is executed. If no ampersand precedes the variable, then the SQL statement must appear as an embedded SQL statement within a PL/SQL program block; the values for the insertion are obtained from the specified program variables; some languages (for example C++) require a colon (:) to precede source program variables.

3. The third format is used when tuples to be inserted are to come from the result of some query.

4. If all the column names are omitted, this is equivalent to specifying them all in the same order as they were specified in the **Create-Table** statement.

```
Insert ::= Insert1 | Insert2 | Insert3

Insert1 ::=
INSERT INTO <TableName> [(<Column> {, <Column>})]
VALUES (<Literal> {, <Literal>});

Insert2 ::=
INSERT INTO <TableName> [(<Column> {, <Column>})]
VALUES ([&] <Pgm-variable> {, [&] <Pgm-variable>});

Insert3 ::=
INSERT INTO <TableName> [(<Column> {, <Column>})]
<Select-statement>;
```

Figure 12-1. *Abridged Form of the Insert Statement*

Example 1: Add a new department to the database with the following details: Code = D500; Name = Engineering; Head = S20:

```
INSERT INTO Dept (Dept#, Dname, Dhead#)
Values ('D500', 'Engineering', 'S20');
```

Example 2: Save all students enrolled in the BSc in MIS program:

```
CREATE TABLE MajorsMIS (Stud# NUMBER(7) NOT NULL, Sname CHAR(15), Fname CHAR(15),
    PRIMARY KEY (Stud#));

INSERT INTO MajorsMIS (Stud#, Sname, Fname)
SELECT Stud#, Sname, Fname FROM Student WHERE Spgm# = 'BSC1';
```

From the above example, the following should be noted:

1. The result of the SELECT is placed into table **MajorsMIS**. When used in this way, the **Insert** statement can insert a set of several rows at once; it illustrates what was referred to as set-at-a-time insertion in Chapter 9.

2. Table **MajorsMIS** is an example of a temporary relation or snapshot as discussed in Chapter 3.

Example 3: The following example illustrates a PL/SQL procedure to insert data into the **Course** table, where the values come from program variables:

```
/* This block allows insertion into a table */
Create Procedure InsertCourse (ThisCourse IN Course.Crs#%Type, ThisCrsname IN Course.Crsname%Type)
IS
BEGIN
 INSERT INTO Course (Crs#, Crsname)
 VALUES (ThisCourse, ThisCrsname);
 /* Note: If the ampersands are removed from the variables, no execution time prompt is done */
EXCEPTION
 WHEN OTHERS THEN /* catch all errors */
 DBMS_Output.Put_Line ('There is an execution error');
END;
```

Note: This procedure can be called from the SQL prompt, or from within an application program by issuing the call statement as in the following example:

```
Call InsertCourse ('CS101', 'Computer Applications');
```

An alternate way of specifying the above procedure is to remove the parameters and write the **Insert-Statement** with *execution-time variables*. An execution-time variable is a variable with an ampersand (&) preceding it. This indicates to the SQL parser that the user will be prompted to supply a value for the variable. You will see examples of the use of such variables in upcoming examples.

12.2 Update Operations

The **Update** statement is used for updating rows of a table. The update may be on a single row or a set of rows, depending on the condition specified in the **Where-Clause**. The abridged general formats of the **Update** statement are shown below (Figure 12-2):

Note:

1. A scalar expression is any combination of columns, arithmetic operators and SQL functions that evaluates to a scalar value (i.e. a number or an alphanumeric value). More will be said about SQL functions later.

2. The first form of the update statement is applicable when the update values are to come from literals that the user (programmer) will supply, or other columns of the table, or a combination of columns and literals.

3. The second form of the update statement is used in an embedded-SQL scenario, or where execution time prompt is desired.

4. Whenever a sub-query is specified within an update statement (the third form), it must provide values for the attributes to be updated.

```
Update1 ::= Update1 | Update2 | Update3

Update1 ::=
UPDATE <TableName>
SET <Column> = <Scalar-expression> | <Literal> {, <Column> = <Scalar-expression> | <Literal>}
[WHERE <Condition>];

Update2 ::=
UPDATE <TableName>
SET <Column> = [&]<Program-Variable> {, <Column> = [&]<Program-Variable>}
[WHERE <Condition>];

Update3 ::=
UPDATE <TableName>
SET (<Column> {,<Column>}) = (<Sub-query>)
[WHERE <Condition>];
```

Figure 12-2. *Abridged Form of the Update Statement*

Example 4: Change the Computer Science department name to 'Department of Computer Science and Mathematics'; change the department head to Professor Hans Gaur (staff code of "S20"):

```
UPDATE Dept SET Dname = 'Department of Computer Science & Mathematics', Dhead# = 'S20'
WHERE DEPT# = 'CSC';
```

Note: This is an example of a simple update (assuming that "CSC" is the unique code for the department). The record that satisfies the condition specified in the Where-Clause is fetched and updated.

Example 5: Assign all male students in the BSC in MIS to Urvine Hall:

```
UPDATE Student SET Hall # = 'Urv' WHERE SPgm# = 'BSC1' AND Sex = 'M';
```

Note: This is an example of a multiple update. All records satisfying the condition specified are fetched and updated. This also illustrates what was referred to as set-at-a-time update in Chapter 9.

Example 6: Change the course code CS100 to CS105:

```
UPDATE Course SET Crs# = 'CS105' WHERE Crs# = 'CS100';
```

Note:

1. It is not a good practice to change codes that are primary key since it increases the possibility of violation of the referential integrity rule.

2. The Oracle DBMS will allow such updates providing that no violation of the referential integrity rule would result; if a violation would result, the instruction would be disallowed (also true for DB2). An alternative to this approach is to restrict the update of primary keys (the system would allow insertion and deletion only), except in the case where the DBMS introduces and maintains surrogates, transparent to the end user. Still another alternative is to allow cascaded update, but this would be very expensive.

Example 7: The following statement uses execution time variable in an **Update** statement:

```
UPDATE Course SET Crsname = &ThisCourse WHERE Crs# = 'CS220' ;
```

Example 8: The following statement uses a query to update a row:

```
UPDATE Course  SET (Crsname, Crsabbr) =
(SELECT Crsname, Crsabbr FROM Course  WHERE Crs# = 'CS220')
WHERE Crs# = 'CS490';
```

12.3 Deletion of Data

To remove rows from a table, the **Delete** statement is used. Alternately, you may use the **Truncate** statement to delete all rows from a table. Figure 12-3 shows the syntax of both statements.

```
Delete ::= DELETE FROM <TableName> [WHERE <Condition>];

Truncate ::= TRUNCATE TABLE <TableName>;
```

Figure 12-3. *The Delete Statement and the Truncate Statement*

Example 9: Delete course 'C9999' from the database:

```
DELETE FROM CourseWHERE Crs# = 'C9999';
```

Note: The DBMS will not allow referenced tuples to be deleted unless DELETE CASCADES was specified when the related foreign key(s) was (were) specified. The default referential integrity for most DBMS suites is DELETE RESTRICTED.

Example 10: Delete all students that belong to Mary Seacole Hall:

```
DELETE FROM Student WHERE Hall# = 'Mars';
```

Example 11: Delete all staff members:

```
DELETE FROM Staff;
```
or
```
TRUNCATE TABLE Staff;
```

Note: Examples 10 and 11 are illustrations of set-at-a-time deletions as mentioned in Chapter 9. In the case of Example 10, all records satisfying the condition are deleted; in the case of Example 11, all records are deleted from the table.

12.4 Commit and Rollback Operations

The **Commit** statement and the **Rollback** statement are both DCL statements that have relevance to data manipulation. They are useful in transaction management: the **Commit** forces a write to the database table while the **Rollback** causes recovery to a safe point. This is particularly important when multiple related tuples are written to different tables (for instance, an invoice may consist of a summary tuple, written to one table, and several detail tuples, written to another table). The syntax for both statements are shown:

```
Commit ::= COMMIT;

Rollback ::= ROLLBACK [TO SAVEPOINT <Save-point-name>];
```

Two related statements are the **Set-Transaction** statement and the **Save-Point** statement. The former is used to define the beginning of a transaction block; the latter is used to create a recovery point in case of catastrophes such as power loss or system failure. The syntax of each is in Figure 12-4:

Note:

1. These statements are typically used in a programming block, not at the SQL prompt.

2. The default transaction mode for Oracle is READ WRITE. However, for application programs that are required to read data only, this should be changed to READ ONLY to prevent record locking. This is particularly important in a multi-user environment.

3. These transaction management statements work the same way for insertions, updates, and deletions.

```
Set-Transaction ::=
SET TRANSACTION <Mode>;
Mode ::= READ ONLY / READ WRITE

Save-Point ::=
SAVEPOINT <Save-point-name>;
```

Figure 12-4. *Syntax For Set-Transaction and Save-Point Statements*

Example 12: A PL/SQL program block for inserting an invoice might look as follows:

```
CREATE PROCEDURE InsertInvoice
AS
Success BOOLEAN; /* A boolean variable */
...
SAVEPOINT InvoicePoint;
SET TRANSACTION READ WRITE; /*This is really redundant; is included for illustration. */
InsertSummary; /* procedure call to insert a row in table InvoiceSummary */
InsertDetail (Success); /* procedure call to insert several related detail rows in table InvoiceDetail */
IF Success THEN
    COMMIT
ELSE
    ROLLBACK TO SAVEPOINT InvoicePoint;
END IF;
...
```

12.5 Basic Syntax for Queries

From an end user perspective, one of the most important services of the database system is the facility to retrieve information and put it to use. This is made possible via the SQL **Select** statement. The **Select** statement is by far, one of the most powerful and complex statements in SQL. It is used to retrieve data from database tables, but as you will soon see, it has many optional clauses. Figure 12-5 provides a general form of the **Select** statement, showing the more commonly used clauses.

```
Select ::=
SELECT [<FunctionSpec>] [DISTINCT] [,] <ItemList>
FROM <RelationList>
[WHERE <Condition>]
[GROUP BY <GroupList>]
[HAVING <Condition>]
[ORDER BY <OrderList>];

ItemList::=
<Attribute> | <ScalarExpression> [[AS] <Alias>] {,<Attribute> | <ScalarExpression> [[AS] <Alias>] }

RelationList ::=
<Table> | <SelectStatement> [<TupleVariable>] {, <Table> | <SelectStatement> [<TupleVariable>]}

Condition ::=
Comparison | NotCondition | AndCondition | OrCondition | ExistsItem

NotCondition ::= NOT <Condition>
AndCondition ::= <Condition> AND < Condition >
OrCondition ::= <Condition> OR <Condition>
ExistsItem ::= EXISTS (<Subquery>)

Comparison::= Comparison1 | Comparison2 | Comparison3 | Comparison4 | Comparison5

Comparison1 ::= <Variable> <Operator> <Variable>
Comparison2 ::= <Attribute> <Operator> <Attribute>
Comparison2 ::= <Attribute> <Operator> <Literal> | <ScalarExpression>
Comparison4 ::= <Attribute> IN (ValuesList | Subquery)
Comparisin5 ::= <Attribute> BETWEEN (<ScalarExpression1> AND <ScalarExpression2>)
ValuesList ::= <Literal> | <ScalarExpression> {,<Literal> | <ScalarExpression>}

Attribute ::=
<TupleVariable.Column> | <Column>

Operator ::= = | < | <= | > | >= | <> | LIKE

OrderList::=    <Column> [ASC/DSC] {,<Column> [ASC/DSC]}

GroupList::=    <Column> {,<Column>}
```

Figure 12-5. *Syntax for the Select Statement*

Observe: Except for a few omissions, the query condition closely mirrors the definition of a well-formed formula, given in Chapter 8. This is not an accident; it is deliberate.

Note:

1. The **Function-Spec-Clause** may involve any combination of a vast list of SQL functions, some of which will be mentioned in subsequent sections. The following are some categories of functions that are applicable:

    - Row functions

    - Date functions

    - Data conversion functions

    - Aggregation (group) functions

    - Programmer defined functions

2. Condition is as discussed in Chapter 8 (WFFs) except for the following:

    a. In SQL, the construct IF <Comparison> THEN WFF is not allowed.

    b. The syntax for using the existential quantifier s slightly different — the tuple variable is implicit rather than explicit.

    c. The universal quantifier is not widely supported in SQL implementations. However, in light of available substitution rules (review section 8.4) we will not pursue its use any further.

3. DISTINCT stipulates that unique tuples will be provided as output where duplicate may occur.

4. A scalar expression is an appropriate combination of columns/literals and arithmetic operators, which results in a scalar value (typically numeric or alphanumeric). The valid scalar operators are multiplication (*), division (/), addition (+), subtraction (-) and concatenation (||).

5. Relational operators used in the **Where-Clause** or **Having-Clause** include the following:

    | < <= > >= = <> LIKE IN BETWEEN |

We will start by looking as simple examples, then pull in additional features as we proceed.

12.6 Simple Queries

We will use the following format for a simple query:

SimpleQuery ::- SELECT <Item-list> FROM <Table> [WHERE <Condition>];

Example 13: List name and ID of students enrolled in "BSC1" program:

SELECT Sname, SFname, Stud# FROM Student WHERE Spgm#= 'BSC1';

Example 14: List all courses offered:

```
SELECT Crs#, Crsname from Course;
/* Since only two attributes are in the relation and we need both, we could have */
SELECT * FROM Course;
/* When the asterisk is used in this way, it is referred to as a wildcard */
```

Example 15: Refer to the supplier-items database of earlier Chapters (3 and 4). Suppose that we have relations **InventoryItem** {Item#, ItemName, ItemPrice, Weight, ...}, **Supplier** {Sup#, Sname, Scity, ...} and **Schedule** {Sup#, Item#, Qty ...}. We wish to show shipment amount on item received. Suppose each shipment is a box of 12 items. We could have the following query:

SELECT Sup#, Item#, Qty, 'Amount=', Qty * 12 FROM Schedule;

The result would look like this:

Sup#	Item#	Qty	
S001	I001	025	Amount = 300
...	...	...	Amount = 999
...	...	...	...

Example 16: Produce a list of students (showing the student's full name and StudentID) from Chancellor Hall sorted on first name within surname:

SELECT Sname || ' ' || Fname AS FullName, Stud# FROM Student WHERE Hall#= 'Chan' ORDER BY Sname, Fname;

Note the use of the concatenation operator in the scalar expression (Sname || ' ' || Fname) and the introduction of the alias (**FullName**). Please be careful not to confuse "alias" as used here, with the term described in Chapter 7. What we are talking about here is a column alias.

12.7 Queries Involving Multiple Tables

Quite often, it will be required to pull data from multiple tables in order to service a particular query. The situation may warrant a natural join, a theta join, an outer join, or a Cartesian product. Oracle supports two different approaches to dealing with queries from multiple tables — the traditional approach, and the newly introduced ANSI (American National Standards Institute) approach.

12.7.1 The Traditional Method

The traditional method for treating queries involving multiple tables is to specify the join condition in the **Where-Clause**. Let us take a few examples:

Example 17: Referring to supplier-items database (of Chapters 3 and 4), suppose we need to multiply quantity by item price to obtain the value of each shipped box. We will display supplier-name and item-name also. The query is shown below:

```
SELECT SH.Sup#, S.Sname, SH.Item#, I.ItemName, SH.Qty, SH.Qty * I.ItemPrice AS Value
FROM Schedule SH, Supplier S, InventoryItem I WHERE SH.Sup# = S.Sup# AND SH.Item# = I.Item#;
```

Note: This is an example of an equijoin. It also includes a scalar expression (**SH.Qty * I.ItemPrice**) and a column alias (**Value**). Note the introduction of explicit tuple variables **SH, S** and **I**, and the new column, **Value**. It is a good habit to introduce tuple variables when the information queried is to come from multiple tables, and/or comparisons are to be made in order to service the query. The result of the above query would look like this:

Sup#	Sname	Item#	ItemName	Qty	Value
S001	ABC Co.	I001	Crank Shaft	10	250.00
...	...	...	...	...	...

Example 18: Show all program-name and course-name combinations.

```
SELECT P.Pgmname, C.Crsname FROM Pgm_Struct PS, Program P, Course C
WHERE PS.PSPgm# = P.Pgm#  AND  PS.PSCrs# = C.Crs#;
```

Example 19: Find department heads that are not division heads:

```
SELECT S.Staff#, S.Staffname FROM Staff S, Dept D, Division DV
WHERE D.Dhead# = S.Staff# AND D.D_Div# = DV.Div# AND DV.DvHead# = S.Staff# AND
        D.Dhead# <> DV.DvHead#);
```

Note: This is an example of a theta-join. Here, we make use of the fact that the table **Division** stores an attribute (**DvHead#**) which indicates the staff member who is head of the division. We also make use of the fact that the table **Dept** stores a similar attribute (**Dhead#**) to indicate the staff member who is head of the department. Further, every department belongs to a division.

Example 20: Get all students who share a birthday with another student.

```
SELECT S1.Stud#, S1.DOB FROM Student S1, Student S2
WHERE S1.Stud# <> S2.Stud# AND S1.DOB = S2.DOB;
```

Note: This is an example of a Cartesian product of a relation with itself. Compare this with Example 8 in section 7.4 and Example 3 in section 8.2.

Caution: If you wish to join relation R1 with relation R2, make sure the R1's foreign key does not allow for null values, since this will produce a spurious result. If in doubt, use an **outer join**, as clarified in the next example.

Example 21: Provide a list of all students and their assigned hall. Assume that it is possible for **Hall#** in the table **Student** to have null values. The following solution would be incorrect, since it could produce a spurious result:

```
SELECT Sname, Hallname FROM Student S, Hall H WHERE S. Hall# = H.Hall#;
```

Note: The results will exclude all students who have not been assigned to a hall (incidentally, this is an example of a natural join). To avoid this situation, use the **outer join** by simply including a parenthesized plus sign (+) on the attribute of the table where there may not be a corresponding row (in this case H.Hall#), when specifying the join condition. The Query should therefore be written as:

```
SELECT Sname, Hallname FROM Student S, Hall H WHERE S. Hall# = H.Hall#(+);
```

Note:

1. The plus sign indicates that rows from the implied relation may have null values (or non-matching values) for the attribute of interest; these rows should be included. If the plus sign is on the right, we have a *left outer join*; if the plus sign is on the left, we have a *right outer join*.

2. Using this approach, you can have the parenthesized plus sign (+)on either but not both sides of the join condition. This means that you have a left outer join, a right outer join, but not a full outer join. To obtain a full outer join, you have to take the union of a left outer join with a right outer join.

3. Left outer joins means take all rows from the table on the left; right outer join means take all rows from the table on the right.

12.7.2 The ANSI Method

Oracle 10g supports the more newly introduced ANSI syntax for handling queries from multiple tables. With this new syntax, the **From-Clause** is modified so that you are forced to explicitly specify the join. The syntax for the modified **From-Clause** is shown in Figure 12-6.

```
From-Clause ::= From1 | From2 | From3 | From4 | From5

From1 ::= FROM <Table> NATURAL [INNER] JOIN <Table>
          {NATURAL [INNER] JOIN <Table>}

From2 ::= FROM <Table> [INNER] JOIN <Table> USING <Column-list>
          {[INNER] JOIN <Table> USING <Column-list>}

From3 ::= FROM <Table> [Alias] [INNER] JOIN <Table> [Alias] ON <Condition>
          {[INNER] JOIN <Table> [Alias] ON <Condition>}

From4 ::= FROM <Table> CROSS JOIN <Table>

From5 ::= FROM <Table> [Alias] [NATURAL] LEFT|RIGHT|FULL [OUTER] JOIN <Table> [Alias] [ON <Condition>]
          {[NATURAL] LEFT|RIGHT|FULL [OUTER] JOIN <Table> [Alias] [ON <Condition>]}
```

Figure 12-6. Modified From-Clause for ANSI Join

Please Note:

1. The first format describes the natural join. For this, the join column(s) in each table must be identical. Moreover, you are not allowed to qualify column names.

2. The second format is useful where more than one column in each table have the same name; you then need to specify which columns should be used for the joining. If you have a properly designed database with unique attribute-names in each table, there will not be many occasions to use this format.

3. The third format is the most widely used, because it is the most flexible. You specify the join condition after the keyword **ON**.

4. The fourth format is for taking Cartesian (cross) products; no join condition is required.

5. The fifth format is for outer joins; there are three types:

    - The left outer join is a join between two tables that returns rows based on the join condition, and unmatched rows from the table on the left.

    - The right outer join is a join between two tables that returns rows based on the join condition, and unmatched rows from the table on the right.

    - The full outer join is a join between two tables that returns rows based on the join condition, and unmatched rows from the table on the left, as well as the table on the right.

6. When the keyword LEFT | RIGHT | FULL is used, the keyword OUTER is implied and is therefore optional. Conversely, when the keyword LEFT | RIGHT | FULL is omitted, the keyword INNER is implied.

7. Left outer join means that all rows from the table on the left are kept; right outer join means that all rows from the table on the right are kept; full outer join means that all rows are kept from both tables (the one on the left and the one on the right).

8. One significant advantage of the ANSI syntax over the traditional is that you can separate join conditions from other conditions that can still be specified in the **Where-Clause**. Another advantage is a much easier achievement of a full outer join (in the traditional approach, you have to take a union of a left outer with a right outer).

Example 22: Example 18 is repeated here using ANSI syntax (show all program-name and course-name combinations).

```
SELECT P.Pgmname, C.Crsname FROM Pgm-Struct PS JOIN Program P ON PS.PSPgm# = P.Pgm#
JOIN Course C ON PS.PSCrs# = C.Crs#;
```

Example 23: Example 21 is repeated here using ANSI syntax (student-name and hall-name combinations, including students not assigned to halls):

```
SELECT S.Sname, H.Hallname FROM Student S LEFT JOIN Hall H ON S. Hall# = H.Hall#;
```

12.8 Queries Involving the use of Functions

SQL allows the use of several functions in order to provide the user (programmer) with flexibility in specifying queries. We will briefly discuss the following categories of SQL functions:

- Row functions

- Date functions

- Data conversion functions

- Aggregation (group) functions

- Programmer defined functions

12.8.1 Row Functions

Row functions are functions that act on rows (tuples) of a query result, typically affecting the value of specific columns of a given row. Figure 12-7 provides a list of commonly row functions that can be used within a query specification. The list is by no means exhaustive.

Function	Explanation
NVL(<Column>, <Literal>)	Replaces null values in the specified column with the literal specified
CONCAT(<Column> | <Literal> ,<Column> | <Literal>)	Concatenates the two columns specified
LOWER(<Column> | <Literal> | <Scalar-expression>)	Converts the alphabetic argument to lower case
UPPER(<Column> | <Literal> | <Scalar-expression>)	Converts the alphabetic argument to upper case
INITCAP(<Column> | <Literal> | <Scalar-expression>)	Converts the first character of each word in the alphabetic argument to upper case
LPAD(<Column>, <Length> [,<PadCharacter>])	Inserts **Length** characters to the left; the default character being **space**
RPAD(<Column>, <Length> [,<PadCharacter>])	Inserts **Length** characters to the right; the default character being **space**
SUBSTR(<Column> | <Literal> | <ScalarExpression>, <Start>, <Length>)	Returns a sub-string of the specified length, starting at the start position
LENGTH(<Column> | <Literal> | <ScalarExpression>)	Returns the length of the string specified
ABS(<Column> | <ScalarExpression>)	Returns the absolute value of the numeric argument
MOD(<Column>	<Scalar-expression >, (<Column> | <ScalarExpression>)	Returns the remainder of the first argument divided by the second
CEIL(<Column> | <Literal> | <ScalarExpression>)	Rounds up to the nearest integer
FLOOR(<Column> |<Literal> | <ScalarExpression>)	Rounds down to the nearest integer
ROUND(<Column> | <Literal> | <ScalarExpression>, <Prec>)	Rounds to the specified precision (expressed as a literal or an expression). If the precision is negative, round to the precision of **Prec** places to the left of the decimal point.
TRUNC(<Column> | <Literal> | <Scalar-expression>, <Prec>)	Truncates to the specified precision (expressed as a literal or an expression). If the precision is negative, truncate to **Prec** places to the left of the decimal point.
GREATEST(<Column> | <Literal> | <ScalarExpression>{,<Column> | <Literal> | <ScalarExpression>})	Returns the highest value from a list of strings, numbers or dates.
LEAST(<Column> | <Literal> | <ScalarExpression>{,<Column> | <Literal> | <ScalarExpression>})	Returns the lowest value from a list of strings, numbers or dates.
SQRT(<Column> | <Literal> | <ScalarExpression>)	Returns the square root of the numeric argument
VSIZE(<Column> | <Literal>)	Returns the size in bytes of the argument
DECODE(<Column> | <ScalarExpression>, <Search>, <Result> {,<Search> , <Result>})	Replaces the search argument with the result for the column specified.

Figure 12-7. Commonly Used SQL Row Functions

Example 24: The following examples illustrate how the row functions may be used (note the use of the pseudo table DUAL for non-database data):

```
SELECT ROUND (136.876, 2) ROUND(136.876, 0), ROUND(136.876, -1) FROM DUAL;
/* produces the result 136.88, 137, 140 */
SELECT TRUNC (136.876, 2) TRUNC(136.876, 0), TRUNC(136.876, -1) FROM DUAL;
/* produces the result 136.87, 136, 130 */

SELECT Stud#, Sname, RPAD(DECODE(Sex, 'M', 'Male', 'F', 'Female'), 6) AS Sexx FROM Student;
/* displays "Male" instead of "M" and "Female" instead of "F" */

SELECT Stud#, SUBSTR(Sname,1,1) || SUBSTR(Fname,1,1) AS Initl FROM Student;
/* displays the initials of students */

SELECT GREATEST(123, 457, 899, 898998, 23000) FROM DUAL;
/* displays 898998 which is the highest value in the specified list */

SELECT Sname, NVL(Spgm#, 'Trial') FROM Student;
/* Displays surname & program code, with "Trial" for unassigned students */
```

Note: You may be surprised by a negative precision used with the rounding function. It simply means that rounding takes place to the left (instead of right) of the decimal point. The following examples should provide clarification:

- ROUND (134.4, -1) = 130

- ROUND (134.4, -2) = 100

- ROUND (134.4, -3) = 0

- ROUND (158.6, -1) = 160

- ROUND (158.6, -2) = 200

- ROUND (158.6, -3) = 0

12.8.2 Date Functions

Date functions constitute a special group of row functions in Oracle. Oracle has an internal representation of date, which stores the day, month, year (including century), hour, minute and second. The default date format is DD-MON-YY. Additionally, Oracle provides a number of date manipulation functions (Figure 12-8):

Function	Explanation
MONTHS_BETWEEN(<Date1>, <Date2>)	Returns the number of months between two dates
ADD_MONTHS(<Date>, <Months>)	Returns a new date after adding a specified number of months
NEXT_DAY(<Date>)	Returns the new date after a specified date
LAST_DAY(<Date>)	Returns the last day of the month specified
ROUND(<Date>, [,<Format>])	Truncates the date given to the nearest day, month or year, depending on the format (which is 'DAY' or 'MONTH' or 'YEAR')
TRUNC(<Date>, [,<Format>])	Truncates the date given to the nearest day, month or year, depending on the format (which is 'DAY' or 'MONTH' or 'YEAR')
SYSDATE	Returns the current system date
NEW_TIME(<Date>, <Zone1>, <Zone2>)	Converts a date and time in time zone **Zone1** to date and time in time zone **Zone2**. Time formats are in the form XST or XDT, (S for Standard, D for Daylight saving) with two exceptions: GMT and there is no NDT for Newfoundland.

Figure 12-8. SQL Date Manipulation Functions

Example 25: The following examples illustrate how the date functions may be used:

```
SELECT SYSDATE FROM DUAL; /* displays the current date */

SELECT Sname, TRUNC( (SYSDATE – DoB)/365.25) AS Age FROM Student;
/* displays students' name and age, assuming DoB is stored internally as type date */

SELECT ADD_MONTHS(SYSDATE, 20) FROM DUAL; /* displays date 20 months beyond current date */

SELECT Sname, MONTHS_BETWEEN(DoB, SYSDATE) AS AgeInMonths FROM Student;
/* displays students' name and age in months, assuming DoB is stored internally as type date */

SELECT LAST_DAY('17-AUG-01') FROM DUAL; /* displays "31-AUG-01" */

SELECT ROUND('22-JUL-98', 'MONTH'), ROUND('22-JUL-98', 'YEAR') FROM DUAL;
/* displays "01-AUG-98" and "01-JAN-99" */

SELECT TRUNC('22-JUL-98', 'MONTH'), TRUNC('22-JUL-98', 'YEAR') FROM DUAL;
/* displays "01-JUL-98" and "01-JAN-98" */
```

To change the default format for system, you can use the **Alter-Session** statement, and change the pseudo column **nls_date_format** as in the following example:

```
ALTER SESSION SET nls_date_format = 'YYYY-MM-DD HH24:MI:SS';
/* If you now display the system date, you will observe the new format of the system date */
```

12.8.3 Data Conversion Functions

Data conversion functions are used to convert data in the following ways:

- Character to number
- Number to character
- Character to date
- Date to character

Figure 12-9 indicates the three common data conversion functions (other less common functions are not discussed in this course). Figure 12-10 shows date formats and numeric formats which are often used with these functions.

```
TO_CHAR((<Column> | <Literal> | <Scalar-expression>[,<Format>])
            /* Converts a number or date to a VARCHAR2 value, based on the format (specified in single quotes) */
TO_NUMBER((<Column> | <Literal> | <Scalar-expression> [,<Format>])
            /* Converts a string with valid digits to number, based on the format specified */
TO_DATE((<Column> | <Literal> | <Scalar-expression>[,<Format>])
            /* Converts a string to date, based on the format specified (default DD-MON-YY) */
```

Figure 12-9. *SQL Commonly Used Data Conversion Functions*

Valid Date Formats:	
YYYY	Four digit year
Y, YY or YYY	Last 1, 2, or 3 digits of year
YEAR	Year spelled out
Q	Quarter of the year
MM	Two digits for month
MON	First three characters of month
MONTH	Month spelled out
WW or W	Week number of year or month
DDD, DD or D	Day of year, month or week
DAY	Day spelled out
DY	Three letter abbreviation of day
DDTH	Ordinal number of day e.g. 7th
HH, HH12, HH24	Hour of day, hour (0-12) or hour(0-23)
MI	Minute (0-59)
SS	Second (0-59)

Valid Numeric Formats:	
9	Number of 9s determine width
0	Displays leading zeros
$	Displays floating dollar sign
L	Displays floating local currency
.	Displays decimal point
,	Displays thousand indicator as specified
PR	Displays negative numbers in parentheses

Figure 12-10. *Valid Date and Numeric Formats*

Example 26: The following examples illustrate how the conversion functions may be used:

```
SELECT Empid, TO_CHAR(Salary, '$99,999.99') AS Salary FROM Emp;
/* displays Salary in the format shown */

SELECT Stud#, TO_CHAR(DoB, 'DD-MM-YYYY' ) AS DoB FROM Student;
/* displays DoB in the format shown */

SELECT TO_NUMBER(SUBSTR(SYSDATE,1,4)) FROM DUAL;
/* displays the current year as a number */
```

12.8.4 Programmer-Defined Functions

Oracle supports programmer-defined functions; these are used in same manner as SQL system functions. Programmer defined functions are written in Oracle's PL/SQL and stored on the server. For more information on how to define them, refer to your Oracle documentation.

Example 27: Below is a programmer defined PL/SQL function to determine y raised to the power x:

```
/* This is a sample function. */
Create Function YPowerX (Y Number, X Number) Return Number
As
K Number(3);
Result Number;
Begin
 If (X = 0) then
   Result := 1;
 Else
   Result := 1;
   For K In 1..X Loop
     Result := Result * Y;
   End Loop;
 End If;
 Return Result;
End;
```

12.8.5 Aggregation Functions

SQL provides several aggregate functions to provide summarized view of data. Some commonly used aggregate (group) functions are described in Figure 12-11:

Note:

1. SUM, AVG, STDDEV and VARIANCE work with numeric values.

2. For MAX and MIN, the DISTINCT option is irrelevant.

3. COUNT works with the DISTINCT option always, except for the case where COUNT (*) or COUNT(1) is used.

Function	Explanation
AVG(<Column>)	Returns average of tuple values for the column specified
COUNT(<Column> | <Scalar-Expression>)	Returns number of tuples in a relation referenced
SUM(<Column> | <Scalar-Expression>)	Returns total of tuple values for the column specified
MAX(<Column>)	Returns largest tuple value for the column specified
MIN(<Column>)	Returns smallest tuple value for the column specified
STDDEV(<Column>)	Returns standard deviation of tuple values for the column specified
VARIANCE(<Column>)	Returns variance of tuple values for the column specified

Figure 12-11. Commonly Used SQL Aggregate Functions

Example 28: How many courses are offered?

```
SELECT COUNT (*) FROM Course;
```

```
SELECT COUNT (1) FROM Course;
```

Note: The second statement is preferred to the first, since it is more efficient.

Example 29: How many programs offer course M100?

```
SELECT COUNT (DISTINCT PSPgm#) FROM Pgm_Struct WHERE PSCrs# = 'M100';
```

Example 30: Referring to the supplier-items database, how many boxes of item 'I100' is supplied? What is the maximum quantity and the minimum quantity?

```
SELECT SUM (Qty) AS SumQty, MAX(Qty) AS MaxQty, MIN(Qty) AS MinQty FROM Schedule
WHERE Item# = 'I100';
```

Aggregate functions are also often used in situations where data is to be grouped, in order to set up control breaks. This is illustrated in the following examples.

Example 31: Referring to the supplier-items database, produce a list showing item number and quantity of items shipped:

```
SELECT Item#, SUM (Qty) AS SumQty FROM Schedule GROUP BY Item#;
```

Sample result:	Item#	SumQty
	I100	600
	I101	700
	...	...

The aggregation functions are often used when grouping data (hence the alternate name, group functions) in order to set up control (summary) lines in reports. The next two examples will illustrate how this is done.

For the next two examples (as well as some of the upcoming ones), consider the section of the sample Oracle database (which is shipped with the Oracle product) consisting of the following tables (table names and column names may vary with different implementations):

Dept{Deptno, Dname, Loc} with primary key [Deptno]
Emp{Empno, Ename, Job, Mgr, Hiredate, Sal, Comm, Deptno} with primary key [Empno]

Assume further that **Emp.Deptno** is a foreign key, which references **Dept.Deptno**.
Example 32: Develop a list from the employee table, showing for each department, the total salary, average salary, minimum salary, maximum salary and standard deviation:

```
SELECT Deptno, SUM(Sal) AS TotalSal, AVG(Sal) AS Average, MAX(Sal) AS MaxSal,
MIN(Sal) AS MinSal, STDDEV(Sal) AS StdDev FROM Emp GROUP BY Deptno;
```

Note: In typical implementations of SQL, it is not permissible to use the GROUP BY clause in a join query. The solution below would therefore be rejected by the SQL compiler. However, there are ways to get around this hurdle (for instance creating a view or snapshot, then writing a query on the view or snapshot). This will be further discussed in Chapter 15).

```
SELECT Deptno, Dname, SUM(Sal) AS TotalSal, AVG(Sal) AS Average, MAX(Sal) AS MaxSal,
MIN(Sal) AS MinSal, STDDEV(Sal) AS StdDev FROM Emp E, DEPT D
WHERE E.Deptno = D.Deptno GROUP BY E.Deptno;
```

The **Having-Clause** may be used to restrict groups. **HAVING...** works after the groups have been selected; **WHERE...** works on rows before group selection.

Example 33: Develop a list from the employee table, showing for each department, the total salary, average salary, minimum salary, maximum salary and standard deviation; show only departments with a total salary of at least $60,000:

```
SELECT Deptno, SUM(Sal) AS TotalSal, AVG(Sal) AS Average, MAX(Sal) AS MaxSal,
MIN(Sal) AS MinSal, STDDEV(Sal) AS StdDev FROM Emp GROUP BY Deptno
HAVING TotSal >= 60000;
/* Note: This will not run in Oracle; you must modify it as follows */
SELECT Deptno, SUM(Sal) AS TotalSal, AVG(Sal) AS Average, MAX(Sal) AS MaxSal,
MIN(Sal) AS MinSal, STDDEV(Sal) AS StdDev FROM Emp GROUP BY Deptno
HAVING SUM(Sal) >= 60000;
```

Note: The question of when a column should be included in a query that involves grouping of data has often troubled inexperienced users of SQL. Here is a simple guide:

```
If you cannot group on the column, then you may not include it in the Select clause of the Select
statement of an aggregation query.
```

12.9 Queries Using LIKE, BETWEEN and IN Operators

The LIKE operator is used to test for the existence of string patterns in a column. The BETWEEN ... AND operator is used to test for column values within a range of values. The IN operator is used to test for column values within a set of values; the set of values may be expressed explicitly, or implied from the result of a sub query (sub-queries will be discussed in the next section).

Example 34: Get names of all courses with code beginning with the acronym "CS" (all computer science courses, for instance):

```
SELECT Crsnames FROM Course WHERE Crs# LIKE 'CS%';
```

Note: The wildcard **%** is used to denote that the string being searched for must begin with the character(s) specified; the characters that follow do not matter.

Example 35: Get names of all second year courses (assuming that a three-digit sequence number after the course acronym, indicates the level of the course):

```
SELECT Crsnames FROM Course WHERE Crs# LIKE '%2__';
```

Example 36: Referring to the Oracle employee-department database (of the previous sub-section), list employees within a salary range of 50,000 and 120,000:

```
SELECT Empno, Ename, Sal FROM Emp WHERE Sal BETWEEN 50000 AND 120000;
```

Example 37: List all students enrolled in MIS, Computer Science or Mathematics (assuming sample data of Figure 7-2):

```
SELECT * FROM Student WHERE Spgm# IN ('BSC1', 'BSC2', 'BSC4');
/* is equivalent to */
SELECT * FROM Student WHERE Spgm# = 'BSC1' OR Spgm# = 'BSC2' OR Spgm# = 'BSC4';
```

Note: In the next section, you will see that the IN operator works quite nicely with sub-queries.

12.10 Nested Queries

A sub-query is a nested query, i.e. a query within another query. A sub-query is particularly useful when a query on a given table depends on data in the table itself. Additionally, nested queries are alternatives to queries involving natural joins (not recommended for complex join conditions). There are two types of nested queries:

- Single-row sub-query: only one row is retrieved

- Multiple-row sub-query: multiple rows are retrieved

The typical format for a sub-query is:

```
SELECT <Item-list> FROM <Relation-list> WHERE <Column> | <Scalar-expression> <Boolean-operator>
   (<Sub-query>);
```

In this format, the following rules apply:

1. The sub-query is another **Select statement**, which cannot include an **Order-By-Clause**.

2. The inner query is executed first, and its result is passed to the outer query.

3. Within the **Where-Clause**, a scalar expression involving at least one column may be specified (immediately following WHERE) instead of a column.

An alternate format for a sub-query is:

```
SELECT <Item-list> FROM <Relation-list> [WHERE <Condition>];
```

In this format, the following rules apply:

1. The relation-list includes at least one sub-query.

2. It is possible to have this format combined with the first.

3. The inner query is executed first, and its result is passed to the outer query.

Example 38: Produce a list showing student name and associated major (program) name (assuming a student's program code is never null):

```
SELECT S.Sname || S.Fname AS Fullname, P.Pgmname FROM Student S, Program P WHERE S. Spgm#
    IN (SELECT Pgm#, Pgmname FROM Program);
/* is equivalent to */
SELECT S.Sname || S.Fname AS Fullname, P.Pgmname FROM Student S, Program P WHERE S. Spgm# =
    P.Pgm#;
```

Example 39: Referring to the Oracle employee-department database, produce a list of employees who earn the maximum salary in their respective departments:

```
SELECT Ename, Job, Sal, Deptno FROM Emp
WHERE Sal IN (SELECT MAX(Sal) FROM Emp GROUP BY Deptno);
// An alternate query follows
SELECT DISTINCT Ename, Job, E1.Sal, E1.DeptNo FROM Emp E1, (SELECT MAX(Sal) AS MaxSal,
    DeptNo FROM Emp GROUP BY DeptNo) E2 WHERE E1.Sal = E2.MaxSal;
```

Note: In queries of this form, do not use the **equal operator** (=) as the connecting operator unless you are sure that the inner sub-query produces only one row. In any event, the **IN operator** is safer.

The **ANY (or SOME) operator** and **ALL operator** both work nicely with nested queries. The expression on the left is compared to *any* row or *all* rows from the sub-query on the right. In using these operators, the following convention must be noted:

- < ANY(...) means less than the maximum value
- = ANY(...) is equivalent to IN (...)
- > ANY(...) means greater than the minimum value
- > ALL(...) means greater than the maximum value
- < ALL(...) means less than the minimum value

Example 40: Referring to the Oracle employee-department database, produce a list of employees who earn less than the maximum salary of a secretary:

```
SELECT Empno, Ename, Sal FROM Emp
WHERE Sal < ANY(SELECT Sal FROM Emp WHERE Job = 'Secretary');
/* which is equivalent to */
SELECT E1.Empno, E1.Ename, E1.Sal FROM Emp E1, (SELECT Job, MAX(Sal) as MaxSal FROM
 Emp GROUP BY Job) E2 WHERE E2.Job = 'Secretary' AND E1.Sal < E2.MaxSal;
```

Example 41: Referring to the Oracle employee-department database, produce a list of employees who earn less than the minimum salary of a secretary:

```
SELECT Empno, Ename, Sal FROM Emp
WHERE Sal < ALL(SELECT Sal FROM Emp WHERE Job = 'Secretary');
/* which is equivalent to */
SELECT E1.Empno, E1.Ename, E1.Sal FROM Emp E1, (SELECT Job, MIN(Sal) as MinSal FROM
 Emp GROUP BY Job) E2 WHERE E2.Job = 'Secretary' AND E1.Sal < E2.MinSal;
```

Example 42: Referring to the Oracle employee-department database (described in section 12.8.5), produce a list of employees who earn more than the average earning for his/her department (show both the employee's salary and his/her department's average salary):

```
SELECT E1.Ename, E1.Sal, E1.Deptno, E2.AvgSal FROM Emp E1, (SELECT Deptno, AVG(Sal) AS
 AvgSal FROM Emp GROUP BY Deptno) E2
WHERE (E1.Deptno = E2.Deptno AND E1.Sal > E2.AvgSal);
```

Note:

1. Several layers of nesting may be constructed; however, this is not recommended.

2. Within nested queries, a scalar variable is confined (known only) to its select block at each level. However, (scalar) variables within a higher block, A, are known to the inner blocks of A. For instance, if a query solution consists of blocks A, B, C, where A consists of B and C, then:

    -   Variables of block C are not known to block B and vice versa.

    -   Variables of blocks B and C are not known to block A.

    -   Variables of block A are known to blocks B and C.

Query Using Exists and NOT Exists

SQL also allows the specification of nested queries that involve the use of the existential quantifiers (EXISTS and NOT EXISTS). As mentioned earlier, the universal quantifier is not supported in some implementations of the language (it is supported in Oracle 10G and Oracle 11G). However, considering the standardization rules of Chapter 8 (section 8.4), this is not a serious deterrent. Moreover, in most cases, the rule of not retrieving a bounded tuple variable, along with its consequences, ensure that SQL statements can be specified without the use of quantifiers. That said, SQL nonetheless supports the use of the existential quantifiers, albeit in a manner that is slightly different from what was discussed in Chapter 8: the tuple variable is usually implicit.

Example 43: Let us revisit the problem of determining program names of programs that include the course M100:

```
The relational calculus solution would be:

RANGE OF P IS Program;
RANGE OF PS IS Pgm_Struct;
P.Pgmname WHERE EXISTS PS (PS.Pgm# = P.Pgm# AND PS.Crs# = 'M100');
```

```
The SQL solution could be any of the following:

SELECT Pgm#, Pgmname FROM Program
WHERE Pgm# IN (SELECT * FROM Pgm_Struct WHERE PSCrs#= 'M100');
/* or */
SELECT Pgm#, Pgmname FROM Program
WHERE EXISTS (SELECT * FROM Pgm_Struct PS WHERE PS.PSPgm# = Program.Pgm#
        AND PS.PSCrs# = 'M100');
/* or */
SELECT PS.PSPgm#, P.Pgmname FROM Program P, Pgm_Struct PS
WHERE PS.PSPgm# = P.Pgm# AND PS.PSCrs# = 'M100';
```

12.11 Queries Involving Set Operators

SQL supports the binary set operators UNION, UNION ALL, INTERSECT and MINUS. Recall from Chapter 7, that a basic requirement for these operations is that (in each case) the two participating relations must have corresponding attributes defined on the same domain. Since from a design perspective, it is highly unlikely that a database will have many base relations that meet this criterion, these set operators are usually used in queries where two sub-queries produce results that meet the compatibility criterion.

The general syntax, therefore, is:

<Query1> <Set Operator> <Query2>;

By way of review (except for UNION ALL), the set operators are explained below:

- UNION: Returns all rows from both queries, but duplicate rows are not displayed.

- UNION ALL: Returns all rows from both queries, including duplicate rows.

- INTERSECT: Returns rows that appear in both query results.

- MINUS: Returns rows that appear in the first query result, but not in the second.

Example 44: Produce a list all students enrolled in MIS, Computer Science or Mathematics (assuming sample data of Figure 7-2), as in Example 37, but this time using the union of sets:

```
SELECT * FROM Student WHERE Spgm# = 'BSC1'
UNION SELECT * FROM Student WHERE Spgm# = 'BSC2'
UNION SELECT * FROM Student WHERE Spgm# = 'BSC4';
// Alternate solution follows:
SELECT * FROM Student WHERE Spgm# = 'BSC1' OR  Spgm# = 'BSC2' OR Spgm# = 'BSC4';
```

Example 45: Find all students from Lenheim Hall who are mathematics majors:

```
SELECT * FROM Student WHERE Hall# = 'Len '
INTERSECT SELECT * FROM Student WHERE Spgm# = 'BSC4';
// Alternate solution follows:
SELECT * FROM Student WHERE Hall# = 'Len ' AND Spgm# = 'BSC4';
```

Example 46: Find all male students from Lenheim Hall who are not mathematics majors:

```
SELECT * FROM Student WHERE Hall# = 'Len ' AND Sex = 'M'
MINUS SELECT * FROM Student WHERE Hall# = 'Len ' AND Sex = 'M' AND Spgm# = 'BSC4';
// Alternate solution follows:
SELECT * FROM Student WHERE Hall# = 'Len ' AND Sex = 'M' AND Spgm# <> 'BSC4';
```

12.12 Queries with Runtime Variables

It has already been established that runtime variables may be specified in an SQL data manipulation statement. This applies to data insertion, update, and deletion statements; it also applies to data retrieval statements (i.e. queries). The rules are unchanged.

Example 47: Produce a list of courses offered, starting from a particular course which the user will specify:

```
SELECT * FROM Course WHERE Crs# >= &InputCode;
```

Note: The ampersand (&) preceding the variable **InputCode** indicates that user will be prompted to specify a value for the variable. This value will then be used to complete the query. A double ampersand indicates (to Oracle) that the input is to be obtained from the previous input value.

Example 48: Search for a course based on name or description, which the user will specify:

```
SELECT * FROM Course WHERE Crsname >= &Search OR CrsDescr >= &&Search;
```

The Oracle PL/SQL **Accept** statement may also be used but it must be specified within a program block. The format is

```
Accept <Variable> [Prompt <String>];
```

Example 49: The following is a program block which includes use of the **Accept** statement:

```
Declare
  ThisDept emp.deptno%Type;
  ThisEmp  emp.empno%Type;
  ThisEmpName emp.ename%Type;
BEGIN
  ACCEPT ThisEmp2 PROMPT 'Enter Employee Number:';
  SET SERVEROUTPUT ON;
  SELECT empno, ename, deptno into ThisEmp, ThisEmpName, ThisDept From Emp
  WHERE empno = '&ThisEmp2';
  ...
  DBMS_output.put_line (ThisEmp);
  DBMS_output.put_line (ThisEmpName);
  DBMS_output.put_line (ThisDept);
  /* set serveroutput off; */
END;
```

12.13 Queries Involving SQL Plus Format Commands

The Oracle SQL Plus environment provides certain format commands that can be used to affect the appearance of outputs from queries. Figure 12-12 shows some of the commonly used format commands, while Figure 12-13 provides a list of valid format codes that may be used in a format specification:

Function	Explanation
TTITLE <Text>/ON/OFF	Sets up title for a query output
BTITLE <Text>/ON/OFF	Sets up footnote for a query
BREAK ON <Column>	Specifies a control break
COLUMN <Column Option>	Specifies how a column is to be displayed. The **Column Option** consists of column commands and optional formats. Column commands include: • CLEAR • FORMAT <Format specification> • HEADING <Text> • JUSTIFY LEFT/CENTER/RIGHT

Figure 12-12. *Commonly Used Format Commands*

```
An    Alphanumeric, e.g. A20
9     Numeric, e.g. 999.99
0     Forces leading zero, e.g. 009.99
$     Floating dollar sign, e.g. $999.99
.     Decimal point
,     Thousand separator, e.g. 999,999.99
```

Figure 12-13. *Valid Format Codes*

Example 50: The following are examples of the use of such commands:

```
TTITLE 'Student Listing';
COLUMN Sname HEADING 'Surname' FORMAT A15 JUSTIFY LEFT;
BREAK ON Spgm#;
...

SELECT Spgm, Sname, Fname, Stud# FROM Student ORDER Spgm, Sname;
/* Produces a list of students, sorted on surname within major, with a control break on major. The list
   will also have a heading as specified. */
```

To clear the format command settings, you use the format clearing statements. The syntax of two such commands are as follows:

```
CLEAR BREAKS | COLUMNS | BUFFER | SCREEN;
TTITLE | BTITLE | REHEADER | REFOOTER OFF;
```

12.14 Embedded SQL

When developing applications for industrial or commercial purposes, SQL is typically used as a database language that is used by the software engineer when it is convenient to do so. What this often means is that an application program may be written in a high level language (such as Pascal, C++, Java, etc.), but containings *embedded SQL statements* to take care of database access issues.

The general convention for embedded SQL is as follows:

- Wherever a column, literal or scalar expression is applicable in an SQL statement, a program variable, or scalar expression involving programming variables, may be applied.

- In many languages, the convention for specifying program variable is to precede the variable with a colon (:). One exception to this rule is Oracle's PL/SQL, where a program variable is preceded either by the ampersand (&) in the case of execution-time variables, or nothing at all.

- In the case where data is to be retrieved into program variables, the **Select** statement is specified with an **Into-Clause**. The required syntax is shown below.

- In the case where a query will produce multiple rows, a *cursor* is set up. Although cursors are implemented differently from one host language to the other, the general principle is somewhat similar: A full discussion of cursors is beyond the scope of this course; suffice it to say that a cursor is a holding area for rows retrieved by a query. Cursors are normally used in stored procedures (in the host language), where multiple rows are retrieved for subsequent usage.

Embedded SQL was mentioned earlier in this chapter (see sections 12.1 and 12.2); in fact, Examples 3 and 12 illustrate embedded SQL relating to data insertion and transaction control respectively. The host language used here is Oracle's PL/SQL. The general syntax for such queries is shown in Figure 12-14, followed by illustrations in Examples 51-53.

```
SELECT <Item-list> INTO <Program-variable> {, <Program-variable>} FROM <Relation-list>
[WHERE <Condition>]
[GROUP BY <Group-list>]
[HAVING <Condition>]
[ORDER BY <Order-list>];
```

Figure 12-14. *Syntax for Embedded Query*

Example 51: The following examples illustrate two PL/SQL program block that each retrieves a single row into program variables (the second more elegantly than the first):

```
Declare
  ThisDept emp.deptno%Type;
  ThisEmp  emp.empno%Type;
  ThisEmpName emp.ename%Type;
BEGIN
-- Accept ThisEmp prompt 'Enter Employee Number:';
  SELECT empno, ename, deptno INTO ThisEmp, ThisEmpName, ThisDept FROM Emp
  where empno = &ThisEmp;
  DBMS_output.put_line (ThisEmp);
  DBMS_output.put_line (ThisEmpName);
  DBMS_output.put_line (ThisDept);
END;
```

```
Declare
  ThisDeptRec Dept%Rowtype;
  ThisEmpRec  emp%Rowtype;
  ThisEmp Emp.empno%Type;
  ThisDept Dept.deptno%Type;

BEGIN
-- Accept ThisEmp prompt 'Enter Employee Number:';
  SELECT * INTO ThisEmpRec FROM Emp where empno = &ThisEmp;
  SELECT * INTO ThisDeptRec FROM Dept where deptno = &ThisDept;
  DBMS_output.put_line (ThisEmpRec); /* Will not work. See the comment below */
  DBMS_output.put_line (ThisDeptRec.Deptno || ' - ' || ThisDeptRec.Dname);
END;
/* The output statement works only with a single string variable. To output a set of variables, first combine them
   into a single string.*/
```

Example 52: The following example illustrates a PL/SQL program block that retrieves multiple rows via a cursor:

```
Declare
 ThisEmp emp.empno%Type;
 ThisEmpRec emp%RowType;
 RecordFound boolean;
 SalaryNull Exception;
 Cursor EmpCursor is
 SELECT * FROM emp WHERE empno >= &ThisEmp;
Begin
 RecordFound := True;
 Open EmpCursor;
 While RecordFound Loop
  Fetch EmpCursor Into ThisEmpRec;
  If EmpCursor%NOTFOUND Then
    RecordFound := False;
  End If;
  If ThisEmpRec.Sal IS NULL Then
    Raise SalaryNull;
  End If;
  DBMS_Output.Put_Line(ThisEmpRec.Empno || ' ' || ThisEmpRec.Ename);
 End Loop;
 Close EmpCursor;
Exception
 When No_Data_Found then  /* Pre-defined (implicit) exception */
  DBMS_Output.Put_Line ('No data found');
 When SalaryNull then    /* User-defined (explicit) exception */
  DBMS_Output.Put_Line ('Salary is null');
 When Others then /* catch all errors */
  DBMS_Output.Put_Line ('There is an execution error');
End;
```

Example 53: The following example performs the same activity as the previous, but here a PL/SQL procedure is used:

```
/* This block does the same operation as the previous. However, it illustrates an alternate way of setting up
    a loop */
Create Procedure QueryEmp (ThisEmp In emp.empno%Type)

As
 ThisEmpRec emp%RowType;
 SalaryNull Exception;
 Cursor EmpCursor is
 select * from emp where empno >= &ThisEmp;
Begin
 Open EmpCursor;
 <<Hunt>>
 Loop
  Fetch EmpCursor Into ThisEmpRec;
  Exit Hunt when EmpCursor%NOTFOUND;
  If ThisEmpRec.Sal IS NULL Then
     Raise SalaryNull;
  End If;
  DBMS_Output.Put_Line(ThisEmpRec.Empno || ' ' || ThisEmpRec.Ename);
 End Loop;
 Close EmpCursor;
Exception
 When No_Data_Found then  /* Implicit exception */
  DBMS_Output.Put_Line ('No data found');
 When SalaryNull then    /* Explicit exception */
  DBMS_Output.Put_Line ('Salary is null');
 When Others then /* catch all errors */
  DBMS_Output.Put_Line ('There is an execution error');
End;
```

12.15 Dynamic Queries

Dynamic queries are used a lot in complex programming environments, where it is either difficult or cumbersome to write a single SQL statement to correspond to each request that the end user is likely to make. Instead of attempting this feat, the application programmer or software engineer writes a sophisticated program (typically in a high level language) which constructs or generates SQL statements that are pertinent to the user request, and passes them on to an SQL parser. Three scenarios for this kind of programming come readily to mind:

- A sophisticated user needs to conduct ad-hoc queries on an underlying database. The user is shielded from implementation details of the database, but is aware of underlying base tables or logical views, and the corresponding data fields (physical and/or logical) that they contain. The user is allowed to determine what details are to be included in his/her query.

- A front-end system (such as Delphi, C++ Builder, Visual Basic, etc.) is being used to construct a user interface for a software system that accesses one or more underlying databases. The software developer incorporates embedded SQL statements in various application queries, based on user input. This request is then sent to the relevant database server to be serviced. The database server processes the request and sends the response back to the client.

- A database administrator needs to periodically back up several components of an Oracle database. Rather than repeatedly issuing backup statements for the different items (for instances tablespaces) he/she may write an SQL script to dynamically generate the required SQL statements needed to perform backup of each component.

Figure 12-15 illustrates an inquiry screen for an application developed in Delphi. The end user is accessing a database for a list of publishers that the institution conducts business with. On the screen, you will notice a push button labeled **Search**, a radio group (with entries **ByCode** and **ByName**), and an input field. This application program works as follows:

- The end user can specify any search argument in the input field, to indicate the starting publisher code or name of interest (blank means start at the beginning of the list of publishers).

- The user will use the radio group to select whether information will be displayed sorted by publisher code or publisher name.

- When the user clicks the **Search** push button, the program will examine the entries made, build an appropriate SQL statement to fetch the information requested, invoke the SQL parser to request this information from the underlying database (which could be in a different back-end system such as Oracle, DB2, etc.). The code for building the SQL statement is shown in the figure.

- The database server that receives this request will process it and return the information to the program. The program will then load the grid shown with the information, display it on screen, and then await the next request from the end user.

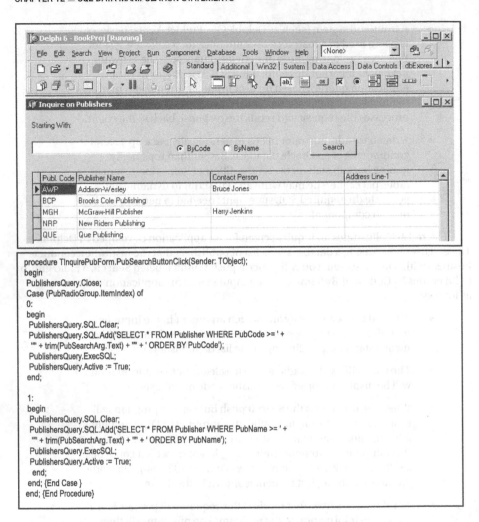

Figure 12-15. *Dynamic SQL For End User Access From Front-end System*

Figure 12-16 provides another illustration of dynamic SQL. A detailed explanation is beyond the scope of this course; however a cursory clarification is in order, and will suffice:

- The SPOOL statement (sixth line down) causes the output of the subsequent query to be redirected to the file specified.

- The SELECT statement causes a series of rows to be written to the spool file. These rows actually contain SQL statements to backup tablespaces found in the current database.

- The spool file can therefore be subsequently run as an SQL script to backup these tablespaces.

```
SET VERIFY OFF;
SET FEEDBACK OFF;
SET TERMOUT OFF;
SET ECHO OFF;
SET PAGESIZE 0;
SPOOL C:\Oracle\Admin\Backup\BackupTS.sql;
SELECT 'ALTER TABLESPACE ' || Tablespace_Name || ' BEGIN BACKUP; ',
  HOST copy ' || File_Name || ' D:\OracleBackup\EFDB ', ' ALTER TABLESPACE ' || Tablespace_Name ||
  ' END BACKUP' FROM DBA_DATA_FILES;

SPOOL OFF;  SET VERIFY ON;  SET FEEDBACK ON;
SET TERMOUT ON; SET ECHO ON;
SET PAGESIZE 20;

/* The instructions will be stored in C:\Oracle\Admin\Backup\BackupTS.sql. We can now run this script */
@ C:\Oracle\Admin\Backup\BackupTS.sql;
```

Figure 12-16. *Automatic Backup of Tablespaces in a Database via Dynamic SQL Statements*

12.16 Summary and Concluding Remarks

Relatively speaking, this has been a rather lengthy chapter. In recognition, the following paragraphs provide a summary of the various related topics covered, followed by some concluding remarks.

The **Insert** statement facilitates insertion of data into a specific table. The statement allows data insertion in one of three ways:

- Insertion by specifying literal column-values for a row of a table

- Insertion via execution-time variables for a row of a table

- Insertion by redirecting the result of a query into a table (multiple records insertion is supported by this strategy)

The **Update** statement facilitates update of rows of a table. Depending on the condition specified (in the **Where-Clause**), the update might affect a single row, multiple rows, or all the rows (if no condition is specified, or all the rows meet the condition specified). The data to be used for the update can be specified in one of three ways:

- By specifying literal column-values for the row(s) of the table that meet(s) the condition specified

- By specifying execution-time variables corresponding to stated columns, for the row(s) of the specified table that meet(s) the condition specified

- By specifying a sub-query that includes columns corresponding to the stated columns, for the row(s) of the specified table that meet(s) the condition specified

The **Delete** statement facilitates deletion of rows from a specified table. Depending on the condition specified (in the **Where-Clause**), the deletion might be for a single row, multiple rows, or all the rows (if no condition is specified, or all the rows meet the condition specified).

The **Commit** and **Rollback** statements facilitate transaction management, and are useful in situations where it is desirable to have a transaction wholly committed, or not recorded, in order to preserve the integrity of the database.

The **Select** statement is one of the most powerful and widely used statements in SQL. It facilitates retrieval of data from one or more tables and presenting the information to the end-user. This process is called querying. It is very flexible and can therefore be used in several different ways:

- Simple queries involve data retrieval (via the **Select** statement) from one table only.

- Queries involving multiple tables can be constructed in one of two ways:

  - The traditional method requires you to specify the join condition in the **Where-Clause** of the **Select** statement.

  - The American National Standard Institute (ANSI) method requires you to specify the join using join keywords. The ANSI method is more verbose but is also more flexible than the traditional method.

- Queries involving the use of functions provide additional functionality and flexibility in data retrieval. The functions can be classified into five categories: row functions, date functions, data conversion functions, aggregation functions, and programmer-defined functions.

- Queries can be constructed using the special operators LIKE, BETWEEN and IN.

- You can have queries containing other queries – nested queries. These queries may involve the use of keywords such as ANY, ALL, EXISTS and NOT EXISTS.

- You can define queries involving the use of set operators — UNION, UNION ALL, INTERSECT, and MINUS.

- You can define queries that make use of execution-time variables.

- You can define queries that make use of various SQL*Plus format commands.

- Typically, software applications do not use SQL only, but embed SQL statements in programs written in another HLL.

- A dynamic query is a query that uses data fed to it to construct a **Select** statement that is then executed. It avoids hard-coding values, thereby providing more flexibility to the end uses that use it.

Complete discussion of all aspects of the **Select** statement could easily take up a considerable portion of a book. The chapter captures and discusses the salient features, which if mastered, will place you on a solid footing in any environment that requires expertise in SQL.

One thing that should be clear is the remarkable power of the language. This can be appreciated if you attempt to write a Java or C++ program to replace any of the examples provided in the chapter. No wonder it is the universal database language. But go on to the next chapter, as there is much more to learn about the language.

12.17 Review Questions

1. Describe three ways in which data may be inserted into base table.

2. Write PL/SQL blocks to allow you to quickly populate the sample college database (created in Chapter 11) with data. Test these out in Oracle.

3. Write PL/SQL blocks to allow you to quickly modify data in your database. Test these out in Oracle.

4. Write PL/SQL blocks to allow you to easily delete data from your database. Test these out in Oracle.

5. Explain the purpose of the **Commit** and **Rollback** statements. Demonstrate how they may be used.

6. Practice writing the following:

   - Simple queries

   - Queries Involving Multiple Tables

   - Queries Involving the Use of Functions

   - Queries Using LIKE, BETWEEN and IN Operators

   - Nested Queries

- Queries Involving Set Operators

- Queries With Runtime Variables

- Queries Involving SQL Plus Format Commands

7. Differentiate between embedded SQL code and dynamic SQL code. Describe a scenario that would warrant the use of each.

12.18 References and/or Recommended Readings

[Connolly, 2002] Connolly, Thomas and Carolyn Begg. *Database Systems: A Practical Approach to Design, Implementation and Management* 3rd ed. New York, NY: Addison-Wesley, 2002. See Chapters 20 and 21.

[Couchman, 1999] Couchman, Jason and Christopher Allen. *Oracle Certified Professional: Application Developer Guide.* New York, NY: Osborne/McGraw-Hill, 1999. See Chapters 1, 2, 5 and 6.

[Elmasri, 2007] Elmasri, Ramez and Shamkant B. Navathe. *Fundamentals of Database Systems* 5th ed. Reading, MA: Addison-Wesley, 2007. See Chapters 8 and 9.

[Garcia-Molina, 2002] Garcia-Molina, Hector, Jeffrey Ullman and Jennifer Widom. *Database Systems: The Complete Book.* Upper Saddle River, NJ: Prentice Hall, 2002. See Chapter 6.

[Martin, 1995] Martin, James, and Joe Leben. *Client/Server Databases: Enterprise Computing.* Upper Saddle River, NJ: Prentice Hall, 1995. See Chapters 16-18.

[Oracle, 2008] Oracle Corporation. *SQL Reference.* http://www.oracle.com/technology/index.html (accessed October 2008).

[Rob, 2007] Rob, Peter and Carlos Coronel. *Database Systems: Design, Implementation & Management* 7th ed. Boston, MA: Course Technology, 2007. See Chapter 8.

[Shah, 2002] Shah, Nilesh. *Database Systems Using Oracle: A Simplified Guide to SQL and PL/SQL.* Upper Saddle River, NJ: Prentice Hall, 2002. See Chapters 5 - 12.

[Ullman, 1997] Ullman, Jeffrey D., and Jennifer Widom. *A First Course in Database Systems.* Upper Saddle River, NJ: Prentice Hall, 1997. See Chapter 5.

CHAPTER 13

■ ■ ■

SQL Views and System Security

Two very powerful and important features of SQL are the facility to create and manage logical views, and the capability to manage security issues of a database. This chapter discusses these two related issues. The chapter proceeds under the following subtopics:

- Traditional Logical Views

- System Security

- Materialized Views

- Summary and Concluding Remarks

13.1 Traditional Logical Views

As pointed out in Chapter 3, a logical view is a virtual relation that allows end users to access information in a manner that is consistent with their requirements. Any creditable DBMS will allow the creation and manipulation of logical views. Following are a few important points about views:

- SQL views allow for logical interpretation of information in the database.

- Views include virtual, named (but not base), and derived relations; these significantly help to comprise the external schema of the database (review chapter 2).

- Like named relations, views are created, and dropped using the **Create** and **Drop** statements. However, views cannot be structurally altered; they are virtual relations that are created and dropped as the situation dictates.

- Views are stored in the system catalog.

- Data modification (insert, update, and delete operations) can be applied through views in the normal (SQL) manner, providing that the view is updateable (more on this later). The view statements are compiled or translated (depending on the DBMS), and the implied base relations are updated at execution time.

- Views can also be queried in a manner that is identical to how base relations are queried.

13.1.1 View Creation

An abridged version of the **Create-View** statement appears in Figure 13-1; the full syntax is shown in Figure 13-2.

```
View-Definition::=
CREATE [OR REPLACE] [FORCE/NOFORCE] VIEW [<Schema>.] <ViewName> [(Column {,Column})] AS <Sub-query>
[WITH CHECK OPTION [CONSTRAINT <Constraint-name>]] | [WITH READ ONLY];
```

Figure 13-1. *Abridged Form of Create-View Statement*

```
Create-View ::=
CREATE [OR REPLACE] [FORCE/NOFORCE] VIEW [<Schema>.] <ViewName>
[Column-Spec | Object-View-Clause | XML-Type-View-Clause | View-Constraint-Spec]
AS <Sub-query>
[WITH CHECK OPTION [CONSTRAINT <Constraint-name>]] | [WITH READ ONLY];

View-Constraint-Spec ::= VCOption1 | VCOption2
VCOption1 ::= (Out-of-line-Constraint)
VCOption2 ::= (<Alias> Inline-Constraint {, Inline-Constraint} {, <Alias> Inline-Constraint {, Inline-Constraint})

/* Inline-Constraint and Out-of-line-Constraint are defined in Create-Table (review chapter 11) */

Object-View-Clause ::= OVOption1 | OVOption2
OVOption1 ::= OF [<Schema>.] <TypeName> UNDER [<Schema>.] <Super-View>
                (Out-of-line-Constraint | [<Attribute> Inline-Constraint]
                {, Out-of-line-Constraint | [<Attribute> Inline-Constraint]})
 OVOption2 ::= OF [<Schema>.] <TypeName> WITH OBJECT IDENTIFIER DEFAULT |
                [<Attribute> {, <Attribute>}]
                (Out-of-line-Constraint | [<Attribute> Inline-Constraint]
                {, Out-of-line-Constraint | [<Attribute> Inline-Constraint]})

XML-Type-View-Clause ::=
OF XMLTYPE XML-Schema-Spec
WITH OBJECT IDENTIFIER DEFAULT |[(<Expression> {, <Expression>})]

XML-Schema-Spec ::=
[XMLSCHEMA <XML-Schema-URL>] ELEMENT [<XML-Schema-URL> #] <Element>

Column-Spec ::=
(<Column> {, <Column>}
```

Figure 13-2. *The Create-View Statement*

Note:

1. Any derivable table (which can be obtained via **Select** statement) can be defined as a view. The sub-query is not allowed to include an **Order-By-Clause**, but this is not a serious omission, as there are alternatives around this constraint.

2. The view is in a way, similar to an insertion with a **Select-Clause**. The difference is that the insertion inserts actual data into a base relation; the view on the other hand, stores virtual data, i.e. it stores the access path to actual data that resides in the underlying base relation(s).

3. The OR REPLACE option replaces an existing view with the same name.

4. The FORCE option creates the view even if the underlying relation does not exist; the default is NOFORCE.

5. The WITH CHECK OPTION applies to the condition specified in the sub-query (in the **Where-Clause**): It allows insertion and update of rows based on the condition. This CHECK OPTION may be given an optional constraint name.

6. The READ ONLY option ensures that the view cannot be used for update of the underlying base relation.

Example 1: Create a logical view **CSCourses** that stores Computer Science Courses only (assume that the first two characters of the Course Code for Computer Science is "CS"):

```
CREATE VIEW CSCourses (Crs#, Crsname)
AS SELECT Crs#, Crsname FROM Course WHERE Crs# LIKE 'CS%';
```

Example 2: Create a logical view that stores for each academic program, a full breakout of all courses included in that program, as they would appear in a college bulletin:

```
CREATE VIEW Bulletin (PsPgm#, Pgmname, PsCrsSeqn, PsCrs#, Crsname)
AS SELECT PsPgm#, Pgmname, PsCrsSeqn, PsCrs#, Crsname FROM Pgm_Struct PS, Program P,
Course C WHERE  PS.PsPgm# = P.Pgm# AND PS.PsCrs# = C.Crs#;
```

13.1.2 View Modification and Removal

To modify a logical view, use the **Alter-View** statement. To remove it from the system catalog, use the **Drop-View** statement. The syntax for each statement is shown in Figure 13-3.

```
Alter-View ::=
ALTER VIEW [<Schema>.] <ViewName>
[ADD Constraint-Clause] |
[MODIFY CONSTRAINT <Constraint> RELY | NORELY] |
[DROP CONSTRAINT <Constraint>] |
[DROP PRIMARY KEY] |
[DROP UNIQUE (<Column> {, <Column>}] |
COMPILE;

// Constraints-Clause is as defined in Create-Table (review chapter 11)

Drop-View ::=
DROP VIEW [<Schema>.] <ViewName> [CASCADE CONSTRAINTS];
```

Figure 13-3. *The Alter-View and Drop-View Statements*

Note:

1. You are not allowed to alter the logical structure of a view, only constraints defined on it. In practice, this statement is seldom used.

2. When a view is dropped, it is removed from the system catalog.

3. The **Cascade-Constraints-Clause** is used to drop all referential integrity constraints that refer to primary and/or unique keys in the view to be dropped. If omitted, and such constraints exist, the **Drop-View** statement will fail.

4. Dropping a base relation automatically drops all associated views on that base relation.

Example 3: Remove the view **CSCourses** from the system:

```
DROP VIEW CSCourses;
```

13.1.3 Usefulness and Manipulation of Logical Views

Logical views are very useful, particularly during development of software systems that access related databases. The following are some advantages of views:

- Provision of some amount of logical data independence in the face of restructuring of the database

- Facilitation of assorted external views of the data stored

- Simplification of the perception of end users — the users concentrate only on data that is of concern to them

- Aiding system security — users have access only to data that concerns them, and cannot access or manipulate in any way, data to which they are not authorized

Data manipulation operations on *updateable views* are converted to equivalent operations on the underlying base table(s). In the case of data retrieval (via the **Select** statement), the conversion is straightforward and traces directly to operations on the underlying base relation(s). In the case of data changes (insertion, update or deletion), more care is required, as explained below.

A logical view is *updateable* if it meets all of the following criteria:

- The view is defined to include attributes that constitute a candidate key of the underlying base relation

- The view does not involve a JOIN*, UNION or INTERSECT operation

- The **Select** statement does not contain the keyword DISTINCT

- The **Select** statement does not include use of any aggregate function, a **Group-By-Clause** or a **Having-Clause**

- The view does not contain derived columns

- The view does not include the **READ ONLY** option

---

*Note: You can actually update an underlying base table through a join logical view, by specifying data (through the view) that will affect one (and only one) of its underlying base tables. However, this is not recommended.

13.2 System Security

In a database system (and many software applications), there are three possible levels of system security:

- Access to the system

- Access to the system resources

- Access to system data

Let us briefly examine each level, and see how they are facilitated in SQL. For the most part, this is examined in the context of an Oracle environment. However, the principles covered are also applicable in non-Oracle database environments as well.

13.2.1 Access to the System

Oracle allows access to the system through user profiles and user accounts. A profile is a working environment for a group of user accounts. When you create a database, Oracle creates a default profile called DEFAULT. When you create a user account, if you do not specify a profile, Oracle assigns the DEFAULT profile to the user account. A user account consists of a user name, a password and other optional parameters. Each user account has an associated profile.

Figure 13-4 shows the syntax for the Create-Profile statement, and example 4 illustrates how it is used. As can be seen from the syntax, the command is used to help create a working environment for the user.

```
Create-Profile ::=
CREATE PROFILE <ProfileName> LIMIT Resource-Parms | Password-Parms {Resource-Parms | Password-Parms};

Resource-Parms :=
[SESSIONS_PER_USER <n> | UNLIMITED | DEFAULT] /* No. of concurrent sessions per user */
[CPU_PER_SESSION <n> | UNLIMITED | DEFAULT] /* CPU time limit for a session, expressed in hundredth of seconds*/
[CPU_PER_CALL <n> | UNLIMITED | DEFAULT] /* CPU time limit for a call (parse, execute or fetch), expressed in
        hundredth of seconds*/
[CONNECT_TIME <n> | UNLIMITED | DEFAULT] /* The total elapsed time limit for a session, expressed in minutes */
[IDLE_TIME <n> | UNLIMITED | DEFAULT] /* Inactive time during a session, expressed in minutes */
[LOGICAL_READS_PER_SESSION <n> | UNLIMITED | DEFAULT]
[LOGICAL_READS_PER_CALL <n> | UNLIMITED | DEFAULT]
[COMPOSITE_LIMIT <n> | UNLIMITED | DEFAULT]  /* The total resource cost for a session, expressed in service units.
        Oracle calculates the total service units as a weighted sum of CPU_PER_SESSION, CONNECT_TIME,
        LOGICAL_READS_PER_SESSION, and PRIVATE_SGA. */
[PRIVATE_SGA [<n> [K|M]] | UNLIMITED | DEFAULT]

Password-Parms :=
[FAILED_LOGIN_ATTEMPTS <Expression> | UNLIMITED | DEFAULT] /* the number of failed attempts to log in to the user
        account before the account is locked */
[PASSWORD_LIFE_TIME <Expression> | UNLIMITED | DEFAULT] /* The number of days the same password can be
        used for authentication. The password expires if it is not changed within this period */
[PASSWORD_REUSE_TIME <Expression> | UNLIMITED | DEFAULT] /* The number of days before which a password
        cannot be reused  */
[PASSWORD_REUSE_MAX <Expression> | UNLIMITED | DEFAULT] /* The number of password changes required before
        the current password can be reused*/
[PASSWORD_LOCK_TIME <Expression> | UNLIMITED | DEFAULT] /* The number of days an account will be locked after
        the specified number of consecutive failed login at */
[PASSWORD_GRACE_TIME <Expression> | UNLIMITED | DEFAULT] /* The number of days after the grace period begins
        during which a warning is issued and login is allowed. The password expires after the grace period. */
[PASSWORD_VERIFY_FUNCTION <Function> | NULL | DEFAULT] /* Function to verify password */
```

Figure 13-4. The Create-Profile Statement

Example 4: The following statement creates a user profile called **InventoryProfile**. The parameters not specified will have default values.

```
CREATE PROFILE InvoryProfile LIMIT
SESSIONS_PER_USER 3
IDLE_TIME 15
FAILED_LOGIN_ATTEMPTS 3
PASSWORD_LIFE_TIME 1
PASSWORD_REUSE_TIME 0
PASSWORD_REUSE_MAX 4
PASSWORD_LOCK_TIME UNLIMITED;
```

As expected, Oracle allows you to modify or drop a profile via the **Alter-Profile** statement, or the **Drop-Profile** statement respectively. The syntax for each is shown below (Figure 13-5).

```
Alter-Profile ::=
ALTER PROFILE <ProfileName> LIMIT Resource-Parms | Password-Parms {Resource-Parms | Password-Parms}

Resource-Parms :=  /* As defined in Create-Profile */

Password-Parms :=  /* As defined in Create-Profile */

Drop-Profile ::=
DROP PROFILE <ProfileName> [CASCADE];
```

Figure 13-5. *The Alter-Profile and Drop-Profile Statements*

Note: The CASCADE option on the **Drop-Profile** statement instructs Oracle to reassign all user accounts formerly assigned to the profile, to the DEFAULT profile.

In addition to profiles, Oracle allows the DBA (or some user with system admin privileges) to create and remove users accounts. Each user account is assigned to a profile. If the profile is not specified at account creation, Oracle assigns the account to the DEFAULT profile. The required syntax for the **Create-User** statement follows:

```
Create-User ::= CUOption1 | CUOption2 | CUOption3
CUOption1 ::=   CREATE USER <UserName> IDENTIFIED BY <Password> User-Spec;
CUOption2 ::=   CREATE USER <UserName> IDENTIFIED EXTERNALLY User-Spec;
CUOption3 ::=   CREATE USER <UserName> IDENTIFIED GLOBALLY AS '<ExternalName>' User-Spec;

User-Spec ::=
[DEFAULT TABLESPACE <Tablespace>]
[TEMPORARY TABLESPACE <Tablespace>]
[QUOTA <n> [K|M] ON <Tablespace>]
[QUOTA UNLIMITED ON <Tablespace>]
[PROFILE <Profile>]
[PASSWORD EXPIRE]
[ACCOUNT LOCK | UNLOCK]
```

Figure 13-6. *The Create-User Statement*

Note:

1. Oracle supports a local database user, a global user (authenticated by Enterprise Directory Service), or an external operating system user.

2. To activate the password expiration (defined in the user's assigned profile), specify PASSWORD EXPIRE.

3. Use the ACCOUNT LOCK / UNLOCK option to lock the account (make it inaccessible by the user) or unlock the account.

4. When you create a user, Oracle creates a schema by the same name as the user. All objects created by that user will be owned by the user's schema.

Example 5: The following statement creates a user called **Bremar**.

```
CREATE USER Bremar IDENTIFIED BY Brem1199
DEFAULT TABLESPACE SampleTBS
QUOTA UNLIMITED ON SampleTBS
PROFILE InvoryProfile
PASSWORD EXPIRE
ACCOUNT UNLOCK;
```

Of course, user accounts may be modified or dropped from the system. The **Alter-User** statement allows you to change all the parameters on the **Create-User** statement, but gives the added flexibility of changing some additional settings for the account. A condensed version of the syntax is shown in Figure 13-7, which also includes the syntax for the **Drop-User** statement.

```
Alter-User ::= AUOption1 | AUOption2 | AUOption3
AUOption1 ::= ALTER USER <UserName> IDENTIFIED BY <Password>
                [REPLACE <OldPassword>] Alter-User-Spec;
AUOption2 ::= ALTER USER <UserName> IDENTIFIED EXTERNALLY Alter-User-Spec;
AUOption3 ::= ALTER USER <UserName>
                IDENTIFIED GLOBALLY AS '<ExternalName>' Alter-User-Spec;

Alter-User-Spec ::=
[DEFAULT TABLESPACE <Tablespace>]
[TEMPORARY TABLESPACE <Tablespace>]
[QUOTA <n> [K|M] ON <Tablespace>]
[QUOTA UNLIMITED ON <Tablespace>]
[DEFAULT ROLE [ALL EXCEPT] <Role> {,<Role>}]
[DEFAULT ROLE NONE]
[PROFILE <Profile>]
[PASSWORD EXPIRE]
[ACCOUNT LOCK | UNLOCK]
[Proxy-Clause] /* See Oracle Documentation */

Drop-User ::=
DROP USER <User> [CASCADE]
```

Figure 13-7. The Alter-User Statement

Note:

1. You can use this command to assign *roles* to the user account. We will discuss *roles* shortly.

2. You can also use the **Proxy-Clause** to grant other privileges to the user (for more on this, see the Oracle documentation for the **Alter-User** statement).

3. The CASCADE option on the **Drop-User** statement drops all objects owned by the user's schema before dropping the user.

Example 6: The following statement removes the user called **Bremar**:

```
DROP USER Bremar CASCADE;
```

13.2.2 Access to the System Resources

In the context of a database, we are concerned with access to system objects such as tables, views, indexes, sequences, synonyms, procedures, and other objects that the DBMS may support. Three possible actions (considered as privileges) may apply to each of these objects: creation, alteration, and dropping. Additionally, any valid SQL statement is considered a privilege. Finally, there are other system-wide privileges and roles (as you will see shortly).

The **Grant** statement is used for granting access of resources to user(s) and/or role(s), while the **Revoke** statement is used for revoking access of resources from user(s) and/or role(s). The basic syntax of each command is shown in Figure 13-8.

```
Grant ::=
GRANT [ALL PRIVILEGES] | [<Privilege> | <Role> {,<Privilege> | <Role>} ]
[(<Column> {,<Column>}] [ON <Object Name>]
To <User> | <Role> | PUBLIC {,<User> | <Role>}
[WITH ADMIN OPTION] [WITH GRANT OPTION];

Revoke ::=
REVOKE ALL/<Privilege>/<Role> {,<Privilege>/<Role>} [On <Object Name>]
FROM <User>/<Role>/PUBLIC {<User>/<Role>} [CASCADE CONSTRAINTS];
```

Figure 13-8. The Grant and Revoke Statements

Note:

1. The **ON Clause** is used if the privilege relates to a database object.

2. The privilege is typically a command name or a role; the recipient of the privilege may be a user or a *role* (roles will be clarified shortly).

3. The WITH ADMIN OPTION enables the recipient (user) to be able to grant/revoke this system privilege to/from other users or roles.

4. The WITH GRANT OPTION enables the recipient (user) to be able to grant/revoke this object privilege to/from other users or roles.

Example 7: Create user **BruceJones** and grant certain privileges to him; also allow user **Scott** to be able to run queries on the **Program** table:

```
CREATE USER BruceJones IDENTIFIED BY BJ999123;

GRANT CREATE TABLE, CREATE VIEW, CREATE INDEX TO BruceJones;
GRANT SELECT ON Program TO BruceJones, Scott WITH GRANT OPTION;
```

Example 8: Remove query access of **Program** from **Bruce Jones** and all privileges from **Stalker:**

```
REVOKE SELECT ON PROGRAM FROM BruceJones;
REVOKE ALL FROM Stalker;
```

Development Privileges

An application developer should have the following system privileges:

Create Session	Create Table	Create Sequence	Create View
Create Trigger	Create Synonym	Create Procedure	Create Tablespace
Analyze Any	Insert Any Table	Select Any Dictionary	

The **Create-Session** privilege is required for logging onto Oracle and starting a work session. The **Analyze-Any** privilege is useful for database performance analysis and tuning (discussed in chapter 21). The **Select-Any-Dictionary** privilege is required in order to query the system catalog (to be discussed in the upcoming chapter). The other privileges are all self-explanatory, and need no further clarification at this point.

Roles

In managing multiple users in different user groups, *roles* are particularly useful. You can define a role to consist of several privileges, and then grant the role to users. Additionally, roles can be granted to other roles. A role is created via the **Create-Role** statement, modified by the **Alter-Role** statement, and removed via the **Drop-Role** statement. Figure 13-9 shows abridged formats of these statements.

```
Create-Role ::=
CREATE ROLE [<Schema>.] <RoleName>
[NOT IDENTIFIED] |
[IDENTIFIED BY <Password>] |
[IDENTIFIED USING [<Schema>.] <Package>] |
[IDENTIFIED EXTERNALLY | GLOBALLY];

Alter-Role ::=
ALTR ROLE [<Schema>.] <RoleName>
[NOT IDENTIFIED] |
[IDENTIFIED BY <Password>] |
[IDENTIFIED USING [<Schema>.] <Package>] |
[IDENTIFIED EXTERNALLY | GLOBALLY];

Drop-Role ::=
DROP ROLE [<Schema>.] <RoleName>;
```

Figure 13-9. Create-Role, Alter-Role and Drop-Role Statements

Note: To create a role, you need to have the **Create-Any-Role** system privilege (the **Any** is optional; if supplied, you can create a role in any schema; if omitted, you can create roles in your schema only). Only role owners and users with **Alter-Any-Role** and **Drop-Any-Role** system privileges can modify or delete a role.

Example 9: Create a role called **Developer** with appropriate privileges and grant the role to Bruce Jones:

```
CREATE ROLE Developer;
GRANT CREATE SESSION, CREATE TABLE,  CREATE SEQUENCE, CREATE VIEW, CREATE ROLE,
CREATE PROCEDURE, CREATE TRIGGER, CREATE TABLESPACE , CREATE SYNONYM,
INSERT ANY TABLE, ANALYZE ANY, SELECT ANY DICTIONARY TO Developer;

GRANT Developer TO BruceJones WITH ADMIN OPTION;
```

You can use terms such as ANY, ALL, NONE and EXCEPT in assigning privileges.

Example 10: The following examples illustrate the use of these keywords:

```
ALTER USER BruceJones DEFAULT ROLE ALL;

ALTER USER Bremar DEFAULT ROLE ALL EXCEPT DBARole;
/*where DBARole is defined */

ALTER USER KClub DEFAULT ROLE Connect, Developer;
/*where Connect and Developer are defined */

GRANT CREATE  ANY ROLE, DROP ANY ROLE to BruceJones;

ALTER USER Stalker DEFAULT NONE;
```

13.2.3 Access to the System Data

Access to system data can be managed in one of three ways:

- Through object privileges

- Through logical views

- Through intricate database design

Security via Object Privileges

Object privileges apply to specific database objects and are sometimes referred to as SUDI (select, update, delete, and insert) privileges. Below (Figure 13-10) is a list of possible object privileges and the relevant types of database object to which they apply:

Privilege	Objects Applicable
ALTER	Table & Sequence
DELETE	Table, View, Sequence, Procedure
EXECUTE	Procedure
INDEX	Table
INSERT	Table & View
REFERENCE	Table
SELECT	Table, View, Sequence
UPDATE	Table & View

Figure 13-10. *Object Privileges*

The **Grant** statement is used to issue object privileges. When used for this purpose, the following rules apply:

- The **ON-Clause** is required.

- The privilege specified must be an object privilege, or the keyword ALL.

Example 11: The following examples assume the prior creation of the user accounts specified:

```
GRANT SELECT, UPDATE ON Student TO BruceJones;
GRANT ALL ON STUDENT TO Boss;
GRANT SELECT ON Pgm_Struct TO PUBLIC; /* granted to all users */
GRANT UPDATE ON Dept TO BruceJones, Developer /*granted to user and role */
```

Example 12: The following statement revokes UPDATE privilege on table Student, for user **BruceJones**.

```
REVOKE UPDATE ON Student FROM BruceJones;
```

Security via Views

As stated in the previous section, views can be used to enhance system security by allowing users to access only what is relevant to them. Conversely, views can be used to prevent users from accessing data for which they have no access privilege.

Example 13: Referring to the college database of earlier discussions, develop a set of logical views that allow department heads to have access to student information if and only if the student is enrolled in a major offered by that department:

```
CREATE VIEW CSMajors (Stud#, Sname, Fname, Sex, Major)
AS SELECT S.Stud#, S.Sname, S.Fname, S.Sex, P.Pgmname AS Major FROM Student S, Program P WHERE
    S.Spgm# IN ('BSC1', 'BSC2', 'BSC5') AND S.Spgm# = P.Pgm#;
...
CREATE VIEW MathMajors (Stud#, Sname, Fname, Sex, Major)
AS SELECT S.Stud#, S.Sname, S.Fname, S.Sex, P.Pgmname AS Major FROM Student S, Program P WHERE
    S.Spgm# IN ('BSC4', 'BSC5') AND S.Spgm# = P.Pgm#;
...

REVOKE ALL ON CSMajors FROM PUBLIC;
GRANT SELECT ON CSMajors TO BruceJones; /* Assume BruceJones is Chair for Computer Science */
...
REVOKE ALL ON MathMajors FROM PUBLIC;
GRANT SELECT ON MathMajors TO TimMaitland; /* Assume TimMaitland Chair for Mathematics */
```

Note: You can block direct access to data in a base table (for example **Student**), and force users to access the data through logical views on the table. These logical views can in turn have restricted access to specific users as illustrated.

Security via Database Design

In addition to views, a database designer may design database tables with security attributes that will subsequently be used to control user access. Only authorized users will have access to these security attributes, but they can be used to block other users from accessing sensitive data. However, you would be required to create and maintain some additional tables (an example of this approach appears in [Foster, 1999]).

13.3 Materialized Views

Oracle supports database objects called *materialized view*s. A materialized view is a database object that stores the results of a query. It differs from the traditional logical view in that whereas the logical view stores the definition of the query, the materialized view stores the result of the query. A materialized view would therefore qualify as a snapshot relation (review chapter 3). A full discussion of materialized views is beyond the scope of this course; however, a brief introduction is worthwhile.

The **From-Clause** of the sub-query that feeds a materialized view can name tables, views, and other materialized views. Collectively these are called *master tables* (a replication term) or *detail tables* (a data warehouse term). Databases that contain the master tables are called the *master databases*.

Materialized views are used in replication environments, as well as in data warehousing (to be discussed in chapter 24). In replication environments, the materialized views commonly created are *primary key views*, *rowed views*, *object views*, and *sub-query views*. For data warehousing purposes, the materialized views commonly created are materialized aggregate views, single-table materialized aggregate views, and materialized join views.

To create a materialized view in your own schema, you need the following system privileges:

- Create Materialized View

- Create Table or Create Any Table

- Select Any Table

To create a materialized view in another user's schema, you need the following system privileges:

- Create Any Materialized View

- Create Table or Create Any Table

- Select Any Table

If you desire to create a materialized view with QUERY REWRITE enabled (see syntax below), then in addition to the above-mentioned privileges, the following must hold:

- The owner of the master tables must have the QUERY REWRITE system privilege.

- If you are not the owner of the master tables, you must have the GLOBAL QUERY REWRITE system privilege or the QUERY REWRITE object privilege on each table outside your schema.

- If the schema owner does not own the master tables, then the schema owner must have the GLOBAL QUERY REWRITE privilege or the QUERY REWRITE object privilege on each table outside the schema.

- If you are defining the materialized view on a pre-built container (see syntax below), you must have the Select privilege WITH GRANT OPTION on the container table.

The user whose schema contains the materialized view must have sufficient quota in the target tablespace to store the materialized view's master table and index, or must have the UNLIMITED TABLESPACE system privilege.

13.3.1 Creating a Materialized View

The Create-Materialized-View statement is used for creating materialized views. The syntax is shown in Figure 13-11.

Create-Materialized-View ::=
CREATE MATERIALIZED VIEW [<Schema>.] <ViewName> [(<ColumnName> {, <ColumnName>})]
[OF [<Schema>.] <ObjectType>] [(Scoped-Table-Ref-Constraint)]
Properties-Spec | Prebuilt-Spec
[Using-Index-Clause] [Create-Mv-Refresh]
[FOR UPDATE] [ENABLE | DISABLE QUERY REWRITE]
AS Subquery;

Using-Index-Clause ::= No-Index-Option | Index-Option
No-Index-Option ::= USING NO INDEX
Index-Option ::= USING INDEX {Physical-Attributes-Clause | Tablespace-Spec}

Tablespace-Spec ::= TABLESPACE <Tablespace>

Scoped-Table-Ref-Constraint ::=
SCOPE FOR (<Ref-Column> | <Ref-Attribute>) IS [<Schema>.] <ScopeTable>
{, SCOPE FOR (<Ref-Column> | <Ref-Attribute>) IS [<Schema>.] <ScopeTable>}

Properties-Spec ::=
Physical-Properties Materialized-View-Props

Prebuilt-Spec ::=
ON PREBUILT TABLE [WITH | WITHOUT REDUCED PRECISION]

Physical-Properties ::= /* as defined in Create-Table statement (see chapter 11) */

Physical-Attributes-Clause ::= /* as defined in Create-Table statement (see chapter 11) */

Materialized-View-Props ::=
[Column-Properties] [Table-Partitioning-Clause] [CACHE | NOCACHE [Parallel-Clause]
[BUILD IMMEDIATE | DEFERRED]

Column-Properties ::= /* as defined in Create-Table statement (see chapter 11) */

Table-Partitioning-Clause ::= /* as defined in Create-Table statement (see chapter 11) */

Parallel-Clause ::= /* as defined in Create-Table statement (see chapter 11) */

Create-Mv-Refresh ::=
REFRESH
[FAST | COMPLETE | FORCE] [ON DEMAND | COMMIT]
[START WITH <Date>] [NEXT <Date>]
[[WITH PRIMARY KEY] | [WITH ROWID]]
[USING DEFAULT [MASTER | LOCAL] ROLLBACK SEGMENT]
[USING [MASTER | LOCAL] ROLLBACK SEGMENT <Rollback-Segment>]

Subquery ::= /* as defined in Select statement (review chapter 12) */

Figure 13-11. *Create-Materialized-View Statement*

Example 14: The views of example 13 are replaced by materialized views below:

```
CREATE MATERIALIZED VIEW CSMajors
AS SELECT S.Stud#, S.Sname, S.Fname, S.Sex, P.Pgmname AS Major FROM Student S, Program P WHERE
    S.Spgm# IN ('BSC1', 'BSC2', 'BSC5') AND S.Spgm# = P.Pgm#;
…

CREATE MATERIALIZED VIEW MathMajors
AS SELECT S.Stud#, S.Sname, S.Fname, S.Sex, P.Pgmname AS Major FROM Student S, Program P WHERE
    S.Spgm# IN ('BSC4', 'BSC5') AND S.Spgm# = P.Pgm#;
…


REVOKE ALL ON CSMajors FROM PUBLIC;
GRANT SELECT ON CSMajors TO BruceJones; /* Assume BruceJones is Chair for Computer Science */
…
REVOKE ALL ON MathMajors FROM PUBLIC;
GRANT SELECT ON MathMajors TO TimMaitland; /* Assume TimMaitland Chair for Mathematics */
```

13.3.2 Altering or Dropping a Materialized View

As you no doubt expect, there is an Alter-Materialized-View statement and a Drop-Materialized-View statement. The respective syntactical structures are shown in Figure 13-12.

```
Alter-Materialized-View ::=
ALTER MATERIALIZED VIEW [ <Schema>.] <Materialized-View>
[Properties-Option]
[Alter-IOT-Clause]
[USING INDEX Physical-Attributes-Clause]
[[MODIFY Scoped-Table-Ref-Constraint] | Alter-Mv-Refresh]
[[ENABLE | DISABLE QUERY REWRITE] | COMPILE | [CONSIDER FRESH]];

Properties-Option ::=
Physical-Attributes-Clause | COMPRESS | NOCOMPRESS | CACHE | NOCACHE | Allocate-Extent-Clause |
Alter-Table-Partitioning | Parallel-Clause | Logging-Clause | LOB-Option | Modify-LOB-Option

LOB-Option ::=  LOB-Storage-Clause {, LOB-Storage-Clause}
Modify-LOB-Option ::=  Modify-LOB-Storage-Clause {, Modify-LOB-Storage-Clause}

Physical-Attributes-Clause ::= /* as defines in Create-Table statement (see chapter 11) */
LOB-Storage-Clause ::= /* as defines in Create-Table statement (see chapter 11) */
Modify-LOB-Storage-Clause ::= /* as defines in Alter-Table statement (see chapter 11) */
Alter-Table-Partitioning ::= /* as defines in Alter-Table statement (see chapter 11) */
Parallel-Clause ::=  /* as defines in Create-Table statement (chapter 11) */
Allocate-Extent-Clause ::=  /* as defines in Alter-Table statement (chapter 11) */
Alter-IOT-Clause ::= /* as defines in Alter-Table statement (chapter 11) */
Scoped-Table-Ref-Constraint ::= /* as defined in Create-Materialized-View */
Alter-Mv-Refresh ::= /* as defined for Create-Mv-Refresh in Create-Materialized-View */

Logging-Clause ::=
LOGGING | NOLOGGING

Drop-Materialized-View ::=
DROP MATERIALIZED VIEW [<Schema>.] <Materialized-View>;
```

Figure 13-12. *Alter-Materialized-View and Drop-Materialized-View Statements*

Example 15: The following statements change methods used for materialized view refresh.

```
ALTER MATERIALIZED VIEW CSMajors
  REFRESH USING DEFAULT MASTER ROLLBACK SEGMENT;
...
ALTER MATERIALIZED VIEW MathMajors
  REFRESH WITH PRIMARY KEY;
```

13.4 Summary and Concluding Remarks

Let us summarize what we have covered in this chapter:

- A logical view is a virtual relation that allows end users to access information in a manner that is consistent with their requirements. The view is created by the **Create-View** statement, which simply allows few required keywords to be inserted ahead of a query (see Figure 13-2).

- The view is treated just like a normal base table. It can be designed to be updateable or read-only.

- The **Alter-View** statement facilitates modification of the view, and the **Drop-View** statement facilitates deletion of the view.

- Views are very beneficial in enhancing logical data independence, facilitation of assorted external views of the database, simplification of the perception of end users, and enhancing system security.

- SQL facilitates the enforcement of a stringent security mechanism at three levels: access to the system, access to system resources, and access to data.

- Access to the system is controlled by profiles and user accounts. SQL provides statements for creating, altering and dropping of profiles as well as user accounts.

- Access to system resources is controlled by privileges and roles. You can grant privileges and/or roles to users via the **Grant** statement, and revoke them via the **Revoke** statement. You can lump privileges together by creating a role via the **Create-Role** statement, and then granting the privileges to the role. The role can then be granted to or revoked from other users. Of course, a role can be altered (via the **Alter-Role** statement) and dropped (via the **Drop-Role** statement).

- Access to system data can be controlled through object privileges to base tables, logical views and object privileges to them, or intricate database design.

- A materialized view is a database view that stores both definition and the result of the related sub-query. It therefore qualifies as a snapshot relation. You can create, alter and drop materialized views via the **Create-Materialized-View** statement, the **Alter-Materialized-View** statement and the **Drop-Materialized-View** statement respectively.

Logical views constitute a very important part of a database, providing a number of conveniences that translate to improved efficiency, flexibility and productivity. As you will see in the upcoming chapter, they also form an integral part of the database system catalog.

13.5 Review Questions

1. What is a logical view? Discuss the importance and usefulness of logical views in a database.

2. When are views updateable and when are they not? Discuss.

3. Practice writing SQL statements to define logical views for various scenarios. Use the sample college database as your model.

4. Briefly explain the three levels of security in a typical database system. Explain how Oracle's implementation of SQL facilitates these three levels.

5. Improve on your college database (from chapter 11) by doing the following:

    a. Create a user profile called **EndUser,** for your database. Create a second profile called **Developer**.

    b. Create two roles: one for each profile (you may call them **EndUserR** and **DeveloperR** respectively). Grant appropriate system privileges to these roles.

    c. Create two users: **BruceEnd** and **BruceDev. BruceEnd** must belong to profile **EndUser**, with default role **EndUserR; BruceDev** must belong to profile **Developer**, with default role **DeveloperR**. Both users must have your tablespace (created from chapter 11) as their default tablespace, with QUOTA UNLIMITED.

      d.   Grant full access of all your database objects created so far to user **BruceDev**. Grant limited access of your database objects to user **BruceEnd**.

      e.   Alternately log on to the system as **BruceDev** and then **BruceEnd**, and check to see whether the privilege restrictions you have set are taking effect.

6.   Practice writing SQL statements to manipulate system and object privileges. Test with your account (assumed to be **System** or **SysDBA**), **BruceDev** and **BruceEnd**.

7.   What are materialized views? Discuss their relevance usefulness. When would you use a materialized view versus a traditional logical view, and vice versa?

8.   Describe a situation that would warrant the use of a materialized view in your college database. Write an SQL statement to define that materialized view.

9.   Practice writing SQL statements to modify materialized views.

13.6 References and/or Recommended Readings

[Connolly, 2002] Connolly, Thomas and Carolyn Begg. *Database Systems: A Practical Approach to Design, Implementation and Management* 3rd ed. New York, NY: Addison-Wesley, 2002. See Chapter 18.

[Couchman, 1999] Couchman, Jason and Christopher Allen. *Oracle Certified Professional: Application Developer Guide.* New York, NY: Osborne/McGraw-Hill, 1999. See Chapter 4.

[Date, 2004] Date, Christopher J. *Introduction to Database Systems* 8th ed. Menlo Park, California: Addison-Wesley, 2004. See Chapters 9 and 17.

[Elmasri, 2007] Elmasri, Ramez and Shamkant B. Navathe. *Fundamentals of Database Systems* 5th ed. Reading, MA: Addison-Wesley, 2007. See Chapter 23.

[Foster, 1999] Foster, Elvis C. *Labour Market Information System: Thesis.* Kingston, Jamaica: Department of Mathematics and Computer Science, University of the West Indies, 1999. See Chapter 4 and appendix 8.

[Oracle, 2008] Oracle Corporation. *SQL Reference.* http://www.oracle.com/technology/index.html (accessed August 2008).

[Shah, 2002] Shah, Nilesh. *Database Systems Using Oracle: A Simplified Guide to SQL and PL/SQL.* Upper Saddle River, NJ: Prentice Hall, 2002. See Chapter 13.

CHAPTER 14

■ ■ ■

The System Catalog

Every reputable DBMS contains a system catalog (also called the data dictionary) of some form. This has been alluded to several times earlier in the course. This chapter discusses this very important component of the database system. The chapter proceeds under the following subtopics:

- Introduction
- Three Important Catalog Tables
- Other Catalog Tables
- Querying the System Catalog
- Updating the System Catalog
- Summary and Concluding Remarks

14.1 Introduction

The system catalog (data dictionary) is perhaps the most important database object in a database system. This is so because it facilitates and supports all or most of the other database objects. The system catalog typically contains *metadata* about the database. By metadata, we mean data about other data. This catalog itself consists of relational tables, which can be manipulated using SQL statements. The system catalog provides the following benefits:

- The system catalog, by maintaining metadata in the form of other relational tables, facilitates most (if not all) of the other database objects. This fulfills the requirements of the Zero Rule of Chapter 9.

- Through the system catalog, the DBMS is able to deliver on the requirements of physical and logical data independence (Chapters 1 and 9) in a sleek manner.

- Through the system catalog, the DBMS is able to deliver on the requirement of integrity independence (Chapters 4, 5 and 9).

- System and object privileges (discussed in the previous chapter) are stored in special catalog tables, thus facilitating the management of the security mechanisms of the database.

- As you will see later in the course (Chapter 22), the system catalog also facilitates the successful implementation of distributed database systems.

The rest of this chapter will focus on aspects of the system catalog, as implemented in Oracle. Note however, that all features of the Oracle catalog may not apply to catalogs of other DBMS suites; also there may be features of others, not included in the Oracle catalog. Note also that a comprehensive discussion of the Oracle data dictionary is beyond the scope and intent of this course; the discussion here is necessarily cursory, but detailed enough to give you a good appreciation of the subject matter.

The Oracle system catalog contains system tables for various database objects: Figure 14-1 provides some of the most commonly referenced objects that are facilitated by the system catalog.

Tablespaces	Datafiles	Tables	Sequences
Tab_Columns	Constraints (on tables)	Cons_columns	Synonyms
Indexes	Users	Roles	Privileges
Tab_comments	Col_comments	Views	

Figure 14-1. *Commonly Referenced Catalog Tables*

These tables are automatically maintained by the DBMS in a manner that is transparent to the user. Oracle allows manipulation of catalog tables only through views. For each table, three views are often available: the view that has the prefix **DBA** (for all database objects), a view that has the prefix **USER** (for the objects owned by the current user), and a view that has the prefix **ALL** (for all objects that are accessible to the current user). However, there are exceptions to this rule. Additionally, views prefixed by **V$** are dynamic performance views which can be queried, irrespective of your schema, provided that you have the appropriate privilege. Finally, views prefixed by **GV$** are global dynamic views.

14.2 Three Important Catalog Tables

To illustrate the importance of the system catalog, let us focus our attention on three important catalog tables: **Tables**, **Tab_Columns** and **Indexes**. We will focus on three views on these tables: **User_Tables, User_Tab_Columns** and **User_Indexes.**

14.2.1 The User_Tables View

This catalog view is based on the underlying table **Tables** (the DB2 equivalent being **Systables**). It contains a row for every base table in the user's schema. When a user account is created, Oracle creates a schema with the same name as the user name.

All objects created by that user are linked to his/her schema, and are eventually stored in a **tablespace,** the default tablespace carrying the name **System** (for a full discussion of tablespaces, see the Oracle production documentation).

To observe the structure of **User_Tables**, you may invoke the describe statement thus:

```
DESCRIBE User_Tables;
```

You will observe that the table contains a number of columns. Among the ones of immediate concern are those indicated in Figure 14-2.

Owner:	The user who created the object
Table_Name:	Name of database table
Tablespace_Name:	Name of tablespace in which it is stored
Num_Rows:	Number of rows

Figure 14-2. *Columns of User_Tables*

14.2.2 The User_Tab_Columns View

This catalog view is based on the underlying table **Tab_Columns** (DB2 equivalent being **Syscolumns**). It contains a row for every column of every table mentioned in **User_Tables**. Figure 14-3 shows the columns of immediate concern.

Table_Name:	Name of database table
Column_Name:	Name of column in the table
Data_Type:	Data type of the column
Data_Length:	Length of the column
Data_Precision:	Number of decimal places of column
Data_Default:	Default value of column

Figure 14-3. *Columns of Tab_Columns*

14.2.3 The User_Indexes View

This catalog view is based on the underlying table **Indexes** (DB2 equivalent being **Sysindexes**). It contains a row for every index in the user's schema. Some columns of interest are mentioned in Figure 14-4.

Index_Name:	Name of index
Table_Owner:	User who created the table
Index_Type:	Type of index
Table_Name:	Name of table indexed
Num_Rows:	Number of rows indexed

Figure 14-4. Columns of User_Indexes

Figure 14-5 provides a simplified illustration of what the catalog data would be, assuming that the database consists of the tables mentioned in the sample college database that we have been referencing (since Chapter 7).

User_Tables:

Table_Name	Tablespace	Num_Rows	...
Student	System	8	
Program	System	2	
Hall	System	2	
Dept	System	4	
Division	System	3	
Course	System	2	
Staff	System	2	
PgmStruct	System	2	

User_Indexes:

Index_Name	Table_Name	Table_Owner	...
xStud	Student	BruceJones	
xStud2	Student	BruceJones	
xProgram	Program	BruceJones	
xProgram2	Program	BruceJones	
xHall	Hall	BruceJones	
xDept	Dept	BruceJones	
xDept2	Dept	BruceJones	
xDept3	Dept	BruceJones	
xDiv	Division	BruceJones	
xDiv2	Division	BruceJones	
xCourse	Course	BruceJones	
xCourse2	Course	BruceJones	
xStaff	Staff	BruceJones	
xStaff2	Staff	BruceJones	
xPgm_Struct	Pgm_Struct	BruceJones	
xPgm_Struct2	Pgm_Struct	BruceJones	

User_Tab_Columns:

Column_Name	Table_Name	Data_Type	...
Stud#	Student	Integer	
Sname	Student	Varchar2	
Fname	Student	Varchar2	
...			
Pgm#	Program	Char	
Pgmname	Program	Varchar2	
...			
Crs#	Course	Char	
Crsname	Course	Varchar2	
...			
Dept#	Dept	Char	
Dname	Dept	Varchar2	
...			

Figure 14-5. *Simplified Illustration of System Catalog for College Database*

14.3 Other Important Catalog Tables

There are several other catalog tables all of which are managed in a manner transparent to the database user. Figure 14-6 provides a .list of commonly used catalog views. This list is by no means exhaustive. However, studying and probing this list will give you a good insight of the usefulness of the catalog views, as you manage the database. Do not feel disconcerted or overwhelmed if you are not familiar with all of the views listed in the figure. These you would normally cover in a course on Oracle database administration. The intent here is to give you a reasonable overview of the role and complexity of the system catalog.

View Name	Contents
V$SYSTEM_PARAMETER	Database system parameters as defined in the parameter file
V$PARAMETER	Database system parameters as defined in the parameter file
V$SESSION	Information on all current sessions running in the database
V$BACKUP	Backup status for datafiles in the database
V$BACKUP_DATAFILE	Information on files backed up via RMAN
V$BACKUP_REDOLOG	Information on archived log files backed up via RMAN
V$BACKUP_PIECE	Information on backed up pieces, updated via RMAN
V$BACKUP_SET	Information on complete, successful backups up via RMAN
V$DATABASE	Information on databases created on the machine
V$DATAFILE_HEADER	Datafile header information
V$DATAFILE	Information on datafiles associated with the database
V$CONTROLFILE	List of controlfiles for the database and their status
V$CONTROLFILE_RECORD_SECTION	Conntrolfile record information (record size, records used, etc.)
V$ARCHIVEED_LOG	Information on archived logs
V$LOGFILE	On-line redo log members of groups
V$LOG	On-line redo log groups
V$LOG_HISTORY	History of log information
V$ARCHIVE_DEST	Information about the five archive destinations, status and failures
V$ARCHIVE_PROCESSES	Status on the ten archive processes
V$PWFILE_USERS	List of users entitled to use SYSDBA and SYSOPER privs.
V$THREAD	Information on log files assigned to each instance
V$INSTANCE	List of database instances running
V$OBJECT_USAGE	List of indexes and their usage
V$PROCESS	List of processes running
V$SESSTAT	Indicates statistics for various sessions
V$LATCHNAME	List of DB latches for various sessions
V$TIMEZONE_NAMES	Valid Time-zones
V$ROLLNAME	List of all online undo segments
V$ROLLSTAT	Undo statistics. Can be joined with V$ROLLNAME
V$TABLESPACE	Information (TBS name, number and backup status) on tablespaces
V$SORT_USAGE	Information (User, Session#, tablespace, segment, extents, etc) on active sorts in the database. Can be joined with V&Session & V&SQL
V$SQL	SQL statements run by the users
V$TEMP-EXTENT-MAP	Extents of all locally Managed temporary tablespaces.
V$TEMP-EXTENT-POOL	Temporary space used and cached for the current instance for locally managed temporary tablespaces.
V$SORT-SEGMENT	Info on sort segments.
V$DATAFILE	Info on data file from the control file.
V$UNDOSTAT	10-minute snapshots reflecting the performance of the undo tablespace.
V$TEMPFILE	Info on temporary files (similar to V&DATAFILE)
V$DISPATCHER	Info on dispatchers.
V$DISPATCHER_RATE	Info on performance statistics for dispatchers.
V$QUEUE	Info on the request queue and response queues.
V$CIRCUIT	Info on Shared Server virtual circuits.
V$SHARED_SERVER	Info on shared servers in the system.
V$SHARED_SERVER_Monitor	Summary info on maximum connections, maximum servers, servers started, servers terminated, high-water level for the shared servers (combined).

Figure 14-6. *Commonly Used Catalog Views*

View Name	Contents
V$SESSION	Info on sessions
V$TIME ZONE-NAMES	Time Zones allowed
V$SORT-SEGMENT	Info about every sort segment in a given instance. Uploaded only for temporary tablespaces.
V$BACKUP_SET	Stores information on backup sets.
RC_BACKUP_SET	Stores information on backup sets. Applicable only if Recovery catalog is in place.
DBA-EXTENTS	Extents allocated for all segments in the database
DBA-FREE-SPACE	Free extents in tablespaces
DBA-SEGMENTS	Segments created in a database, their size, tablespace, type, storage forms, etc.
DBA_DATA_FILES	Information on datafile(s) for each tablespace. An alternative to joining V$TABLESPACE and V$DATAFILE.
DBA-8K-CACHE-SIZE	For Shareland block size of 8K
DBA-16K-CACHE-SIZE	For BOTHRACK size of 16 C
DBA-CACHE-SIZE	Block Size for the db
DBA_PROFILES	List of profiles.
XXX_SOURCE	The source code for programs running
XXX_OBJECTS	Objects belonging to a database
XXX_TABLES	Tables belonging to a database
XXX_TAB_COLUMNS	Columns of database tables
XXX_TAB_PRIVS	Table privileges granted to users and roles
XXX_COL_PRIVS	Column privileges granted to users and roles
XXX_INDEXES	Indexes defined on database tables
XXX_IND_COLUMNS	Columns included in each index
DBA_CONSTRAINTS	List of constraints
DBA_CONS_COLUMNS	Columns for each constraint
XXX_SYS_PRIVS	System privileges granted
DBA_ROLES	List of roles
SESSION_ROLES	Roles for the session
XXX_ROLE_PRIVS	Role privileges granted
XXX_ROLLBACK_SEGS	Information on undo segments
ROLE_SYS_PRIVS	System privileges granted to roles
ROLE_ROLE_PRIVS	Role privileges granted to other roles
ROLE_TAB_PRIVS	Table privileges granted to roles
XXX_TABLESPACES	Information (TBSName, Block-Size, Extent Info) Tablespace in the database
XXX-FREE-SPACE	Free extents available in tablespaces (for each data-file in each tablespace). Locally Managed temporary tablespaces are not included.
XXX-SEGMENTS	Info on segments and their storage parameters
XXX-EXTENTS	Info on extents (Size, assorted segments, associated tablespace).
XXX-DATAFILES	Info on data-files belongings do tablespaces
XXX-TEMP-FILES	Info no temporary files belongs to locally managed temporary tablespaces
XXX-USERS	Info (Including default tablespace allocation) on users.
XXX_VIEWS	Info on logical views
XXX-TEMP-FILES	Info on data files belonging to locally managed temporary tablespaces.
XXX-USED-EXTENTS	Info on used extents for tablespaces
XXX-ROLLBACK_SEGS	Info on rollback segments for tablespaces
DBA-UNDO-EXTENTS	Info on undo extents for tablespaces
Note: Prefix XXX means DBA, USER or ALL, e.g. DBA_SYS_PRIVS or USER_SYS_PRIVS.	

Figure 14-6. *Commonly Used Catalog Views (continued)*

14.4 Querying the System Catalog

The system catalog can be queried using SQL **Select** statements in a manner similar to any created relational table. This is one of the many remarkable features of the relational DBMS, and a powerful witness to the potency of Date's Zero Rule (see Chapter 9).

Example 1: What columns does the table **Student** have?

```
SELECT Column_Name FROM USER_TAB_COLUMNS WHERE Table_Name = 'STUDENT';
/* is equivalent to */
DESCR Student;
```

Example 2: What relation(s) contain(s) the attribute Pgm#?

```
SELECT Table_Name FROM USER_TAB_COLUMNS WHERE Column_Name IN ('Pgm#', 'PGM#');
```

Example 3: What relation(s) contain(s) an attribute that is CHAR(7)?

```
SELECT Table_Name FROM USER_TAB_COLUMNS
WHERE Data_Type = 'CHAR' AND Data_Length = 7;
```

Example 4: The catalog may be used to keep track of certain related tables, defined for a particular system. For instance, if the tables of interest are prefixed 'CMP' then the following statement will yield a list of tables of interest:

```
SELECT Table_Name FROM USER_TABLES WHERE Table_Name LIKE 'CMP%';
```

Example 5: List all logical views in the system, and all valid users:

```
SELECT * FROM DBA_VIEWS;

SELECT * FROM DBA_USERS;
```

14.5 Updating the System Catalog

Direct update (via INSERT, UPDATE, DELETE) of system catalog record, is not allowed as this would be an avenue for compromising the integrity of the database.

The system catalog is automatically updated by the system DBMS when statement such as CREATE TABLE, ALTER TABLE, DROP TABLE, CREATE VIEW, DROP VIEW, CRETE INDEX, DROP INDEX, CREATE SYNONYM, DROP SYNONYM, etc. are issued. In short, whenever a database object is created or modified, the system catalog is automatically updated by the DBMS.

The **Comment** statement is the only SQL statement that allows direct update of the system catalog by a user. It allows update of the **Comments** column in either the **Tab_Comments** table or the **Col_Comments** table. The format of the command is:

```
Comment-Satement::= COMMENT ON TABLE | COLUMN  <TableName> | <ColumnName> IS <String>;
```

Note: The column-name specified must be qualified by its table-name. The string supplied is enclosed in single quotes.

In order to understand how this statement works, you need to familiarize yourself with the structure and purpose of the catalog tables **Tab_Comments** and **Col_Comments**. The **Describe** statement will allow you to view the structure (left as an exercise). You will observe the following columns in respective tables:

```
Tab_Comments {Table_Name, Table_Type, Comments}
Col_Comments {Table_Name, Column_Name, Comments}
```

The Tab_Comments table is used to store comments on tables of the database; the Col_Comments table is used to store comments on table columns of the database. The Comment statement allows modification of these comments.

Example 6: Store comments on tables and columns of the database:

```
COMMENT ON TABLE Course IS 'The Course Relation';
COMMENT ON COLUMN Course.Crs# IS 'Course Code';
COMMENT ON COLUMN Course.Crsname IS 'Course Name';
...
/* Do this for each table in the database */
```

To access these comments, you may query any of the following the views:

- **DBA_Tab_Comments:** All table comments for the database.

- **USER_Tab_Comments:** All table comments owned by the current user.

- **ALL_Tab_Comments:** All table comments to which the current user has access.

- **DBA_Col_Comments:** All column comments for the database.

- **USER_Col_Comments:** All column comments owned by the current user.

- **ALL_Col_Comments:** All column comments to which the current user has access.

Example 7: The following statement lists table comments for tables owned by schemas beginning with the name **Bruce**:

```
SELECT SUBSTR(table_name,1,12) TabName, SUBSTR(comments,1,40) TabComment
FROM DBA_Tab_Comments WHERE Owner LIKE 'Bruce%';
```

14.6 Summary and Concluding Remarks

It is now time to summarize what has been discussed in this chapter:

- The system catalog is the most important database object in a database system. This is so because it facilitates and supports all or most of the other database objects. The system catalog typically contains metadata about the database.

- The Oracle system catalog contains system tables for various database objects including (but not confined to) tablespaces, datafiles, tables, views, table columns, constraints, indexes, users, roles, privileges, etc. Oracle does not allow direct access of its catalog tables; rather, it provides views prefixed by **DBA, ALL, USER**, and **GC$**.

- Three commonly used Oracle catalog views are **User_Tables**, **User_Tab_Columns**, and **User_Indexes**. In actuality, the Oracle catalog contains scores of catalog views (review section 14.3).

- You can query catalog views just as you would any other table. This often provides useful information to the DBA or software engineer.

- As a rule, Oracle does not allow direct update of its catalog tables. However, note that the catalog is automatically updated every time the physical or logical structure of the database is modified. The only exception to this rule is the **Comment** statement. This statement allows the specification of comments for database tables and columns.

If you consider what has been said about the system catalog in light of Date's Zero Rule and Codd's twelve rules for relational DBMS suites, you will soon realize the catalog is an absolute necessity if the DBMS is to stand up to the lofty industry expectations. To be more direct, if you are evaluating a DBMS suite and discover that it does not host a comprehensive system catalog, you are pursuing a product that is not going to stand up to much rigor; you'd be well advised to save your effort for some more meaningful project.

As powerful as useful as SQL is, the language is not without limitations. The next chapter discusses some of these limitations.

14.7 Review Questions

1. Discuss the importance of the system catalog in a database system.

2. State some commonly referenced catalog tables.

3. Discuss three important catalog tables, and explain how their use can help in the management of a database.

4. The PL/SQL **Describe** statement allows you to view the structure of a database table. Write an equivalent **Select** statement on the system catalog, that provides the same information. Use one of the tables in the sample college database as your frame of reference.

5. Review the as many of the catalog views listed in Figure 14-6 as possible, and practice writing **Select** statements on them.

6. Explain clearly, how the system catalog is maintained. Provide useful examples.

14.8 References and/or Recommended Readings

[Couchman, 1999] Couchman, Jason and Christopher Allen. *Oracle Certified Professional: Application Developer Guide.* New York, NY: Osborne/McGraw-Hill, 1999. See Chapter 3.

[Martin, 1995] Martin, James, and Joe Leben. *Client/Server Databases: Enterprise Computing.* Upper Saddle River, NJ: Prentice Hall, 1995. See Chapter 5.

[Oracle, 2008] Oracle Corporation. *SQL Reference.* http://www.oracle.com/technology/index.html (accessed August 2008).

[Ullman, 1997] Ullman, Jeffrey D., and Jennifer Widom. *A First Course in Database Systems.* Upper Saddle River, NJ: Prentice Hall, 1997. See Chapter 7.

CHAPTER 15

■ ■ ■

Some Limitations of SQL

As can be seen from Chapters 11 – 14, SQL is a very powerful programming language, ideally suited for the management of databases. However, like all languages, SQL has limitations. This chapter briefly examines some of these limitations. The chapter proceeds as follows:

- Programming Limitations
- Limitations on Views
- Foreign Key Constraint Specification
- Superfluous Enforcement of Referential Integrity
- Limitations on Calculated Columns
- If-Then Limitation
- Summary and Concluding Remarks

15.1 Programming Limitations

While SQL is a very sophisticated fourth generation language (4GL) for database management, it does not have many facilities that are normally present in a traditional high-level language (HLL). These include user interface programming and traditional internal processing facilities for basic data structures. The truth is, SQL was never intended for these facilities. SQL is therefore most effective in an environment where it is embedded in HLL code. The HLL may be the host language of a DBMS, or some other language that the DBMS supports.

Quite often, in complex software development projects, the developer will encounter situations where a single SQL statement is inadequate to service the needs of the user. What is required is a series of SQL statements (and possibly non-SQL statements). The limitations on logical views (discussed in the following section) provide a case in point. Again, an HLL support is often a perfect antidote for these scenarios.

15.2 Limitations on Views

The limitations on logical views were mentioned in Chapter 13 (sections 13.1 and 13.2), without much elaboration. Let us revisit this matter here.

291

15.2.1 Restriction on use of the Order-By-Clause

When a view is created, the **Order-By-Clause** is not supported in the sub-query. This means that you cannot create a view that orders data. The rationale for this limitation is that a view is a virtual relation, and therefore ordering of the data would only increase system overheads. The obvious response to this argument is this: since a view merely stores a definition, why not include data ordering in the definition?

The work-around for this limitation is to create the view (obviously without ordering data), then when the view is being accessed via a query, employ the **Order-By-Clause** on the query.

Example 1: Creation of the College Bulletin from the college database of earlier discussions:

```
CREATE VIEW Bulletin (PsPgm#, Pgmname, PsCrsSeqn, PsCrs#, Crsname)
AS SELECT PsPgm#, Pgmname, PsCrsSeqn, PsCrs#, Crsname FROM Pgm_Struct PS, Program P, Course
    C WHERE  PS.PsPgm# = P.Pgm# AND PS.PsCrs# = C.Crs#;
...
SELECT * FROM Bulletin ORDER BY PsPgm#, PsCrsSeqn;
```

15.2.2 Restriction on Data Manipulation for Views involving UNION, INTERSECT or JOIN

As pointed out in Chapter 13, a view is not updateable if it involves a JOIN, a UNION or an INTERSECT operation. A little thought will reveal that while this is an understandable constraint, it is not always a prudent one, as there are situations that could warrant updateable views involving these operations (for more elaboration, see [Date, 2004]).

The example above is a useful illustration: it should be possible for a user to modify **Pgmname** and/or **Crsnme** for a logical row in **Bulletin** as follows:

- If **Pgmname** is modified, the DBMS should use **Pgm#** to access the correct row in the table **Program** and modify its corresponding column for **Pgmname**.

- If **Crsname** is modified, the DBMS should use Crs# to access the correct row in the table Course and modify its corresponding column for **Crsname**.

In either case, the search for a corresponding column must not be made merely on the column name (since queries can rename columns), but the name as well as characteristics of the column (which can be obtained from the system catalog).

Note: Administering changes (insertion, update or deletion of rows) to join logical views of this sort is by no means a trivial matter, hence SQL does not support it. The point to note here is that it is thinkable and indeed doable, though complex. A similar argument applies to logical views involving UNION and INTERSECT operations.

15.3 Foreign Key Constraint Specification

Some implementations of SQL (example early versions of Gupta SQL-Windows) do not provide the designer the flexibility of specifying which attribute(s) of a referenced table are to be considered when a foreign key constraint is defined.

Example 2: Referring to the college database of Chapter 7, the following is what a Gupta SQL-Windows specification for the foreign keys of the **Pgm_Struct** table would look like:

```
ALTER TABLE Pgm_Struct FOREIGN KEY (PsPgm#) REFERENCES Program;
ALTER TABLE Pgm_Struct FOREIGN KEY (PsCrs#) REFERENCES Course;
```

Note: Gupta SQL-Windows has since been upgraded to Team Developer; therefore, this example is not a commentary on the current product. The [previous SQL] syntax did not allow for the designer to specify which attribute in the referenced relation is to be used. Rather, the DBMS chose the attribute with similar characteristics to the referencing attribute (i.e. the foreign key). This idea is good for basic scenarios; however, if there are more than one attribute in the referenced relation with similar characteristics to the foreign key, confusion could arise.

Work-around: The obvious work-around for a scenario like this is to allow the designer to explicitly specify which attribute of the referenced relation is to be used in the foreign key constraint. Oracle does this quite nicely; the specification for this scenario might be as follows:

```
ALTER TABLE Pgm_Struct
ADD CONSTRAINT PSForeign1 FOREIGN KEY (PsPgm#) REFERENCES Program (Pgm#)
ADD CONSTRAINT PSForeign2 FOREIGN KEY (PsCrs#) REFERENCES Course (Crs#);
```

15.4 Superfluous Enforcement of Referential Integrity

Some implementations of SQL exhibit a superfluous enforcement of the referential integrity rule with respect to update of non-key attributes of tuples in a referenced relation.

Example 3: Suppose that we have a course — M100 College Algebra — that occurs in all academic programs. We wish to change the description of the course to "Elementary Algebra", thus:

```
UPDATE Course SET CrsName = 'Elementary Algebra' WHERE Crs# = 'M100';
```

Note: Some DBMSs (e.g. Oracle) will forbid this update, since M100 would be a referenced tuple. This might be considered imprudent. What might be required is a restriction on deletion, not update of this sort.

Work-around: Oracle avoids this situation quite elegantly, by allowing the designer to temporarily **disable** a constraint, and **enable** it at a subsequent time. If your DBMS does not have this kind of facility, what you may have to do is drop the foreign key constraint from the referencing table(s), make the update, and then reintroduce the foreign key constraint.

Example 4: Here is an illustration of how you could circumvent the problem in Oracle:

```
ALTER TABLE Pgm_Struct DISABLE CONSTRAINT PSForeign2;
/* or   ALTER TABLE Pgm_Struct MODIFY CONSTRAINT PSForeign2 DISABLE; */

UPDATE Course SET CrsName = 'Elementary Algebra' WHERE Crs# = 'M100';

ALTER TABLE Pgm_Struct ENABLE CONSTRAINT PSForeign2;
/* or   ALTER TABLE Pgm_Struct MODIFY CONSTRAINT PSForeign2 ENABLE; */
```

15.5 Limitations on Calculated Columns

In most implementations of SQL (that this writer has worked with), you are forbidden to specify a virtual (calculated) column in a Group-By-Cause, Having-Clause, or a Where-Clause in the same Select statement (this excludes accessing virtual columns in nested queries as demonstrated in section 12.10 of Chapter 12). Neither can you define a virtual (calculated) column in terms of another calculated column in the same Select statement.

Example 5: Consider a table that is keyed on a numeric attribute, **Trans_Date**, that stores the date (YYYYMMDD format). One might want to create a virtual attribute, **Trans_Year**, that stores the year only (first four bytes of **Trans_Date**), and cumulate another column of the table, based on **Trans_Year**. In the writer's experience, this cannot be done in a straightforward manner.

Work-around: One obvious work-around would be as follows:

1. Create a logical view with the virtual column;

2. Write a query on the view, grouping on the virtual column.

Alternate Work-around: An alternate work-around is to simply restate the calculated expression wherever it is needed within the query.

Example 6: Example 33 from Chapter 12 is repeated here to illustrate the point: We desire a list from the employee table (of the Oracle default database), showing for each department, the total salary, average salary, minimum salary, maximum salary and standard deviation; we want to show only departments with a total salary of at least $600,000:

```
// This will not run in Oracle
SELECT Deptno, SUM(Sal) AS TotalSal, AVG(Sal) AS Average, MAX(Sal) AS MaxSal,
MIN(Sal) AS MinSal, STDDEV(Sal) AS StdDev FROM Emp GROUP BY Deptno
HAVING TotalSal >= 60000;

// This will run in Oracle
SELECT Deptno, SUM(Sal) AS TotalSal, AVG(Sal) AS Average, MAX(Sal) AS MaxSal,
MIN(Sal) AS MinSal, STDDEV(Sal) AS StdDev FROM Emp GROUP BY Deptno
HAVING SUM(Sal) >= 60000;
```

Notice that in the **Having-Clause**, the calculated column **TotSal** cannot be used. You have to specify the expression used for the derived column.

Example 7: Referring to the default Oracle database, suppose we want to list employees beyond a certain hire year. Following is an incorrect SQL statement followed by a correct SQL statement for the problem:

```
SELECT Empno, Ename, SUBSTR(TO_CHAR(Hiredate, 'YYYYMMDD'),1,4) HireYear FROM Emp
WHERE HireYear >= 1985; /* Will not run. You cannot use a calculated column in this way */

SELECT Empno, Ename, SUBSTR(TO_CHAR(Hiredate, 'YYYYMMDD'),1,4) HireYear FROM Emp
 WHERE SUBSTR(TO_CHAR(Hiredate, 'YYYYMMDD'),1,4) >= 1985; /*This will run successfully */
```

15.6 If-Then Limitation

In Chapter 8 (section 8.2), it was mentioned that one form of a WFF is as follows:

> If <Condition> then <WFF>

It appears that this format is seldom implemented in typical SQL implementations (though there are deviations of it). The work-around is to apply the appropriate standardization rule (review section 8.4 of Chapter 8), which is shown below:

> If A then B <=> (A)' or B.

This is by no means a significant setback. One can get by without ever using an if-then construct, and simply using its equivalent.

15.7 Summary and Concluding Remarks

Here is a summary of what was covered in this chapter:

- SQL is a powerful language, but not without limitations. The first is that SQL is a database language by design and intent. It does not include features for building complex user interfaces, because it was not intended to.

- You are not allowed to use the **Order-By-Clause** on SQL views. Additionally, a view is not updateable if it includes the use of the set operator UNION, INTERSECT, or JOIN.

- Some implementations of SQL do not provide the designer the flexibility of specifying which attribute(s) of a referenced table are to be considered when a foreign key constraint is defined.

- Some implementations of SQL exhibit a superfluous enforcement of the referential integrity rule with respect to update of non-key attributes of rows in a referenced relation.

- You are not allowed to define a calculated column in terms of another calculated column in the same query, or to reference a calculated column in the same **Select** statement.

- It appears that the if-then construct is not widely supported in SQL.

Fortunately, there is a work-around for each limitation. This is perhaps why SQL is so popular: its benefits far outweigh its limitations. We can therefore expect that SQL will continue to be the universal database language a long time yet.

This brings us to the end of our study of SQL. The next five chapters provide an overview of five commonly used DBMS suites.

15.8 Review Questions

1. What are the programming limitations of SQL? As a software engineer, how do you make up for these limitations?

2. Discuss the limitations of SQL with respect to logical views. What are the implications of these limitations?

3. What problems relating to referential integrity are often present in implementations of SQL? How are these problems addressed in Oracle 10g?

4. Describe the SQL limitation on calculated columns. Carefully explain how it can be circumvented.

15.9 Recommended Readings

[Date, 2004] Date, Christopher J. *Introduction to Database Systems* 8th ed. Menlo Park, CA: Addison-Wesley, 2004. See Chapters 4 and 10.

[Oracle, 2008] Oracle Corporation. *SQL Reference.* http://www.oracle.com/technology/index.html (accessed August 2008).

PART D

■ ■ ■

Some Commonly Used DBMS Suites

This division allows you to peruse through a professional summary of six commonly used DBMS suites. Two of the products are regarded as comprehensive (front-end and back-end) products; two are regarded as a back-end products; one is regarded as a front-end product. While the products chosen are widely regarded as leaders in their respective categories, these chapters are not to be regarded as promotion of the products. In fact, it should be noted that the software engineering industry is rich with excellent alternatives to the products discussed in the division.

The primary purpose of the division is to expose you to six excellent DBMS alternatives. The chapters to be covered include:

- Chapter 16 — Overview of Oracle
- Chapter 17 — Overview of DB2
- Chapter 18 — Overview of Microsoft SQL Server
- Chapter 19 — Overview of MySQL
- Chapter 20 — Overview of Delphi

There are several other products that time will not allow for us to explore. Included in this list are the following

- Ingres
- Informix
- Sybase

It is hoped that the ones covered will provide you with the impetus to go on and explore more about them, as well as others not covered in the text.

PART D

Some Commonly Used DBMS Suites

CHAPTER 16

■ ■ ■

Overview of Oracle

This chapter provides an overview of the Oracle DBMS. Actually, you have been exposed to Oracle throughout division three, since the implementation of SQL that we have studied is Oracle-based. The chapter proceeds under the following subheadings.

- Introduction
- Main Components of the Oracle Suite
- Shortcomings of Oracle
- Summary and Concluding Remarks

16.1 Introduction

Oracle is widely regarded as one of the world's leading RDBMS suites. The product was developed by a company that bears the same name as the product. The product, unlike many of its competitors has benefited from a very focused corporate mission. The Oracle DBMS was first introduced in the 1980's. By the early 1990's Oracle Corporation was the world's leading software engineering company. Today it consistently shares an overall second position with IBM (behind the phenomenal Microsoft), and first in the areas of database management systems and internet applications.

The Oracle suite is a comprehensive package of software development tools for developing, as well as managing an information system with an underlying Oracle database. The product has been through several stages of revision and upgrade. The latest version is Oracle11G, which supports grid computing and no upper limit on database size. By the time this volume is published, Oracle 11G will be in production in many organizations.

In terms of connectivity, Oracle communicates with all the major alternate DBMS suites in the industry (typically via ODBC) — DB2, Sybase, Informix, Ingress, MS SQL Server, and MySQL.

The Oracle suite is marketed for major modern operating systems including, Windows, Unix, and Linux. The following are the Oracle product editions currently marketed:

- Enterprise Edition
- Standard Edition
- Standard Edition One

- Express Edition

- Personal Edition

These editions all come with various components and features to service different needs. Typically, when you purchase Oracle, you specify what edition you are interested in. You will be allowed to install the appropriate edition when you access the Oracle CDs.

Some advantages of the Oracle DBMS suite are:

- The product is recognized as one of the leading DBMS suites in the industry.

- Oracle provides a comprehensive and at times innovative implementation of SQL.

- The product supports RAD (though limited).

- The Oracle DBMS handles large databases very effectively.

- Oracle handles distributed databases quite well.

- Oracle also handles object databases quite well.

- Oracle facilitates the construction and management of small, medium sized, and large data warehouses.

- Oracle facilitates communication with other databases.

- The Oracle DBMS hosts a comprehensive system catalog, thus allowing it to effectively handle complex databases consisting of different types of objects.

- Oracle provides a user interface that encourages Oracle experts, while facilitating novices.

- Oracle provides availability and scalability with grid computing, industry-leading security, lower costs with its self-managing database.

16.2 Main Components of the Oracle Suite

The Oracle 11G product family includes the several main components. The more visible ones are:

- Oracle Server

- Oracle PL/SQL

- Oracle Developer

- Oracle Database Configuration Assistant (DBCA)

- Oracle Network Services

- Oracle Admin Assistant

- Oracle Database Upgrade Assistant

- Oracle Enterprise Manager (OEM) Database Control

- Oracle Enterprise Manager Grid Control

- Oracle Enterprise Manager Configuration Assistant

- Oracle HTTP Server

- Oracle Documentation

- Oracle Transparent Gateways

- Oracle Development Kit

- Oracle JDBC/OCI Interfaces

- Oracle iSQL *Plus and SQL *Plus

- Oracle Real Application Clusters

- Oracle Enterprise Integration Gateways

- Oracle Application Server

- Oracle Integration

- Oracle Internet File System

- Oracle Recovery Manager

- Oracle Warehouse Builder

- Oracle OLAP Client

In addition, there are several other add-ons as well as less visible but significant components in the Oracle suite. A brief discussion (overview) of a few of these components follows.

16.2.1 Oracle Server

The Oracle Server is the central database engine of the Oracle Suite. It hosts a fairly comprehensive implementation of SQL, supporting all major SQL statements, and with enhancements of its own.

The developer typically writes SQL statements in an SQL *Plus environment. This environment provides:

- Additional commands which can be used along with standard SQL commands

- A default editor (notepad), which may also be used to key in commands

- A line editor, which may be used to key in commands

The Oracle Server supports a very comprehensive system catalog. There are system tables for all the database object types supported. These include (but are not confined to):

- Databases

- Tablespaces

- Datafiles

- (Database) Tables

- Sequences

- Columns of tables

- Constraints (Cons-tables and Cons-columns)

- Synonyms

- Logical views

- Indexes

- Privileges (Role_privs and Table_privs)

- Table_Comments

- Column_Comments

These tables are typically accessed indirectly via logical views prefixed by 'DBA', 'User' or 'All' (e.g. we have DBA_tables, User_tables and All_tables).

16.2.2 Oracle PL/SQL and SQL *Plus

Oracle has its own host language, PL/SQL. This high level language (very Pascal-like) is what is typically used to develop an application (although Java is supported).

PL/SQL was specifically developed for Oracle applications and is portable on Oracle Servers. It exhibits all the main features of a classical HLL, but avoids ambiguities (for instance about the If-Statement). PL/SQL is a limited HLL; it focuses solely on database application development. It has limited treatment of arrays and pointers.

Oracle provides a standard SQL Editor through SQL *Plus. SQL *Plus is a basic line editor that allows you to enter and SQL statements. You were introduced to basic SQL *Plus commands in section 11.1. Due to its limitations, many Oracle users tend to use other text editors to specify SQL instructions and integrate them into SQL *Plus. This process is seamless and is handled quite well by SQL *Plus.

16.2.3 Oracle Developer Suite

Oracle Developer is a sophisticated suite component that facilitates rapid application development (RAD). Like most RAD tools, Oracle Developer provides several facilities in a GUI environment. Following is a summary of the prominent subsystems:

Oracle Business Intelligence Beans: This subsystem provides a set of standard JavaBeans components to build business intelligence applications.

Oracle Designer: This subsystem provides a complete toolset to be employed in modeling the requirements and design of enterprise applications.

Oracle Discoverer: This subsystem is an ad-hoc query and reporting tool for publishing information drawn from data marts, data warehouses, online transaction processing systems, and other Oracle back-end systems on the Web.

Oracle Forms Developer: This subsystem is a PL/SQL-based development environment for building GUI-based applications that may be designed to be *Web-accessible* (see chapter 25).

Oracle JDeveloper: This subsystem is a Java-based alternative to the Forms Developer, facilitating the development of a GUI-based application that may be designed to be Web-accessible. It provides an Interactive Development Environment (IDE) that mirrors that of the Sun Microsystems equivalent product called NetBeans. With the recent acquisition of Sun Microsystems, we can expect further improvement of the related services and capabilities in this area. This is a huge acquisition for the Oracle Corporation.

Oracle Reports Developer: This subsystem provides report-building tools for designing attractive reports by pulling information from an Oracle database.

Oracle Software Configuration Manager: This subsystem facilitates management of structured and unstructured data and all types of files throughout the software development life cycle.

Oracle Warehouse Builder: This subsystem provides tools required for the construction and management of a *data warehouse* (see chapter 24).

16.2.4 Oracle Enterprise Manager Database Control and SQL Developer

The Oracle Enterprise Manager (OEM) Database Control is a component that provides a user friendly GUI environment for the DBA to perform administrative work on the database. Through OEM, the DBA can manage a given database, or a group of databases in a cluster. Moreover, OEM is Web-accessible; through it, you can access your database from any computer that has an internet connection via the URL address http://<Machine.Domain>:5500/em (you supply the machine name and domain name for your network).

When you access a database through OEM, all its component objects (schemas, users, tablespaces, tables, procedures, triggers, indexes, constraints, etc.) are available in a hierarchical manner. Each of these database components can be accessed, and their properties changed. OEM then generates the required SQL code or database scripts, in order to effect these changes, and executes them. OEM can also be used to create database objects (user accounts, tables, views, tablespaces, indexes, constraints, etc.). The productivity of the DBA is therefore greatly enhanced. Of course, you will need a valid user account, password, and appropriate privileges.

Oracle also provides a GUI-based component called Oracle SQL Developer (OSQLD). It provides functions similar to OEM. Students as well as practitioners will find this component very effective in providing a shield from the slightly gorier rigor of SQL syntax (but the truth is, SQL syntax is by no means a tragedy; we could live with it).

Still, Oracle provides another GUI-based component called iSQL *Plus, which facilitates Web-accessibility to the database in a manner that is similar to OEM. You can also access your database server from any machine that has an internet connection, via the URL http://<Machine.Domain>:5560/isqlplus (again, you supply the machine name and domain name for your network).

16.2.5 Oracle Enterprise Manager Grid Control

Oracle Enterprise Manager Grid Control is an HTML-based interface that provides complete monitoring across the entire Oracle technology stack — business applications, application servers, databases, and the E-Business Suite — as well as non Oracle components. The components of Grid Control include:

- Oracle Management Service (OMS)

- Oracle Management Agents

- Oracle Management Repository

These components communicate with each other through HTTP and we can achieve secure communications between tiers within firewall-protected environments by enabling the secure socket layer (SSL) protocol. Using Grid Control, an administrator can view alerts, overall system status, performance metrics, and be alerted when failure occurs.

16.2.6 Oracle Database Configuration Assistant

Earlier versions of Oracle did not have OEM, only Oracle Database Configuration Assistant (DBCA). Unfortunately, creating, configuring and managing Oracle databases can be quite complex. DBCA helps to take some complexity out of this by automating the process. The user is shielded from gory syntactical details via a user interface, which generates the requisite SQL and database scripts, based on the user responses to friendly prompts.

DBCA and OEM are complimentary products; the former is particularly useful for database creation and initial configuration; the latter is extremely helpful during database administration and monitoring.

16.2.7 Oracle Warehouse Builder

The Oracle Warehouse Builder (OWB) is comprised of a number of components that facilitate the construction and management of a *data warehouse* environment. You will learn more about data warehousing in chapter 24. For now, you may consider a data warehouse as a database consisting of read-only information obtained by extracting, aggregating, and possibly reformatting data from multiple source databases. With OWB, you can construct a simple data warehouse for a set of departmental databases, as well as a complex data warehouse for an entire enterprise or group of enterprises.

16.3 Shortcomings of Oracle

Oracle, despite its apparent monopoly on the industry, has a few significant shortcomings, primarily in the area of its user interface:

SQL Environment: The standard SQL environment provided through SQL *Plus is unfortunately not graphical, but command-based. This means that the developer has to memorize SQL syntax rules in order to be productive. Out of recognition of this shortcoming, Oracle provides three complimentary alternatives to SQL *Plus — DBCA, OEM, and Oracle SQL Developer (OSQLD).

Oracle Forms Developer: In earlier versions of Oracle Forms Developer (OFD), the user interface needed improvement. Direct manipulation was not always provided in an elegant manner. Case in point: when an object was created on a form:

- The user had to access the Property Palette in order to change certain attributes about the object. The problem was, changes made on the Property Palette were not always obvious to the user (e.g. color scheme selection).

- The user had to constantly switch among Object Navigator, Layout Editor and Property Palette. Although the three perspectives were automatically connected, the process of constant switching was counter-productive.

- Form Builder was not as easy to learn as equivalent components in other products.

At the time of writing, these problems were not thoroughly checked in OFD 11G. However, it is hoped that they have been corrected in this new version. Moreover, the introduction of Oracle JDeveloper (OJD) in Oracle 10G, as an alternative to earlier versions of OFD, has effectively circumvented these problems, since such problems do not exist in OJD.

PL/SQL Support: Like SQL support, Oracle's support of its own PL/SQL is somewhat lacking: no GUI or interactive command prompt. The developer has to memorize PL/SQL command syntax, and there are no context sensitive prompts to help.

System Integration: As stated earlier, the Oracle suite consists of several components. Two observed problems here:

- There are (in the writer's view) too many splinter components, many of which could be merged.

- These components are not all gracefully integrated (one example of this is OJD of Oracle 10G; this component requires some caution in order to be properly installed and configured).

The reason for this is that Oracle shows signs of after-thought evolution, rather than purposeful planning. This problem becomes evident when one considers for example, pre-10G versions of OEM and DBCA. These two products could have been easily merged with a third — Recovery Manager (RMAN) — into one product, providing comprehensive coverage of database administration. The problem of integration becomes very glaring when full installation of Oracle (particularly so on Unix and Linux platforms) is attempted. You will observe that in Oracle10G and 11G, the OEM has been greatly improved. This was not always the case.

Code Generation: Earlier versions of Oracle provided very negligible automatic code generation. For instance, early versions of Form Builder provided a useful environment for application development, but did not generate much PL/SQL code. The developer was still required to memorize SQL and PL/SQL syntax. It must be said, however, that components such as OEM, OSQLD, and DBCA do generate a considerable amount of code. It is hoped that this trend will continue in the future.

Database Management: Most DBMS suites have a simple, straightforward way of dealing with creating a database and populating it with database objects. Oracle does not. To achieve this objective, you have to follow the following procedure:

- Create an Oracle database.

- Create one or more tablespaces. Each tablespace will consist of at least one datafile.

- Create user(s) and grant appropriate quotas to the tablespace(s).

- Populate the tablespace(s) with database objects.

The DBA or someone with DBA privileges typically does the first three steps. Each of these steps is multifaceted, involving several subservient steps. By using DBCA and OEM, these steps have been greatly simplified, but they can still be thought intensive. The final step can be done by users with appropriate privileges.

Affordability: Traditionally, Oracle solutions have been prohibitively expensive for small and medium size companies. In recognition of this, Oracle Corporation provides a special educational program for colleges and universities in North America. This program is called the Oracle Academic Initiative (OAI). Under this program, enrolled institutions pay a nominal membership fee; this entitles them to free access to Oracle products, which they are authorized to use for education and research purposes.

Combined Effect: When we combine the effect of all the flaws mentioned, the end result is that Oracle remains a product that is relatively difficult to learn and use. On the other hand, if these problems were to be corrected, the product would truly qualify as a "killer application" [Downes, 1998]. Moreover, Oracle 9I, 10G, and 11G represent significant improvements over its earlier versions of the product.

16.4 Summary and Concluding Remarks

Let us summarize what we have covered in this chapter:

- Oracle is widely regarded as one of the world's leading RDBMS suites. The product runs on all the major operating system platforms, except OS-400, is marketed under five editions — Enterprise Edition (EE), Standard Edition (SE), Standard Edition One (SE1), Express Edition (XE), and Personal Edition (PE).

- The Oracle suite includes a number of components. These include (but are not confined to) Oracle Server, Oracle PL/SQL, Oracle JDeveloper, Oracle Database Configuration Assistant, Oracle Enterprise Manager, Oracle SQL Developer, Oracle SQL*Plus, and Oracle iSQL*Plus.

- Oracle has some shortcomings relating to the component integration, limited code generation, complex database creation, and affordability.

Notwithstanding the shortcomings, Oracle is an excellent DBMS suite, and for this reason, it is expected to continue to dominate the database systems arena well into the foreseeable future. Oracle's recent acquisition of Sun Microsystems represents a significant possession for the company. This means that we can expect to see greater integration of Java-based interfaces in the Oracle products (something Oracle has been working on for some time), as well as increased platform independence.

16.5 Review Questions

1. What are the main editions of Oracle that are marketed?

2. What are the main components of an Oracle suite? Briefly discuss how these components are related.

3. Identify some benefits and drawbacks of the Oracle suite.

16.6 References and/or Recommended Readings

[Couchman, 1999] Couchman, Jason and Christopher Allen. *Oracle Certified Professional: Application Developer Guide*. New York, NY: Osborne/McGraw-Hill, 1999.

[Downes, 1998] Downes, Larry and Chunka Mui. *Unleashing the Killer App - Digital Strategies For Market Dominance*. Boston: Harvard Business School Press, 1998.

[Oracle, 2008] Oracle Corporation. *SQL Reference*. http://www.oracle.com/technology/index.html (accessed August 2008).

[Shah, 2002] Shah, Nilesh. *Database Systems Using Oracle: A Simplified Guide to SQL and PL/SQL*. Upper Saddle River, NJ: Prentice Hall, 2002.

CHAPTER 17

■ ■ ■

Overview of DB2

This chapter provides an overview of the DB2 DBMS. The chapter proceeds under the following captions:

- Introduction
- Main Components of the DB2 Suite
- Shortcomings of DB2
- Summary and Concluding Remarks

17.1 Introduction

DB2 is another leading RDBMS suite in the software engineering industry (Oracle being its main arch rival). Developed by IBM Corporation, the DB2 RDBMS was first introduced for MVS/370 and MVS/XA in 1983 and for MVS/ESA in 1988. In 1996 The DB2 Universal Database, the industry's first fully scalable, Web-accessible database management system was announced by IBM. It is called "universal" because of its ability to sort and query alphanumeric data as well as text documents, images, audio, video, and other complex objects. Also, DB2 supports the two dominant database models — the relational model and the object-oriented model, hence the term universal DBMS (UDBMS). Like Oracle, the DB2 suite is quite comprehensive.

DB2 Universal Database (UDB) offers many database and information management enhancements. The most recent version of the product is DB2 UDB version 9.7. It is the database of choice for the development and deployment of critical solutions in areas such as:

- E-business
- Business intelligence
- Content management

- Enterprise Resource Planning

- Customer Relationship Management

- Data Warehousing

Being a leading DBMS product, DB2 provides a wide range advantages. The following are some of the more widely acclaimed advantages of the DB2 UDB suite:

- The product is recognized as one of the leading DBMS suites in the industry.

- DB2 provides a comprehensive and at times innovative implementation of SQL.

- The DB2 suite includes a number of front-end RAD tools that all seamlessly support DB2.

- The DB2 UDB handles large databases very effectively.

- DB2 UDB handles distributed databases and object databases quite well.

- DB2 UDB facilitates the construction and management of small, medium, and large data warehouses.

- DB2 UDB facilitates communication with other databases.

- The DB2 UDB hosts a comprehensive system catalog, thus allowing it to effectively handle complex databases consisting of different types of objects.

- DB2 UDB provides a user interface that encourages experts, while facilitating novices.

- DB2 facilitates seamless integration of various products.

The DB2 suite is marketed for major modern operating systems including i5/OS, Windows, AIX (IBM's implementation of UNIX), Solaris, Linux, HP-UX, and Mac OS-X. The following are the DB2 UDB product editions currently marketed:

- DB2 UDB Everyplace Edition

- DB2 UDB Personal Edition

- DB2 UDB Workgroup Server Edition

- DB2 UDB Express Edition

- DB2 UDB Enterprise Server Edition

These editions all come with various components and features to service different needs. IBM uses the mantra "DB2 is DB2 is DB2" to mean, all DB2 database applications are platform independent across the above-mentioned editions and operating systems [IBM, 2009a].

17.2 Main Components of the DB2 Suite

The DB2 product family includes the following main components:

- DB2 Universal Database Core

- IBM InfoSphere Information Server

- IBM Data Studio

- IBM InfoSphere Warehouse

Depending on the edition of the DB2 UDB, various other components may be included. Additionally, there are several other components comprising these main components. Some of these DB2 UDB components are summarized in Figure 17-1. This list is not comprehensive. However, it should convey the reality that the DB2 UDB suite is quite comprehensive.

Component	Summary
DB2 Universal Database Core	This is the core product for creating and managing a relation/object database.
DB2 High Performance Upload (DB2 HPU)	Enables the DBA to manage large quantities of data, and efficiently manage functions such as backup, data upload, recovery, and data migration.
DB2 Performance Expert for LUW	Useful in optimizing the performance of the database environment
Data Encryption Expert	Facilitates encryption and compression of data for both on-line and offline environments.
InfoSphere Data Architect	Facilitates the modeling, designing, and standardization of various distributed data resources.
InfoSphere DataStage	Facilitates the extraction and transformation of data from multiple sources, and loading them into a staging area.
InfoSphere Federation Server	Facilitates the amalgamation of data from multiple heterogeneous sources into a single virtual view for end users.
InfoSphere Information Analyzer	For analyzing the structure, content, and quality of the information from heterogeneous data sources.
InfoSphere Connectivity Software	Provides the necessary protocol for efficient cross-platform connections to multiple sources.
InfoSphere Metadata Workbench	Allows for tracing of relationships and attributes from source databases to a target database where they are used (even across editions and platforms).
InfoSphere QualityStage	Facilitates analysis of data from source databases, based on established business rules, in order to determine the data quality; also includes data cleansing features.
InfoSphere Replication Server	Enables data consolidation and/or replication in support of data availability.
Optim Database Administrator for Linux, Unix, and Windows (LUW)	Used for various administrative activities such as data migration, structural database changes, disaster recovery, etc.
Optim Database Relationship	Used for managing groups of related tables in support of a set of business operation(s).
Optim Development Studio	A development environment for Oracle, DB2, and Informix, supporting SQL, XQuery, stored procedures, Web services, and Java data access.
Optim pureQuery Runtime for LUW	Used for building high performance database applications.
Optim Query Tuner for LUW	Provides expert advice for writing high performance queries, and improving database design.
Optim Test Data Management Solution for Custom and Packaged Application	Facilitates the thorough testing of database applications for data quality.
InfoSphere Warehouse Departmental Edition	For constructing and managing a data warehouse, typically at the departmental level.
InfoSphere Warehouse Enterprise Edition	For constructing and managing a data warehouse at the enterprise level.

Figure 17-1. *DB2 Components*

Following is a summary of the main components mentioned above. As the DB2 product documentation is a much more comprehensive source than this chapter, you are advised to check that source (see [IBM, 2008], [IBM, 2009a], and [IBM, 2009b]) for additional information.

314

17.2.1 DB2 Universal Database Core

The DB2 Universal Database Core (also called the DB2 Common Code) contains the core database services. Superimposed on top of this is a layer of code that is specific to the operating system (OS) platform that the DBS suite runs on. This approach gives the product the platform independence that it enjoys. When you purchase DB2, you must specify and choose the OS platform that will be used for your implementation, as well as the desired edition. Depending on the edition chosen, you will have other features and components bundled together in a seamless whole (for more information on this, see the production documentation via [IBM, 2009a]).

Irrespective of the edition and OS platform, all DB2 applications are accessible with each other, and from IBM software development tools such as Rational and WebSphere. Additionally, through ODBC, other non-DB2 databases can be reached.

17.2.2 IBM InfoSphere Information Server

The InfoSphere Information Server (previously called the Information Integrator in earlier versions) is a collection of technologies that combines database management systems, Web services, replication, federated systems, and data warehousing functions into a common platform. It also includes a variety of programming interfaces and data models. It is used for data integration from heterogeneous data sources (hence the name). Using the Information Integration technology, you can access diverse types of data (structured, unstructured, and semi-structured). The source data may reside on different back-end systems (example Oracle, Microsoft SQL Server, Informix, etc.). You can transform that data into a format that provides easy access to information across the enterprise, while giving the end user the illusion that all the data resides on their machine.

Information integration enables the integration of data from multiple sources with the following functions:

- Provision of real-time read and write access

- Transformation of data for business analysis and data interchange

- Management of data placement for performance, currency, and availability

The DB2 information integration strategy includes the following goals for users:

- To provide users with the ability to continue to more easily manipulate legacy data

- To provide users with the ability to take advantage of familiar software to use known assets and resources

- To provide users with the ability to acquire and easily maintain new data

- To provide users with the ability to use existing data management tools to access data wherever it is located

Figure 17-2 provides a list of some of the prominent components comprising the InfoSphere Information Server (these were earlier clarified in Figure 17-1).

- InfoSphere Metadata Workbench
- InfoSphere Information Analyzer
- InfoSphere DataStage
- InfoSphere QualityStage
- InfoSphere Federation Server
- InfoSphere Connectivity Software
- InfoSphere Data Architect
- InfoSphere Replication Server

Figure 17-2. *Prominent Constituent Components of the InfoSphere Information Server*

17.2.3 IBM Data Studio

The Data Studio spans the entire life cycle (design, development, implementation, deployment, and management) for all DB2 applications, irrespective of editions and OS platform. Among the services provided are the following:

- Accelerated solution delivery

- Integrated database administration

- Data growth management

- Optimized performance

- Data privacy

- Streamlined data test management

- Streamlined upgrades and migration

Under these services, a number of components have been bundled. Figure 17-3 provides a list of some of the more prominent ones.

- InfoSphere Data Architect
- Optim Database Administrator
- Optim Database Relationship
- Optim Development Studio
- Optim pureQuery Runtime for LUW
- Optim Query Tuner for LUW
- Optim Database Administrator for LUW
- Optim Test Data Management Solution for Custom and Packaged Applications
- DB2 High Performance Upload
- DB2 Performance Expert for LUW
- Data Encryption Expert

Figure 17-3. *Prominent Constituent Components of the Data Studio*

17.2.4 IBM InfoSphere Warehouse

The DB2 UDB suite provides four editions of a data warehousing software. The editions of InfoSphere Warehouse provided are tailored to meet the varied needs of the organization. They are as follows:

- InfoSphere Warehouse Departmental Edition

- InfoSphere Warehouse Departmental Base Edition

- InfoSphere Warehouse Enterprise Edition

- InfoSphere Warehouse Enterprise Base Edition

With these resources, you can construct simple departmental data warehouses from departmental databases, or more complex data warehouses for an entire enterprise or group of enterprises.

17.3 Shortcomings of DB2

DB2 represents a huge effort by IBM to develop and market a top quality product. To a large extent the company has succeeded. There have not been many serious complaints about the product. Nonetheless, as the saying goes, there is no perfect software. A few complaints have been made against the product, as summarized below:

Backup and Recovery: DB2 offers a very basic set of backup and recovery capabilities, but lacks the completeness and depth of high availability functionality required by most e-businesses today. One is therefore forced to rely on cold backups at the operation system level. More improvement is needed in this area.

Support of Domains: Some users would like to see DB2 support domain-based calculus. It is felt that by adding domains to the DBMS, stronger data integrity constraints can be achieved.

Affordability: Like Oracle, DB2 is prohibitively expensive for small and medium size companies. In recognition of this, IBM provides a special educational program for colleges and universities in North America. Under this program, enrolled institutions purchase the products for a nominal fee, and are able to use them for education and research purposes. Additionally, IBM provides the public with the flexibility of choosing from five different editions according to prevailing needs and financial constraints.

317

Documentation: IBM provides a Web-accessible information center for the DB2 product family (see [IBM, 2008]). It must be stated that compared to other similar resources, this site could benefit from some improvements. In the experience of this author, one has to spend considerable time in finding the information sought.

Combined Effect: DB2 is on the verge of becoming a truly superb product. It is hoped that IBM can address the few problem areas for the product.

17.4 Summary and Concluding Remarks

It is now time to summarize what we have covered in this chapter:

- DB2 is widely regarded as one of the world's leading UDBMS suites. The product runs on all the major operating system platforms, and is marketed under five editions: DB2 UDB Everyplace Edition, DB2 UDB Personal Edition, DB2 UDB Workgroup Server Edition, DB2 UDB Express Edition, and DB2 UDB Enterprise Server Edition.

- The DB2 suite includes a number of components. These include (but are not confined to) DB2 Universal Database Core, IBM InfoSphere Information Server, IBM Data Studio, and IBM InfoSphere Warehouse.

- DB2 has some shortcomings relating to backup and recovery, and affordability.

Not withstanding the shortcomings, DB2 is an excellent DBMS suite, and is arguably the one with the most comprehensive and coherent design. For these and other reasons, it is expected that the product will continue to dominate the database systems arena well into the foreseeable future.

17.5 Review Questions

1. What are the main editions of DB2 that are marketed?

2. What are the main components of the DB2 suite? Briefly discuss how these components are related.

3. Identify some benefits and drawbacks of the DB2 suite.

17.6 References and/or Recommended Readings

[Downes, 1998] Downes, Larry and Chunka Mui. *Unleashing the Killer App — Digital Strategies For Market Dominance*. Boston: Harvard Business School Press, 1998.

[IBM, 2008] IBM Corporation. IBM DB2 Database for Linux, UNIX, and Windows Information Center. `http://publib.boulder.ibm.com/infocenter/db2luw/v9r5/index.jsp` (accessed August 2008).

[IBM, 2009a] IBM Corporation. Compare the Distributed DB2 9.5 Data Servers. `http://www.ibm.com/developerworks/db2/library/techarticle/0301zikopoulos/0301zikopoulos1.html` (accessed August 2009).

[IBM, 2009b] IBM Corporation. IBM Data Management. `http://www-01.ibm.com/software/data/management/` (accessed August 2009).

CHAPTER 18

■ ■ ■

Overview of MS SQL Server

This chapter provides an overview of the Microsoft SQL Server DBMS. Relatively speaking, SQL Server represents the most recent introduction of a major DBMS suite in the marketplace. It is also somewhat different from other products. For these two reasons, we will deviate slightly from the structure of the previous two chapters, as we cover additional but relevant information about the product. The chapter therefore proceeds under the following captions:

- Introduction
- Main Features of SQL Server
- Editions of SQL Server
- Main Components of the SQL Server Suite
- SQL Server Default databases
- SQL Server Default Logins
- Named versus Default Instances
- Removing SQL Server
- Shortcomings of SQL Server
- Summary and Concluding Remarks

By the time this volume is available to the public, many of components mentioned will likely be outdated. The focus therefore is to describe the general product environment that an MS SQL Server user is likely to see. The discussion will be broadly based on products MS SQL Server 2005 and MS SQL Server 2008.

18.1 Introduction

MS SQL Server (version 8.0) is Microsoft's flagship relational database engine product. The product was developed by Microsoft for its Windows operation system platform, and has been through several stages of revision.

18.1.1 Brief History

Microsoft SQL Server uses a version called Transact-SQL (T-SQL). Microsoft initially developed SQL Server (a database product that implements the SQL language) with Sybase Corporation for use on the OS/2 platform. After the IBM-Microsoft collaboration broke down, Microsoft abandoned OS/2 in favor of its then new network operating system, Windows NT Advanced Server. At that point, Microsoft decided to further develop the SQL Server engine for Windows NT by itself. The resulting product was Microsoft SQL Server 4.2, which was updated to version 4.2.1.

After Microsoft and Sybase parted ways, Sybase further developed its database engine to run on Windows NT (currently known as Sybase Adaptive Server Enterprise), and Microsoft developed SQL Server 6.0, then SQL Server 6.5, which also ran on top of Windows NT. SQL Server 7.0 introduced the capability to run on Windows NT as well as on Windows 95 and Windows 98. With SQL Server 7.0, Microsoft dramatically rewrote and modified the Sybase code. The company redesigned the core database engine and introduced a sophisticated query optimizer and an advanced database storage engine. SQL Server 2005 enhanced this new code line, adding significant new features. The most recent version of the DBMS is MS SQL Server 2008.

18.1.2 Operating Environment

As mentioned earlier, MS SQL Server has been specifically designed, developed, and tailored to operate in, and maximize the use of the features of the Windows operating system. The DBMS can run as a Windows service. As you are no doubt aware, a service is an application that Windows can start either automatically when booting up, or manually on demand. Services on Windows have a generic application programming interface (API) that can be controlled programmatically. Services facilitate the running of applications such as MS SQL Server without requiring that a user be logged in to the server computer.

Technically speaking, MS SQL Server is a back-end system. However, being developed and marketed by Microsoft, all the front-end Microsoft RAD tools are designed to integrate with SQL server. The effect is that when SQL Server is implemented in a Microsoft Windows environment (as it must be), one has a choice from several front-end tools that will seamlessly integrate with the SQL Server database.

18.1.3 MS SQL Server and the Client-Server Model

Like most modern DBMS suites, Microsoft's SQL Server is a client-server software system. The server side of the application provides database security, fault tolerance, database performance, concurrency, and reliable backups. The client side provides the user interface that facilitates access to the database via reports, queries, and forms. Various clients can connect to MS SQL Server, including the utilities that come with SQL Server, such as SQL Server Query Analyzer. Non-Microsoft applications can also access the backend via ODBC.

18.2 Main Features of MS SQL Server

According to Microsoft, MS SQL Server provides a number of significant features, some of which are mentioned below:

Database Support: The SQL Server database engine provides facilities for supporting relational databases as well as unstructured data (via XML). It also includes security features and other related features required to create and support complex Web-accessible databases.

Replication Services: The SQL Server relational database engine supports the features required to support demanding data processing environments. The database engine protects data integrity while minimizing the overhead of managing thousands of users who may be concurrently modifying the database. SQL Server distributed queries facilitate referencing of data from multiple sources as if the data all resided in the local SQL Server database. At the same time, the distributed transaction support protects the integrity of any updates of the distributed data. Replication facilitates maintenance of multiple copies of data, while ensuring that the separate copies remain synchronized.

Ease of Installation and Usage: SQL Server includes a set of administrative and development tools that improve upon the process of installing, deploying, managing, and using SQL Server across several sites. SQL Server also supports a standards-based programming model integrated with the Microsoft Distributed interNet Applications (DNA) architecture, allowing for easy integration with the World Wide Web (WWW). These features allow software engineers to rapidly deliver SQL Server applications that customers can implement with a minimum of installation and administrative overhead.

Interoperability: SQL Server includes facilities for communicating with heterogeneous databases.

Notification Services: These services come in the form of capabilities for the development and deployment of applications that can deliver personalized, timely information updates to a variety of connected and mobile devices.

Integration Services: These services include data extraction, transformation, and loading (ETL) capabilities for data warehousing and enterprise-wide data integration.

Analysis Services: These services include online analytical processing (OLAP) capabilities for the rapid and sophisticated analysis of large and complex datasets using multidimensional storage.

Reporting Services: These services provide a comprehensive solution for creating, managing, and delivering both traditional, paper-oriented reports and interactive, Web-based reports from pre-existing databases.

Management Tools: SQL Server includes integrated management tools for administering and tuning the database. Two significant products provided are Microsoft Operations Manager (MOM) and Microsoft Systems Management Server (SMS).

Development Tools: SQL Server ships with various integrated development tools for the database engine, data extraction, transformation, and loading, data mining, OLAP, and application development through Microsoft Visual Studio.

18.3 Editions of MS SQL Server

Microsoft markets two server editions (Enterprise and Standard, both in 32 bit and 64 bit flavors) of SQL Server and several specialized editions of SQL Server. After examining their requirements and specifications, it should be obvious which one to use. However, regardless of the edition of SQL Server that one chooses, they are all built on a common code base (except for the version for Windows CE), so the same rules, conditions, and administration apply. A brief summary of each edition follows.

SQL Server Standard Edition: The Standard Edition is what most people mean when they refer to SQL Server. This version of the product supplies the essential functionality needed for e-commerce, data warehousing, and line-of-business solutions. It is intended to run on Windows platforms, starting at Windows Server 2003 (SP2) to more contemporary versions of the operating system including Windows Server 2008. Among the prominent features are the following:

- Support of 16 multiple instances

- Support of 4 concurrent processors

- RAM of 3 GB

- Compliant with 64 bit architecture

- Unlimited database size
- Notification services

SQL Server Enterprise Edition: Enterprise Edition (64-bit) provides the most scalable data platform. Addressing more memory than any other edition of SQL Server, it scales to the performance levels required to support the largest data warehousing and analysis applications, ecommerce websites and enterprise business systems. This edition runs on various Windows platforms ranging from Microsoft Windows 2003 Server with Service Pack (SP) 2 or later to Windows Server 2008. This edition includes the full range of features in the SQL Server suite. Among the prominent features are the following:

- Support of 50 multiple instances
- No limit on concurrent processors
- RAM of 512 GB, or based on the underlying operating system
- Compliant with 64 bit architecture
- Unlimited database size
- Table and index partitioning
- Indexed views
- Parallel index operations
- Database snapshots
- Integration services
- Notification services

SQL Server Workgroup Edition: The Workgroup Edition is the data management solution for small organizations or workgroups within larger entities. It includes the entire core database features needed for data management in an affordable and simple-to-manage package. The platform requirements are similar to that of the Enterprise Edition. Among the prominent features are the following:

- Support of 50 multiple instances
- Can support 2 concurrent processors
- RAM of 3 GB
- Unlimited database size

SQL Server Express Edition: The Express Edition helps developers to use a lightweight version of the product to build robust and reliable applications. The product is free and can be downloaded from the Microsoft Web site. Among the prominent features are the following:

- Support for 1 processor only
- RAM of 1 GB
- Database size of 4 GB

SQL Server Compact Edition: The Microsoft SQL Server 2008 Compact Edition is also a free lightweight version of SQL Server that facilitates a low maintenance, compact embedded database for single-user client applications for all Windows platforms including tablet PCs, pocket PCs, smart phones and desktops.

SQL Server Developer Edition: The Developer Edition is designed to enable developers to build any type of application on top of SQL Server 2008. It includes all the functionality of the Enterprise Edition but with a special development and test license agreement that prohibits production deployment.

18.4 Main Components of MS SQL Server Suite

In this section, we shall briefly examine the main components of the SQL Server suite. We shall do so under the following categorizations:

- Server Components

- Management Tools

- Client Connectivity

- Development Tools

- Code Samples

- Optional Components

18.4.1 Server Components

The main server components are as follows:

- The SQL Server (also known as SQL Server Agent) is the core database engine and the management support service. This option is enabled by default.

- The Upgrade Tools is the database upgrade support, so one can run the Version Upgrade Wizard to upgrade a SQL Server 6.5 installation. This option is enabled by default.

- Replication Support should be left enabled (as it is by default) if you plan to use replication.

- Full-Text Search uses technology from Microsoft Index Server to build indexes on textual data. This option is installed by default and supports full-text search in a fail-over cluster configuration.

- Debug Symbols, enabled by default, provides debug files should one ever need to troubleshoot SQL Server with Microsoft Product Support. This option should be left enabled.

- Performance Counters should be left enabled (as it is by default) if one wants the ability to monitor SQL Server's performance with the performance monitor utility that Windows provides.

18.4.2 Management Tools

The management tools are enabled by default; they consist of the following:

- Enterprise Manager is the graphical management interface for both development and administration of SQL Server.

- The SQL Server Profiler is a great tool for monitoring SQL Server activities, including queries and how these queries are run. It also provides performance measurements.

- Query Analyzer is the component used to enter and run Transact-SQL statements. One can also view how SQL Server will optimize and run queries. Experienced T-SQL developers tend to use this tool.

- DTC Client Support allows you to use the Distributed Transaction Coordinator to run data modification queries across multiple systems.

- Conflict Viewer is the conflict resolution wizard for merge replication.

18.4.3 Client Connectivity

Client Connectivity is a set of components that facilitates communication with the SQL Server. This set includes components for Open Database Connectivity (ODBC), Object Linking and Embedding Database (OLE DB), and DB-Library. Each library allows you to write or use programs that connect to SQL Server. Collectively, they are known as the MDAC (Microsoft Data Access Components).

18.4.4 Development Tools

The main development tools are described below:

- Headers and Libraries are the C++ files needed for development of SQL Server programs.

- MDAC system development kits (SDKs) are the Software Development Kits for XML and the Microsoft Data Access Components. These SDKs allow enable and support the development of programs using XML and MDAC.

- Backup/Restore API includes a sample program, necessary C/C++ files, and documentation on how to build backup and restore programs.

- Debugger Interface installs the components necessary to allow Microsoft Visual Studio components and the SQL Server Query Analyzer utility the capability to debug stored procedures. This option is selected by default.

18.4.5 Code Samples

None of the code samples is installed by default. However, depending on your choice, their inclusion could serve to enrich your SQL Server environment. The following are the main options:

- ADO includes programming examples for ActiveX Data Objects (ADO).

- DBLIB includes programming examples for the DB-Library API. DB-Library was the native Database Application Programming Interface (API) of SQL Server in earlier releases, and is supported in SQL Server for backward compatibility.

- Desktop includes code samples on setting up unattended install operations for the Microsoft SQL Server Desktop Engine (MSDE).

- DTS includes programming examples for data transformation services (DTS). DTS provides a way to move data from one data source to another.

- ESQLC includes the programming examples for Embedded SQL for the C programming language.

- MSDTC includes the programming examples for the Microsoft Distributed Transaction Coordinator.

- ODBC includes the programming examples for the open database connectivity programming API in SQL Server.

- ODS includes the programming examples for the open data services (ODS) API for SQL Server.

- OLE Automation includes the programming examples to support OLE Automation for SQL Server.

- Replication includes the programming examples for SQL Server replication.

- SQLDMO includes programming examples for the SQL-Distributed Management Objects administrative programming interface.

- SQLNS includes programming examples for the SQL Name Space administrative programming interface.

18.4.6 SQL Server Optional Components

After installing SQL Server, you can install three additional services: the Microsoft Search Service, the Microsoft SQL Server Analysis Services, and Microsoft English Query. Although you can the Microsoft Search Service (full-text indexing) during the default setup of SQL Server, you also have the option of installing the other two services after the initial setup is complete. This can be done independent of SQL Server if so desired.

Microsoft SQL Server Analysis Services: Microsoft SQL Server Analysis Services comprise a set of technologies to extend data warehousing into SQL Server. The Server Analysis Services help us build OLAP (On Line Analytical Processing) data to perform detailed trend analysis in many ways, as well as support data mining. The services provide the capability to build and control these cubes, and a user interface to build, administer, and query these cubes is also installed. The server side installs only on Windows 2003 (or later). The client components and user interface are also available on Windows clients.

Microsoft English Query: Microsoft English Query allows an administrator to configure a database schema and allows end users to run their database queries in English instead of Transact-SQL. This capability is particularly beneficial for Internet-based applications that don't want to force users to run SQL statements. For example, we can say, "Show me the number of books sold for each author this year," rather than use a complicated SQL statement.

18.5 MS SQL Server Default Databases

When you install SQL Server, the following databases are installed. You can add additional databases later, but these databases are guaranteed to be there. Some of them (**master, model, tempdb**, and **MSDB**) are system databases — they cannot be dropped without causing serious harm to SQL Server. The other two, **pubs** and **Northwind**, are simply samples to help we learn SQL Server. These can be safely dropped from production SQL Servers.

The master Database: The **master** database is the key database for running SQL Server. It contains a pointer to the primary data file for every other database installed on system, as well as key server wide information. This server wide information includes such items as system wide error messages, login information, system stored procedures, and connected or linked servers. The master database can be recovered only in the event of a disaster with special techniques.

The model Database: The **model** database is best thought of as a template database. Each time a new database is created, the **model** database is actually copied, and then the size and other changes requested for new database are applied. Therefore, any object that exists in the model database is copied to the new database at the time of creation. For example, you can place a table, a username, and other essential objects in this database right after installation of SQL Server. Each time a new database is created after that, these essential objects are automatically included. The **model** database is about 768KB after installation. Because the model is copied to create each new database, no database can be smaller than the **model**.

The tempdb Database: The **tempdb** database is the place where sorts, joins, and other activities that require temporary space are performed. It's approximately 2MB after installation, but as is the case with all databases in SQL Server by default, it can grow as more space is required. The **tempdb** database is reinitialized each time SQL Server (the SQL Server service) is started.

The MSDB Database: The MSDB database supports the SQL Server Agent service, including storing information about jobs, alerts, events, and replication. A history of all backup and restore activity is also kept in this database. The MSDB database is about 12MB by default.

The pubs Database: The **pubs** database is meant to be a learning tool. It contains a sample database about a publisher, including information about authors, books, and sales. Most of the examples in the SQL Server Books Online are based on the **pubs** database. Most database features are highlighted via their implementation in the **pubs** database. The **pubs** database is just under 2MB in size after installation.

The Northwind Database: The **Northwind** database is an alternative learning database to the **pubs** database. Northwind has been the sample database supplied with Microsoft Access for some time now. Because more and more Microsoft Access users are migrating to SQL Server, the **Northwind** database was brought over to assist them in learning the features of the product with a familiar database. **Northwind** is about 3.5MB by default.

18.6 MS SQL Server Default Logins

One of the first things you should do after installing SQL Server is to log in. If you went with the default and selected Windows Authentication Mode, you simply need to select the Windows NT Authentication option on any dialog that asks you to connect to SQL Server. If you choose to use Mixed Mode, you could either do that or use the default login for SQL Server, **sa** (lowercase on case-sensitive sort-order servers). The letter **sa** stands for system administrator.

> **sa:** The **sa** user account is a member of the **sysadmin** fixed server role. As a member of this role, **sa** can do anything in SQL Server. The **sa** account always exists and cannot be dropped. However, you cannot use it when we are in Windows Authentication Mode. If you are in Mixed Mode, you can select to login using this account. Still, it is more likely you will use the next option, logging in via membership in local administrators group.

> **Windows Local Administrators Group:** If you are on a Windows computer and are a member of the local administrators group, you do not have to use the SQL Server authentication. During setup, SQL Server adds the local Windows Administrators group to the **sysadmin** role, just as **sa** is added. As a result, all local administrators are made SQL Server administrators by default. On earlier versions of Windows platforms (prior to 2003), Windows authentication is not available, so you must use **sa**. Password control is not necessary in SQL Server when we are using Windows authentication; SQL Server simply uses Windows login credentials.

18.7 Named versus Default Instances

SQL Server has introduced the capability to run multiple, independent copies of the database server on a single Windows-based computer. Microsoft supports up to 16 copies of SQL Server installed on a single computer.

Default Instance: One can connect to the default instance of SQL Server (there is only one per machine) by specifying only the server name when connecting via an application program. In earlier versions, connection to the SQL Server was done this way — the SQL Server instance was specified as the machine name on which SQL Server was running. For instance, if the computer is named **BDServ**, then to connect to the default instance, you would specify **DBServ** when prompted for the SQL Server name. The program files install to the default path of **MSSQL**. The service names for the actual SQL Server services are as follows:

- SQL Server: **MSSQLServer**

- SQL Server Agent: **SQLServerAgent**

Named Instance: A named instance of SQL Server is one that is named during setup. When you want to connect to a named instance, you specify both the server name and the instance name that was entered during setup. The services are created with unique names as well:

- SQL Server: **MSSQL$Instancename**

- SQL Server Agent: **SQLAgent$Instancename**

Common Components: Some common components are shared between installations of SQL Server; they do not really belong to either the default or any of the named instances that might have been installed on the computer. They include the SQL Server tools, as well as system components such as MDAC 2.6. For more information on these, please refer to the MS SQL Server product documentation.

18.8 Removing MS SQL Server

If, for some reason, you need to remove SQL Server, simply use Control Panel's Add/ Remove Programs — just like any other application on your computer. Selecting this option removes all files and Registry keys related to SQL Server, but does not remove shared components that were installed, such as the MDAC components. Also, if this is not the last instance of SQL Server to be removed, the tools will remain. When you remove the last instance of SQL Server, the tools are also removed.

We need to address one important issue regarding upgrade from to SQL Server from an earlier version of the software. If for instance, you desire to upgrade from SQL Server 6.5, do not run the 6.5 setup program to remove the previous release of SQL Server; this can damage your SQL Server installation. Microsoft provides a special uninstall program for SQL Server 6.5; it is accessible via a shortcut in the Microsoft SQL Server Switch menu; it is called **Uninstall SQL Server 6.x**.

18.9 Shortcomings of MS SQL Server

SQL Server represents a huge effort by Microsoft to develop and market a top quality product. Whether the company will succeed in this venture is a bit too early to tell; we will have to wait and see. There are however, a few areas of concern as summarized below:

Support Only for Microsoft Windows: Almost all Windows operating systems provide support for SQL Server. If you have anything other than Microsoft Windows as your operating system platform, however, you will have to forego using this product, and instead look to another RDBMS vendor. It is obvious why Microsoft has taken this course of action, but it would be nice to have the ability to install the product on other operating systems. Platform independence or some semblance of it would certainly add credence to MS SQL Server, as it competes in the DBMS industry.

No Native Load Balancing Capabilities: SQL Server provides any built-in support for load balancing.While it is possible to achieve a "load-balanced" solution with horizontal data portioning, this is not true load balancing. The DBMS provides no logic that analyses the load on one server and then passes the request to another based on the results of the analysis. This does not mean that load balancing cannot be achieved with SQL Server; it can be achieved via a third party solution such as Cisco's Content Services Switch.

No Version Control on Database Objects: SQL Server provides no versioning support of stored procedures, views, or even any Data Definition Language (DDL). You have to script your database and objects, and then use a product such as Visual SourceSafe (VSS) to version the scripts. This is not good, particularly if you have developers who come along and change the structure slightly, without updating the external source control repository.

Poor Performance and Configuration Out of the Box: Most DBAs know that to improve performance of your RDBMS, you should separate your program, data, and transaction log files onto physically separate disk drives. With SQL Server, you can split the data and program files from each other at installation time, but the transaction log files are installed by default with the data partition. This results in poor performance.

Cannot Read Transaction Log Files: There is no capability with SQL Server's own tools to read the transaction logs. This means that you need to either buy a third-party tool, or take a wild guess and restore the database to a point in time. Transaction logs are used only during recovery of database, if the database is corrupt. The ability to read the transaction logs is valuable for debugging purposes. This therefore represents a serious omission.

No Support for Java: Microsoft's non-support stance on Java is well known. Unfortunately, this has meant that your Java code is not portable from other DBMS platforms. Code that has been written for your DB2 or Oracle installation will need to be translated into T-SQL to be used within SQL Server. This creates a challenge when migrating from other RDBMS platforms. In fact, SQL Server doesn't offer any support for any programming language, except of course SQL. To use VBScript in SQL Server, you need to develop DTS packages that interface with the RDBMS. These related limitations constitute a serious handicap to the product.

Combined Effect: MS SQL Server has made a reasonably impressive entrance to the DBMS market place. The product is scalable to some degree; its robustness and stability is yet to be tested; however, there are a few success stories that Microsoft will hasten to point out.Given the fact that for better or for worse, the Windows operating system has become a household name, and that MS SQL Server seamlessly integrates with that operating system (both products produced and marketed by Microsoft), MS SQL Server is guaranteed a promising future.

18.10 Summary and Concluding Remarks

Here is a summary of what we have covered in this chapter:

- MS SQL Sever is an emerging DBMS suite that is seeking to increase market share in the database systems market. The product runs on Windows platforms. The product is marketed under six editions: Standard Edition, Enterprise Edition, Workgroup Edition, Express Edition, Compact Edition, and Developer Edition.

- The MS SQL Sever suite includes a number of components. These components have been classified under Server Components, Database Management Tools, Client Connectivity Tools, Development Tools, Code Samples, and Optional Components.

- MS SQL Sever is shipped with the following default databases: **master**, **model**, **tempdb**, **MSDB**, **pubs**, and **Northwind**.

- MS SQL Sever has a number of shortcomings relating to platform dependence (running only on Windows platform), no load-balancing, poor performance, difficult reading transaction logs, security, lack of support for Java.

MS SQL Sever has made a fair entry into a very competitive market. If not for any other reason, we expect it to be around for the foreseeable future, due to its marriage to the Windows platform.

18.11 Review Questions

1. What are the main editions of MS SQL Server that are marketed?

2. What are the main components of the MS SQL Server suite? Briefly discuss how these components are related.

3. Describe the default databases and logins that are provided by MS SQL Server.

4. Identify some benefits and drawbacks of the MS SQL Server suite.

18.12 References and/or Recommended Readings

[Beauchemin, 2005] Beauchemin, Bob, Niels Berglund, and Dan Sullivan. *A First Look at Microsoft SQL Server 2005 for Developers.* Microsoft Press, 2005.

[DeBetta, 2005] DeBetta, Peter. *Introducing Microsoft SQL Server (TM) 2005 for Developers (Pro – Developer).* Microsoft Press, 2005.

[Microsoft, 2008] Microsoft. *SQL Server 2005.*
http://www.microsoft.com/sql/2005/default.mspx (accessed October 2008).

[Microsoft, 2008] Microsoft, *SQL Server 2008.*
http://msdn.microsoft.com/en-us/library/bb418432(SQL.10) aspx
(accessed October 2008).

CHAPTER 19

■ ■ ■

Overview of MySQL

This chapter provides an overview of MySQL. The chapter proceeds under the following captions:

- Introduction to MySQL
- Main Features of MySQL
- Main Components of MySQL
- Shortcomings of MySQL
- Summary and Concluding Remarks

19.1 Introduction to MySQL

MySQL has become the most popular open source DBMS and the fastest growing DBMS in the industry. The product is an attractive alternative to higher-cost, more complex DBMS suites. Its award-winning speed, scalability and reliability, combined with the fact that it is free, are some of the reasons for the product's increasing popularity. The current production release series is MySQL 5.0, which was declared stable for production use in October 2005.

MySQL is currently marketed in three editions:

- MySQL Standard Edition
- MySQL Enterprise Edition
- MySQL Cluster Edition

Figure 19-1 provides the salient differences between these editions, in terms of their characteristic services and features. The editions and features are clarified on the MySQL website (see [MySQL, 2010]).

Characteristic Services and Features	MySQL Editions		
	Standard	Enterprise	Cluster
Continuous Support	Yes	Yes	Yes
Maintenance, Updates, and Patches	Yes	Yes	Yes
Knowledge Base	Yes	Yes	Yes
MySQL Core Database	Yes	Yes	Yes
MySQL Connections (via ODBC, JDBC, and .Net)	Yes	Yes	Yes
MySQL Replication	Yes	Yes	Yes
MySQL Partitioning	No	Yes	Yes
MySQL Workbench	Yes	Yes	Yes
MyISAM Storage Engine	Yes	Yes	Yes
InnoDB Storage Engine	Yes	Yes	Yes
NDB Storage Engine	No	No	Yes
MySQL Enterprise Monitor (for MySQL servers)	No	Yes	Yes
MySQL Enterprise Backup	No	Yes	Yes
MySQL Cluster Manager	No	No	Yes
MySQL Cluster Geo-Replication	No	No	Yes

Figure 19-1. Prominent Services and Features of the MySQL Editions

The original creator of MySQL is a Swedish company called MySQL AB. The company had been in operation for over ten years (1995 – 2008), before being acquired by Sun Microsystems, which has been recently acquired by Oracle. In the early stages, MySQL was used primarily for internal purposes. Over the past five years, the product's ascendancy to international acclaim has been quite noticeable. MySQL runs on multiple platforms, including Unix, Linux, Windows, Solaris, and MacOS. The maximum tablespace size supported is 64 TB. Database tables can be of any size up to this limit.

MySQL brings a number of advantages to the database arena. These are summarized in Figure 19-2.

- **Reliability and Performance:** In its relatively short existence, the product has established itself as being fairly reliable. Also, due to its relatively small size, MySQL databases tend to be relatively high on performance, when compared to larger, more complex products.

- **MySQL Software is Open Source:** Because MySQL is open source, it is free, and it brings all the benefits of open sourse products. For this reason, the product is enjoying increased popularity in the academic community as well as among small businesses.

- **Platform Independence**: MySQL runs on multiple operating system platforms. This provides users with felexibility in terms of project development and implementation.

- **Ease of Use and Deployment:** Because of the above-mentioned benefits, MySQL is very easy to deploy. The product is also easy to learn and use.

Figure 19-2. Main Benefits of MySQL

19.2 Main Features of MySQL

In order to fully MySQL, it is important to take note of the underlying features of the product. These are summarized in Figure 19-3. These features were adopted from the official MySQL Web site [MySQL AB, 2008]; minor modifications have been added to improve readability. From the list of features provided, it is clear that the intent of MySQL AB is to develop and market a comprehensive DBMS.

Internals and Portability:
- MySQL was written in C and C++.
- The product has been tested with a broad range of different compilers.
- MySQL runs on many different operating system platforms.
- Includes APIs for C, C++, Eiffel, Java, Perl, PHP, Python, Ruby, and Tcl are available.
- Implements a fully multi-threaded using kernel threads. It can easily use multiple CPUs if they are available.
- Provides transactional and non-transactional storage engines.
- Uses very fast B-tree disk tables with index compression.
- It is relatively easy to add other storage engines. This is useful if you want to add an SQL interface to an in-house database.
- Implements a very fast thread-based memory allocation system.
- Implements very fast joins using an optimized one-sweep multi-join.
- Employs in-memory hash tables, which are used as temporary tables.
- SQL functions are implemented using a highly optimized class library and should be as fast as possible. Usually there is no memory allocation at all after query initialization.
- The MySQL code is tested with Purify (a commercial memory leakage detector) as well as with Valgrind, a GPL tool (*http://developer.kde.org/~sewardj/*).
- The server is available as a separate program for use in a client/server networked environment. It is also available as a library that can be embedded (linked) into standalone applications. Such applications can be used in isolation or in environments where no network is available.

Data Types:
- MySQL supports several data types, including signed/unsigned integers 1, 2, 3, 4, and 8 bytes long, **FLOAT, DOUBLE, CHAR, VARCHAR, TEXT, BLOB, DATE, TIME, DATETIME, TIMESTAMP, YEAR, SET, ENUM,** and OpenGIS spatial types.
- Fixed-length and variable-length records.

Statements and Functions:
- Full operator and function support in the SELECT and WHERE clauses of queries.
- Full support for SQL **GROUP BY** and **ORDER BY** clauses. Support for group functions (**COUNT(), COUNT(DISTINCT ...), AVG(), STD(), SUM(), MAX(), MIN(),** and **GROUP_CONCAT()**).
- Support for LEFT OUTER JOIN and RIGHT OUTER JOIN with both standard SQL and ODBC syntax.
- Support for aliases on tables and columns as required by standard SQL.
- **DELETE, INSERT, REPLACE,** and **UPDATE** return the number of rows that were changed (affected).
- The MySQL-specific **SHOW** command can be used to retrieve information about databases, database engines, tables, and indexes.
- The **EXPLAIN** command can be used to determine how the optimizer resolves a query.
- Function names do not clash with table or column names. For example, ABS is a valid column name. The only restriction is that for a function call, no spaces are allowed between the function name and the '(' that follows it.
- You can mix tables from different databases in the same query.

Security:
- A stringent but flexible privilege-based security mechanism that allows host-based verification. Passwords traffic is encrypted when you connect to a server.

Scalability and Limits:
- Handles small as well as large databases. MySQL database server with 60,000 tables and about 5,000,000,000 rows are possible. Maximum tablespace size is 64 TB.
- Up to 64 indexes per table are allowed (32 before MySQL 4.1.2). Each index may consist of 1 to 16 columns or parts of columns. The maximum index width is 1000 bytes; before MySQL 4.1.2, the limit was 500 bytes. An index may use a prefix of a column for **CHAR, VARCHAR, BLOB,** or **TEXT** column types.

Figure 19-3. *Main Underlying Features of MySQL*

337

Connectivity:
- Clients can connect to the MySQL server using TCP/IP sockets on any platform. On Windows systems in the NT family (NT, 2000, XP, or 2003), clients can connect using named pipes. On Unix systems, clients can connect using Unix domain socket files.
- In MySQL 4.1 and higher, Windows servers also support shared-memory connections if started with the **--shared-memory** option. Clients can connect through shared memory by using the **--protocol=memory** option.
- The Connector/ODBC (MyODBC) interface provides MySQL support for client programs that use ODBC connections. For example, you can use MS Access to connect to your MySQL server. Clients can be run on Windows or Unix. MyODBC source is available. All ODBC 2.5 functions are supported, as are many others.
- The Connector/J interface provides MySQL support for Java client programs that use JDBC connections. Clients can be run on Windows or Unix. Connector/J source is available.
- MySQL Connector/NET enables developers to easily create .NET applications that require secure, high-performance data connectivity with MySQL. It implements the required ADO.NET interfaces and integrates into ADO.NET aware tools. Developers can build applications using their choice of .NET languages. MySQL Connector/NET is a fully managed ADO.NET driver written in 100% pure C#.

Geographic Localization:
- The server can provide error messages to clients in many languages.
- Full support for several different character sets, including **latin1 (cp1252)**, **german**, **big5**, **ujis**, and more. For example, the Scandinavian characters 'å', 'ä' and 'ö' are allowed in table and column names. Unicode support is available as of MySQL 4.1.
- All data is saved in the chosen character set. All comparisons for normal string columns are case-insensitive.
- Sorting is done according to the chosen character set (using Swedish collation by default). It is possible to change this when the MySQL server is started. To see an example of very advanced sorting, look at the Czech sorting code. MySQL Server supports many different character sets that can be specified at compile time and runtime.

Clients and Tools:
- MySQL Server has built-in support for SQL statements to check, optimize, and repair tables. These statements are available from the command line through the **mysqlcheck** client. MySQL also includes **myisamchk**, a very fast command-line utility for performing these operations on **MyISAM** tables.
- All MySQL programs can be invoked with the **--help** or **-?** option to obtain online assistance.

Figure 19-3. *Main Underlying Features of MySQL (continued)*

19.3 Main Components of MySQL

Compared to other DBMS suites on the market, MySQL is relatively simple, and therefore does not include a sophisticated (or convoluted) list of components. Rather, there is a list of important programs that make up the MySQL suite. The most important programs are summarized in Figure 19-4. The information provided here was adopted from the MySQL AB Web site (with minor changes to improve readability and clarity). For a more detailed discussion, the reader is referred to that site. Each program provides a help option that allows you to access useful documentation on the program in question.

mysqld: This is the SQL daemon (that is, the MySQL server). To use client programs, **mysqld** must be running, because clients gain access to databases by connecting to the server.

mysqld_safe: This is a server startup script. **mysqld_safe** attempts to start **mysqld**. **mysqld_safe** is the recommended way to start a **mysqld** server on Unix and NetWare. **mysqld_safe** adds some safety features such as restarting the server when an error occurs and logging runtime information to an error log file.

mysql.server: This is a server startup script. This script is used on systems that use System V-style run directories containing scripts that start system services for particular run levels (Linux, Solaris and Mac OS X). It invokes **mysqld_safe** to start the MySQL server. The **mysql.server** component can be found in the **support-files** directory under your MySQL installation directory or in a MySQL source distribution.

mysqld_multi: This is a server startup script that can start or stop multiple servers installed on the system. **mysqld_multi** is designed to manage several **mysqld** processes that listen for connections on different Unix socket files and TCP/IP ports. It can start or stop servers, or report their current status.

mysqlmanager: This is an alternative to the **mysql_multi** program; it is called the MySQL Instance Manager (IM). This program is a daemon running on a TCP/IP port that serves to monitor and manage MySQL Database Server instances. MySQL Instance Manager is available for Unix-like operating systems, as well as Windows.

MySQL Instance Manager can be used in place of the mysqld_safe script to start and stop the MySQL Server, even from a remote host. MySQL Instance Manager also implements the functionality (and most of the syntax) of the **mysqld_multi** script.

mysql_install_db: This script creates the MySQL database and initializes the grant tables with default privileges. It is usually executed only once, when first installing MySQL on a system.

After installing MySQL on Unix, you need to initialize the grant tables, start the server, and make sure that the server works satisfactorily. You may also wish to arrange for the server to be started and stopped automatically when your system starts and stops. You should also assign passwords to the accounts in the grant tables. On Unix, the grant tables are set up by the **mysql_install_db** program. For some installation methods, this program is run for you automatically:

mysql_fix_privilege_tables: This program is used after a MySQL upgrade operation. It updates the grant tables with any changes that have been made in newer versions of MySQL. Some releases of MySQL introduce changes to the structure of the system tables in the MySQL database to add new privileges or support new features. When you update to a new version of MySQL, you should update your system tables as well to make sure that their structure is up to date. Note: As of MySQL 5.1.7, this program has been superseded by **mysql_upgrade**.

mysql_upgrade: This program is used after a MySQL upgrade operation. It checks tables for incompatibilities, repairs them if necessary, and updates the grant tables with any changes that have been made in newer versions of MySQL. The **mysql_upgrade** program should be executed each time you upgrade MySQL. It checks all tables in all databases for incompatibilities with the current version of MySQL Server. If a table is found to have a possible incompatibility, it is checked. If any problems are found, the table is repaired. **mysql_upgrade** also upgrades the system tables so that you can take advantage of new privileges or capabilities that might have been added.

All checked and repaired tables are marked with the current MySQL version number. This ensures that next time you run **mysql_upgrade** with the same version of the server, it can tell whether there is any need to check or repair the table again. **mysql_upgrade** also saves the MySQL version number in a file named **mysql_upgrade.info** in the data directory. This is used to quickly check if all tables have been checked for this release so that table-checking can be skipped. To ignore this file, use the – **force** option.

make_binary_distribution: This program makes a binary release of a compiled MySQL database.

Figure 19-4. Important MySQL Component Programs

19.4 Shortcomings of MySQL

Like all software products, MySQL does have some limitations in its current production release (version 5.1). What is most impressive about the MySQL venture is that the developers readily admit the limitations and document them. Following is a summary of these limitations:

19.4.1 Limitation on Joins and Views

Limitation on Joins: The maximum number of tables that can be referenced in a single join is 61. This also applies to the number of tables that can be referenced in the definition of a view. This is a reasonable threshold that should not cause anyone to lose sleep.

Limitations on Views: View processing is not optimized in MySQL. Three restrictions have been documented by MySQL AB:

- You are not allowed to create indexes on views. This is significant, so MySQL AB would do well to remove it in the near future.

- Indexes can be used for views processed using MySQL's **merge** algorithm. However, a view that is processed with the **temptable** algorithm is unable to take advantage of indexes on its underlying tables (although indexes can be used during generation of the temporary tables). This is also a significant restriction that should be lifted in the future.

- Subqueries cannot be used in the **From-Clause** of a view. MySQL AB promises to lift this limitation in the future.

19.4.2 Limitations on Sub-queries

MySQL AB lists a number of restrictions on sub-queries, and promises to address them in the near future. Some of the more prominent ones are mentioned below (for a full list, go to the MySQL AB site [MySQL AB, 2008]):

1. If you compare a null value to a sub-query using operators ALL, ANY, or SOME, and the subquery returns an empty result, the comparison might evaluate to the non-standard result of NULL rather than to TRUE or FALSE.

2. A subquery's outer statement can be any one of the following: SELECT, INSERT, UPDATE, DELETE, SET, or DO.

3. Sub-query optimization for the IN (<sub-query>) construct is not as effective as for the equal (=) operator or for IN (<value-list>) constructs. A typical case for poor performance of the IN (<sub-query>) construct is when the sub-query returns a small number of rows but the outer query returns a large number of rows to be compared to the sub-query result. The problem is that, for a statement that uses an IN (<sub-query>) construct, the optimizer rewrites it as a correlated sub-query.

Example 1: The following example illustrates:

```
SELECT ... FROM Table1 t1 WHERE t1.a IN (SELECT b FROM Table2);
// The optimizer rewrites the statement to a correlated subquery:
SELECT ... FROM Table1 t1 WHERE EXISTS (SELECT b FROM Table2) t2 WHERE t2.b = t1.a);
```

If the inner and outer queries return **M** and **N** rows, respectively, the execution time becomes on the order of **f(M×N)**, rather than **f(M+N)** as it would be for an uncorrelated subquery. An implication is that query construct with IN (<sub-query>) can be much slower than a query written using an IN(<value-list>) construct that lists the same values that the sub-query would return. Obviously, this is a very undesirable situation.

4. The optimizer is more mature for joins than for subqueries, so in many cases a statement that uses a subquery can be executed more efficiently if you rewrite it as a join. An exception to this occurs for the case where an IN (<sub-query>) construct can be rewritten as a SELECT DISTINCT join construct.

Example 2: The following example illustrates:

```
SELECT <ColumnsList> FROM <Table1> WHERE <ID_col> IN (SELECT <ID_col2>
FROM <Table2> WHERE <Condition>);
// The above statement format can be rewritten as follows:
SELECT DISTINCT <ColumnsList> FROM <Table1> t1, <Table2> t2
WHERE t1.<ID_col> = t2.<ID_col> AND <Condition>);
```

Note however, that in this case, the join requires an extra DISTINCT operation and is not more efficient than the subquery. If you are not looking for distinct values in the result set, then the **Select** statement with the join is preferred to the **Select** statement with a subquery.

19.4.3 Limitations on server-side Cursors

Server-side cursors are implemented in the C programming language via the **mysql_stmt_attr_set()** function. The same implementation is used for cursors in stored routines. A server-side cursor allows a result set to be generated on the server side only; the entire result set is not necessarily transferred to the client, but only for the rows requested by the client. For example, if a client executes a query but is only interested in a few rows, the remaining rows are not transferred. In MySQL, a server-side cursor is materialized into a temporary table. Initially, this is a memory table, but is converted to disk table if its size reaches the value of the **max_heap_table_size** system variable. One limitation of the implementation is that for a large result set, retrieving its rows through a cursor might be slow.

19.4.4 Other Limitations

There are other restrictions relating to stored procedures, functions, triggers and *XA transactions*. (The acronym *XA* means *extended architecture*. The term *XA transactions* is often used to describe transactions involving different systems or databases. For instance, a client application program acting as a transaction manager in one system, may request information from a database server acting as a resource manager in another system.) These will not be discussed here; the interested reader is referred to the MySQL AB Web site [MySQL AB, 2008].

19.5 Summary and Concluding Remarks

Let us summarize what has been discussed in this chapter:

- MySQL is the most popular open source DBMS. It runs on Windows and Unix platforms, and is marketed under three editions: Standard Edition, Enterprise Edition, and Cluster Edition.

- The MySQL suite consists of a number of important component programs, including but not confined to: **mysqld**, **mysqld_safe**, **mysql.server**, **mysqlmanager**, **mysql_multi**, etc.

- The official MySQL Web site reports a number of shortcomings that are being addressed. These include but are not confined to limitations on joins, limitations on views, limitations on sub-queries, limitations on server-side cursors, etc.

MySQL has made an impressive entry into the software engineering industry, and for this reason, it is expected that the product will be around for the foreseeable future.

19.6 Review Questions

1. Briefly account for the history of MySQL.

2. Outline the characteristic features of MySQL.

3. What are the main components of the MySQL suite? Briefly discuss the functional responsibilities of each component.

4. Discuss the benefits and shortcomings of MySQL.

19.7 References and/or Recommended Readings

[Downes, 1998] Downes, Larry and Chunka Mui. *Unleashing the Killer App – Digital Strategies For Market Dominance*. Boston, MA: Harvard Business School Press, 1998.

[Dubois, 2005] Dubois, Paul. *MySQL* 3rd ed. Indianapolis, IN: Sams, 2005.

[Kofler, 2005] Kofler, Michael. *The Definitive Guide to MySQL 5* 3rd ed. Berkely, CA: Apress, 2005.

[MySQL AB, 2008] MySQL AB. *Documentation: MySQL.* http://dev.mysql.com/doc/ (accessed October 2008).

[MySQL, 2010] MySQL. MySQL Editions: http://www.mysql.com/products/ (accessed August 2010).

CHAPTER 20

■ ■ ■

Overview of Delphi

This chapter looks at the second front-end system that we will consider — Delphi. The chapter provides an overview of the product under the following subheadings:

- Introduction
- Main Components of the Delphi Suite
- Shortcomings of Delphi
- Summary and Concluding Remarks

20.1 Introduction

Delphi is an object-oriented RAD tool, which allows the software engineer to develop applications for Windows platforms. Delphi also provides a simple cross-platform solution when used in conjunction with Kylix, the equivalent RAD tool for the Linux platform. Kylix understands most of the code developed under a Delphi environment, making cross-platform software development more accessible to developers.

Delphi was developed by Borland in the early 1990s. The product evolved from Borland Turbo Pascal after the company decided to make an object-oriented Pascal version of the popular product and simplify greatly the software development process. Since 2003, the market has seen several releases including Delphi V7, Delphi V8, Delphi 2005, Delphi 2007, and Delphi 2009. The rest of the chapter will be based on a review of Delphi 2005 and Delphi 2007. However, since the chapter deliberately avoids implementation details, you will find that the information provided also applies to earlier versions all the way back to Delphi V6, as well as more recent versions. Since 2008, the Borland Software Development Division (responsible for the Delphi product line) has been acquired by software engineering firm called Embarcadero Technologies. The contemporary version of the product is called Delphi Delphi XE2, and is marketed by Embarcadero.

Delphi is best described as a front-end RAD tool that interfaces with various databases through at least one of the following strategies:

- Database drivers for Paradox, Interbase, MS SQL Server, Oracle, DB2, Informix, MySQL, Sybase, Blackfish SQL, and SQL Anywhere
- Borland Database Engine (BDE) for local database drivers
- Borland Data Provider (BDP) for .NET (this includes Interbase 7.5, MS SQL Server, Oracle, DB2, Sybase, and MS Access)

Delphi allows you to wrap an object-oriented GUI around a relational database. Figure 20-1 summarizes some of the different types of projects that Delphi can be used for, and Figure 20-2 summarizes the main strengths of the product.

Standard Delphi Projects:
- Package
- Dynamic Link Library (DLL)
- Console Application
- Visual component Library (VCL) Forms Application
- Windows Logo Application
- (Single Document Interface (SDI) Application
- Multiple Document Interface (MDI) Application

Delphi for .NET Projects:
- DB Web Control Library
- Web Control Library
- ASP.NET Web Server Application
- Enterprise Core Object (ECO) ASP.NET Web Server Application
- ECO ASP.NET Web Application
- ASP.NET Web Application
- Dynamic Link Library (DLL)
- Package
- Windows Forms Application
- VCL Forms Application
- Console Application
- ECO WinForms Application
- WinForm Controls Package

C# Projects:
- DB Web Control Library
- Web Control Library
- ASP.NET Web Server Application
- ECO ASP.NET Web Server Application
- ECO ASP.NET Web Application
- ASP.NET Web Application
- Control Library
- Class Library
- Windows Forms Application
- Console Application
- ECO Package in DLL
- ECO WinForms Application

Figure 20-1. Some Common Delphi Project Alternatives

- **Object-Oriented:** The object-oriented approach to software development, as supported by the product, enhances productivity in application development and maintenance. In particular, the effects of reusability of code (and objects), polymorphism and encapsulation are marked. Also, understandability of the system is greatly enhanced. Thus, system development becomes more exciting, challenging and meaningful.
- **Ease of Usage:** Automatic code generation (which can be easily accessed and modified) significantly allows for a significant reduction in the development time for an application. One-touch key or click allows quick access to code or changing back to visual editing of application. Code is easy to traverse, visualize, and modify, with very useful highlighters and code completion features.
- **Comprehensive Tool Palette:** Delphi provides a tool palette of over 160 reusable, customizable and extensible CLX components (in various categories) for rapidly building sophisticated internet, database and GUI applications.
- **Code Generation:** Delphi generates a fair amount of code - in fact you can build quite sophisticated applications without writing a single line of code. In more complex situations where the software engineer needs to write code, he/she gets a jump-start, which may account for anywhere between 40% and 80% of coding.
- **Ease of Learning:** The code is generated in Object Pascal, a very easy-to-learn language.
- **Scalability:** Delphi allows building large corporate-level applications either from scratch, or from using existing Delphi applications and scaling up.
- **Cross Platform Portability:** Code developed under Windows (using CLX), can be used natively under Linux using Kylix, reducing development time and cost while enlarging the potential market of developed applications.
- **Database Support:** Support for a wide cross section of databases including MS Access, DB2, dBase, FoxPro, InterBase, Informix, MS SQL, MySQL, MyBase, Oracle, Paradox, and Sybase.
- **Comprehensive Help System:** The help system is comprehensive and well organized, with context sensitivity features.
- **Operating System Integration:** The product integrates seamlessly into the MS Windows and Linux environment, utilizing the power of the operating system, rather than trying to take on tasks traditionally done by an operating system.
- **Easy Database Creation & Management:** The creation and management of databases is a case which emphasizes the previous advantage. Delphi allows you to create a database alias which points to a Windows folder containing the related database objects. Those database objects could be native database objects (for instance in Paradox), or they may be Oracle databases, or some other external database requiring access through ODBC. This is the extent to database creation and management in Delphi: it passes the job of object management to the operating system on which it is running.

Figure 20-2. *Areas of Strength of Delphi*

20.2 Major Components of the Delphi Suite

Delphi has the following major components:

- Database Development Environment
- Integrated Development Environment (IDE) and Visual Component Library (VCL)
- Borland Database Engine (BDE)
- Component Library for Cross-Reference (CLX)
- Enterprise Core Object (ECO) Subsystem
- Documentation Subsystem

20.2.1 The Database Development Environment

The available tools for manipulating databases are as follows:

- **Database Desktop:** A simple interface for creating and managing local databases.

- **Database Explorer:** An intuitive interface to the different databases, allowing the user to view all the different settings, as well as performing SQL queries and data manipulation.

- **Borland Database Engine (BDE):** A subsystem that allows programmatic access and modification of databases and the data contained in them. It is the engine between the application and the data, and facilitates access to various databases. It also provides access to non-native databases using ODBC, and other vendor products using their respective drivers.

Through the database development environment, the user can carry out the following functions:

- Create a database alias

- Create tables

- Modify table structures

- Create and modify indexes

- Create and modify logical views

- Create and modify queries, which include graphic interpretation of data

- Create and modify reports which include graphic interpretation of data

Additionally, the developer has the option of writing original SQL statements and storing these in files for later use. In summary, the main database object types facilitated are database aliases, tables, indexes, views and query files.

20.2.2 Interactive Development Environment

The Interactive Development Environment (IDE) is the Delphi component that is used for application development for Delphi, Delphi for .NET, or C++. It provides a number of useful features:

- A GUI with a number of predefined application building blocks, located on over 30 tool palettes. More commonly used tool palettes include Standard, Additional, Data Access, Data Controls, dbExpress, BDE, ActiveX, COM+, and ADO (ActiveX Data Objects).

- Context sensitive prompts to guide the application development process.

- Interactive command prompts so the developer does not have to memorize the syntax for using certain built-in procedures.

- Automatic code generation: A fairly sophisticated application can be developed with negligible coding from the developer. Code is generated in Object Pascal or C++.

- Code accessibility: For more complex/sophisticated applications, the developer can easily access the generated code and modify it.

Each Delphi project may include several types of files. The more common file types are: project files (extensions BDSPROJ and DPR), a Pascal unit file (extension PAS) with Object Pascal code for each operation with a corresponding form, and a form file (extension DFM) for each operation with a corresponding Pascal unit. By using the tool palettes and applying Object Pascal (or C++) code, other components can be easily added to the project. Some commonly used application building blocks are mentioned in Figure 20-3.

Form	MainMenu	PopupMenu	Label	EditField
Memo	OKButton	CheckBox	RadioButton	ListBox
ComboBox	ScrollBar	RadioGroup	Image	OLE Container
Timer	DataSet	DataSource	DBGrid	DBNavigator
DBText	DBEditField	DBImage	Query	SQL
Table	StoredProc	Database	ADODataSet	ADOTable
ADOQuery	RDSConnection			

Figure 20-3. *Commonly Used Building Blocks in Delphi*

Theses tools provide software engineers and application developers with much flexibility; the tools can be used to build a wide range of software applications including:

- Traditional database applications

- Client-server applications

- E-Business applications

- Web applications and services using W3C compliant technologies such as SOAP, XML, WSDL

- Web applications frameworks compatible with Apache, IIS and Netscape Web servers

- Text editors and other GUI-based applications

Delphi generates all code in Object Pascal. The code can be easily accessed and modified by the application developer. In practice, this is normally done, in order to create an acceptable user interface.

20.2.3 Database Engine

The Borland Database Engine (BDE) was the original component that allowed programmatic access and modification of databases and data. It was the engine between the application and the physical database. In application mode, the developer would typically superimpose BDE building blocks (via the BDE Tool Palette) onto forms to facilitate database access. The BDE also provided access to non-native databases using ODBC and other vendor products using their drivers. In more contemporary versions of Delphi, the DBE has been replaced by three alternatives that provide identical functionality: one is called Absolute Database; the other is called Accuracer Database system; the third component is called dbExpress.

20.2.4 Component Library for Cross Reference

Through its Component Library for Cross-Referencing (CLX), Delphi allows developing applications that can later be recompiled and used in the Linux platform (using Kylix). These libraries include:

- Traditional database applications

- Client-server applications

- E-Business applications

- Web applications

20.2.5 Enterprise Core Object Subsystem

The Enterprise Core Object (ECO) subsystem facilitates code visualization and the development and maintenance of class diagrams for an application. This component is fairly new and therefore still needs refinement.

20.2.6 Documentation

Delphi is marketed with a comprehensive help system, which covers all aspects of the software. The help system is in hypermedia format. Additionally, context sensitive help can be obtained by pressing the F1 key from anywhere during application or database development. Borland also maintains on-line documentation of the product.

20.3 Shortcomings of Delphi

Figure 20-4 provides a summary of some observed flaws about Delphi. The flaws are mainly superficial, relating to the product's user interface.

- There is not a simple SQL interface to perform complex interactive queries. However, the programmatic manipulation is very powerful and allows performing more than by interactive queries.
- Support for local databases such as dBase and Paradox is not as good as support for large-scale systems such as InterBase, MySQL, and Oracle. In fact, support for the local databases tends to be lacking (thus confirming that Delphi is really a front-end system which will facilitate the construction of an application which accesses a back-end database).
- The documentation provided by the product is suited for experienced developers. It assumes the user is familiar with the Delphi environment. There are several books on Delphi software development available at bookstores that attempt to address this problem.
- The installation of Delphi in a networked environment where workstations are shared among many people (computer lab setting, for example) gives a lot of problems since the product requires registration of the software suite. The software assumes a user is going to use the same workstation all the time.

Figure 20-4. *Some Observed Flaws of Delphi*

Delphi provides a RAD tool that once learned, can cut down development greatly, it simplifies Windows application development, and it gives the freedom to use assembler instructions, or object oriented constructs and components that promise modularity and reduced maintenance in the long run. With its good performance at compile and run time, scalability and good database support, Delphi competes with the best software developments tools in the market.

20.4 Summary and Concluding Remarks

It is now time to summarize what has been discussed in this chapter:

- Delphi is best described as a front-end RAD tool that connects to any back-end database via ODBC; but it also provides limited back-end database services. The product runs on Windows, Linux and Unix platforms.

- The Delphi suite includes the following components: Database Development Environment, Integrated Development Environment (IDE), Visual Component Library (VCL), Borland database Engine (BDE), Component Library for Cross-Reference (CLX), and the Delphi Documentation.

- A few shortcomings have been observed about Delphi; they relate to support for dBase and Paradox databases, the documentation, and product registration.

Delphi is an excellent product that has been tested and refined over time. It is anticipated that this product will be around for the foreseeable future.

20.5 Review Questions

1. Identify some benefits of running a Delphi database (front-end) environment.

2. Identify and briefly discuss the main components of the Delphi suite.

3. Discuss some of the observed shortcomings of Delphi.

20.6 References and/or Recommended Readings

[Embarcadero, 2008] Embarcadero Technologies. *Delphi*. http://www.embarcadero.com/products/delphi/ (accessed October 2008).

[Cantu, 2005] Cantu, Marco. *Mastering Delphi 2005*. Sybex Publishing, 2005.

[Intersimone, 2007a] Intersimone, David. *Antique Software: Turbo Pascal 1.0* http://bdn.borland.com/article/0,1410,20693,00.html (accessed October 2008).

[Intersimone, 2007b] Intersimone, David. *Antique Software: Turbo Pascal 5.5* http://bdn.borland.com/article/0,1410,20803,00.html (accessed October 2008).

PART E

■ ■ ■

Advanced Topics

This division of the text covers some advanced topics in database system that you should be familiar with.

The objectives of this division are

- to introduce you to the salient issues related to database administration;

- to introduce you to the theory, advantages, and challenges of distributed databases;

- to provide an overview of object databases, and point out the challenges faced by the approach;

- to provide an overview of data warehousing;

- to provide an overview of Web-accessible databases, and the supporting technologies.

The division includes five chapters, each providing an overview of an area of database systems that could be further explored.

The chapters to be covered include the following:

- Chapter 21 — Database Management

- Chapter 22 — Distributed Database Systems

- Chapter 23 — Object Databases

- Chapter 24 — Data Warehousing

- Chapter 25 — Web-Accessible Databases

Please note that for each of these topics, several texts have been written. It will therefore not be possible to cover them in detail. Rather, in each case, an overview is provided, outlining the salient issues.

■ ■ ■

CHAPTER 21

Database Administration

We have established the importance of a database as a valuable information resource in the organization. This resource must be carefully administered (managed) in order to ensure the continued operation and success of the organization. In this regard, the database administrator is extremely important (database administrators are among the highest paid IT professionals).

This chapter provides an overview of database administration. It discusses (from an administrative view point) the following issues:

- Database Installation, Creation and Configuration

- Database Security

- Database Management

- Database Backup and Recovery

- Database Tuning

- Database Removal

- Summary and Concluding Remarks

Please note that a solitary chapter which overviews database administration will not make you a good database administrator (DBA). To achieve that objective, you will need to apply the knowledge in this course, combined with additional knowledge gained from a special course in database administration. This chapter helps to prepare you for that vocation by providing an overview of database administration issues.

21.1 Database Installation, Creation, and Configuration

Before any work can be done, the database software must be installed. This is usually a straightforward, but time consuming process. For large, sophisticated products such as Oracle and DB2, installation could get complicated, since decisions have to be made about what components to install, where (in terms of directories or folders) to store certain resources, and what environmental or configuration settings to choose. For simpler products like MySQL and Delphi, the installation process is correspondingly simpler.

Next, the database must be created and configured. Depending on the DBMS suite that is in use, database creation and configuration may be very simple or quite complicated. In some systems (for example Delphi), database creation is a simple act of creating a directory (in the Linux environment) or folder (in the Windows environment), and then creating database aliases that point to that directory or folder. In others such as MySQL, there is a highly simplified **Create-Database** statement that allows you to create a database within seconds. On the other end of the spectrum, there are systems such as Oracle, for which you must first complete a course before you know how to properly create a database (review Oracle's version of the **Create-Database** statement in Chapter 11). And there are those products in between the two extremes.

Once you have created the database, there are issues that must be determined as part of the database configuration. These issues include the following:

- Location of the database and its related files

- Communication issues for server and client (for client-server databases) in a multi-user environment

- Physical structure of the database

- Logical structure of the database

- Users of the database and their access rights

Like database creation, the complexity of these issues, and the flexibility with which they can be addressed, will depend to a large extent on the products involved, as well as the complexity of the database itself.

21.2 Database Security

Database security is a very important aspect of database administration. Ideally, the security mechanism must be multi-tiered, controlling access to the system, the system resources, and the system data. The DBA must ensure the following:

- Access to the system is controlled.

- Authorized users must be able to access (insert, modify, retrieve or delete) data that they are authorized to access.

- Authorized users must be restricted to the data and resources that they are duly authorized to access and nothing more.

- Unauthorized users must have absolutely no access.

In order to achieve this, the DBA must be fully conversant with SQL facilities (commands) for managing database users and objects. The information covered in Chapter 13 is particularly relevant here. Some DBMS suites are marketed with a GUI, which is superimposed on the basic SQL interface, and provides a more user-friendly environment for working, by generating SQL code (which can be subsequently accessed and modified) to GUI-based instructions. Examples of this in the Oracle suite include Oracle Enterprise Manager (OEM), iSQL Plus, and Oracle SQL Developer (OSQLD).

To further reinforce the security mechanism of the database, more sophisticated products provide the facility to encrypt data stored in database files. In other products, the conventional wisdom is to rely on the encryption feature provided by the underlying operating system.

21.3 Database Management

As mentioned in Chapter 11, once the database has been created, it must be populated with database objects. Database objects include tablespaces (specific to Oracle), tables, indexes, views, synonyms, procedures, triggers, packages, sequences, users, roles, etc. Most of these database objects are dynamic and will grow or shrink in size, with the passing of time. The database and its objects must therefore be managed.

Database management is a complex matter that covers a wide range of activities; among these are the following:

- Reorganizing existing database tables and indexes

- Deleting unnecessary indexes or moving other objects

- Making alterations to the database itself

- Making alterations to database components (tablespaces, datafiles, tables, procedures, etc.)

- Creating additional database objects (tablespaces, datafiles, tables, users, indexes, procedures, etc.)

- Training users

- Backup and recovery of database objects

- Database performance tuning

Most of these issues have been discussed in previous chapters. The last two issues — backup and recovery, and database performance tuning — deserve some attention. They will be addressed in the next two sections.

21.4 Database Backup and Recovery

In general, the term database backup and recovery refers to the various strategies and procedures involved in protecting a database against data loss, and reconstructing the data should that loss occur. The reconstructing of data is achieved through media recovery, which refers to the various operations involved in restoring, rolling forward, and rolling back a backup of database files. Like database installation, creation and configuration, backup and recovery can be quite simple or very complex, depending on the database environment, and the desired objectives. For the remainder of this section, we shall consider, as case study, backup and recovery in the Oracle environment (it does not get any more complicated than this).

21.4.1 Oracle Backups: Basic Concept

A backup is a copy of data. This backup may include important parts of the database such as the control file, datafile(s), or tablespace(s); alternately, it may involve the entire database. A backup is a safeguard against unexpected data loss and application errors. If you lose the original data, then you can reconstruct it by using a backup.

Backups are divided into physical backups and logical backups. Physical backups, which are the primary concern in a backup and recovery strategy, are copies of physical database files. You can make physical backups with either the Oracle Recovery Manager (RMAN) utility or operating system utilities. In contrast, logical backups contain logical data (for example, tables and stored procedures) extracted with the Oracle Export utility and stored in a binary file. You can use logical backups to supplement physical backups.

21.4.2 Oracle Recovery: Basic Concept

Recovery is the opposite of backup. A database recovery is effected from a database backup, so if the backup was not done, the recovery is not an option. Like backup, recovery may involve a component or section of the database (from a control file, datafile(s) or tablespace(s)), or it may involve an entire database.

To restore a physical backup of a datafile or control file is to reconstruct it and make it available to the Oracle database server. To recover a restored datafile is to update it by applying archived redo logs, and online redo logs, that is, records of changes made to the database after the backup was taken. If you use RMAN, then you can also recover restored datafiles with incremental backups, which are backups of a datafile that contain only blocks that changed after a previous incremental backup.

After the necessary files are restored, media recovery must be initiated by the user. Media recovery can use both archived redo logs and online redo logs to recover the datafiles. If you use SQL*Plus, then you can run the RECOVER command to perform recovery. If you use RMAN, then you run the RMAN RECOVER command to perform recovery.

21.4.3 Types of Failures

Several circumstances can halt the operation of an Oracle database. The most common types of failure are described in Figure 21-1. Oracle provides for complete recovery from all possible types of hardware failures, including disk crashes. Options are provided so that a database can be completely recovered or partially recovered to a specific point in time.

Failure Type	Comment
User error	User errors can require a database to be recovered to a point in time before the error occurred. For example, a user may accidentally drop a table. To enable recovery from user errors and accommodate other unique recovery requirements, Oracle provides exact point-in-time recovery. For example, if a user accidentally drops a table, the database can be recovered to the instant in time before the table was dropped.
Statement Failure	**Statement failure** occurs when there is a logical failure in the handling of a statement in an Oracle program (for example, the statement is not a valid SQL construction). When statement failure occurs, the effects (if any) of the statement are automatically undone by Oracle and control is returned to the user.
Process Failure	A **process failure** is a failure in a user process accessing Oracle, such as an abnormal disconnection or process termination. The failed user process cannot continue work, although Oracle and other user processes can. The Oracle background process PMON automatically detects the failed user process or is informed of it by SQL*Net. PMON resolves the problem by rolling back the uncommitted transaction of the user process and releasing any resources that the process was using.
	Common problems such as erroneous SQL statement constructions and aborted user processes should never halt the database system as a whole. Furthermore, Oracle automatically performs necessary recovery from uncommitted transaction changes and locked resources with minimal impact on the system or other users.
Instance Failure	**Instance failure** occurs when a problem arises that prevents an instance from continuing work. Instance failure can result from a hardware problem such as a power outage, or a software problem such as an operating system crash. When an instance failure occurs, the data in the buffers of the system global area is not written to the datafiles.
	Instance failure requires **crash recovery** or **instance recovery**. Crash recovery is automatically performed by Oracle when the instance restarts. In an Oracle9*i* Real Application Clusters environment, the SMON process of another instance performs instance recovery. The redo log is used to recover the committed data in the SGA's database buffers that was lost due to the instance failure.
Media (disk) Failure	An error can occur when trying to write or read a file that is required to operate the database. This is called disk failure because there is a physical problem reading or writing physical files on disk. A common example is a disk head crash, which causes the loss of all files on a disk drive.
	Different files can be affected by this type of disk failure, including the datafiles, the redo log files, and the control files. Also, because the database instance cannot continue to function properly, the data in the database buffers of the system global area cannot be permanently written to the datafiles.
	A disk failure requires **media recovery**. Media recovery restores a database's datafiles so the information in them corresponds to the most recent time point before the disk failure, including committed data in memory that was lost because of the failure. To complete a recovery from a disk failure, the following is required: backups of the database's datafiles, and all online and necessary archived redo log files.

Figure 21-1. *Types of Database Failures*

If some datafiles are damaged during a disk failure, but most of the database is intact and operational, the database can remain open while the required tablespaces are individually recovered. Therefore, undamaged portions of a database are available for normal use while damaged portions are being recovered. This is a very desirable feature, especially for large corporate databases that must be up and running "twenty four by seven."

21.4.4 Database Backups

Because one or more files can be physically damaged as the result of a disk failure, media recovery requires the restoration of the damaged files from the most recent operating system backup of a database. There are several ways to back up the files of a database.

Whole Database Backups

A whole database backup is an operating system backup of all datafiles, online redo log files, and the control file of an Oracle database. A whole database backup is performed when the database is closed and unavailable for use.

Partial Backups

A partial backup is an operating system backup of part of a database. The backup of an individual tablespace's datafiles and the backup of a control file are examples of partial backups. Partial backups are useful only when the database's redo log is operated in ARCHIVELOG mode.

A variety of partial backups can be taken to accommodate any backup strategy. For example, you can back up datafiles and control files when the database is open or closed, or when a specific tablespace is online or offline. Because the redo log is operated in ARCHIVELOG mode, additional backups of the redo log are not necessary. The archived redo log is a backup of filled online redo log files.

21.4.5 Basic Recovery Steps

Because of the way the Oracle Database Writer (DBWn) writes database buffers to datafiles, at any given time, a datafile might contain some tentative modifications by uncommitted transactions and might not contain some modifications by committed transactions. Therefore, two potential situations can result after a failure:

- Data blocks containing committed modifications were not written to the datafiles, so the changes appear only in the redo log. Therefore, the redo log contains committed data that must be applied to the datafiles.

- Because the redo log can contain data that was not committed, uncommitted transaction changes applied by the redo log during recovery must be erased from the datafiles.

To solve this situation, two separate steps are used by Oracle during recovery from an instance or media failure: rolling forward and rolling back.

Rolling Forward

The first step of recovery is to **roll forward**, which is to reapply to the datafiles all of the changes recorded in the redo log. Rolling forward proceeds through as many redo log files as necessary to bring the datafiles forward to the required time.

If all necessary redo information is online, Oracle rolls forward automatically when the database starts. After roll forward, the datafiles contain all committed changes as well as any uncommitted changes that were recorded in the redo log.

Rolling Back

The roll forward is only half of recovery. After the roll forward, any changes that were not committed must be undone. After the redo log files have been applied, then the undo records are used to identify and undo transactions that were never committed yet were recorded in the redo log. This process is called **rolling back**. Oracle completes this step automatically.

21.4.6 Oracle's Backup and Recovery Solutions

There are two methods for performing Oracle backup and recovery: Recovery Manager (RMAN) and user-managed backup and recovery. RMAN is a utility automatically installed with the database that can back up any Oracle8 or later database. RMAN uses server sessions on the database to perform the work of backup and recovery. RMAN has its own syntax and is accessible either through a command-line interface or though the Oracle Enterprise Manager GUI. RMAN comes with an API that allows it to function with a third-party media manager.

One of the principal advantages of RMAN is that it obtains and stores metadata about its operations in the control file of the production database. You can also set up an independent recovery catalog, which is a schema that contains metadata imported from the control file, in a separate recovery catalog database. RMAN performs the necessary record keeping of backups, archived logs, and so forth using the metadata, so restore and recovery is greatly simplified.

An alternative method of performing recovery is to use operating system commands for backups and SQL*Plus for recovery. This method, also called user-managed backup and recovery, is fully supported by Oracle Corporation, although use of RMAN is highly recommended because it is more robust and greatly simplifies administration.

Whether RMAN is used, or user-managed methods, physical backups can be supplemented with logical backups of schema objects made using the Oracle Export utility. The utility writes data from an Oracle database to binary operating system files. You can later use Oracle Import to restore this data into a database.

21.5 Database Tuning

To maintain acceptable database performance, it is necessary to carry out periodic performance tuning. As the database is being used, it will exhibit a natural tendency to degraded performance. The current database system may not be performing acceptably, based on user-defined criteria, due to any of the following:

- Poor database design

- Database growth

- Changing application requirements (possibly including a redefinition of what acceptable performance is)

Note however, that there might be occasions when database tuning efforts are not fully effective. When components that are external to the database, yet vital to the entire client-server application performance, fail to perform acceptably, database tuning might not help without the corresponding tuning of these other application infrastructure pieces. The main components external to the backend database are the backend operating system, the network, and the client operating system. The major examples are the following:

- Very weak clients (PCs)

- Network saturation

- Very weak, saturated, or poorly tuned operating system

21.5.1 Tuning Goals

There are different ways of determining the goals of a performance tuning effort. A DBA should consider them all. Database systems can be sampled on various quantitative measures; the most important of these are the following:

- Throughput: This is the accomplished work per unit time, as measured by transactions per second (tps); higher is better.

- Response time: This is the time it takes for an application to respond, as measured in milliseconds or seconds, lower is better.

- Wait time: This is the elapsed time a program takes to run; lower is better.

In any system, throughput and response time usually run counter to one another as tuning goals. If response time is high (bad), throughput might be high (good). If throughput is low (bad), response time might be low (good).

Common sense helps when sorting out these two conflicting measures. The more users that are concurrently using a system within a certain amount of time, the more likely it is that each user will experience longer delays than normal, but the number of transactions going through the system will be greater. On the other hand, if you decrease the number of concurrent users accessing the system within a certain time window, each user will enjoy faster response time at the expense of fewer overall transactions completing in that duration.

Typically, on-line transaction processing (OLTP) systems (also called operational databases) want low response time or high throughput, in terms of transactions per second, depending on the application needs. A decision support system (DSS) also wants low response time. However, a DSS might also want high throughput in terms of data blocks read or written per unit time. This type of throughput is not necessarily counterproductive to high concurrency and low response times. A batch (production) system typically wants lower wait times. For example, everyone likes for the payroll application to complete on time!

It is important to always consider the following two central tuning goals:

- Maximize your return on investment (ROI). Invest your time and effort wisely by working on the problems most likely to yield the optimum improvement.

- Minimize contention. Bottlenecks are characterized by delays and waits; eliminate or reduce these whenever possible.

Finally, the following general-purpose database tuning goals should be considered:

- Minimize the number of data blocks that need to be accessed; review and rewrite database access code as necessary.

- Use caching, buffering, and queuing whenever possible to compensate for the electro-mechanical disadvantage (memory is faster than disk).

- Minimize the data transfer rates (the time it takes to read or write data); fast disks, RAID, and parallel operations help do this.

- Schedule concurrent programs that complement instead of compete with each other.

21.5.2 Tuning Methodology

It is best to approach tuning with a structured methodology. After ensuring that the operating system is performing at its peak and that sufficient operating system resources have been allocated to your database system, you should tune following in this order:

- Database design
- Database application
- Memory management
- I/O management
- Database contention

Database Design Tuning: In database design tuning, you are concerned with the physical and logical structure of the database. During this exercise, the DBA examines and takes decisions about refining the logical and physical structure of the database. Among the issues that may be addressed are the following:

- Determining whether critical database components (tablespaces, datafiles, log-files, etc) need to be redefined and/or relocated (to different directories/folders).

- Determining whether critical database objects (primarily tablespaces and tables) need to be partitioned (i.e. fragmented into different partitions).

- Determining whether critical database tables need to be restructured.

- Determining whether additional database objects (tables, logical views, etc.) are required, and if so, where they should be placed.

Database Application Tuning: In database application tuning, the concern is on end-user access to the database. During this exercise, the DBA determines ways to better facilitate access to the database by the various applications that need to use it. Among the issues that may be addressed are the following:

- Ascertaining whether existing database application objects (procedures, triggers, etc.) are performing according to expectations.

- Determining whether additional database application objects (procedures, triggers, etc.) are required and where to place them.

- Determining whether adequate database access points (including ODBC connections, database service connections, etc.) are in place and are working acceptably.

Memory and I/O Management Tuning: Memory management tuning in closely related to database design tuning. This is critical because poor database design could lead to poor memory performance which in turn leads to poor database performance. Among the issues that may be addressed are the following:

- Storage allocations for database objects (primarily tablespaces, datafiles, and tables).

- Storage allocations for the database itself (these parameters are set at database creation or database alteration).

Oracle provides a number of utilities for managing memory performance of database tables. However, a full discussion of these is beyond the scope of this course. Suffice it to say that the database fault rate on each table can be monitored. If the fault rate is high, the table needs to be reorganized.

Database Contention: Database contention relates to how the database is handling multi-user access as well as concurrent access. Like memory management, there are specific utilities for managing this issue; these utilities are typically provided by the DBMS suite.

21.6 Database Removal

Sometimes, it becomes necessary to remove a database. Often, there is no specific command for this, for obvious reasons: The database exists under the auspices of the host operating system. Database removal is therefore an operating system command.

Depending on the DBMS being used, database removal may be a trivial matter, or one requiring a few steps. For instance, removal of a Delphi or MySQL database involves a single step. On the other hand, removing an Oracle database involves several steps of deleting related folders/directories managed by the DBMS in collaboration with the underlying operating system. These folders/directories were created when the database was created (or altered).

Once a database has been deleted, it is completely gone, and can only be reintroduced via a recovery operation.

21.7 Summary and Concluding Remarks

Here is a summary of what has been discussed in this chapter:

- Depending on the DBMS being used, database creation may be complex or simple. Delphi and Oracle are at the two extreme ends of the spectrum — database creation is very simple in Delphi, and very complex in Oracle.

- Database security must ideally be multi-tiered. It must address access to the system, access to the system resources, and access to data.

- Database management must continue after database creation. It must address issues relating to the performance of the database system in the face of growing data collection and changing user needs. Database tuning is and integral part of this.

- Backup must be carefully planned and methodically implemented, in order to minimize or eliminate data loss due to system failures. The recovery procedures must also be reviewed as required.

- Like database creation, depending on the DBMS used, database removal may be trivial or complex.

21.8 Review Questions

1. What are the main issues to be considered when creating a database?

2. What are the critical issues to be addressed when configuring the security mechanism of a database?

3. What are the main issues to be addressed during the management of a database?

4. Why are backups important? Discuss how backup and recovery are handled in Oracle.

5. Why is performance tuning of a database important? Identify basic tuning guidelines to be observed.

21.9 References and/or Recommended Readings

[Hoffer, 2007] Hoffer, Jeffrey A., Mary B. Prescott and Fred R. McFadden. *Modern Database Management* 8th ed. Upper Saddle River, NJ: Prentice Hall, 2007. See Chapter 12.

[Mullins, 2002] Mullins, Craig S. *Database Administration: The Complete Guide to Practices and Procedures*. Reading, MA: Addison-Wesley, 2002.

[Oracle, 2008] Oracle Corporation. *Documentation: Oracle10G Database Release 2 Documentation*. http://technet.Oracle.com (accessed October 2008).

[Rob, 2007] Rob, Peter and Carlos Coronel. *Database Systems: Design, Implementation & Management* 7th ed. Boston, MA: Course Technology, 2007. See Chapters 11 and 15.

CHAPTER 22

■ ■ ■

Distributed Database Systems

As wonderful as database systems are, they would not be delivering on their true potential, if they could not be networked in a distributed environment. This chapter discusses distributed database systems under the following subheadings:

- Introduction

- Advantages of Distributed Database Systems

- Twelve Rules for Distributed Database Systems

- Challenges to Distributed Database Systems

- Database Gateways

- The Future of Distributed Database Systems

- Summary and Concluding Remarks

22.1 Introduction

The concept of a distributed system was introduced in Chapter 2. A distributive database system consists of a collection of sites, connected via a communication network in which:

- Each site is a database system in its own right.

- The sites work together (if necessary) so that a user at any given site can access data at any other site as if the data resides of the host (user's) site.

Section 2.7 of Chapter 2 mentioned some connectivity possibilities. Here are a few noteworthy points to remember:

1. From the definition, the user is given the notion of virtual database systems consisting of data that may reside anywhere in the network.

2. The sites may be distributed over a wide geographical area, or in a local area/building. A distributed database system can therefore be a LAN (local area network), a MAN (metropolitan area network), or a WAN (wide area network).

3. Distributed database systems are not to be confused with remote access systems, sometimes called distributive processing systems. The latter has been around for some time. In such systems, the user accesses data at remote sites but the operation is not seamless; the user is aware and the consequences may be obvious. In a distributed database system, access across sites is seamless.

The literature [on electronic communications and computer networks] documents several alternate approaches to setting up a distributed database. Three prevalent ones are as follows:

- Using client-server technology to set up a federated database

- Setting up a virtual private network (VPN)

- Setting up a data warehouse

There is no shortage of information on client-server technology and VPNs. Exploration of this is beyond the scope of this course; however, references [Martin, 1995] and [Ozsu, 1999] should provide you with a useful start. Suffice it to say that Oracle as described earlier (Chapters 10-16) qualifies as a distributed DBMS. When you install Oracle Server on a node in a network, that node acts as a database server. If you then install Oracle Client on other nodes in the network, your database server can be accessed from anywhere in the network (as well as from other network systems with Web accessibility) in a seamless manner. Also, Chapters 24 and 25 provide overview of data warehousing and Web-accessible databases respectively.

22.2 Advantages of Distributed Database Systems

Figure 22-1 provides some benefits that distributed database systems provide. The benefits may be summarized in three categories:

- Efficiency and Productivity

- Convenience

- Reliability

Efficiency and Productivity:

1. Improved response time and throughput since processing (front-end and back-end as well as at different sites) can be done in parallel.
2. Data (from foreign sites) can be replicated (locally) to improve access time.
3. Easy and fast communication over relatively long distances.
4. Distributive database systems can ensure that the best resources are brought together and utilized in such systems.

Convenience:

5. The systems used (back-ends and front-ends, and at different sites) may be different according to the needs and circumstances of the (users of) respective sites.
6. The structure of the database can mirror the structure of the enterprise — local data is stored locally; access is available to other data over the network.
7. Due to information sharing, the integrated system provides for more data storage, (possibly) increased functionality and features than a single database system.
8. The system is more easily designed to facilitate multiple users (this could lead to improved productivity).

Reliability:

9. Reduction of dependence on a central system (also, this might not be practical).
10. Improved reliability: if one machine fails, the whole system does not fail (there is no reliance on a central system).

Figure 22-1. *Benefits of Distributed Database Systems*

When weighed against the challenges posed by distributed database (discussed later), they outweigh them by a huge margin; we therefore expect the continued proliferation of distributed databases.

22.3 Twelve Rules for Distributed Database Systems

In his classic text, *Introduction to Database Systems,* Christopher Date discusses twelve rules (objectives) for distributed database systems [Date, 2004]. Let us take a brief look at these rules.

Rule 1: Local Autonomy

The sites should be autonomous to the maximum possible extent. All operations at a site are governed by that site alone. This is not always entirely possible, but is an objective to strive for.

Rule 2: No Reliance on Central Site

This is a consequence of objective 1. The sites must be treated as equals. There is no reliance on a central site. Reliance on a central site would make the system vulnerable to the central site (bottleneck could occur or the central site could go down). This is undesirable.

Rule 3: Continuous Operation

The system must be able to run continuously. There should be no need for a planned shut down in order to carry out any function (for instance backup or tuning).

Rule 4: Location Independence (Transparency)

Users should not need to know where data is physically stored in order to access it; the system should operate as if all the data resided at the local site. The distributed nature of the database must be transparent to the end end users.

Rule 5: Fragmentation Independence

The system should support data fragmentation — it should be possible to partition a given relation into fragments that are stored at different sites. Thus, data can be stored where it is most frequently used. Network trafficking is therefore reduced. Fragmentation should be transparent to the end users.

Example 1: Suppose that a large organization has employee records in an **Employee** relation. The departments are at different localities. Records for each department are stored at different sites in those respective departments. This can be easily facilitated in Oracle or DB2 by *partitioning* the **Employee** table. A full discussion of table partitioning is beyond the scope of this course. However, suffice it to say that that this is the technique used by several leading DBMS suites to facilitate fragmentation independence.

Rule 6: Replication Independence

A given relation (or fragment of a relation) can be replicated at different sites. Replication may improve access time and hence performance. The drawback however, is that at update, all copies have to be updated simultaneously. Replication should be transparent to the end users.

Rule 7: Distributed Query Processing

Distributed query processing must be facilitated among different sites. Records are transmitted set (relation) at a time instead of record at a time.

Example 2: Suppose we have an international company, IBM, say, where employees are stored in the relation **Employee**, fragmented in various countries, where there are IBM offices. IBM Canada, issues the request: "Find all Jamaican male employees." Then:

a. Suppose there are n records that satisfy this request. If the system is relational, the query will involve tw o messages one from Canada to Jamaica and one from Jamaica to Canada. If the system is not relational, but record-at-a-time, the query will involve $2n$ messages — n from Canada to Jamaica and n from Jamaica to Canada.

b. Query optimization of the request occurs before execution (record-at-a -time requests cannot be optimized).

Due to these two points, distributive database systems are usually relational.

Rule 8: Distributed Transaction Management

Each transaction must be atomic — fully committed or fully rolled back. This objective must be met irrespective of the agents (constituent processes) of the transaction. Concurrency control must be ensured (usually by data locking).

Rule 9: Hardware Independence

It should be possible to integrate the system across different hardware platforms. It should therefore be possible to run the DBMS on different hardware systems.

Rule 10: Operating System Independence

It should be possible to integrate the system across different operating system platforms. It should therefore be possible to run the DBMS on different operating systems.

Rule 11: Network Independence

The system should be able to support different sites with different hardware and different operating systems and networking protocols.

Rule 12: DBMS Independence

The DBMS suites used may be different. For instance DB2 and Oracle both support SQL and open database connectivity (ODBC); it should therefore be possible to link databases running on the two DBMS suites. The same argument should apply for other DBMS suites.

22.4 Challenges to Distributed Database Systems

Distributed databases did not come easily; neither were they easy to maintain. Fortunately, the software engineering industry has figured out how to address these challenges. However, improving the algorithms used, and finding new ones are always topical research issues. There are five well known challenges to distributed database systems. These are:

- Query Optimization
- Catalog Management
- Update Propagation
- Concurrency Control
- Transaction Management

Query Optimization

Query optimizing processing must be distributed in order to minimize network trafficking. To illustrate, consider a query Qa of site A, accessing to relations in a natural join: Rb of site B and Rc of site C. The optimizer must decide on one of the following strategies:

    a.   Move copies of Rb and Rc to site A

    b.   Move copy of Rb to site C and process the join there

    c.   Move copy of Rc to site B and process the join there

    The optimizer must be able to calculate what would be most economical alternative (given the structure and configuration of the underlying network) and choose that alternative. For example, Oracle implements two query optimization strategies — a rule-based optimization and a cost-based optimization. Before executing a query, the query optimizer optimizes the query by converting it to an internal format (based on an Oracle algorithm) that will ensure the most efficient execution.

Catalog Management

Catalog management is one of the most complex issues that a distributed database must resolve. This is so since additional information must be stored for the database objects (e.g. fragmentation, replication, location etc.). Where and how the catalog should be stored is a complicated issue. Below are some alternatives:

- **Centralized:** The catalog is stored at a centralized location, and is accessible to the other participating sites.

- **Fully Replicated:** The catalog is replicated at each participating site.

- **Partitioned:** Each site maintains its own catalog. The total catalog is the union of each site catalog.

- **Hybrid:** Each site maintains its own catalog; additionally, a central site maintains the global catalog.

    Each of these approaches has its related advantages and challenges. Resolving this issue is often done with the use of simulation software, and much research into the matter.

Update Propagation

In the case where data is replicated at different sites, it may not be possible to effect update to all replicas at the desired time. How is this resolved? The *primary copy* approach is a common method of resolution:

- One replica is deemed the primary copy. As soon as that copy is updated, the update process is deemed completed.

- The site with the primary copy is responsible for updating the other sites as son as possible.

This somewhat contradicts the objectives of transaction independence and redundancy control. As was emphasized in chapter 4, once data replication is introduced in a database, with it come various other data integrity problems. Resolution is therefore a matter of tradeoff.

Concurrency

Concurrency is another issue that must be resolved. To illustrate, consider what might happen if user X tries to retrieve a particular data set for update purposes, but that data set is being updated by another user Y. Consider that in a distributed system, there might be thousands of users, so that this kind of contention could easily develop among several users. Typically, the DBMS handles this problem by *record locking*: a record or data set that is retrieved for update is *locked* to that transaction until the update is completed; it is then released (unlocked) for other users. Requests to release (*unlock*) objects in a distributed database system must be managed. This is a serious overhead.

In application development where distributed databases are accessed, or there is multi-user access of a single database, the application programmer must check for record lock on a data set before attempting to lock that data set. The application programmer must program a graceful recovery from a record lock situation (normally done by issuing an appropriate message to the end user and allowing them to defer that particular request until some subsequent time).

Transaction Management

Issues such as when to lock records, and when to commit or rollback transactions are critical in a distributed database. The application developer must be familiar with the facilities provided by the DBMS and SQL (COMMIT and ROLLBACK) for managing transactions.

22.5 Database Gateways

Traditionally, a database gateway is a software component that links two different DBMS suites. It could run on either of the two systems running the dissimilar DBMS suites, or on a separate machine for that purpose. The simplest configuration is to run the software on either system as a driver for the other DBMS. Another alternative is to use the software called Open Database Connectivity (ODBC). ODBC is marketed with the Windows operating system, and is readily available for other operating systems.

Suppose for instance, that Oracle and DB2 both support SQL (as in fact, they do). It should therefore be possible to link the two DBMS suites, as illustrated in Figure 22-2. In reality, each product includes an ODBC driver that in effect acts as the gateway. Following are some functions of the gateway:

- Mapping between the two different protocols (formats)

- Mapping between the two different dialects of SQL (e.g. Oracle's dialect versus DB2's dialect)

373

- Mapping between the two different system catalogs so that users of one DBMS (Oracle) can access all files from the other DBMS (DB2)

- Mapping between the two different sets of data used

- Resolution of semantic mismatches across the two systems (e.g. attribute **Employee.Empno** in a DB2 table may map to **Empl.Emp#** in an Oracle table)

- Resolution of transaction management issues such as data locking, updates, commit and rollback

- Resolution of security and accessibility issues across the two different systems

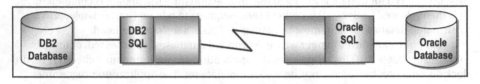

Figure 22-2. *Illustrating the Function of a Database Gateway*

By way of example, Oracle operates a very sophisticated gateway system that allows connectivity to other non-Oracle databases either directly through its gateway, or indirectly through ODBC (see [Oracle, 2008]). Among the many features of the Oracle gateway system are the following:

- Location independence and transparency

- Data-type translations between Oracle and non-Oracle systems

- Data dictionary between Oracle and non-Oracle systems

- Read/write access

- Support for large objects (LOBs)

- Support for non-Oracle stored procedures

- Transmission of pass-through SQL between Oracle and non-Oracle system

- Data encryption services

22.6 The Future of Distributed Database Systems

Since the mid-1990's, two significant technologies have significantly influenced the development and direction of distributed databases. These are:

- Object Technology (OT)

- Electronic Communication Systems (ECS)

22.6.1 Object Technology

In a few short years, OT has come to dominate the contemporary software engineering industry. New products are forced by industry demands to support OT in some form. Much work has been done by the Object Management Group (OMG) in establishing the Common Object Request Broker Architecture (CORBA) standards for distributed database systems. The Microsoft equivalents of CORBA are Component Object Model (COM), Distributed COM (DCOM), and more recently, the .NET framework.

CORBA standards span a wide range of specifications from user interface to object-object communication. They are supported by some of the leading software engineering firms in the industry. With the emergence of Java, the software industry has made significant progress in the area of platform independent software components than ever before. As mentioned in chapter 6, Java (through JDBC) supports both CORBA and ODBC.

22.6.2 Electronic Communication Systems

Complimentary to the advances in OT, the past decade has seen much achievement in the arena of *electronic communication systems* (ECS). Contemporary operating systems are more sophisticated, supporting a wider range of communication protocols. The protocols and their underlying technology have been refined to provide much higher transmission rates. Also, communication protocols provide much more services than previously.

With a refinement of, and emphasis on standards, interoperability is now a much more attainable goal than in the previous decade. These advances, when combined with those in OT, will contribute to the proliferation of heterogeneous information models.

22.7 Summary and Concluding Remarks

Let us summarize what we have covered in this chapter:

- A distributed database systems is a conglomeration of database systems in which each system operates as an autonomous system on its own, or collaborates with other systems as required.

- Distributed databases systems provide a number of benefits in the areas of efficiency and productivity, convenience, and reliability.

- Distributed database systems should strive to conform to the standards outlined in Date's twelve rules for such systems.

- Distributed databases face challenges in the areas of query optimization, catalog management, update propagation, concurrency control and transaction management.

- A database gateway is a software component that links two different DBMS suites.

- Distributed databases have been significantly affected by developments in object technology and electronic communications technology. This is expected to continue in the foreseeable future.

Distributed databases have helped to transform our world in a significant way. To fully appreciate the power of distributed databases, just consider for a moment, a world without them: no World Wide Web; minimized reliability on critical company databases; reduced capabilities on operating systems; limited remote access to databases. The next chapter takes a closer look at object databases.

22.8 Review Questions

1. Define a distributed database system. Discuss the advantages of such systems.

2. Outline and clarify the twelve rules for distributed database systems.

3. Discuss the challenges to distributed database system.

4. As an IT professional (perhaps in training), what are your future expectations for distributed database systems?

22.9 References and/or Recommended Readings

[Chung, 1997] Chung, P. Emerald, Yennun Huang, Shalini Yajnik, Deron Liang, Joanne C. Shih, Chung-Yih Wang, and Yi-Min Wang. *DCOM and CORBA Side by Side, Step by Step and Layer by Layer.* http://research.microsoft.com/~ymwang/papers/HTML/DCOMnCORBA/S.html (accessed October 2008).

[Date, 2004] Date, Christopher J. *Introduction to Database Systems* 8th ed. Menlo Park, CA: Addison-Wesley, 2004. See Chapter 21.

[Elmasri, 2007] Elmasri, Ramez and Shamkant B. Navathe. *Fundamentals of Database Systems* 5th ed. Reading, MA: Addison-Wesley, 2007. See Chapter 25.

[Kifer, 2005] Kifer, Michael, Arthur Bernstein, and Philip M. Lewis. *Database Systems: An Application-Oriented Approach* 2nd ed. New York, NY: Addison-Wesley, 2005. See Chapter 16.

[Martin, 1995] Martin, James, and Joe Leben. *Client/Server Databases: Enterprise Computing.* Upper Saddle River, NJ: Prentice Hall, 1995. See Chapters 7-9.

[Oracle, 2008] Oracle Corporation. *Oracle Database Gateways.* http://www.oracle.com/technology/products/gateways/index.html (accessed October 2008).

[Ozsu, 1999] Ozsu, M. Tamer, and Patrick Velduriez. *Principles of Distributed Database Systems.* 2nd ed. Eaglewood, NJ: Prentice Hall, 1999.

[Rob, 2007] Rob, Peter and Carlos Coronel. *Database Systems: Design, Implementation & Management* 7th ed. Boston, MA: Course Technology, 2007. See Chapter 12.

[Silberschatz, 2006] Silberschatz, Abraham, Henry Korth, and S. Sudarshan. *Database System Concepts* 5th ed. Boston, MA: McGraw-Hill, 2006. See Chapter 22.

CHAPTER 23

■ ■ ■

Object Databases

The previous decade has witnessed the advancement of several so-called object database management systems (ODBMS) and universal database management systems (UDBMS). This Chapter discusses such systems under the following subheadings:

- Introduction

- Overview of Object Oriented Database Management Systems

- Challenges to Object Oriented Database Management Systems

- Hybrid Approaches

- Summary and Concluding Remarks

23.1 Introduction

Object Technology (OT) has been dominating the software engineering industry in recent times. For better or worse, there has been a heightened interest and indulgence in object-oriented methodologies (OOM). Full treatment of OT and OOM is better handled in another course on the subject. However, for completeness, a brief introduction is made here.

OT provides obvious advantages to application programming, with benefits of encapsulation, polymorphism and complexity (information) hiding, code reusability, etc (Figure 23-1 summarizes the commonly mentioned advantages). By contrast, an OO approach to database design may or may not bring significant benefits, depending on the situation. Data structure encapsulation may or may not be desirable; besides, the principle of encapsulation often contradicts the principle of data independence in database design.

1. **Reusability of Code:** A tested system component can be reused in the design of another component.
2. **Stability and Reliability:** Software can be constructed from tested components. Organizations can be assured of guaranteed performance of software.
3. More complex systems can be constructed.
4. **Understandability:** Designer and user think in terms of object and behavior rather than low-level functional details. This results in more realistic modeling that is easier to learn and communicate.
5. **Faster Design:** Most RAD tools and contemporary CASE tools are object oriented to some degree. Also code reusability enhances faster development.
6. **Higher Quality Design:** New software can be constructed by using tested and proven components.
7. **Easier Maintenance:** Since systems are broken down into manageable component objects, isolation of system faults is easy.
8. **Dynamic Lifecycle:** I-OO-CASE tools integrate all stages of the software development life cycle (SDLC).
9. **Interoperability:** Generic classes may be designed for multiple systems.
10. **Design Independence:** Classes may be designed to operate and/or communicate across different platforms.
11. **Clarity:** OT promotes better communication between IS professionals and business people.
12. **Better CASE Tools:** OT leads to the development of more sophisticated and flexible CASE and RAD tools.
13. **Better Machine Performance:** OT leads to more efficient use of machine resources.

Figure 23-1. *Benefits of Object Technology*

It is widely believed that an OO approach to database design and implementation is preferable for complex applications such as:

- CAD/CAM systems

- CASE tools

- Geographic information systems (GIS)

- Document Storage and retrieval systems

- Artificial intelligence (AI) systems and expert systems

Which approach is the better? This is a difficult question to answer. It depends on the situation at hand, but the following is a summary of the alternatives:

- Truly function oriented systems with relational database and procedural application development

- Truly OO systems involving (encapsulation of) both data structure and operation

- Hybrid approach A with relational database and OO user interface

- Hybrid approach B with object/relational database and OO user interface

The first approach is a well-known traditional approach, and will not be discussed further. The latter three approaches are more aligned to current practices in the software engineering industry. They will be discussed in the upcoming sections.

23.2 Overview of Object-Oriented Database Management Systems

In a truly object-oriented DBMS (OO DBMS), the following concepts hold (for more details, see the references):

- An object type is a concept or thing about which data is to be stored, and a set of operations is to be defined.

- An object is an instance of an object type.

- An operation is a set of actions to be performed on an object.

- A method specifies the way an operation is to be performed.

- Encapsulation is the packaging of data structure and operations, typically into a class. The internal structure of the class is hidden from the outside, and only members (member functions) of the class have access to it.

- A subclass may inherit properties (structure or operations from a subclass. Also a class may be comprised of several component classes).

- Polymorphism is the phenomenon where a given object or operation may take on a different form, depending on the context of usage.

- Objects communicate by sending messages to each other. These messages are managed via events; an object therefore responds to events.

23.3 Challenges for Object-Oriented Database Management Systems

A number of challenges stand in the way of achieving purely object-oriented DBMSs, some of which have been articulated in [Date, 2004]. Figure 23-2 provides a brief summary of these challenges.

1. OT as proposed by its ardent proponents, encourages generalization and the building of inheritance hierarchies where objects consist of other objects (as in subtype, component and aggregation relationships. If pursued to their logical conclusion without pragmatic deviations (as discussed in chapter 3), the system could break down into a convoluted mess. Another related problem is that hierarchies, as we know, do not lend themselves to representation of M:M relationships. Consider, for instance, an M:M relationship between **Academic Program** and **Course**. How do we model and implement this in the OO paradigm? Do we assume that academic programs contain courses or vice versa?. History has shown that hierarchical based systems (such as CODASYL) are unsuited for complex distributed databases. For this reason, purely OO databases have been criticized as "CODASYL warmed over."

2. The OO model does not encourage the introduction of keys to uniquely identify objects, since object identifiers (OIDs) are generated (as internal address) at the point of instantiation. Note however, that OIDs do not obliterate the need for user keys, since end users still need to have a way of identifying objects separate and apart from internal addresses. The problem is further compounded when we have intermediate transient objects, or what in relational terminology is referred to as logical (virtual) objects such as a natural join record. In the OO model, there is no way to negotiate these situations without duplicating data into separate storage variables which must be maintained by the running program, thus increasing system overheads.

   The relational model gracefully handles these situations by allowing the user to define keys and surrogates (note that surrogates are not identical to OIDs). Then thanks to data independence, you can define multiple logical views on physical data. It has been argued that encapsulation is to the OO model what data independence is to the relational model. However, when analyzed, encapsulation is not a perfect replacement for data independence.

3. The OO model does not promote data sharing, a fundamental tenet of the relational model. At best, we could have encapsulated objects sharing their data contents with other objects, but in a distributed environment database (or mere network with one database server and several users), this would significantly increase the system overheads.

4. The matters of class, instance and collection are particularly difficult to negotiate. In the OO paradigm as we know, a class is essentially a complex data type; an instance is a specific object which belongs to at least one class. Without intense programmatic intervention, it would be difficult to determine a collection of objects belonging to a given class.

   The relational model has no such problem. A relational table defines the type and contains the collection of related data (objects) all in the same place. And as you are aware, this data can be shared and used to construct any number of logical perspectives as required by external end users.

5. The perfect encapsulation of data structure and operation in a data model is still for the most part, an ideal. We have seen complete achievement of this objective in the programming domain, but seldom in the database domain.

Figure 23-2. *Challenges to Object-Oriented Database Management Systems*

23.4 Hybrid Approaches

Due to the above-mentioned challenges, it is unlikely that we will see a proliferation of purely object- oriented DBMS suites involving only encapsulated database objects in the immediate future. The benefits of OT are therefore likely to continue to be more significant in the area of user interface than database (of course with a few exceptions as mentioned earlier). The relational model on the other hand, has long proven its worth. The best we can therefore expect is a peaceful coexistence of both OO systems and relational databases — a kind of hybrid. The next two subsections describe two hybrid approaches.

23.4.1 Hybrid Approach A

In the Hybrid Approach A, a relational database is accessed by an OO user interface. This means that the application development is done via an OO Programming Language (OOPL), CASE tool, or RAD tool.

There is no shortage of OOPL (some of them pure OOPLs, others are hybrid OOPLs). The more popular ones include C++, Java, C#, and Object Pascal. There are many object-oriented CASE (OO-CASE) tools and RAD tools that support this approach. They include (but are not confined to) products such as Team Developer, Delphi, Oracle JDeveloper, WebSphere, NetBeans etc.

Three advantages of this approach are as follows:

1. It can facilitate *legacy systems* (software systems based on old technology), which are prevalent in large organizations.

2. It facilitates peaceful coexistence of traditional and more contemporary system approaches.

3. It reaps the benefits of a relational database and OO application development.

The main disadvantage of the approach is that it does not address the earlier mentioned situations that warrant OO database design. However, the skillful database designer can use techniques mentioned in Chapter 3 for implementing relationships such as subtype, component and aggregation.

23.4.2 Hybrid Approach B

In this approach, a relational/object database (often referred to as a universal database) is accessed via an OO user interface. Like the Hybrid Approach A, application development is done via an OOPL, OO-CASE tool, or RAD tool.

The universal database supports both the relational database as well as the OO database. The designer can therefore make critical decisions as to which approach is preferred, given the scenario. The skillful database designer also has the flexibility of employing techniques mentioned in Chapter 3 for implementing relationships such as sub-type, component and aggregation.

Several of the leading software engineering companies have in recent times, introduced products that support object databases. Examples include:

- IBM's DB2 Universal

- Oracle Universal Database Server

- Informix's Universal Data Option for its Dynamic Server

Advantages of the approach are as follows:

1. The strengths of the relational model and the OO model can be emphasized, and the respective weak points avoided.

2. Legacy systems can be facilitated.

3. It facilitates peaceful coexistence of traditional and more contemporary system approaches.

One possible disadvantage is that the database designer could be sometimes forced to make difficult decisions on database design.

23.5 Summary and Concluding Remarks

It is time to summarize what we have discussed in this Chapter:

- OT provides several huge benefits to the software engineering arena.

- An OO approach to database design may or may not bring significant benefits, depending on the situation. In some situations the OO approach is ideal; in others it is not.

- There are a number of challenges to object databases that do not exist in a relational database.

- The most pragmatic approach for merging the benefits of the relational model and the OO model is to superimpose an OO user interface on a relational or universal database.

The strength of the relational model lies in its firm mathematical foundations, its huge benefits, and the immense financial outlay that have been placed in relational systems. This third fact is significant: Several large corporations have invested millions of dollars hugely in relational databases. They are not likely to discard these investments. The strength of the OO model lies in its huge benefits in certain situations, and its intuitiveness. Given the strength of both models, we can expect them to continue to peacefully coexist in the foreseeable future, complementing instead of rivaling each other.

23.6 Review Questions

1. Identify the main benefits that object technology brings to the arena of database systems.

2. Describe the main features of the OO DBMS model.

3. Discuss the main challenges to the object-oriented database management systems.

4. Discuss the hybrid approach to database systems.

23.7 References and/or Recommended Readings

[Date, 2004] Date, Christopher J. *Introduction to Database Systems* 8th ed. Menlo Park, CA: Addison-Wesley, 2004. See Chapters 25–26.

[Elmasri, 2007] Elmasri, Ramez and Shamkant B. Navathe. *Fundamentals of Database Systems* 5th ed. Reading, MA: Addison-Wesley, 2007. See Chapters 20–22.

[Kifer, 2005] Kifer, Michael, Arthur Bernstein and Philip M. Lewis. Database Systems: An Application-Oriented Approach 2nd ed. New York, NY: Addison-Wesley, 2005. See Chapter 14.

[Lee, 2002] Lee, Richard C. and William M. Tepfenhart. *Practical Object-Oriented Development With UML and Java*. Upper Saddle River, NJ: Prentice Hall, 2002.

[Martin, 1993] Martin, James and James Odell. *Principles of Object Oriented Analysis and Design*. Englewood Cliffs, NJ: Prentice Hall, 1993.

[Rumbaugh, 1991] Rumbaugh, James, et. al. *Object Oriented Modeling And Design*. Eaglewood Cliffs, NJ: Pretence Hall, 1991.

[Silberschatz, 2006] Silberschatz, Abraham, Henry Korth, and S. Sudarshan. *Database System Concepts* 5th ed. Boston, MA: McGraw-Hill, 2006. See Chapter 9.

CHAPTER 24

■ ■ ■

Data Warehousing

Since the mid1990s, database technology has expanded into a new area of interest — the development and management of data warehouses. It is a fascinating field of study that deserves some attention. This chapter provides an overview of data warehousing and information extraction. The chapter proceeds under the following subheadings:

- Introduction
- Rationale For Data Warehousing
- Characteristics of a Data Warehouse
- Data Warehouse Architectures
- Extraction, Transformation and Loading
- Summary and Concluding Remarks

24.1 Introduction

The concept of a data warehouse springs from the combination of two sets of needs:

- The business requirement for a global view of information, independent of and despite its source or underlying structure
- The need of information systems (IS) professionals to manage large volumes of company data in a more effective manner

The data warehouse has been approached many times and from many directions in the last decade; many implementations exist today. In order to proceed, we must make a distinction between data and information:

- Data is the computerized representation of business information.
- Information is the assimilation of data to convey meaning as understood and used by end users.

A data warehouse is an *integrated, subject-oriented, time-variant, nonvolatile,* consistent database, constructed from multiple sources, and made available (in the form of read-only access) to support decision making in a business context. As you will soon see (in section 24.3), the highlighted terms in this definition are deliberate because of their significance.

Here is an alternate definition: A data warehouse is a relational database that is typically constructed from multiple transactional databases (called *source databases*), and designed for query and analysis rather than transaction processing. The data warehouse usually contains historical data that is derived from transaction data from multiple sources. It separates analysis workload from transaction workload, and enables a business to consolidate data from several sources.

In addition to a relational database, a data warehouse environment often consists of an ETL (extract, transformation, and load) solution, an OLAP (on-line analytical processing) engine, client analysis tools, and other applications that manage the process of gathering data and delivering it to business users. End users typically require some kind of catalog that describes the data in its business context, and acts as a guide to the location and use of this information. Finally, end users require a set of tools to analyze and manipulate the information thus made available.

As you are no doubt aware by now, achieving comprehensiveness and consistency of data in today's business environment is often a complex and challenging undertaking. This is also true for a data warehouse. The following steps are necessary for the construction of a data warehouse:

1. Conduct an information infrastructure analysis to determine the required structure of the data warehouse.

2. Identify the source databases that will feed the data warehouse.

3. Design the integrated logical data model and determine the architecture of the data warehouse.

4. Develop and implement a comprehensive meta-data methodology.

5. Determine, and then implement the physical structure of the data warehouse.

6. Design and implement an integrated staging area for the data warehouse.

7. Extract, transform and load the data (from various sources) into the data warehouse. This involves first cleansing the source data of various structural and content errors.

8. Conduct comprehensive post-implementation review(s) to ensure that the data warehouse is performing acceptably.

9. Maintain the data warehouse.

Data mining is the act of extracting data/information from assorted sources and presenting information in a manner that is consistent with user requirement. Data mining often implies the existence of data warehouses, so the two terms are closely related. Another related term is *information extraction* (IE) —the extraction of structured information from unstructured text. IE sometimes involve access of data warehouse(s) either as the source or destination of information.

24.2 Rationale for Data Warehousing

Data warehousing is a technology that is fast enhancing more traditional decision support systems (DSS), because of the added flexibility and benefits that the new technology brings. Let us briefly examine the problems that DSS end users tend to have from two perspectives — user constraints and information system (IS) constraints.

User Constraints: In the absence of data warehousing, users of traditional decision support systems developed using the traditional application-driven approach, commonly complained of the following difficulties:

- Difficulty in finding and accessing information needed

- Difficulty in understanding information found

- Information obtained is not as useful as expected

IS Constraints: In the absence of data warehousing, IS personnel also complained of a variety of problems:

- Developing copy programs is often very challenging

- Maintaining copy programs and copy databases presents serious integrity and work scheduling problems

- Data storage volumes tend to grow rapidly

- Database administration also tends to become quite complex

The solution to the above-mentioned problems is the implementation of a data warehouse. A data warehouse provides the decision support benefits that a traditional DSS provides, while providing more flexibility for expansion beyond the confines of the company. This is so for two reasons:

- The data warehouse has the capacity to attract interest in the salient facts about the organization, without providing unnecessary details.

- While companies may be hesitant about putting their transaction database(s) into the public domain (due to security and confidentiality concerns), they are more likely to be willing to put their data warehouse into the public domain (via the World Wide Web).

24.3 Characteristics of a Data Warehouse

In the definition of a data warehouse, a number of terms were deliberately highlighted. These terms convey important characteristics about a data warehouse. These will be clarified in the next subsection. Next, we will examine what kind of data that is typically stored in a data warehouse. We also examine the processing requirements of a data warehouse. Finally, we will review twelve rules that govern data warehouses.

24.3.1 Definitive Features

In the introduction, it was established that a data warehouse is an integrated, subject-oriented, time-variant, nonvolatile database. Let us briefly examine what these adjectives mean.

Subject-Oriented: Data warehouses are designed to aid the analysis of data in order to make decisions. For example, to learn more about your company's sales data, you can build a warehouse that concentrates on sales. Using this warehouse, you can answer questions like "Who was our best customer for this item last year?" This ability to define a data warehouse by subject matter, sales in this case, makes the data warehouse subject-oriented.

Integrated: Integration is closely related to subject orientation. Data warehouses typically contain data from disparate sources into a consistent format. They must resolve such problems as naming conflicts and inconsistencies among units of measure. When a data warehouse achieves this, it is said to be integrated.

Nonvolatile: Nonvolatile means that, once entered into the warehouse, data should not change. This is logical because the purpose of a warehouse is to enable you to analyze historical data.

Time-Variant: A data warehouse's focus may change over time; also, it could grow (in terms of data volume, data structure and complexity).

24.3.2 Nature of Data Stored

Of importance also, is the nature of data stored in a data warehouse. A data warehouse differs from an operational database in the nature of data stored. An operational database consists of a set of normalized relational tables that store atomic data. A data warehouse on the other hand, stores decision support data, often in non-normalized, aggregated formats. Three distinctions can be made between operational data and decision support data:

> **Time Span:** Operational data represent atomic transactions at specific points in time. Decision support data represent (aggregated) data over a period of time.

> **Granularity:** Operational data is atomic; decision support data is often aggregated. Data warehouses contain decision support data that have been aggregated from various sources and transformed to its intended format.

> **Dimension:** Operational data is instamatic; decision support data is multi-dimensional, typically involving the dimension of time as well as other factors of concern.

24.3.3 Processing Requirements

Data warehouses have very different processing requirements from OLTP systems and operational databases, as explained below.

Workload: Data warehouses are designed to accommodate ad hoc queries. The workload of the data warehouse might not be known in advance, so a data warehouse should be optimized to perform well for a wide variety of possible query operations. OLTP systems and operational databases support only predefined operations. Your applications might be specifically tuned or designed to support only these operations.

Data Modifications: A data warehouse is updated on a regular basis by the ETL process (run nightly or weekly) using bulk data modification techniques. The end users of a data warehouse do not directly update the data warehouse. In OLTP systems and operational databases, end users routinely issue individual data modification statements to the database. The OLTP database is always up to date, and reflects the current state of each business transaction.

Schema Design: Data warehouses often use non-normalized or partially normalized schemas (such as a *star schema*) to optimize query performance. OLTP systems and operational databases often use fully normalized schemas to optimize update/insert/delete performance, and to guarantee data consistency.

The star schema was introduced in Chapter 5 (section 5.6); it is so widely mentioned in database literature, it deserves a bit of attention: A star schema describes a mechanism where there is a "central" table referred to as a *fact table*, and other so-called *dimensional tables* that relate to the fact table via 1:M relationships. The dimensional tables contain dimensional data about details stored in the fact table. While the star schema is widely used in data warehouses, it is also applicable in operational databases as well. Figure 24-1 provides an illustration of a star schema of five relational tables for tracking the graduation statistics from a regional university that operates multiple schools and programs in multiple locations. Tables **Location**, **AcademicProgram**, **TimePeriod**, and **School** qualify as dimensional tables, while table **GraduationSummary** qualifies as the fact table.

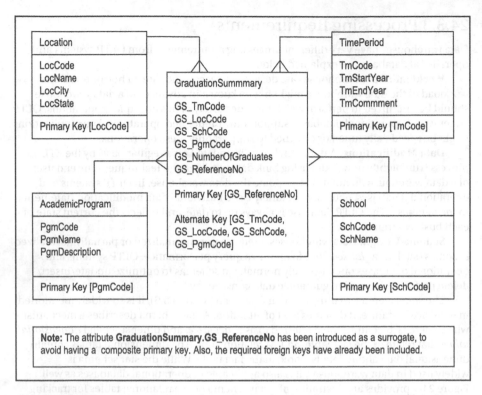

Figure 24-1. *Illustration of a Star Schema for Graduations from a Regional University*

Typical Operations: A typical data warehouse query may scan thousands or millions of rows of data. For example, a data warehouse query may involve determining the total sales for all customers in a specific time period. Except for sophisticated queries, a typical OLTP or operational database operation accesses only a small percentage of records, relative to the amount stored. For example, an operational query may involve retrieving the current purchase order for a particular customer, from a table storing hundreds of thousands of purchase orders.

Figure 24-2 provides a summary of what we have established so far: that a data warehouse is typically constructed for various operational databases (sources), and possesses certain characteristics.

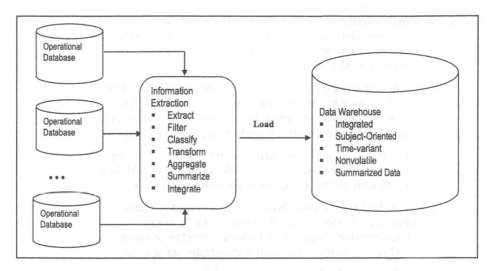

Figure 24-2. *Constructing a Data Warehouse*

24.3.4 Twelve Rules That Govern a Data Warehousing

Data warehouse was first introduced by William Inmon in the 1990s; he still operates as an expert in the field (see [Inmon, 2002] and [Inmon, 2007]). Like E.F. Codd and C. J. Date of the relational model, Inmon introduced twelve rules for governing data warehouses. These rules aptly summarize the previously mentioned characteristics of the data warehouse. Many of these rules have been subsumed in the foregoing discussions. Nonetheless, for emphasis, they are paraphrased below:

1. **Separation:** The data warehouse and operational database environments should be separated.

2. **Integration:** The data warehouse data are integrated from various operational sources.

3. **Time Horizon:** The data warehouse typically contains historical data with an extended time horizon. This is in contrast to a significantly shorter time horizon for the operational databases that may be used as sources for the data warehouse.

4. **Nature of Data:** The data in a data warehouse represent snapshot captures (from operational data sources) at specific points in time.

5. **Orientation:** The data contained in the warehouse are subject-oriented.

6. **Accessibility:** The data warehouse is a predominantly read-only database, with periodic batch updates from the operational databases that are connected to it. It does not support on-line interactive updates.

7. **Life Cycle:** The data warehouse development life cycle differs from classical approach to database development in that whereas the data warehouse development is data-driven, the classical database approach tends to be process-driven.

8. **Levels of Detail:** In a typical data warehouse, there may be several levels of detail. These include current detail, old detail, lightly summarized data, and highly summarized data.

9. **Data Set:** The data warehouse is characterized by read-only transactions on very large data sets. This is in contrast to the operational database, which is characterized by numerous update transactions on a more narrowly defined data set.

10. **Relevance:** The data warehouse environment has a system that keeps track of all data sources, transformations and storage. This is essential if the data warehouse is to maintain its relevance.

11. **Metadata:** The data warehouse's metadata forms a critical component of its environment. The metadata provides the following functions: definitions of data elements in the warehouse; identification of data source, transformation, integration, storage, usage, relationships, and history of each data element.

12. **Resource Usage:** The data warehouse typically enforces optimal usage of the data by enforcing some form of chargeback mechanism for resource usage.

24.4 Data Warehouse Architecture

The architecture of a data warehouse varies depending upon the specifics of an organization's situation. Three common architectures have been identified:

- Basic Data Warehouse

- Data Warehouse With a Staging Area

- Data Warehouse With Staging Area and Data Marts

24.4.1 Basic Data Warehouse Architecture

Figure 24-3 shows a simple architecture for a data warehouse. End users directly access data derived from several source systems through the data warehouse.

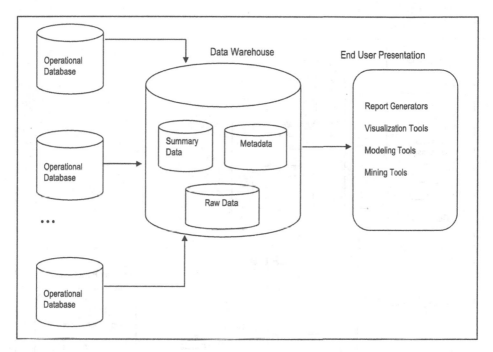

Figure 24-3. *Basic Data Warehouse*

The data warehouse consists of raw data (from operational databases), summary data and metadata. Summaries are very valuable in data warehouses because they pre-compute long operations in advance. For example, a typical data warehouse query may be to retrieve something like aggregate sales for a specific period. In Oracle, this may be implemented as a materialized view or snapshot relation set up for that purpose.

24.4.2 Data Warehouse Architecture with a Staging Area

In the basic data warehouse, you need to clean and process your operational data before putting it into the warehouse. You can do this programmatically, although most data warehouses use a staging area instead. A staging area simplifies building summaries and general warehouse management. Figure 24-4 illustrates this typical architecture.

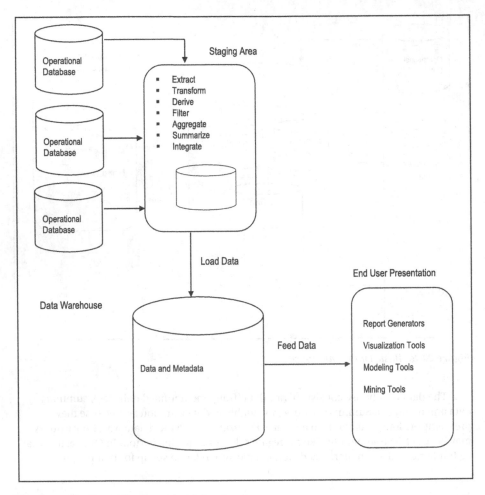

Figure 24-4. *Data Warehouse with Staging Area*

24.4.3 Data Warehouse Architecture with a Staging Area and Data Marts

Although the data warehouse with staging area is quite common, you may want to customize your warehouse's architecture for different groups within your organization, or across different related organizations. You can do this by adding *data marts*. A data mart is a small, single-subject data warehouse that provides decision support for a particular aspect (line) of the business. Figure 24-5 summarizes the approach for three data marts. For example, the data marts may respectively represent information relating to purchasing, sales, and inventory for an organization. A financial analyst would then be able to conduct separate analysis on purchasing, sales and inventory, and then a global analysis on the three aspects combined.

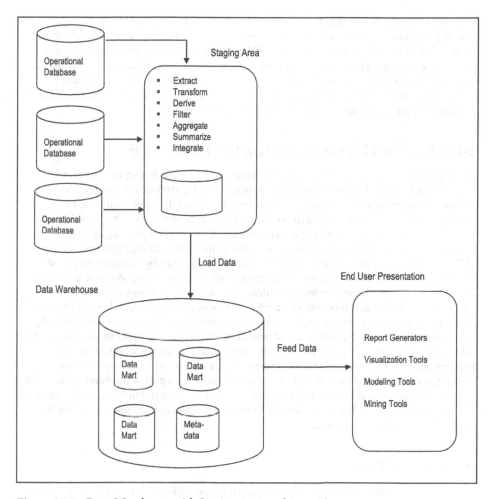

Figure 24-5. *Data Warehouse with Staging Area and Data Marts*

24.5 Extraction, Transformation, and Loading

The data warehouse must be loaded regularly so that it can serve its purpose of facilitating business analysis. To do this, data from one or more operational databases needs to be extracted, transformed (where necessary), and copied into the warehouse. The acronym ETL is often used to refer to this extraction, transformation and loading of data. The acronym is perhaps too simplistic, since it omits the transportation phase and implies that each of the other phases of the process is distinct. We refer to the entire process, including data loading, as ETL. However, you should understand that ETL refers to a broad process, and not three well-defined steps.

The methodologies and tasks of ETL have been well known for many years, and are not necessarily unique to data warehouse environments. A wide variety of proprietary applications and database systems are used as the IT backbone business enterprises.

Data are shared between applications or systems, trying to integrate them, giving at least two applications the same picture of the world. This data sharing was mostly addressed by mechanisms similar to what we now call ETL. Data warehouse environments face the same challenge with the additional burden that they not only have to exchange, but to integrate, rearrange and consolidate data over many operational systems, thereby providing a new unified information base for business intelligence. Additionally, the data volume in data warehouse environments tends to be very large.

24.5.1 What Happens During the ETL Process

During extraction, the desired data is identified and extracted from many different sources, including database systems and applications. Very often, it is not possible to identify the specific subset of interest, therefore more data than necessary has to be extracted, so the identification of the relevant data will be done at a later point in time.

Depending on the source system's capabilities (for example, operating system resources), some transformations may take place during this extraction process. The size of the extracted data varies from hundreds of kilobytes up to gigabytes, depending on the source system and the business situation. The same is true for the time difference between two (logically) identical extractions: the time span may vary between days/hours and minutes to near real-time. Web server log files for example can easily become hundreds of megabytes in a very short period of time. After extracting data, it has to be physically transported to the target system or an intermediate system for further processing. Depending on the chosen mode of transportation, some transformations can be done during this process, too. For example, an SQL statement that directly accesses a remote target through a gateway can concatenate two or more columns as part of the **Select** statement.

After transportation to the target system, the data may undergo transformation into the desired formats for the target system. Once this process is completed, the data is loaded into the data warehouse.

24.5.2 ETL Tools

Designing and maintaining the ETL process is often considered one of the most difficult and resource-intensive portions of a data warehouse project. Many data warehousing projects use ETL tools to manage this process.

Oracle Tools

Oracle Warehouse Builder (OWB) provides ETL capabilities and takes advantage of inherent database abilities. Other data warehouse builders create their own ETL tools and processes, either inside or outside the database.

Besides the support of extraction, transformation, and loading, there are some other tasks that are important for a successful ETL implementation as part of the daily operations of the data warehouse and its support for further enhancements. The OWB is quite a sophisticated component that facilitates the construction simple as well as complex data warehouses, the population of them via the ETL process, and the management of them.

DB2 Tools

As mentioned in Chapter 17, DB2 provides four main products for managing data warehouses:

- InfoSphere Warehouse Departmental Edition

- InfoSphere Warehouse Departmental Base Edition

- InfoSphere Warehouse Enterprise Edition

- InfoSphere Warehouse Enterprise Base Edition

Each of these products (the latter being an upgrade of the former) consists of related components that allow for the creation, population (via ETL transactions), and management of data warehouses, according to organizational requirements.

24.5.3 Daily Operations and Expansion of the Data Warehouse

Successive ETL transactions to the data warehouse must be scheduled and processed in a specific order. Depending on the success or failure of the operation or parts of it, the result must be tracked and subsequent, alternative processes might be started. The control of the progress and the definition of a business workflow of the operations are typically addressed by special ETL tools provided by the DBMS suite.

As the data warehouse is an active information system, data sources and targets are not beyond the prospect of change. These changes must be maintained and tracked through the lifespan of the system without overwriting or deleting the old ETL process flow information. To build and keep a level of trust about the information in the warehouse, the process flow of each individual record in the warehouse can be reconstructed at any point in time in the future. With time, the data warehouse could therefore expand into something larger and different.

24.6 Summary and Concluding Remarks

Here is a summary of what we have discussed in this chapter:

- A data warehouse is an integrated, subject-oriented, time-variant, nonvolatile, consistent database, obtained from a variety of sources and made available to support decision making in a business context.

- A data warehouse is a relational database that is designed for query and analysis rather than transaction processing.

- The data warehouse is updated via the ETL process.

- A data warehouse provides the decision support benefits that a traditional DSS provides, while providing more flexibility for expansion beyond the confines of the company.

- Data warehouses often use non-normalized or partially normalized schemas to optimize query performance.

- Data warehouses should conform to Inmon's twelve rules for data warehouses.

- Three common data warehouse architectures are the basic data warehouse, data warehouse with a staging area, and data warehouse with a staging area and data marts.

The field of data warehousing is a fascinating breakthrough and is the subject of many contemporary researches. Since it is relatively new, vast opportunities for data warehouse architecture and ETL transaction optimization still abound. Data warehousing is studied as an advanced course in several undergraduate degree programs, as well as graduate programs. The supporting technologies are provided via products from the three leading software engineering companies — IBM's DB2, Oracle (from Oracle Corporation), and Microsoft's SQL Server. Additionally, these companies provide readily available documentation on the topic.

With the advancement of the WWW and Web-accessible databases, it is anticipated that the fascination in data warehousing will continue into the foreseeable future. And speaking of Web-accessible databases, the next chapter discusses this topic.

24.7 Review Questions

1. Give the definition of a data warehouse. Clearly outline what data warehousing entails.

2. Provide a rationale for data warehousing.

3. Describe a scenario that would warrant the use of a data warehouse.

4. Discuss the main characteristics of a data warehouse in terms of:

   - Definitive features

   - Nature of data stored

   - Processing requirements

   - Rules that govern the data warehouse

5. State the three architectural approaches to data warehouse design. For each approach, describe the basic architecture, and provide a scenario that would warrant such an approach.

6. Clearly explain the ETL process. Give examples of ETL tools.

24.8 References and/or Recommended Readings

[Adelman, 2000] Adelman, Sid and Larissa Terpeluk Moss. *Data Warehouse Project Management.* Boston, MA: Addison-Wesley, 2000.

[Connolly, 2002] Connolly, Thomas and Carolyn Begg. *Database Systems: A Practical Approach to Design, Implementation and Management* 3rd ed. New York, NY: Addison-Wesley, 2002. See Chapters 30-32.

[Date, 2004] Date, Christopher J. *Introduction to Database Systems* 8h ed. Menlo Park, CA: Addison-Wesley, 2004. See Chapter 22.

[Elmasri, 2007] Elmasri, Ramez and Shamkant B. Navathe. *Fundamentals of Database Systems* 5th ed. Reading, MA: Addison-Wesley, 2007. See Chapters 28 and 29.

[Hoffer, 2007] Hoffer, Jeffrey A., Mary B. Prescott and Fred R. McFadden. *Modern Database Management* 8th ed. Upper Saddle River, NJ: Prentice Hall, 2007. See chapter 11.

[IBM, 2008] IBM Corporation. *Data Warehouse.* http://www-01.ibm.com/software/data/infosphere/warehouse/ (accessed October 2008).

[Inmon, 2002] Inmon, William. *Building the Data Warehouse* 3 rd ed. New York, NY: John Wiley, 2002.

[Inmon, 2007] Inmon Associates Inc. http://www.billinmon.com/ (accessed October 2008).

[Oracle, 2008] Oracle Corporation. *Oracle10g Database Release 2.* http://technetOracle.com (accessed October 2008).

[Rob, 2007] Rob, Peter and Carlos Coronel. *Database Systems: Design, Implementation & Management* 7th ed. Boston, MA: Course Technology, 2007. See Chapter 13.

[Silberschatz, 2006] Silberschatz, Abraham, Henry Korth, and S. Sudarshan. *Database System Concepts* 5th ed. Boston, MA: McGraw-Hill, 2006. See Chapters 18 – 19.

■ ■ ■

CHAPTER 25

Web-Accessible Databases

Another new area of database systems that has become widespread since the 1990s is Web-accessible databases. The proliferation of these databases is strongly correlated to the growth of the World Wide Web (WWW or W3); both phenomena have become part and parcel of twenty-first century lifestyle, and both promise to be an integral part of life in the foreseeable future. This Chapter provides an overview of Web-accessible databases. The Chapter proceeds under the following subheadings:

- Introduction
- Web-Accessible Database Architecture
- Supporting Technologies
- Implementation with Oracle
- Implementation with DB2
- Generic Implementation via Front-end and Back-end Tools
- Summary and Concluding Remarks

25.1 Introduction

A Web-accessible database is simply a database that is accessible via the WWW. The rationale for web-accessible databases can be easily appreciated when one considers the huge benefits that they bring to the business community. Figure 25-1 provides a brief discussion of some of the significant benefits.

Electronic Commerce: Through electronic commerce (E-commerce), companies are able to market their products and services via on-line stores in a manner that was impossible prior to the WWW.

Broadening of Company Scope: The on-line market is not constrained by space, time, or geographic region. Companies that trade in this market have virtually joined a global village in which resources and services are only seconds away.

Convenience: Companies that use Web-accessible databases afford themselves easy access to critical company information (preferably without sacrificing security) in very cost-effective way. These conveniences would have much more expensive (if at all possible) if pursued via more traditional methods.

Improved Productivity: By using Web-accessible databases, companies often improve their productivity by making use of resources that otherwise would have been more expensive (financially and in terms of time).

Improved Competitiveness: By using Web-accessible databases, companies often improve their competitive advantage in the marketplace.

Other Benefits: In many cases, Web-accessible databases involve the use of distributed databases. In such cases, the benefits of distributed databases (review section 22.2) also apply.

Figure 25-1. *Significant Benefits of Web-Accessible Databases*

25.2 Web-Accessible Database Architecture

In sections 2.6 and 2.7, we discussed the idea of separating a database system into front-end and back-end. This principle is commonly used in implementing Web-accessible databases. Two approaches are common: the two-tiered approach as represented in Figure 25-2, and the three-tiered approach as represented in Figure 25-3. In the two-tiered approach, client applications send requests to the DBMS, which is running on a database server. These requests are processed according to some scheduling algorithm. In the three-tiered approach, additional sophistication is provided by an intersecting application server, which services client requests from various (heterogeneous) applications and filters them to the DBMS for processing. This provides additional flexibility and functionality to the system.

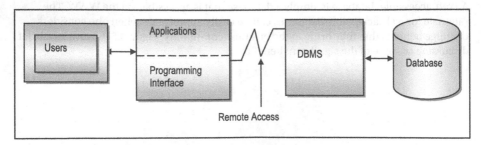

Figure 25-2. *Two-Tiered Approach to Web-Accessible Database*

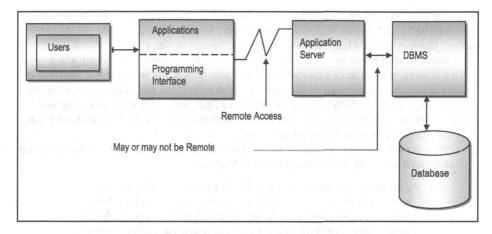

Figure 25-3. *Three-Tiered Approach to Web-Accessible Database*

As you view these two figures, bear in mind that users (in the figures) include end-users as well as businesses making electronic requests from other Web-accessible databases. This is so because there are two types of Web-accessible database systems that are prevalent:

- Consumer-to-business (C2B) systems facilitate individual users accessing a company database.

- Business-to-business (B2B) systems facilitate businesses accessing other Web-accessible databases of other businesses in a manner that is often transparent to the end-user. This relatively new market provides huge opportunities for companies to improve their efficiency and productivity by concentrating on what they do best, and outsourcing non-essential functions that other businesses provide more efficiently. This gives them the opportunity to also forge powerful alliances for more effective operation.

25.3 Supporting Technologies

The usefulness of separating front-end and back-end subsystems was illustrated in the previous section. This strategy allows us to design and secure the database as a separate activity from developing applications that access that database. Web applications could be one of the many different applications that access the database. Following are some supporting technologies for Web-accessible databases.

Web Servers: A Web server is a sophisticated software system that allows a computer to provide various services to multiple client requests made via the WWW. The server runs on an operating system (which runs on a computer). However, loosely speaking, we usually refer to the entire package of machine and software as the Web server.

Popular Web server software products include Apache, Microsoft's Internet Information Service (IIS), CERN server, NCSA (National Center for Supercomputing Applications) server, Spinner server, Plexus server, Perl server, Tomcat server, etc.

Server-side Extensions: A server-side extension is a software that communicates with a Web server to handle assorted client requests. Often, the server-side extension program acts as an intermediary between the Web server and the database, farming out all SQL requests to the DBMS. Both the DBMS and the server-side extension program must be ODBC-compliant. Products such as ColdFusion, Delphi, Java Studio Enterprise, etc. qualify as server-side extension programs.

Web Server Interfaces: Web server interfaces facilitate the display of information on dynamic Web pages. There are two popular categories:

- Common Gateway Interface (CGI) is a set of rules that specify how parameters are passed between client programs and Web servers. A client program that can run on a Web server is called a script, hence the term CGI script. Common scripting languages include JavaScript, Active Server Pages (ASP), and PHP. However, high-level languages such as C++, Java, Perl, etc. also qualify.

- Application Program Interface (API) is a set of routines, protocols and tools that facilitate easy software construction. Since APIs are typically shared code that is resident in memory (in the case of Web technology, they reside on the Web server), they tend to be more efficient than CGI scripts.

Extensible Markup Language (XML): XML is a meta-language that was designed specifically to facilitate the representation, manipulation and transmission of structured data over the WWW. It was first published by the WWW Consortium (W3C) in 1998, and to no surprise, has become the de facto data exchange standard for e-commerce, thus circumventing the pre-existing problem of interoperability among different Web servers.

XML was developed from an earlier standard called the Standard Generalized Markup Language (SGML). And as expected, other XML-based languages are emerging. Three examples are Extensible Business Reporting Language (XBRL), Structured Product Labeling (SPL), and Extensible Style Language (XSL).

Simple Object Access Protocol (SOAP): The original emphasis of SOAP was to support remote procedure calls (RPC). However, the norm is for SOAP messages to be sent by web servers as XML documents (synchronous as well as asynchronous). SOAP messages are frequently transmitted as the data portion of HTTP (hyper-text transport protocol) messages.

Hypertext Transport Protocol (HTTP): HTTP is the protocol used to transfer of information over the WWW. It is characterized by a simply request-response structure that represents interactions between a client (Web browser) and a Web server. It is assumed that you are familiar with the Internet, basic Web page construction, Uniform Resource Locators (URLs), domain names and other related issues.

Web Services Description Language (WSDL): The original authors of WSDL define it as "an XML format for describing network services as a set of endpoints operating on messages containing either document-oriented or procedure-oriented information" [Ariba, 2001] WSDL can be construed as an interface definition language (IDL) with bindings that clearly specify how the various components of a message are mapped. WSDL messages are frequently transmitted as SOAP messages over HTTP.

Client-side Extensions: These add functionality to the Web browsers. Client-side extensions are available in various forms. Following is a summary of the most commonly encountered ones:

- **Plug-ins:** A plug-in is an external application program that is automatically invoked by the Web browser when required. For example, a Web browser, upon receiving a PDF (portable document format) document will invoke the available PDF-reader on the host operating system.

- **Java:** As you are no doubt aware, Java is a platform independent programming language. Most operating systems have a *Java Virtual Machine* (JVM), which allows Java code to execute on the local machine (if there isn't a JVM in the operating system, this is readily available from the Sun Microsystems Web site). Calls to Java routines are often embedded in HTML pages. When a Web browser encounters this, it invokes the local JVM to execute the code.

- **JavaScript:** JavaScript is a Java-like scripting language (developed by Netscape), but is much simpler. JavaScript code is often embedded in Web pages. It is downloaded whenever the Web page is activated, as well as on certain specific events (such as loading of a specific page from the server, or a mouse-click, etc.) Whenever the browser encounters this, it invokes the JavaScript plug-in to execute this code.

- **ActiveX:** ActiveX is Microsoft's alternative to Java. It works perfectly in a Windows environment. Although possible in other languages, C++ and Visual Basic are well known for their facilitation of ActiveX controls.

- **VBScript:** VBScript is another Microsoft product that is often used to add functionality to the Web browser. Like JavaScript, VBScript code is often embedded in Web pages. Invocation and execution are also similar to JavaScript.

- **Cookies:** Cookies are used to expedite user requests when the user visits a site more than once. When the site is first visited, the Web server creates a cookie with basic user information (such as e-mail) and sends it to the browser. When the browser is subsequently used to visit that site, the cookie, upon recognition by the Web server, is used to expedite the user request.

25.4 Implementation with Oracle

Oracle implements a database that is by definition, Web-accessible (this applies since Oracle 10G). This is achieved through the products Oracle Enterprise Manager, (OEM), iSQL*Plus, Oracle JDeveloper, and Oracle SQL Developer in the following ways:

- When you install the Oracle Server suite (including OEM) on a node in your company or home network, the machine is automatically configures as a database server.

- Oracle automatically installs and configures a database listener on database server to respond to incoming requests from client nodes (running Oracle 10G or 11G Client) in the network, on the internet, or an extranet.

- Typically, your database server should have at least one database. This can be created during installation, or subsequently via the Oracle Database Configuration Assistant (DBCA) component.

- You can access your database server from any machine that has an internet connection, through OEM via the URL http://<Machine.Domain>:5500/em (you supply the machine name and domain name for your network). Of course, you will need a valid user account, password, and appropriate privileges.

- You can also access your database server from any machine that has an internet connection, through Oracle's iSQL*Plus via the URL http://<Machine.Domain>:5560/isqlplus (again, you supply the machine name and domain name for your network). Again, you will need a valid user account, password, and appropriate privileges.

- Through Oracle JDeveloper (OJD), Oracle allows Web-accessible Java-based applications to be constructed. These applications may access local or remote Oracle (or heterogeneous) databases.

- Through Oracle Forms Developer (OFD), Oracle also allows Web-accessible PL/SQL-based applications to be constructed. These applications may access local or remote Oracle (or heterogeneous) databases.

This development represents a huge step forward for Oracle, and has no doubt fuelled its invigorated claim of being the leading software engineering firm for Web-accessible databases.

25.5 Implementation with DB2

Like Oracle, DB2 implements a Web-accessible database (this applies to DB2 8 and subsequent versions). This is achieved through the products DB2 Connect, DB2 Everyplace and WebSphere in the following ways:

- If you configure a mainframe, or mini computer to be a DB2 server, and create your DB2 database on it, you can access the database over an intranet, the Internet, or an extranet by running DB2 Connect from your client machine. As in the case of the Oracle database, you will need to know the machine name, the domain name and port number that the database server listens on, in order to connect to it.

- DB2 Everyplace is a miniscule version of DB2 that runs on mobile devices such as *personal digital assistants* (PDAs), cell phones, etc. DB2 Everyplace can be used as a local independent DBMS, or to query information residing at a remote database server, via the WWW.

- Through WebSphere, IBM allows Web-accessible Java-based applications to be constructed. These applications may access local or remote DB2 (or heterogeneous) databases. There is also a WebSphere Everyplace version for PDAs, cell phones and other pervasive devices.

Like Oracle, IBM also claims to be the leading software engineering firm for Web-accessible databases. The truth is, both companies are archrivals at the top of the database systems market.

25.6 Generic Implementation via a Front-end and a Back-end Tool

This section describes a generic approach to constructing a Web-accessible database system, based on front-end and back-end tools. The operation can be summarized in two steps:

1. Create the database using an appropriate back-end tool. The tool used must support ODBC, JDBC, or both. Of course, it is assumed that appropriate planning and design as discussed in earlier Chapters, have taken place.

2. Create the Web-application using an appropriate front-end tool that incorporates the requisite Web-supporting technologies as discussed in section 25.3. The tool must support ODBC and/or JDBC, and must facilitate code in at least one of the accepted scripting languages (JavaScript, PHP, ASP, etc.). It must also support XML. Again, the basic assumption is that sound principles of software engineering will be used to design the user interface as a pre-requisite to this activity.

Figure 25-4 provides a list of commonly used tools. They have been listed in three categories: front-end tools, back-end tools, and programming languages. In each, it is recommended that you use the most current version of the stated software product (for the RAD tools and DBMS suites, the versions stated are simply safe starting points).

Product	Parent Company
Front-end RAD Tools that Support Web-Accessible Databases	
Delphi 2005	Embarcadero Technologies
WebSphere 6.0	IBM
NetBeans 6.0	Sun Microsystems
ColdFusion MX7	Macromedia
Oracle JDeveloper 10G	Oracle
Visual Studio 2005	Microsoft
Relational and/or Universal DBMS Suites	
DB2 8.2	IBM
Oracle 10G	Oracle
SQL Server 2005	Microsoft
Informix 10	IBM
MySQL 5.0	MySQL AB
Programming/Scripting Languages	
Java, C++, Object Pascal, JavaScript, PHP, XML, ASP, VBScript, Perl	

Figure 25-4. *Commonly Used Tools for Web-accessible Databases*

25.7 Summary and Concluding Remarks

Let us summarize what we have covered in this Chapter:

- A Web-accessible database is simply a database that can be accessed via the WWW.

- Web-accessible databases provide a number of benefits to companies and individuals that implement and/or use them. Among the benefits are facilitation of e-commerce, broadening of the company's scope of operation and market reach, a wide range of conveniences, improved productivity, and improved competitive advantage.

- A Web-accessible database may be implemented as a two-tiered system or a three-tiered system. Additionally, they may be C2B or B2B.

- The supporting technologies for Wed-accessible databases include Web servers, server-side extensions, server interfaces, XML, SOAP, WSDL, and client-extensions.

- Both Oracle and DB2 implement Web-accessible databases as a matter of policy.

- Implementation of a Web-accessible database can be summarized into two simple but profound steps: creating the database and creating the Web-accessible user interface. The tools used must meet minimum industry standards.

Web-accessible databases are among one of the technology-related phenomena that have transformed life in the twenty-first century. They are expected to continue to be an integral part of life in the foreseeable future.

This takes us to the end of the chapters for the course. If you understand most of the issues discussed, and now have a desire to delve more deeply into some aspects of the field, then the course has succeeded in its intent. If you find that you now have a strong desire to make database systems one of your areas of expertise, then welcome to the community! You will find it a wonderfully rewarding and progressive field.

25.8 Review Questions

1. Give the definition of a web-accessible database. Provide justification for their existence.

2. Discuss two example of the usefulness of Web-accessible databases.

3. Discuss the two-tiered approach to implementing Web-accessible database. When should you use such an approach?

4. Discuss the three-tiered approach to implementing Web-accessible database. When should you use such an approach?

5. Briefly describe the main supporting technologies for Web-accessible databases.

6. Describe how Oracle implements Web-accessible databases.

7. Describe how DB2 implements Web-accessible databases.

8. Describe a generic approach for implementing a Web-accessible database. What precautions must be taken?

25.9 References and/or Recommended Readings

[Ariba, 2001] Ariba, IBM Corporation, and Microsoft. *Web Services Description Language (WSDL) 1.1.* http://www.w3.org/TR/wsdl (accessed August 2009).

[Date, 2004] Date, Christopher J. *Introduction to Database Systems* 8th ed. Menlo Park, CA: Addison-Wesley, 2004. See Chapter 27.

[Elmasri, 2007] Elmasri, Ramez and Shamkant B. Navathe. *Fundamentals of Database Systems* 5th ed. Reading, MA: Addison-Wesley, 2007. See Chapters 26 and 27.

[Hoffer, 2007] Hoffer, Jeffrey A., Mary B. Prescott and Fred R. McFadden. *Modern Database Management* 8th ed. Upper Saddle River, NJ: Prentice Hall, 2007. See Chapter 10.

[Kifer, 2005] Kifer, Michael, Arthur Bernstein and Philip M. Lewis. Database Systems: An Application-Oriented Approach 2nd ed. New York, NY: Addison-Wesley, 2005. See Chapter 17.

[Riccardi, 2003] Riccardi, Greg. *Database Management With Web Site Development Applications.* Boston, MA: Addison-Wesley, 2003. See Chapters 12-15.

[Rob, 2007] Rob, Peter and Carlos Coronel. *Database Systems: Design, Implementation & Management* 7th ed. Boston, MA: Course Technology, 2007. See Chapter 14.

[Silberschatz, 2006] Silberschatz, Abraham, Henry Korth, and S. Sudarshan. *Database System Concepts* 5th ed. Boston, MA: McGraw-Hill, 2006. See Chapter 10.

[W3C, 2003] World Wide Web Consortium. *Extensible Markup Language (XML).* http://www.w3.org/XML/ (accessed August 2009).

PART F

■ ■ ■

Final Preparations

This penultimate division has two objectives:

- to help you to review and assimilate the concepts and principles covered in the course so that you will be able to apply them to real situations;

- to help you prepare for final examinations.

The division consists of a final chapter that includes sample examination questions and case studies for your usage.

■ ■ ■

CHAPTER 26

Sample Exercises and Examination Questions

This final chapter of sample exercises, examinations, and case studies, will proceed under the following captions:

- Introduction
- Sample Assignment 1A
- Sample Assignment 2B
- Sample Assignment 3A
- Sample Assignment 4A
- Sample Assignment 5A
- Sample Assignment 6A
- Sample Assignment 7A
- Sample Assignment 8A
- Sample Interim Examination A
- Sample Interim Examination B
- Sample Final Examination A
- Sample Final Examination B
- Sample Final Examination C

26.1 Introduction

This chapter provides you with some sample examination questions and case studies, designed to help you solidify in your mind, the concepts and principles covered in the course. The problems are arranged in assignments and examinations. The intent is to enlighten you to the type of problems they are likely to be asked to solve.

Generally speaking, assignment questions are more demanding than examination questions, and require more time. You will also observe that most of the examination questions are drawn from actual assignments. You should therefore do the assignments before attempting the examinations. The suggested weight (in points) for each question is indicated immediately following the question in curly brackets.No solution is provided for the problems posed in this chapter, for the following reasons:

- The problems are intended to test your understanding of the materials covered. If you find that you are struggling with the solution to a problem, then you need to review the relevant sections before continuing.

- In some cases (particularly where you are asked to design a database), there may be more than one solution to the problem(s) posed. This in typical in software engineering as well as in database systems, where you analyze alternate solutions to a problem, and choose the most prudent one.

- If your are using this book as a prescribed text for a course in database systems, your professor will want to have a say in what questions you ought to focus on.

26.2 Sample Assignment 1A

Zealot Industries Inc. is a manufacturing firm with over 2000 employees. The firm has been expanding well beyond the founders' expectations. However, it faces a severe hindrance to additional expansion — the absence of a computerized Human Resource Management System (HRMS) that could facilitate management of human resource related issues.

Precision Software Inc. is a software engineering firm contracted to develop and implement the HRMS project. After a preliminary meeting with Zealot's senior management, the lead software engineer on the Precision Software team documents his findings as follows:

- A detailed employee profile consists of the employee's personal information, employment history, education history and beneficiary information.

- Every employee belongs to a department, and is assigned a specific job description (there may be several employees with the same job description).

- Employees are classified according to the salary range that they fall in.

- Each employee has a compensation package which outlines basic salary and other benefits. Benefits include health insurance, retirement plan, life insurance, professional development allowance, housing allowance, traveling allowance, entertainment allowance, vacation allowance, and education allowance.

- A payroll log keeps track of remuneration paid out to employees.

- Each employee is assigned to at least one project; the number of employees assigned to a project depends on the size and complexity of the project.

1. Identify all information entities (object types) mentioned or implied in the case.   {10}

2. Identify all relationships among the entities (object types) and represent them on an ERD or ORD.   {20}

3. Use the information in the case, combined with the information conveyed by the E-R diagram and your own intuitive design skills to propose relations and their associated attributes for each of the entities represented on the E-R diagram. You may also introduce additional relation(s) to take care of M:M relationship(s) which may exist.   {60}

26.3 Sample Assignment 2B

1. What are the possible advantages of using distributive processing in a database system environment?   {06}

2. What are the problems that can be experienced from having non-normalized files in a system?   {06}

3. Relation R(A B C . . . K) is in 1NF only. The following FDs hold:

    a. Primary key is (ABC)

    b. A → D

    c. B –> E

    d. F → G,H,I

    e. J → B

    f. K → C

    g. (AF) –>> J/K

    By repeatedly using Heath's or Fagin's theorems, decompose R into a set of 5NF relations. Show how the new relations will be keyed.   {15}

4. The following atomic data elements were taken from the data dictionary of an inventory system:

Item Number [ITM#]	Item Name [ITMNAME]
Item Last Price [ITMLP]	Item On Hand Quantity [ITMQOH]
Item Average Price [ITMAP]	Item Category Code [ITMCTG]
Category Description [CTGDES]	Item Supplier [ITMSPLR]
Order# [ORD#]	Order Date [ORDDATE]
Item Ordered [ORDITM]	Quantity Ordered [ORDQTY]
Order Status [ORDSTS]	Invoice Number [INV#]
Invoice Received Date [RCVDATE]	Item Received [RCVITM#]
Quantity Received [RCVQTY]	Invoice's Related Order [INVORD#]
Requisition Date [RQSDATE]	Requisition Number [RQS#]
Department Requesting [RQSDEPT]	Issue Date [ISSDATE]
Requisition Honor Date [RQSHDATE]	Quantity Issued [ISSQTY]
Issue Number [ISS#]	Item Issued [ISSITM]
Department Receiving the Issue [ISSDPT]	Item Issue Price [ISSPRC]

Group the attributes into related entities. Then for each entity, identify the FDs, then normalize it. Grade may be assigned as follows:

Identification of all possible FDs.   {11}

Putting the elements into normalized relations. You may introduce elements as required with appropriate explanation.
                                                       {44}

26.4 Sample Assignment 3A

1. Define the following terms:

   Candidate key   {02}

   Foreign key   {02}

   Functional dependence   {03}

   Transitive dependence   {03}

2. Give the primary key and the highest normal form of each of the following relations. State any assumptions made and give reasons for your answers.

   Student {Student#, Name, Address, Gender, Age DOB}
                                                       {03}

   Flight {Flight#, Date, Seats-Available, Flight-Time, From-City, To-City}   {03}

Account {Account#, Customer#, Customer-Name, Balance}
{03}

Supply {Part#, Quantity, Supplier#, Supplier-Address}
{03}

3. In the relation **Participation**, are attributes Manager, Project, Hours (spent on project per month), Salary. A manager's salary is fixed, and he/she can work on many projects.

3a. Draw a FD diagram of the relation.   {03}

3b. Would you store **Participation** as defined?
Justify your answer.   {04}

3c. Provide some sample data for the relation.   {04}

3d. What is the highest normal form of **Participation**?   {03}

3e. Show how you would design a conceptual schema to store the data mentioned for relation **Participation**?   {11}

4. A scientific research establishment organizes its work in projects, each project consisting of several experiments. For each experiment, the following is recorded:

Project number

Project manager

Project name

Experiment number

Experiment name

Lab in which experiment is to be conducted

List of scientists to work on the project

Note: A project manager may work on an experiment. A scientist may work on more than one experiment, provided that they are done in the same lab. A manager may manage more than one project.

4a. From the information given, develop an ERD.   {10}

4b. Using the XR model, derive a set of BCNF relations for the system. Use self- explanatory relation and attribute names (you may introduce new attributes).   {20}

419

5. Figure 26-1 provides a snapshot of a live database. Primary keys are highlighted. Based on the data, derive an E-R diagram (state any assumptions made). {10}

Warehouse

WhNo	City	Size (Sq.ft.)
WH1	Seattle	37,000
WH2	New York	50,000
WH3	Miami	20,000
WH4	Boston	13,000
...	...	...

Employee

WhNo	EmpNo	Salary ($US)
WH2	E1	42,000
WH1	E3	61,000
WH2	E4	65,000
WH3	E6	63,000
WH1	E7	55,000
...	...	...

Supplier

SNo	Sname	Location
S3	Wilson	Jamaica
S4	Barnes	USA
S6	Jones	UK
S7	Lewis	Singapore
...	...	...

PurchaseOrder

EmpNo	SNo	OrderNo	OrderDate
E3	S7	OR67	840623
E1	S4	OR73	840728
E7	S4	OR76	840525
E6	S6	OR77	840619
E3	S4	OR79	840623
E1	S6	OR80	840729
E3	S6	OR90	850622
E3	S3	0R91	850713
...	...	...	...

Figure 26-1. *Snapshot of a Database*

26.5 Sample Assignment 4A

Figure 26-2 provides basic specifications for a music database. Carefully analyze the figure, and answer the questions that follow.

Relational Table	Primary Key or Candidate Keys
Musicians {MNO, MNAME, DOB, MCOUNTRY}	Primary key [MNO]
Compositions {CNO, TITLE, MNO, CDATE}	Primary key [CNO]
Ensembles {ENO, ENAME, ECOUNTRY, MNO_MGR}	Primary key [ENO]
Performances {PNO, PDATE, CNO, CITY, PCOUNTRY, ENO}	Candidate keys [PDATE, ENO], [PNO]
Ensemble_Members {ENO, MNO ,INSTRUMENT}	Primary key [ENO, MNO]

Figure 26-2. *Basic Specifications Music Database*

1. Write relational calculus statements to realize the following:

1a. Registered musicians (MNO and MNAME) from USA or JAM (where "USA" and "JAM" are abbreviated codes for United States and Jamaica respectively). {03}

1b. List every ensemble (ENO) that includes a SAXAPHONE or CLARINET player. {03}

1c. Give the ENO of every ensemble that includes a SAXAPHONE but not a CLARINET player. {04}

1d. List all compositions (CNO and TITLE) by MOZART. {04}

1e. List all performances (PNO, CNO, MNO, and PCOUNTRY) of compositions in the country of origin. {06}

1f. Give the ENO of every ensemble that includes a SAXAPHONE or CLARINET player, but not both. {06}

1g. Find CNO for compositions all of which have been performed in USA. {03}

1h. List countries in which MOZART's compositions have been performed. {03}

1i. Give ENAME of ensembles whose manager is RUSSIAN. {03}

2. Write relational algebra statements corresponding to each of the relational calculus statements of question #1. {35}

26.6 Sample Assignment 5A

The (cross-section of the) college database introduced in chapter 7 (and discussed in subsequent chapters) is repeated here (Figure 26-3).

Student {Stud#, Sname, Fname, Sex, Addr, Spgm#, S_Hall#, DoB ...}
      Primary Key [Stud#]
Program {Pgm#, Pgmname ...}
      Primary Key [Pgm#]
Hall {Hall#, Hallname ...}
      Primary Key [Hall#]
Dept {Dept#, Dname, Dhead#, D_Div#}
      Primary Key [Dept#]
      Dhead# references **Staff.Staff#**
      D_Div# references **Division.Div#**
Staff {Staff#, Staffname ...}
      Primary Key [Staff#]
Course {Crs#, Crsname ...}
      Primary Key [Crs#]
Pgm_Struct {PSPgm#, PSCrs#, PSCrsSeqn)
      Primary Key [PsPgm#-PsCrs#]
      PsPgm# references **Program.Pgm#**
      Pscrs# references **Course.Crs#**
Division {Div#, Divname, Dvhead# ...}
      Primary Key [Div#]
      Dvhead# references **Staff.Staff#**

Figure 26-3. *Cross Section of College Database Requirements*

1. Write SQL statements to create these tables in your schema of the class database. You may add additional attributes to the structure of each database table, as you deem appropriate. Store these statements in an SQL script file.   {40}

2. Use your SQL script file to create the tables in the class database.   {16}

3. Populate your tables with sample data (at least six records per table).   {16}

26.7 Sample Assignment 6A

Figure 26-2 is repeated as Figure 26-4 for ease of reference. Carefully analyze the figure, and answer the questions that follow.

Relational Table	Primary Key or Candidate Keys
Musicians {MNO, MNAME, DOB, MCOUNTRY}	Primary key [MNO]
Compositions {CNO, TITLE, MNO, CDATE}	Primary key [CNO]
Ensembles {ENO, ENAME, ECOUNTRY, MNO_MGR}	Primary key [ENO]
Performances {PNO, PDATE, CNO, CITY, PCOUNTRY, ENO}	Candidate keys [PDATE, ENO], [PNO]
Ensemble_Members {ENO, MNO ,INSTRUMENT}	Primary key [ENO, MNO]

Figure 26-4. *Basic Specifications for Music Database*

1. Write appropriate SQL statements to create the tables specified in the figure (you may assign appropriate column types and lengths). Also include important integrity constraints. {30}

2. Write SQL statements to realize the following:

2a. Registered musicians (MNO and MNAME) from USA or JAM (where "USA" and "JAM" are abbreviated codes for United States and Jamaica respectively). {03}

2b. List every ensemble (ENO) that includes a SAXAPHONE or CLARINET player. {03}

2c. Give the ENO of every ensemble that includes a SAXAPHONE but not a CLARINET player. {04}

2d. List all compositions (CNO and TITLE) by MOZART. {04}

2e. List all performances (PNO, CNO, MNO, and PCOUNTRY) of compositions in the country of origin. {06}

2f. Give the ENO of every ensemble that includes a SAXAPHONE or CLARINET player, but not both. {06}

2g. Find CNO for compositions all of which have been performed in USA. {03}

2h. List countries in which MOZART's compositions have been performed. {04}

2i. Give ENAME of ensembles whose manager is RUSSIAN. {03}

3. Define and specify SQL views to realize the above requirements. {36}

4. Given the above database, and assuming an Oracle 10g environment, show what the contents of the system catalog tables **User_Tables** (attributes **Table_Name** and **Tablespace_ Name**) and **User_Columns** (attributes **Column_Name** and **Table_Name**) would be. {10}

5. The above database may be refined by introducing a **Countries** table, and adjusting three other tables to each have a foreign key that references this table. Show the required SQL statements to make this adjustment. {12}

26.8 Sample Assignment 7A

For each question, show the SQL statement(s) that you have used in order to address the question.

1. Create a test table called **JonesB_TestTable** (where "JonesB" represents your user name) and populate it with some sample data. {10}

2a. Create a role and for its name, use the concatenation of your user account and the word "Role." For instance, the role may be called **JobesB_Role** (where "JonesB" represents your user name). {02}

2b. Grant to your role the system privileges that facilitate application development (see section 13.2.2 for guidelines on this). {11}

2c. Grant to your role, SUDI privileges on **JonesB_TestTable** (review section 13.2.3 for the SUDI privileges). {04}

2d. There is a catalog table that you can access to see all the system privileges granted to all roles in the system. Its name is **Role_Sys_Privs**. Study its structure, and then issue an appropriate SQL statement to display the system privileges associated with your role. Show the SQL statement used. {06}

3. Create a test user account called **JonesB_User** (where "JonesB" represents your user name). Assign the user to your tablespace; also use a password that you will remember. Your current tablespace name is **TBS_JonesB** (where "JonesB" represents your user name). {04}

3a. Try logging on to the database as **JonesB_User**. Record the result of your attempt, and provide an explanation for this observation. {04}

3b. Log on with your normal user account and grant your role (created in 2a) to user **JonesB_User**. {02}

3c. Try logging on as **JonesB_User** once more and record the result of your attempt. Provide an explanation for this observation. {04}

3d. Log on as **JonesB_Useer** and try running a query on your test table. To do this, you must either create synonym for **JonesB_TestTable** in the schema of **JonesB_User**, then run the query on the synonym, or you must qualify the table name when you run the query on **JonesB_TestTable.** Record the result of your attempt, and explain why you obtained that result. {10}

3e. Switch to your normal user account and revoke the SUDI privileges on **JonesB_TestTable** from your role. {04}

3f. Log on as **JonesB** again and try running a query on your **JonesB_TestTable**. Record the result of your attempt. Provide an explanation for this result. {06}

26.9 Sample Assignment 8A

1. Identify and summarize five issues to be addressed in database administration. {12}

2.1 Give the definition of a distributed database system. {03}

2.2 What is the difference between database fragmentation and database replication? Cite a situation that would warrant each. {04}

2.3 State and clarify four of Date's twelve rules for distributed databases. {12}

2.4. Discuss two challenges to distributed databases, and alternate approaches for addressing each challenge.   {08}

3.1. Describe two challenges to OO database management systems.   {06}

3.2. Describe one hybrid approach that facilitates the peaceful coexistence of relational databases and object technology.   {04}

26.10 Sample Interim Examination A

Instruction: Answer all four questions.

1a. What are the main components of a Database System? With the aid of a diagram, show how they are related.
          {10}

1b. State six objectives of a database system.   {06}

1c. What is meant by data independence? Using example(s) explain its importance.   {04}

2a. Clarify the terms external schema, conceptual schema and internal schema.   {06}

2b. Clarify the terms data sub language (DSL), data definition language (DDL) and data manipulation language (DML). Relate SQL to these terms.   {08}

3a. What are the main functions of the DBMS?   {06}

3b. Give two examples of a DBMS.   {02}

3c. What are the functional components of the DBMS? By use of a diagram, show how they are related.   {12}

4a. Define the following terms:

Primary key   {02}

Foreign key   {02}

Attributes   {02}

Relation   {02}

Domain   {03}

4b. Figure 26-5 is an excerpt from the database design proposal for a college administrative management system:

Relation	Attributes	Primary Key
Program	ProgNum, ProgName	ProgNum
Course	CrsCode, CrsName, CrsCredit	CrsCode
Pgm_Struct	ProgNum, CrsCode, CrsSequence	ProgNum & CrsCode
Chapterr	LectNum, LectName	LectNum
Class	ClassCode, ClassDescr	ClassCode
Class_Sched	Period, CrsCode, LectNum, ClassCode	Period & ClassCode

Figure 26-5. *Excerpt from College Database Proposal*

Study the figure and answer the following questions:

Identify all foreign keys. {02}

Describe verbally how you could obtain a list of course names and chapterr names, lecturing these courses at specific times. {02}

Explain verbally how you could obtain a list of program names and course names in appropriate order for the college bulletin. {02}

26.11 Sample Interim Examination B

Instruction: Answer all five questions.

1a. What is a database? {02}

1b. State four primary objectives and four secondary objectives of a database system. {08}

1c. What is data independence? Explain its importance in the design of a database. {06}

1d. State four advantages that a DBS has over traditional file processing systems. {04}

2a. Briefly describe the three levels of architecture in a database system. You may use diagram(s) in your explanation. {10}

2b. With the use of diagram(s) where necessary, explain how communication is achieved among end users, the database, application programs, DBMS and the hardware. {10}

3a. State four functions of the DBMS. {04}

3b. ITC Software Inc. is developing a database system for one of its clients, X-Don Inc., based in Miami, Florida. X-Don has experienced Windows users. They use the Oracle RDBMS. Additionally, X-Don has very experienced Oracle Programmers. However, it is strategically imprudent for ITC Software to design and develop the database in Oracle or on the Windows platform. They prefer to work on the Linux platform, using a product called Kylix and PHP. To complicate matters, ITC Software operates out of Port of Spain, Trinidad. ITC Software therefore desires to access the X-Don's database, hosted in Miami, via telecommunication linkage. Is the project feasible? Using block diagram, explain how the project could be implemented. {08}

3c. Briefly explain the following: Data Definition Language (DDL); Data Manipulation Language (DML); Data sub-language (DSL); Structured Query Language (SQL) {08}

4. Developing an inventory management system is standard in most organizations. The main entities to be identified are Purchase Orders, Receipts (of goods), Inventory (Items), Inventory Categories, Inventory Requisitions, Departments, Inventory Issues. Next, we identify relationships among the entities:

- Departments make requisitions for inventory items;

- Issues of inventory are made to departments in response to requisitions;

- Purchase orders are made to suppliers for inventory items;

- Goods received are normally accompanied by an invoice, specifying the items and cost (of course, invoices come from suppliers);

- Each inventory item is assigned a category.

4a. From the information given, draw an ERD for the inventory management system described. {10}

4b. For each relationship, state whether mandatory or optional; 1:1 or 1:M or M:M or M:1. {10}

5a. Write brief notes on five of the terms in following list (Figure 26-6): {10}

Entity	Relation	Attributes
Entity set	Tuples	Candidate Key
Primary Key	Foreign Key	Degree
Cardinality	Domain	Scalar Values

Figure 26-6. *Basic Terms Used in the Relational Model*

5b. Complete the following triplets with the most appropriate words or expressions to be taken from the list provided below (Figure 26-7). {10}

Relation   _____   _____

_____   Rows   _____

_____   _____   Number of Fields

Attributes   _____   _____

_____   Number of Rows   _____

List od Terms:

Binary	Number of columns	Decomposable
N-ary	File	Degree
Table	Spurious	Number of records
Fields	Elements	Base
Records	Snapshot	Tuples
Columns	Cardinality	Normalized

Figure 26-7. Database Terminology Puzzle

26.12 Sample Final Examination A

This examination consists of nine (9) questions distributed over four (4) sections. You are required to do four (4) questions, but no more than one question from a section.

Section A: Do all questions from this section.

1.

1a. What are the main components of a database system? With the aid of a diagram, show how they are related. {10}

1b. State six (6) objectives of a database system. {06}

1c. Give four (4) examples of popular DBMS suites. {04}

2.

2a. Briefly clarify the terms *external schema, conceptual schema* and *internal schema.* By use of an appropriate diagram, show how the three terms are related. {10}

2b. Explain what is meant by *data sub-language (DSL), data definition language (DDL)* and *data manipulation language (DML).* How does SQL relate to these terms? {04}

2c. State four (4) significant roles/functions of the DBMS. {04}

2d. What is the difference between a DBMS and a compiler? {02}

Section B: You may do one question from this section.

3.

The following atomic data elements were taken from the data dictionary of an inventory management system:

Item Number [ITM#]	Item Name [ITMNAM]
Item Last Price [ITMLP]	Item On Hand Quantity [ITMQOH]
Item Average Price [ITMAP]	Item Category Code [ITMCTG]
Category Description [CTGDES]	Item Supplier [ITMSPLR]
Order# [ORD#]	Order Date [ORDDAT]
Item Ordered [ORDITM]	Quantity Ordered [ORDQTY]
Order Status [ORDSTS]	Invoice Number [INV#]
Receipt Date [RCVDAT]	Item Received [RCVITM]
Quantity Received [RCVQTY]	Invoice's Related Order [INVORD]
Requisition Date [RQSDAT]	Requisition Number [RQS#]
Department Requesting [RQSDPT]	Issue Date [ISSDAT]
Requisition Honor Date [RQSHDT]	Item Issued [ISSITM]
Issue Number [ISS#]	Quantity Issued [ISSQTY]
Item Issue Price [ISSPRC]	
Department Receiving the Issue [ISSDPT]	

Figure 26-8a. *Excerpts from Inventory Management System*

Put the elements into normalized relations, clearly stating the basis for your decision. You may introduce data elements as required. Clearly state any assumptions or observations made. {20}

4.

4a. Complete the following triplets with the most appropriate words or expressions to be taken from the list provided in Figure 26-8b. {10}

4b. Give a formal definition of a relation. Clarify any ambiguity that may exist between an entity and a relation. {04}

4c. State three (3) kinds of relations that may be found in a database; explain what each is with an example. {06}

Relation	_____	_____
	Rows	_____
_____		
_____	_____	Number of Fields
Attributes	_____	_____
_____	Number of Rows	_____

List od Terms:

Binary	Number of columns	Decomposable
N-ary	File	Degree
Table	Spurious	Number of records
Fields	Elements	Base
Records	Snapshot	Tuples
Columns	Cardinality	Normalized

Figure 26-8b. *Database Terminology Puzzle*

5.

5a. State and briefly clarify two integrity rules that must govern a database.   {04}

5b. How should deletion of referenced tuples be treated? Give an appropriate example.   {06}

5c. Suppose that it is desirable to record the following information in a normalized database:

Course	[C]
Teacher	[T]
Hour	[H]
Room	[R]
Student	[S]
Grade	[G]

Assume that the following dependencies hold:

[H+R]→ C

[H+T] → R

[C+S] → G

[H+S] → R

[C] → T

By completing closure, determine the candidate key
in the given relation. {03}

Derive a set of 4NF relations. {07}

Section C: Examine the section of a college/university database, shown in Figure 26-9 and answer one question from this section.

6.

Write relational calculus statements that will produce the
results specified below:

6a. List all students (name, ID, and gender) who share
surname with other students {03}

6b. List all program-names and related course-
names {04}

6c. List the names of all programs that include the course (code)
'CS100' {03}

6d. List the names of all programs that do not include course
(code) 'ENGL101' {03}

6e. List all Canadian (country code 'CAN') students (name,
ID, Hall-name) enrolled in the B.S. in Computer Science
(program code 'P11SC') {04}

6f. List the name of each department along with the name
of its chair-person {03}

7.

Write relational algebra statements that will produce the
results specified below:

7a. List all students (name, ID, and gender) who share
surname with other students {03}

7b. List all program-names and related course-names 04}

7c. List the names of all programs that include the
course (code) 'CS100' {03}

7d. List the names of all programs that do not include course
(code) 'ENGL101' {03}

7e. List all Canadian (country code 'CAN') students (name,
ID, Hall-name) enrolled in the B.S. in Computer Science
(program code 'P11SC') {04}

7f. List the name of each department along with the name
of its chair-person {03}

Section D: Examine the section of a college/university database, shown in Figure 26-9 and answer one question from this section.

Table Name	Attributes
Student	**Stud#**, LName, FName, Sex, DOB, Pgm#, CntryCode, Hall#
Program	**Pgm#**, PgmName
Department	**Dept#**, DName, Chair#
Course	**CrsCode**, CrsName
Hall	**Hall#**, HallName
Staff	**Staff#**, StaffName
Pgm_Struct	**Pgm#, Crscode**, PgmSequence
Country	**CntryCode**, CntryName

Note:
- Primary-key attributes are highlighted.
- Pgm# in the table **Student** stores the program-code of the student's (academic) major.
- Chair# in the table **Department** stores the staff-number of the department's chairperson.

Figure 26-9. *Section of a College Database*

8.

Write SQL statements that will produce the results specified below:

8a. List all students (name, ID, and gender) who share surname with other students   {03}

8b. List all program-names and related course-names   {04}

8c. List the names of all programs that include the course (code) 'CS100'   {03}

8d. List the names of all programs that do not include course (code) 'ENGL101'   {03}

8e. List all Canadian (country code 'CAN') students (name, ID, Hall-name) enrolled in the B.S. in Computer Science (program code 'P11SC')   {04}

8f. List the name of each department along with the name of its chair-person   {03}

9.

9a. How important are (logical) views in a database (cite possible advantages)?   {04}

9b. Identify four (4) scenarios that could render a logical view non-updateable.   {04}

9c. Referring to the college database of Figure 26-9, define a view that "stores" Computer Science courses only (assume that all Computer Science course-codes begin with the acronym 'CS').   {03}

9d. How important is the system catalog in a DBMS? Describe three important tables that are usually included in the system catalog (use the Oracle DBMS as a frame of reference).   {06}

9e. Given the information provided in Figure *26-9*, illustrate what might be the contents of one of the catalog tables mentioned in (9d) above. Explain how the system catalog is maintained.   {03}

26.13 Sample Final Examination B

This examination consists of four (4) sections. You are required to do all questions in section A, and three additional questions — one from each of the other three sections.

Section A: Answer all questions in this section. For multiple-choice questions, simply highlight the responses that you deem to be correct.

1. State six significant objectives of a database system.   {06}
   a.

   b.

   c.

   d.

   e.

   f.

2. State three advantages of a database system.
                                    {03}
   a.

   b.

   c.

3. State three primary functions of a DBMS.   {03}

   a.

   b.

   c.

4. Which of the following is not a valid example of a DBMS?
                                    {01}
   a.   Oracle

   b.   DB2

   c.   Java Development Kit

   d.   Informix

5. A record is to a file: {01}

    a. What a mouse is to a computer

    b. What a tuple is to a relation

    c. What a procedure is to a program

    d. What peach is to a fruit salad

6. Cardinality of a relation refers to: {01}

    a. The age (in months) of the relation

    b. The sexual orientation of parties in the relation

    c. The number of tuples in the relation

    d. None of the above

7. A foreign key may be defined as: {01}

    a. An attribute or combination of attributes that uniquely
        identify tuples of a relation

    b. An attribute or combination of attributes that ought not
        to have been included in a relation

    c. An attribute that may contain null values

    d. An attribute or combination of attributes of a relation R1
        that forms the primary key in some other relation R2

8. Let R1[A,B,C] and R2[C,D,E] be two relations with R1.C being
    defined on the same domain as R2.C. Assume further that the
    primary key of R1 is A and the primary key of R2 is C. Which of
    the following statements are valid?   {02}

    a. SELECT * FROM R1, R2 WHERE R1.C = R2.C

    b. SELECT * FROM R1, R2 WHERE R1.C = R2.D

    c. There is a M:M relationship between R1 and R2

    d. There is a 1:M relationship between R2 and R1

9. Based on the principle of data independence, which of the
    following can be concluded?   {02}

    a. One can decompose a relation into smaller projections in
        any way he/she chooses

    b. Structural changes to a database should not affect the
        application programs that access the database

    c.   Different users of a database will have different external perspectives of its data

    d.   All of the above

10. Which of the following statements regarding the results of normalization are false?   {02}

    a.   Redundancy and data anomalies are reduced

    b.   Redundancy and data anomalies are exacerbated

    c.   Data integrity and data independence are enhanced

    d.   Data integrity and data independence are compromised

11. Let R1[A,B,C] and R2[C,D,E] be two relations with R1.C being defined on the same domain as R2.C. Assume further that the primary key of R1 is A and the primary key of R2 is C. R2 consists of N2 tuples each of which is referenced by at least one of the N1 tuples of R1. Which of the following assertions are plausible/true?   {02}

    a.   N1 > N2

    b.   N1 < N2

    c.   In order to purge (empty) both relations, one must purge in the order {R1, R2}

    d.   In order to purge (empty) both relations, one must purge in the order {R2, R1}

12. How many standard normal forms are there?   {01}

    a.   Three

    b.   Four

    c.   Five

    d.   Six

13. A relation that is in BCNF is automatically in: {02}

    a.   3NF, 2NF and 1NF

    b.   3NF and 2NF

    c.   4NF and 5NF

    d.   None of the above

14. In database systems, a surrogate: {02}

   a. Is a relational table that is not related to other tables in the database

   b. Is a system-controlled primary key, introduced by the designer

   c. Is sometimes introduced to avoid using a cumbersome composite primary key.

   d. Is a database designer that gets no credit for his/her work

15. An ERD is useful to: {01}

   a. Show the interrelationships among application programs of a system

   b. Represent the relationships among application programs and database tables

   c. Illustrate the various external view that users of a database might have

   d. Illustrate the main entities and relationships of a database system

Section B: Answer one question from this section.

16.

16a. Give a formal definition of a relation. Clarify any ambiguity that may exist between an entity and a relation. {04}

16b. State three (3) kinds of relations which may be found in a database; for each type, explain what it is and give an appropriate example. {06}

16c – 16e. The following is an excerpt from a college database design proposal (Figure 26-10):

Relation	Attributes	Primary Key
Program	ProgNum, ProgName	ProgNum
Course	CrsCode, CrsName, CrsCredit	CrsCode
Pgm_Struct	ProgNum, CrsCode, CrsSequence	ProgNum & CrsCode
Chapterr	LectNum, LectName	LectNum
Class	ClassCode, ClassDescr	ClassCode
Class_Sched	Period, CrsCode, LectNum, ClassCode	Period & ClassCode

Figure 26-10. Except From a College Database

16c. Based on the Figure 26-10, clearly identify all relationships and foreign keys. {06}

16d. Based on Figure 26-10, describe, how you could obtain a list showing course names and the corresponding names of lecturers who teach these courses. {02}

16e. Based on Figure 26-10, describe, how you could obtain a list showing program names and the corresponding course names in appropriate order for the college bulletin. {02}

17.

17a. Define the following terms:

Functional Dependence	{02}
Transitive Dependence	{02}
Non-loss decomposition	{02}
Boyce-Codd Normal Form	{02}
Multi-valued Dependence	{02}
Fourth Normal Form	{02}

17b. As Database Manager or Information Systems Manager in a software engineering firm, what standards would you set in respect of logical database design? Justify your position. {08}]

Section C: Answer one question from this section.

Figure 26-2, which provides an excerpt from the specification of a music database, is repeated here (as Figure 26-11) for ease of reference. Carefully analyze the figure, and answer the questions that follow.

Relational Table	Primary Key or Candidate Keys
Musicians {MNO, MNAME, DOB, MCOUNTRY}	Primary key [MNO]
Compositions {CNO, TITLE, MNO, CDATE}	Primary key [CNO]
Ensembles {ENO, ENAME, ECOUNTRY, MNO_MGR}	Primary key [ENO]
Performances {PNO, PDATE, CNO, CITY, PCOUNTRY, ENO}	Candidate keys [PDATE, ENO], [PNO]
Ensemble_Members {ENO, MNO ,INSTRUMENT}	Primary key [ENO, MNO]

Figure 26-11. *Basic Specifications of Music Database*

18.

Provide sample data of the above relations.   {bonus 04}
Write relational calculus statements to realize the following:

18a.   List registered musicians from CUB or CAN (where "CUB"
and "CAN" are abbreviated codes for Cuba and Canada
respectively).   {03}

18b.   Give the ENO of every ensemble that includes a Violin or
Violin player.   {03}

18c.   Give the ENO of every ensemble that includes a Violin
player but not a Guitar player.   {04}

18d.   List all compositions (CNO and TITLE) by
David Foster.   {04}

18e.   List all performances (PNO CNO MNO & PCOUNTRY)
of compositions that have been performed in the
country of origin.   {06}

19.

Provide sample data of the above relations.   {bonus 04}
Write relational algebra statements corresponding to
specifications of 18a – 18e above.   {20}

Section D: Answer one question from this section.

20.

20a.   How important are logical views in a database?   {04}

20a – 20f.   The college database of question 16 is repeated
here for ease of reference.

Based on the schema provided in Figure 26-12, write SQL statements
to do the following:

20b.   Create a view which will allow three of the above tables to
be joined as one, so as to provide information for the college
bulletin. The information required should include Program
Code, Program Name, Course Sequence, Course Number,
and Course Name.   {04}

20c.   Assuming the existence of a program with code "P01" and
name "BS. in Mathematics," extract from the system, the
program structure for this program with courses listed
in order of sequence number. The data fields required
are outlined in 20b above.   {04}

Relation	Attributes	Primary Key
Program	ProgNum, ProgName	ProgNum
Course	CrsCode, CrsName, CrsCredit	CrsCode
Pgm_Struct	ProgNum, CrsCode, CrsSequence	ProgNum & CrsCode
Lecturer	LectNum, LectName	LectNum
Class	ClassCode, ClassDescr	ClassCode
Class_Sched	Period, CrsCode, LectNum, ClassCode	Period & ClassCode

Figure 26-12. *Except From a College Database*

20d. Establish a class-course-lecturer relationship, stored as a view, so that for each class, it will be known what course is offered, and who is the lecturer. {04}

20e. List all courses offered by the college. {01}

20f. Create a view for chemistry majors, which enables them to have read-only access to the chemistry curriculum only (assume that chemistry course codes are prefixed by the string "CHEM"). {03}

21.

21a. Write SQL statement(s) to create a role called **Developer** and give it all the privileges required for application development. {04}

21b. Write SQL statement(s) to assign the **Developer** role to users **GrantFord** and **HarryLim**, and deny the user **Stalker** all privileges. {03}

21c. Assume that your database contains a table called **Payroll**, which has confidential information about the salary of employees. As the DBA, you want to restrict access to this table as follows: User **JohnHenry** must have query access only; user **BruceJones** must have query as well as modification access; no one else must have any access to the table. Write SQL statement(s) to realize this. {06}

21d. Write an SQL statement to query the Oracle 10G system catalog and provide a list of all tables in a given database (your display must include the name of the table, the owner of the table and the tablespace it belongs to). {03}

21e. Describe two limitations of SQL and briefly explain how they can be circumvented. {04}

26.14 Sample Final Examination C

This examination consists of four (4) sections. You are required to do all questions in section A, and three additional questions — one from each of the other three sections.

Section A: Answer all questions in this section

1. State six (6) significant objectives of a database system.

   {06}

   a.

   b.

   c.

   d.

   e.

   f.

2. State the components of a database system.   {05}

   a.

   b.

   c.

   d.

   e.

3. State four (4) primary functions of a DBMS.   {04}

   a.

   b.

   c.

   d.

4. Give the meaning of the acronyms DSL, DDL, DML and DCL. Briefly explain their importance in a database system. Provide an example of a DSL.   {05}

   DSL:

   DDL:

   DML:

   DCL:

   Example:

5. Give three (3) examples of popular and modern DBMS suites. {03}

   a.

   b.

   c.

6. State and briefly clarify three (3) types of relations that are likely to be found in a database. {03}

   a.

   b.

   c.

7. Clarify the terms *relation, foreign key, candidate key,* and *degree.* {04}

   Relation:

   Foreign Key:

   Candidate Key:

   Degree:

8. State four (4) types of objects that are typically defined in a database that supports SQL. {04}

   a.

   b.

   c.

   d.

9. State two (2) strong points about SQL and describe two (2) limitations of the language. {04}

   a.

   b.

   c.

   d.

10. What are the two dominant contemporary models for
database design, implementation and management?

{02}

a.

b.

Section B: Answer one question from this section

11.

Precision Software Inc. is a software engineering firm
contracted to develop and implement a Human Resource
Management System (HRMS) for Zealot Industries Inc. After
a preliminary meeting with Zealot's senior management,
the lead software engineer on the Precision Software team
documents his findings as follows:

- A detailed employee profile consists of the employee's
  personal information, employment history, education
  history and beneficiary information.

- Every employee belongs to a department, and is assigned
  a specific job description (there may be more than one
  employees with the same job description).

- Employees are classified according to the salary range that
  they fall in.

- Each employee has a compensation package which outlines
  basic salary and other benefits. Benefits include health
  insurance, retirement plan, life insurance, professional
  development allowance, housing allowance, traveling
  allowance, entertainment allowance, vacation allowance,
  and education allowance.

- A payroll log keeps track of remuneration paid out to
  employees.

- Each employee is assigned to at least one project; the
  number of employees assigned to a project depends on the
  size and complexity of the project.

11a. Identify all information entities (object types) mentioned or
implied in the case.   {05}

11b. Identify all relationships among the entities (or object types)
and represent them on an ERD or ORD.   {15}

12.

A scientific research est. For each experiment, the following is recorded:

- Project number
- Project manager
- Project name
- Experiment number
- Experiment name
- Lab in which experiment is to be conducted
- List of scientists to work on the project

Note: A project manager may work on an experiment. A scientist may work on more than one experiment, provided that they are done in the same lab. A manager may manage more than one project.

From the information given, use the XR model to derive a set of BCNF relations for the system.

Use self-explanatory relation and attribute names (you may introduce new attributes). {20}

Section C: Answer one question from this section

Examine the section of a college/university database, shown in Figure 26-13, and answer one question from this section.

13.

Write relational calculus statements that will produce the results specified below:

13a. List all students (name, ID, and gender) who share surname with at least another student {03}

13b. List all program-names and related course-names {04}

13c. List the names of all programs that include the course (code) 'CS100' {03}

13d. List of the names of all programs that do not include the course (code) 'ENGL101' {03}

13e. List all Canadian (country code 'CAN') students (name, ID, Hall-name) enrolled in the B.S. in Computer Science (program code 'P11SC') {04}

13f. List the name of each department along with the name of its chairperson {03}

14.

Write relational algebra statements that will produce the results specified below:

Write relational calculus statements that will produce the results specified below:

14a. List all students (name, ID, and gender) who share surname with at least another student {03}

14b. List all program-names and related course-names {04}

14c. List the names of all programs that include the course (code) 'CS100' {03}

14d. List of the names of all programs that do not include the course (code) 'ENGL101' {03}

14e. List all Canadian (country code 'CAN') students (name, ID, Hall-name) enrolled in the B.S. in Computer Science (program code 'P11SC') {04}

14f. List the name of each department along with the name of its chairperson {03}

Section D: Answer one question from this section

Examine the section of a college/university database, shown in Figure 26-13, and answer one question from this section.

15.

Write SQL statements that will produce the results specified below:

15a. List all students (name, ID, and gender) who share surname with at least another student {03}

15b. List all program-names and related course-names {04}

15c. List the names of all programs that include the course (code) 'CS100' {03}

15d. List of the names of all programs that do not include the course (code) 'ENGL101' {03}

15e. List all Canadian (country code 'CAN') students (name, ID, Hall-name) enrolled in the B.S. in Computer Science (program code 'P11SC') {04}

15f. List the name of each department along with the name of its chairperson {03}

16.

16a. State three (3) advantages of logical views.　　　　　{03}

16b. State three (3) scenarios that could render a logical view non-updateable.　　　　　{03}

16c. Referring to the college database of Figure 26-13, define a view that "stores" computer science courses only (assume that all computer science course-codes begin with the acronym 'CS').　　　　　{03}

16d. Assuming that the program code for Computer Science is 'P11SC', construct a second logical view for computer science majors only. Your view must include all attributes of the student record, the full descriptive name of the computer science program, and the descriptive name of the hall dormitory that the students reside in.　　　　　{05}

16e. Provide the SQL statement that will create the **Student** table of Figure 26-13, with its primary key and foreign keys appropriately defined (assume that referenced tables have been previously defined).　　　　　{06}

Table Name	Attributes
Student	**Stud#**, LName, FName, Sex, DOB, Pgm#, CntryCode, Hall#
Program	**Pgm#**, PgmName
Department	**Dept#**, DName, Chair#
Course	**CrsCode**, CrsName
Hall	**Hall#**, HallName
Staff	**Staff#**, StaffName
Pgm_Struct	**Pgm#, Crscode**, PgmSequence
Country	**CntryCode**, CntryName

Note:
- Primary-key attributes are highlighted.
- Pgm# in the table **Student** stores the program-code of the student's (academic) major.
- Chair# in the table **Department** stores the staff-number of the department's chairperson.

Figure 26-13. Section of a College Database

PART G

■ ■ ■

Appendices

This final division contains three review topics from your data structures and software engineering courses:

- Appendix 1 — Review of Trees
- Appendix 2 — Review of Hashing
- Appendix 3 — Review of Information Gathering Strategies

APPENDIX 1

■ ■ ■

Review of Trees

This appendix provides a brief review of trees. You should pay specific attention to the section on B-trees, since most DBMS suites implement them by default. Note: This appendix is not meant to replace a full course (and text) in data structures. It should therefore be regarded as an overview, not a final authority on the subject matter. This review covers the following sub-topics:

- Introduction to Trees

- Binary Trees

- Threaded Binary Trees

- Binary Search Trees

- Height-Balanced Trees

- Heaps

- M-way Search Trees and B-trees

- Summary and Concluding Remarks

A1.1 Introduction to Trees

The main difference between $O(N^2)$ sorting algorithms and $O(N \log N)$ sorting algorithms is that the latter repeatedly reduce (by approximately one half) the number of keys remaining to be compared with each other, while the former does not. Trees are excellent sources of f (N log N) sorts.

As you are no doubt aware, in computer science, we use trees (and graphs) to represent and implement complex data structures. Here is a working definition of a tree: A tree T is a finite set of nodes $(V_1, V_2 ... V_n)$ such that:

a. There is one designated node called the root

b. The remaining nodes are partitioned into $M \geq 0$ disjoint sets $T_1, T_2 ... T_n$ such that each T_i is itself a tree.

c. Except for the root, each node has a parent node.

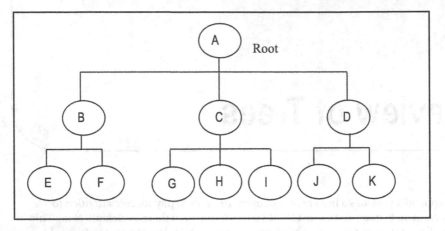

Figure A1-1. *An Example of a Tree*

Here are a few additional conventions about trees:

- The *leaves* are the terminal nodes.
- Parent nodes are said to have *siblings*.
- A forest is a combination (abundance) trees.

Level, Height and Weight of a Tree

- The root is at level zero (0).
- The height is therefore determined by the formula
  $$H = \text{Highest level} + 1$$
- Weight = Number of leaves

A1.2 Binary Trees

A1.2.1 Overview of Binary Trees

A binary tree is a tree in which each node is either empty or consists of two disjoint binary trees: the left *sub-tree* and the right *sub-tree*. Figure A1-2 illustrates this concept.

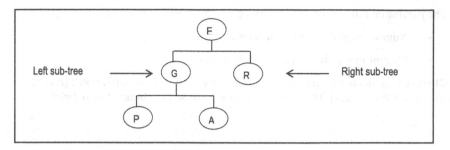

Figure A1-2. *Illustrating a Binary Tree*

Note:

- No parent has more than two children.

- A *full* (also called *perfect*) binary tree is a binary tree that contains the maximum number of nodes possible. Figure A1-3 shows a complete binary tree.

- A *complete* binary tree is a binary tree that is full down to the penultimate level, and with nodes at the final level filled in from left to right.

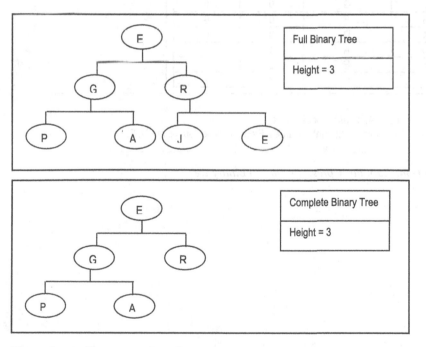

Figure A1-3. *Illustration of a Full Binary Tree and Complete Binary Tree*

The maximum number of nodes of a tree may be determined as follows:

- Number of nodes at the ith level is 2^i

- Maximum number of nodes = $\sum [0..k]$ of 2^i

Observe that this is a geometric series of first term 1 and common ration 2 (review your discreet mathematics). The sum is therefore $2^k - 1$. So for a binary tree of height k,

Maximum nodes = $2^k - 1$

Example 1: In the example above (Figure A1-3), maximum nodes = $2^3 - 1 = 7$.

A1.2.2 Representation of Binary Trees

Binary trees may be represented by arrays or preferably linked lists. Figure A1-4a illustrates a tabular representation of a binary tree while Figure A1-4b illustrates the graphic representation.

Location	Information	Left	Right
1	B	4	6
2	G	0	0
3	F	0	0
4	D	0	0
5	A	1	7
6	E	0	0
7	C	3	2

Note:
1. The root is node A. It has no pointer to it.
2. Leaves do not have left or right sub-trees. From the table, leaves are D, E, F, G.

Figure A1-4a. *Tabular Representation of a Binary Tree*

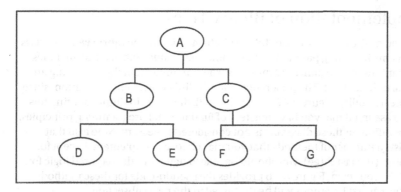

Figure A1-4b. *Graphic Representation of a Binary Tree*

A1.2.3 Application of Binary Trees

Binary trees are typically applied in the following ways:

- Binary trees (and extensions of binary trees) are used extensively in database management systems (DBMS) and operating system (OS) construction to effectively manage indexes of data files.

- Binary trees are used in calculation of expressions during compilation.

- Binary trees are used in data compressions, example, Huffman Coding Tree.

A1.2.4 Operations on Binary Trees

The following are the main operations that are normally defined on a binary tree:

- **Creation:** At creation the tree either has no nodes or a dedicated root-node.

- **Insertion:** We may allow insertion at the root, after terminal nodes only, or we may allow insertion anywhere in tree.

- **Deletion:** Again, we may allow deletion of terminal nodes only, or we may allow deletion of nodes from anywhere in tree.

- **Clear:** Remove all nodes from the binary tree, thus leaving it empty.

- **Check-Size:** Return the size of the tree.

- **Check-Empty:** Check if the tree is empty.

- **In-order:** In-order traversal of the tree.

- **Pre-order:** Pre-order traversal of the tree.

- **Post-order:** Post-order traversal of the tree.

A1.2.5 Implementation of Binary Trees

Suppose that you desire a binary tree of **LibraryPatron** objects. The **LibraryPatron** class includes data items including patron number, name, major, and status; it also includes methods for manipulating instances of the class. You can implement this tree using an array, array-list, or linked-list. The preference is for the linked-list implementation, since it provides more flexibility. Figure A1-5 shows the UML diagrams for implementing this binary tree. It is assumed that you have mastery of fundamental programming principles; therefore, elaboration on these diagrams is not considered necessary. Note also that Figure A1-5c lists a number of methods that you may choose to implement. Except for traversal methods (the last three), you should be able to figure out the required logic for these methods ob your own. Figure A1-6 provides the pseudo-code for these methods. The logic for the traversal methods will be discussed in the next subsection.

LibraryPatron
protected int PatronNumber protected String Name protected String Major private String Status
LibraryPatron() LibraryPatron(int ThisNumber) void Modify(LibraryPatron ThisPatron) void InputData(int x) String PrintMe() int GetPatronNumber()

Figure A1-5a. *The UML Diagram of the LibraryPatron Class*

PatronNode
protected LibraryPatron Info protected PatronNode Left, Right
PatronNode() void Modify(PatronNode ThisNode) void InputData(int x) String PrintMe()

Figure A1-5b. *The UML Diagram of the PatronNode Class*

PatronsBinaryTree
protected PatronNode Root protected int Size, TravRef LibraryPatron[] Traversal
public PatronsBinaryTree() public void addRoot(LibraryPatron ThisPatron) /* Inserts at the root, assuming previously empty tree */ public void addLeftLeaf(PatronNode ThisLeaf, LibraryPatron ThisPatron) /* Inserts at the specified leaf */ public void addRightLeaf(PatronNode ThisLeaf, LibraryPatron ThisPatron) /* Inserts at the specified leaf */ public void addLeftSubtree(PatronNode ThisNode, PatronNode NewNode) /* Inserts at the specified node */ public void addRightSubtree(PatronNode ThisNode, PatronNode NewNode) /* Inserts at the specified node */ public void removeSubtree(PatronNode ThisNode) public void Modify(PatronNode ThisNode, LibraryPatron ThisPatron) public void clearTree() public LibraryPatron getInfo(PatronNode ThisNode) public PatronNode getNode(PatronNode ThisNode) public int getSize() public boolean isEmpty() public void inOrderTraversal(PatronNode ThisNode) public void preOrderTraversal(PatronNode ThisNode) public void postOrderTraversal(PatronNode ThisNode)

Figure A1-5c. The UML Diagram of the PatronsBinaryTree Class

PatronsBinaryTreeMonitor
public static PatronsBinaryTree PatronsTree public static final String HEADING = "Library Patrons Tree" public static final int DEFAULT_NUMBER = 0
public static void main(String[] args) public static void InputPatrons() public static void TraverseTree() public static void RemovePatrons() public static void CheckSize() public static void InitializeTree() public static void Empty()

Figure A1-5d. The UML Diagram of the PatronsBinaryTreeMonitor Class

Assume that each node consists of the following:
- Info // Euphemism for details of the node
- Left // Pointer to the left sub-tree
- Right // Pointer to the right sub-tree

Also assume that Root always points to the root of the tree

---

addRoot(LibraryPatron ThisPatron)
START
 If (Root = NULL)
   Root.Info := ThisPatron;
   Set Root.Left and Root.Right to NULL;
   Add 1 to Size;
 End-If;
STOP

addLeftLeaf(PatronNode ThisLeaf, LibraryPatron ThisPatron)
START
 Let NewNode be a PatronNode;
 Instantiate NewNode;
 NewNode.Info := ThisPatron;
 Set NewNode.Left and NewNode.Right to NULL;
 ThisLeaf.Left := NewNode; // No longer a leaf, but now a sub-tree
 Add 1 to Size;
STOP

addRightLeaf(PatronNode ThisLeaf, LibraryPatron ThisPatron)
START
 Let NewNode be a PatronNode;
 Instantiate NewNode;
 NewNode.Info := ThisPatron;
 Set NewNode.Left and NewNode.Right to NULL;
 ThisLeaf.Right := NewNode; // No longer a leaf, but now a sub-tree
 Add 1 to Size;
STOP

addLeftSubtree(PatronNode ThisNode, PatronNode NewNode)
START
 Let Temp, LeftEnd be PatronNode references;
 Temp := ThisNode.Left;
 LeftEnd := NewNode;
  While (LeftEnd.Left <> NULL) LeftEnd := LeftEnd.Left; End-While;
 ThisNode.Left := NewNode;
 LeftEnd.Left := Temp;
 Increase Size by the size of the sub-tree;
 STOP

Figure A1-6. *Binary Tree Algorithms*

```
addRightSubtree(PatronNode ThisNode, PatronNode NewNode)
START
 Let Temp, RightEnd be PatronNode references;
 Temp := ThisNode.Right;
 RightEnd := NewNode;
 While (RightEnd.Right <> NULL) RightEnd := RightEnd.Right; End-While;
 ThisNode.Right := NewNode;
 RightEnd.Right := Temp;
 Increase Size by the size of the sub-tree;
STOP


removeSubtree(PatronNode ThisNode)
START
 If (ThisNode.Left = ThisNode.Right = NULL) // a leaf
        Kill(ThisNode); Subtract 1 from Size;
 End-If;
 Else
        If (ThisNode.Left <> NULL) removeSubtree(ThisNode.Left); End-If;
        If (ThisNode.Right <> NULL) removeSubtree(ThisNode.Right); End-If;
        Kill(ThisNode);
 End-Else;
STOP


Modify(PatronNode ThisNode, LibraryPatron ThisPatron)
START
 ThisNode.Info := ThisPatron;
STOP


clearTree()
START
 removeSubtree(Root);
STOP


getInfo(PatronNode ThisNode): Returns LibraryPatron
START
 Return ThisNode.Info;
STOP


getNode(PatronNode ThisNode): Returns PatronNode
START
 Return ThisNode;
STOP


getSize(): Returns integer
START
 Return Size;
STOP
```

Figure A1-6. *Binary Tree Algorithms (continued)*

```
isEmpty(): Returns Boolean
START
  Return whether Size is 0 or not;
STOP

setSize (PatronNode ThisNode, Size)
START
  // Assume that this method is first called with ThisNode pointing to Root
  Let Current, HoldLeft, and HoldRight be PatronNode instances;
  Current := ThisNode;
  If (Current <> NULL)
          Add 1 to Size;
          Holdeft := Current.Left;
          HoldRight := Current.Right;

          If (HoldLeft <> NULL)
                  Current := HoldLeft;
                  setSize(Current, Size);
          End-If;
          If (HoldRight <> NULL)
                  Current := HoldRight;
                  setSize(Current, Size);
          End-If;
    End-If;
STOP
```

Figure A1-6. *Binary Tree Algorithms (continued)*

A1.2.6 Binary Tree Traversals

There are three traversal algorithms for binary trees: Pre-order, In-order and Post-order.

Pre-order traversal (also called prefix walk or polish notation) obeys the algorithm shown in Figures A1-7a and A1-7b.

```
Visit the root;
Traverse the left sub-tree in Pre-order;
Traverse the right sub-tree in Pre-order;
```

Figure A1-7a. *Summary of the Pre-order Traversal Algorithm*

```
preOrderTraversal(PatronNode ThisNode)
START // Assume the UML diagram of figure A1.5
  // Assume that Traversal is a global array of Size LibraryPatron objects;
  If (ThisNode is not NULL)
    Append ThisNode.Info to Traversal;
    preOrderTraversal(ThisNode.Left);
    preOrderTraversal(ThisNode.Right);
  End-If;
STOP
```

Figure A1-7b. *Detailed Pre-order Traversal Algorithm*

Example 2: Figure A1-7c provides an example of the application of the pre-order algorithm.

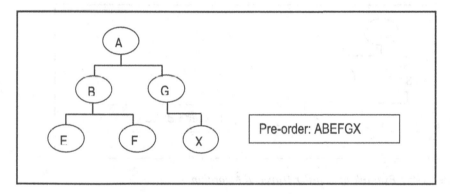

Figure A1-7c. *Example of Pre-order Traversal Algorithm*

In-order traversal (also called symmetric order or infix notation) obeys the algorithm shown in Figures A1-8a and A1-8b.

```
Traverse the left sub-tree in In-order;
Visit the root;
Traverse the right sub-tree in In-order;
```

Figure A1-8a. *Summarized In-order Traversal Algorithm*

```
inOrderTraversal(PatronNode ThisNode)
START // Assume the UML diagram of figure A1.5
 // Assume that Traversal is a global array of Size LibraryPatron objects;
 If (ThisNode is not NULL)
   inOrderTraversal(ThisNode.Left);
   Append ThisNode.Info to Traversal;
   inOrderTraversal(ThisNode.Right);
 End-If;
STOP
```

Figure A1-8b. *Detailed In-order Traversal Algorithm*

Example 3: Figure A1-8c provides an example of the application of the in-order algorithm.

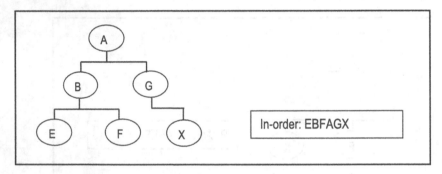

Figure A1-8c. *Example of In-order Traversal Algorithm*

Post-order traversal (also called suffix walk or reverse polish notation) obeys the algorithm shown in Figures A1-9a and A1-9b.

```
Traverse the left sub-tree in Post-order;
Traverse the right sub-tree in Post-order;
Visit the root;
```

Figure A1-9a. *Summarized Post-order Traversal Algorithm*

460

```
postOrderTraversal(PatronNode ThisNode)
START // Assume the UML diagram of figure A1.5
  // Assume that Traversal is a global array of Size LibraryPatron objects;
  If (ThisNode is not NULL)
    postOrderTraversal(ThisNode.Left);
    postOrderTraversal(ThisNode.Right);
    Append ThisNode.Info to Traversal;
  End-If;
STOP
```

Figure A1-9b. *Detailed Post-order Traversal Algorithm*

Example 4: Figure A1-9c provides an example of the application of the post-order algorithm.

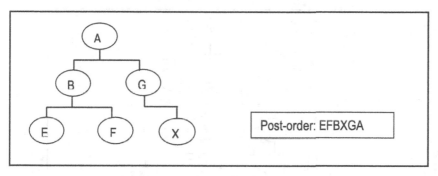

Figure A1-9c. *Example of Post-order Traversal Algorithm*

A1.2.7 Using Binary Tree to Evaluate Expressions

We can use binary trees to evaluate expressions by following a simple convention: All operands are leaves of the tree and the operators are parent nodes.

Example 5: The expression (a - b) * c is represented on a binary tree as shown in Figure A1-10a. To load an expression to tree, repeatedly select the operator that divides the expression into two, as the root. In the end leaves are operands and roots are operators.

461

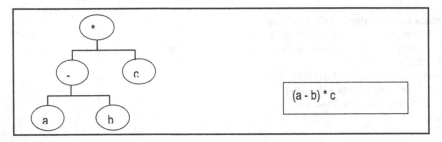

Figure A1-10a. *Using Binary Tree to Represent Arithmetic Expressions*

Example 6: The expression $[(((a+b)*c)/d) + e^f]/g$ is represented on a binary tree as shown in Figure A1-10b. Note that in the figure the symbol ↑ is used for exponent.

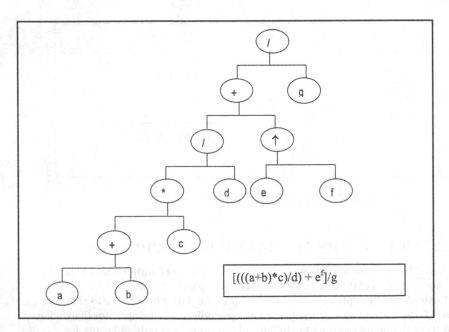

Figure A1-10b. *Using Binary Tree to Represent Arithmetic Expressions*

Observe: You should be able to convince yourself that a post-order traversal of a binary tree for arithmetic expressions of this sort, produces the expression in postfix notation. This is left as an exercise for you.

A1.3 Threaded Binary Trees

In order to facilitate easy traversal of a binary tree, the tree may be threaded with pointers that explicitly show a traversal ordering. The threads link the nodes in the sequence of the traversal method.

Types of Threads:

- Right thread links a node to its successor

- Left thread links a node to its predecessor

A tree can only be threaded according to one traversal method at a time.

Threaded for In-order Traversal

To illustrate, if a binary tree is threaded for In-order processing, the following conventions are observed:

- Left threads (except for leftmost leaf) point to predecessor nodes in in-order.

- Left thread from leftmost leaf points to the root.

- Right threads (except for rightmost leaf) point to successor nodes in in-order.

- Right thread of rightmost leaf is NULL.

A1.4 Binary Search Trees

A binary search tree (BST) is a binary tree in which the following properties hold:

a. All nodes in the left sub-tree of R_i precede (by way of ordering) R_i so that, If $R_j = R_i.Left$, then $R_j.Info < R_i.Info$

b. All nodes in the right sub-tree of R_i succeed (by way of ordering) R_i so that, If $R_j = R_i.Right$, then $R_j.Info >= Ri.Info$

Note: In-order traversal of a BST produces a sorted list (in ascending values). Moreover, it can be shown that this sort algorithm is an $O(N \log N)$ algorithm on the average.

A BST provides the following advantages:

- It facilitates an $O(N \log N)$ sort, which is more efficient sort than N^2 sort algorithms.

- It facilitates faster (binary) search than searching a linear linked list.

The disadvantages associated with a BST are as follows:

- It takes up more space than linear link list.

- It can degenerate into a linked list (see next section).

- As nodes are added, there is no control on the height (hence structure) of the tree. This is often undesirable.

Example 7: Suppose we wish to load the string HBXAM to a BST. We obtain a BST as follows:

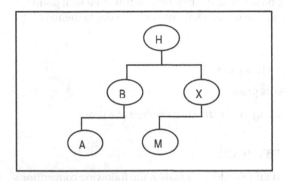

Figure A1-11. *Example of BST*

Assuming the conventions of Figure A1-5, the algorithms of Figure A1-6 would still be applicable but with two extensions: We need to introduce an algorithm for inserting a node in the tree while preserving its properties. Secondly, we need to be able to search for a particular value in the tree. Figures A1-12 and A1-13 provide the insertion algorithm, and the search algorithm respectively. Note that the order in which nodes are added to the BST affects the structure of the tree. In fact, if a sorted list is added to the BST, it degrades to a linear linked list.

```
Insert (PatronNode ThisNode, LibraryPatron ThisPatron)
START
  /* ThisNode represents the point in the BST where an assessment for insertion begins.
    ThisPatron represents the information to be inserted in the BST. Typically, this algorithm will be called
    with the argument for ThisNode being Root. However, it could called with any node as the starting point. */

Let NewNode and Current be instances of PatronNode;
If (ThisNode = NULL) // BST is empty
    Instantiate NewNode; NewNode.Info := ThisPatron;
    Set NewNode.Left and NewNode.Right to NULL;
    Root := NewNode;
End-If;
Else
    // Find the insertion point and insert the node there
    Current := FindInsertionPoint(ThisNode, ThisPatron);
    If (ThisPatron < Current.Info)  addLeftLeaf(Current, ThisPatron); End-If; // See figure A1.6
    Else addRightLeaf(Current, ThisPatron);   End-Else;
End-Else;
  // Add 1 to Size; // This is already done
STOP
```

Figure A1-12a. *Algorithm to Insert a Node in the BST*

```
FindInsertionPoint(PatronNode ThisNode, LibraryPatron ThisPatron): Returns PatronNode
START
  Let Point be a PatronNode;
  Point := ThisNode;
  If (ThisPatron < Point.Info)
    If (Point.Left <> NULL)
      Point := FindInsertionPoint(Point.Left, ThisPatron);
    End-If;
    Else // ThisPatron >= Point.Info
    If (Point.Right <> NULL)
      Point := FindInsertionPoint(Point.Right, ThisPatron);
    End-If;
  End-If;
  Return Point;
STOP
```

Figure A1-12b. *Algorithm to Find the Insertion Point in the BST*

```
Search(LibraryPatron SearchValue): Returns PatronNode
START
  Let Current and Sought be PatronNode instances;
  Current := Root; Sought := NULL;
  While (Current.Info <> SearchValue) AND (Current.Info <> NULL) do the following:
        If (SearchValue < Current.Info)
                Current := Current.Left;
        End-If;
        Else      Current := Current.Right; End-Else;
  End-While;
  If (Current.Info = SearchValue) Sought := Current; End-If;
  Return Sought;
STOP
```

Figure A1-13. *Algorithm to Search the BST*

Example 8: Adding the sorted list A B C D E F G to a BST results in the following:

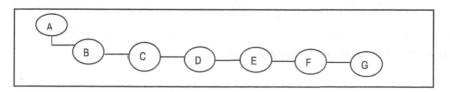

Figure A1-14. *Loading a Sorted List to a BST*

Searching for a node in this BST would be reduced to searching a linear linked list! Solving this problem is not trivial. It is generally referred to as balancing the tree. Several algorithms have been proposed for balancing a BST.

A1.5 Height-Balanced Trees

A height-balanced k-tree (denoted (HB (k)) is a BST in which the maximum allowable difference in height between any two sub-trees sharing a common root (not necessary a parent) is k. Put another way, the maximum possible difference in height between leaves of the tree is k.

An AVL tree (named after Adelson-Velskii and Landis, the Russian founders) is a HB (1) tree, that is, the maximum possible difference in height between any two sub-trees sharing a common root is 1. Put another way, leaves are either at level m or level m + 1. Figure A1-14 provides some illustrations. Heaps (discussed next) are also examples of HB trees.

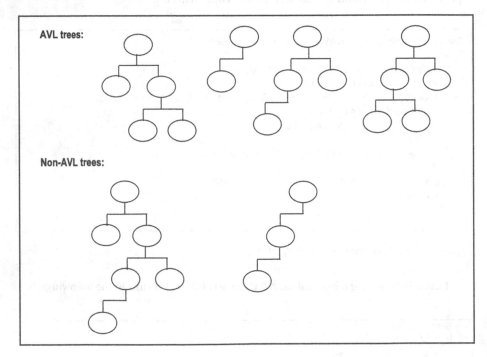

Figure A1-15. *Illustrating AVL and non-AVL Trees*

A1.6 Heaps

A heap is an almost complete binary tree, such that:

a. Every leaf of the tree is at level m or m + 1, where m is an integer (AVL requirement).

b. If a node has a right descendant at level l, it also has a left descendant at level l (converse, not necessarily true).

c. There is some established relationship between the parent-value and each child-value.

Figure A1-16 provides some illustrations. From the definition, observe that there are two types of heaps: *max-heaps* and *min-heaps*:

- **Max-heap:** Every node stores a value that is greater than or equal to the value of either of its children. The root therefore stores maximum value of all nodes in the tree.

- **Min-heap:** Every node stores a value that us less than or equal to the value of either of its children. The root therefore stores the minimum value of all nodes in the tree.

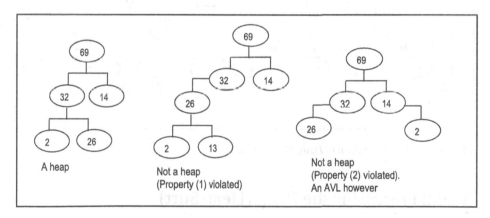

Figure A1-16. *Illustrations of Heap*

The heap-sort algorithm utilizes a max-heap. Heap-sort involves two phases:

- Creating (building) the heap
- Processing the heap

A1.6.1 Building the Heap

Figure A1-17 provides a summarized form of the algorithm to construct a heap.

---

1. Start at left and gradually build the heap;
2. For each node, introduce left sub-tree whenever possible before introducing a right sub-tree at each level;
3. If addition of a node results in any heap principle being violated, rotate node(s) until the anomaly is resolved;

Figure A1-17. *Heap Construction Algorithm*

Example 9: Figure A1-18 shows how a maximum heap is constructed with the following nodes:6 25 7 2 14 10 9 22 3 16.

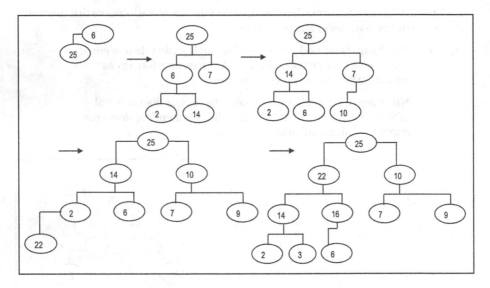

Figure A1-18. *Illustration of Heap Construction*

A1.6.2 Processing the Heap (Heap Sort)

The algorithm for processing the heap (also called heap-sort because it produces a sorted list) is shown in Figure A1-19. The algorithm shown assumes a max-heap; it progressively removes the root of the heap until it is empty. Heap-sort performs as well as quick-sort on the average and better than quick-sort at worst; it is an O(N Log N) algorithm.

---

1   Repeatedly remove the maximum value from the heap (that, is the root);
2   Place this at end of a growing list (growing backwards);
3   Re-arrange the tree so that the heap properties are maintained;
4   Continue until the heap is empty.

Figure A1-19. *Heap-sort Algorithm*

Example 10: Figure A1-20 illustrates how the heap of Example 9 would be processed to yield a sorted list.

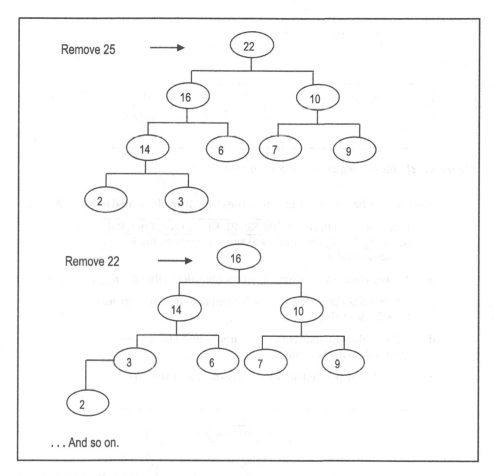

Figure A1-20. Illustrating Heap-sort

A1.7 M-Way Search Trees and B-Trees

An m-way search tree is a tree in which each node has out-degree ≤ m. The out-degree of a node is the number of sub-trees that it has. Figure A1-21 illustrates an m-way search tree in which the root has out-degree 2, the left node has out-degree 3 and the right node has out-degree 3. The leaves (always) have out-degree 0. Figure A1-22 illustrates a 3–way search tree.

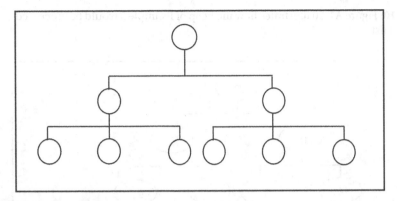

Figure A1-21. *Illustrating an m-way Search Tree*

The M-Way tree has the following properties (which are illustrated in Figure A1-22):

a. Each node is of the form [P0, K0, P1, K1, . . . Pn-1, Kn-1, Pn] where P_o, P_1 ... P_n are pointers to successor nodes and K_o, K_1 ... K_{n-1} are key values.

b. The key values in a node are in ascending order so that $K_i \leq K_{i+1}$.

c. All key values in nodes of the sub-tree pointed to by P_i are less than the key value K_i.

d. All key values in nodes of the sub-tree pointed to by P_i are greater than the key value k_{i-1}.

e. The sub-tree pointed to by P_i are also m-way search trees.

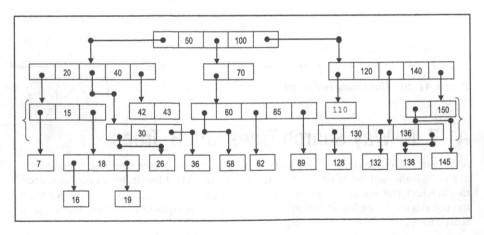

Figure A1-22. *A Three-way Search Tree*

470

A1.7.1 Definition of B-tree

A B-tree of order m is an m-way search tree with the following properties:

a.   Except for the root and leaves, each node of the tree has at least [m/2] sub-trees and no more than m sub-trees so that [m/2] ≤ number of sub-trees ≤ m. Note: [x] ≡ the smallest integer greater than x (e.g. [1.5] = 2).

b.   The root of the tree has at least two sub-trees, unless it is itself a leaf.

c.   All leaves of the tree are at the same level.

Figure A1-23 illustrates a B-tree of order 3, constructed from the 3-way search tree of Figure A1-22.

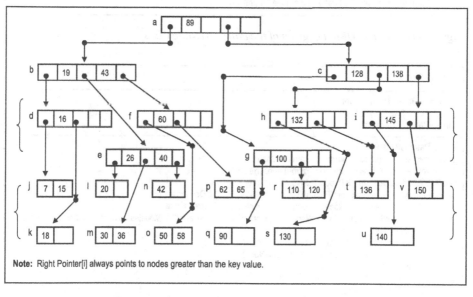

Note: Right Pointer[i] always points to nodes greater than the key value.

Figure A1-23. *B-tree of order 3 (Corresponding to 3-way Search Tree)*

A1.7.2 Implementation of the B-tree

The main operations we desire for the B-tree include:

- Creation
- Direct Search
- Sequential Search
- Insertion
- Deletion

471

A possible implementation of a B-tree of **LibraryPatron** objects is shown in Figure A1-24. As you may well imagine, maintaining such a tree is much more challenging than a BST or heap, but by no means insurmountable. We will look more closely at some of these algorithms shortly.

PatronBTNode
protected LibraryPatron [] Info protected PatronBTNode [] Pointer

PatronBTNode()
void Modify(PatronBTNode ThisNode) /* Modifies the current node based on ThisNode */
void Modify(int hostItem, LibraryPatron ThisPatron) /* Modifies an item in the node based on ThisPatron */
void InputData(int x)
String PrintMe(int Item) // Prepares an item in the node for printing
String PrintMe() // Prepares all items in the node for printing

Figure A1-24a. *The UML Diagram of the PatronBTNode Class*

PatronsBTree
protected PatronBTNode Root protected int Size, TravRef LibraryPatron[] Traversal

public PatronsBTree()
public void addRoot(LibraryPatron ThisPatron) // Inserts an item at the root
public void addItem(LibraryPatron ThisPatron) // Inserts an item
public void addNode(PatronBTNode ThisNode) // Inserts a node
public LibraryPatron removeItem(PatronBTNode ThisNode, int x) // Deletes an item
public PatronBTNode removeNode(PatronBTNode ThisNode) // Deletes a node
public void Modify(PatronBTNode ThisNode, int x, LibraryPatron ThisPatron) /* Modifies an item based on **ThisPatron** */
public void clearTree()
public LibraryPatron getInfo(PatronBTNode ThisNode, int x)
public PatronBTNode getNode(PatronBTNode ThisNode)
public int getSize()
public boolean isEmpty()
public void inOrderTraversal()
public PatronBTNode diretSearch(LibraryPatron SearchValue)

Figure A1-24b. *The UML Diagram of the PatronsBTree Class*

Sequential search of the B-tree is achieved by an In-order traversal. Several values may be sought simultaneously. Note however, that internal nodes will be visited more than once since they contain several keys. Performance is therefore poor.

The direct search algorithm is shown in Figure A1-25. It is used to find a specific node in the tree. It is a very efficient algorithm. On the average, searching for an item among 1,000,000 items takes just about 20 comparisons! B-trees are also excellent for storing large volumes of data without deteriorating. For these reasons, B-trees are widely used as the file systems for compilers, database management systems, and operating systems.

```
diretSearch(LibraryPatron SearchValue): Returns PatronBTNode
START // Assume that the maximum number of items per node is N
  Current := Root;
  i :=    0;
  While (SearchValue <> Current.Info[i]) do the following:
         If (SearchValue < Current.Info[i]) OR (i = N)
                  Current := Current.Pointer[i];  i := 0;
         End-If;
         Else  If ((i + 1) <= N)  i :=  i + 1; End-If; End-Else;
  End-While;

  // Current now points to the correct node
  Return Current;
STOP
```

Figure A1-25. *Direct Search Algorithm*

Figure A1-26 provides the summarized form of the B-tree insertion algorithm. This algorithm is easier described than implemented. Fortunately, you do not need to implement it in a typical data structures course. However, you do need to be able to demonstrate an understanding of the algorithm, so let us take an example:

1. Search for and locate appropriate insertion node;
2. If the node is not full, insert the data item;
3. If the node is full, node splitting occurs as follows:
   - Introduce a new node;
   - Place half of the keys in the new node, and half of the keys in the original node;
   - Move the remaining value up to the parent node;

Note In the worst case, node splitting continues up to the root and the tree height increases by one.

Figure A1-26. *Summary of B-tree Insertion Algorithm*

Example 11: Referring to the B-tree of Figure A1-23, consider inserting the following items: 22, 41, 59, 57, 54. Figure A1-27 illustrates how these items would be added.

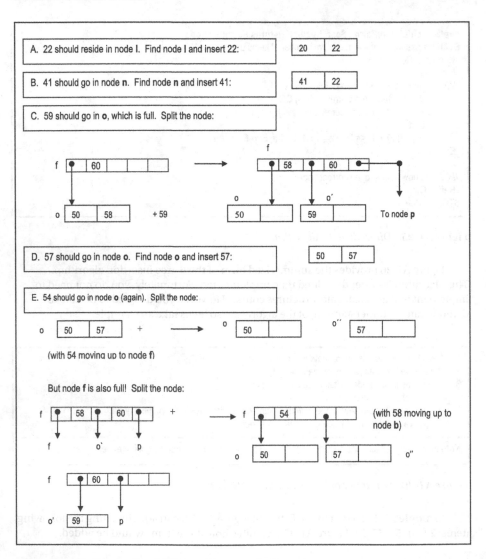

Figure A1-27. *Illustrating Addition of Items to the B-tree*

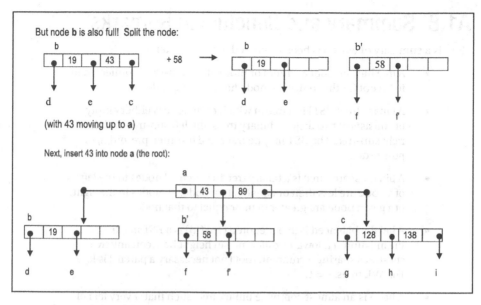

Figure A1-27. *llustrating Addition of Items to the B-tree (continued)*

The summarized item deletion algorithm is shown in Figure A1-28. Note that as in the case of insertion, deletion may lead to significant adjustment of the tree.

1. Search for and locate the appropriate node;
2. Remove the item;
3. If resultant node is now empty, adjust the tree, by moving up a key value from one of its sub-tree giving preference to the leftmost sub-tree. The worst-case scenario is that the tree looses a leaf.

Figure A1-28. *B-tree Item Deletion Algorithm*

Example 12: Referring to the B-tree of Figure A1-23, consider deleting the following items: | 65   7   16 |

   a.   65 is in node **p**, remove it: p | 62 | | | | |

   b.   7 is in node **j**, remove it: j | 15 | | | | |

   c.   16 is in node **d**, remove it. Move up 15 from node **j** and place a dummy (null) value at node **j**.

A1.8 Summary and Concluding Remarks

Here is a summary of what has been discussed in this chapter:

- A tree has one root and zero or more other sub-trees connected to it. Except for the root, each node has a parent node.

- A binary tree (BST) is a tree in which each node is either empty or consists of two disjoint binary trees: the left sub-tree and the right sub-tree. The BST may be traversed in-order, pre-order, or post-order.

- A binary search tree is a binary tree in which all nodes to the left of a node are less then or equal to that node; all nodes to the right of a given node are greater than or equal to that node.

- A height-balanced k-tree (denoted (HB (k)) is a BST in which the maximum allowable difference in height between any two sub-trees sharing a common root (not necessary a parent) is k. For AVL trees, k = 1.

- A heap is an almost complete binary tree, such that: Every leaf of the tree is at level m or m + 1, where m is an integer; if a node has a right descendant at level l, it also has a left descendant at level l; there is some established relationship between the parent-value and its two children-values.

- An m-way search tree is a tree of out-degree less than or equal to m, i.e. a maximum of m pointers point from a node. The tree has the following properties: Each node has a maximum of m pointers and m-1 key values; in any node, the key values are in ascending order; the pointer to the left of key value k[i] points to a node with values less than or equal to k[i]; the pointer to the right of key value k[i] points to a node with values greater than or equal to k[i].

- A B-tree is a special type of m-way search tree with the following properties: Except for the root and leaves, each node of the tree has at least m/2 sub-trees and no more than m sub-trees; the root of the tree has at least two sub-trees, unless it is itself a leaf; all leaves of the tree are at the same level.

Trees (and particularly BSTs, heaps, and B-trees) are widely used in software engineering to solve various programming problems related to the organization and retrieval of data.

A1.9 References and/or Recommended Readings

[Carrano, 2006] Carrano, Frank and Janet Prichard. *Data Abstraction & Problem Solving with Java*. Boston, MA: Addison-Wesley, 2006. See Chapter 11.

[Carrano, 2007] Carrano, Frank. *Data Structures & Abstraction with Java* 2nd ed. Upper Saddle River, NJ: Prentice Hall, 2007. See Chapter 25 – 29.

[Drake, 2006] Drake, Peter. *Data Structures and Algorithms in Java*. Upper Saddle River, NJ: Prentice Hall, 2006. See Chapter 10.

[Folk, 1998] Folk, Michael, Bill Zoellick & Greg Riccardi. File Structures: An Object-Oriented Approach with C++, 3rd ed. Reading, Massachusetts: Addison-Wesley, 1998. See Chapters 8 and 9.

[Ford, 2005] Ford, William H. and William R, Topp. *Data Structures with Java*. Upper Saddle River, NJ: Prentice Hall, 2005. See Chapters 16 – 18, 22.

[Knuth, 1973] Knuth, D. The Art of Computer Programming volume 3, "Searching and Sorting". Reading, Massachusetts: Addison-Wesley, 1973.

[Kruse, 1999] Kruse, Robert and Alex Ryba. Data Structures and Program Design in C++ 1st ed. Upper Saddle River, New Jersey: Prentice Hall, 1999.

[Langsam, 2003] Langsam, Yedidya, Moshe Augenstein, and Aaron M. Tanenbaum. *Data Structures Using Java*. Upper Saddle River, NJ: Prentice Hall, 2003. See Chapter 5.

[Main, 2006] Main, Michael. *Data Abstraction & Other Objects Using Java*. Boston, MA: Addison-Wesley, 2006. See Chapters 9 and 10.

[Standish, 1980] Standish, T. A. Data Structure Techniques. Reading, Massachusetts: Addison-Wesley, 1980.

[Venugopal, 2007] Venugopal, Sesh. *Data Structures Outside In with Java*. Upper Saddle River, NJ: Prentice Hall, 2007. See Chapters 9 – 11.

[Weis, 2007] Weiss, Marl Allen. *Data Structures and Algorithm Analysis in Java* 2nd ed. Boston, MA: Addison-Wesley, 2007. See Chapter 4 and 7.

APPENDIX 2

■ ■ ■

Review of Hashing

Hashing is a technique for mapping data from a large set to limited space in a much smaller set. This appendix provides an overview of the subject. The appendix covers the fundamentals of hashing under the following captions:

- Introduction

- Hash Functions

- Collision Resolution

- Hashing in Java

- Summary and Concluding Remarks

A2.1 Introduction

In computer science, it is always important to establish mapping functions between (what is called) the conceptual user view of data and actual physical storage reality in the computer system. The former is what the end-user sees; the latter is what is actually stored on the storage media. For reasons that will become clear in your courses in software engineering, database systems, and operating systems, the two perspectives are seldom identical.

Another equally important issue is how to find data that is stored. For example, consider a transaction file for a financial institution, with millions of records. As you can well imagine (based on earlier discussions), sequential access of records in this file, would be suitable for a non-interactive program running in batch mode. However, it would not be suitable for a program that needs to provide interactive responses to the end used, based on different customers. You certainly would not want to process this file relying solely on an array, linked list, queue, or stack. You could use a BST, a heap, or better yet, a B-tree! But how would you determine where on the storage media to actually store records of your file so they can be easily retrieved when needed? Hashing is one technique for addressing this problem.

Hashing is a technique that addresses the problems of where (on a physical storage medium) to store data and how to retrieve the data stored. In hashing, there is a predictable relationship between a key value used to identify a record, and the record's location on a storage medium.

A hash function takes a key value, applies an algorithm to determine its location. Mathematically, we represent this as follows (Figure A2-1):

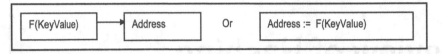

Figure A2-1. *Basic Concept of Hashing*

The hash function maps key values from a relatively large domain to a relatively smaller range of address locations. Because of this, collision may occur and must be resolved. Collision occurs when two or more keys map to the same address, as illustrated in Figure A2-2.

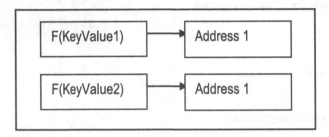

Figure A2-2. *Illustrating Collision*

Since two records cannot be stored in the same location, the collision must be resolved. Various collision resolution techniques have been proposed. These will be discussed shortly.

A2.2 Hash Functions

A good hash function should exhibit two important features: Firstly, it should be easy and fast to compute. Secondly, it must attempt to scatter the key values (random or non-random) evenly over the address space. Various hash functions have been proposed and tested with varying results. Among the commonly discussed hash functions are the following: absolute addressing, direct table lookup, division-remainder, mid-square, folding, and truncation. We will briefly discuss each technique.

A2.2.1 Absolute Addressing

In absolute addressing, the address is the key value. Thus,

```
Address := KeyValue Mod Divisor
```

This is a simplistic approach to hashing; it will only work for trivial cases. In most practical cases, this approach will be inadequate, since storage will be limited.

A2.2.2 Direct Table Lookup

In direct table lookup, the following steps are taken:

- The addresses are initially generated via some method. The method used to generate these addresses could be any of the techniques discussed in this section, or some other technique.

- The keys and addresses are stored as a separate index (directory).

- To access a record, the index is first consulted to determine its address.

Figure A2-3 provides an example of an index lookup table for an employee file. The assumptions here are as follows:

- The file is keyed on the employee's identification number.

- Each employee record occupies 128 bytes of space.

- A means of determining the address for each record is in place.

- The notation TnSn is used to denote the track number and sector number on a hard drive (for instance T1S1 means track 1, sector 1).

- Each sector can store up to 4096 bytes of data.

Key Value (ID_Number)	Address on Storage Medium
2001000	T1S1-0000
2001010	T1S1-0128
2001020	T1S1-0256
2001030	T1S1-0384
2001040	T1S1-0512
2001050	T1S1-0640
2001060	T1S1-0768
2001070	T1S1-0896
2001080	T1S1-1024
...	...

Figure A2-3. *Example of Table Lookup for Employee Records*

The technique is applied as follows:

- When a record is first written, its address is determined and logged into the index (lookup) table.

- When a record is to be retrieved, the index is consulted for its exact location.

The technique has three significant advantages: Table lookup is a very efficient way of storing small to medium sized files. Additionally, the technique is simple and easy to implement. Finally, the technique avoids the problem of collision (by presumably addressing it up front). For these reasons, the technique is widely used in database management system (DBMS) suites and operating systems.

The approach has two problems: Firstly, storing a data file requires management of two separate physical files on the storage medium. Secondly, as the size of the data file grows, so does the size of the index (table lookup) file.

A2.2.3 Division-Remainder

The division-remainder technique prescribes that you divide the key value by an appropriate number, then use the remainder of the division as the address for the record. In computer science, we refer to the operation that yields the remainder of an integer division as the modulus (commonly abbreviated as mod). Thus,

```
Address := KeyValue Mod Divisor
```

Note:

- If the divisor is N, then address space must be of minimum size N (that is 0 to N-1).

- To minimize the number of collisions, the divisor is typically a large number that does not contain any prime factors less than 20. For example, 997 or 1011 is preferred to 1024.

The technique is applied as follows: When a record is to be stored or retrieved, its address is first determined via the hash function.

The technique has three significant advantages:

- It is simple and easy to implement.

- It is very efficient for small files.

- It avoids using two physical files for a single data file.

The technique has three significant disadvantages that discourage widespread use as a primary hash function:

- It offers no guarantee against collision (though it can be minimized by carefully choosing the divisor).

- It does not perform very well in attempting to distribute keys evenly across the address space.

- As the size of the data set increases, so does the likelihood of collision.

A2.2.4 Mid-Square

In the mid-square technique, the key value is squared, and then a specific number of digits is extracted from the "middle" of the result to yield the hash address. If an address space of N digits is desired, then digits are truncated at both ends of the squared key value, leaving N digits from the middle.

As an example, suppose that we need a 4-digit address, and we have a key value of 7895. The address could be determined as follows:

```
Address := Mid-square(7895) = 62331025 = 3310
```

Like the division-remainder technique, when a record is to be stored or retrieved, its address is first determined via the hash function.

The technique is a slight improvement over the division-remainder technique, providing the following advantages:

- It is simple and easy to implement.

- It is very efficient for small files as well as large files.

- It performs reasonably well in attempting to distribute the keys evenly over the address space.

- It avoids using two physical files for a single data file.

The technique has one significant disadvantage: It offers no guarantee against collision (but the performance is better than the division-remainder technique).

A2.2.5 Folding

The folding technique involves partitioning the key into several parts and combining the parts in a convenient way (via multiplication, addition or subtraction) to obtain a hash address.

To illustrate this technique, suppose that the folding method is addition and the address space is for four digits. Then, we may derive a hash address from the key value of 625149 via one of the following means:

Address := 625 + 149 = 0774	Or	Address := 6251 + 49 = 6300

The advantages and disadvantages of folding are similar to those of the mid-square technique. Figure A2-4 shows a comparison of how both techniques forms on data set of key-values. For this particular data set, folding appears to distribute the key-values more gracefully over the address space. On the other hand, the mid-square technique appears to distribute the key-values more randomly over the address space. Of course, this simple experiment is not enough for us to make conclusion as to how the techniques will perform on other data sets.

Key-Values:	2001010	2001020	2001030	2001040	2001050	2001060	2001070	2001080
Folding Address:	2011	2021	2031	2041	2051	2061	2071	2081
Mid-square Address:	4102	8104	2106	6108	0110	4112	8114	2116

Figure A2-4. *Comparing Folding with Mid-square on a Data Set*

A2.2.6 Truncation

In the truncation technique, part of the key is ignored, and the other part is used as the hash address. To illustrate this technique, suppose that the address space is for four digits. Then, we may derive a hash address from the key value of 625149 via one of the following means:

Address := 625149 = 6251	Or	Address := 625149 = 5149

Truncation, like absolute addressing is too simplistic for practical purposes. It could result in repeated collisions, and it does not come close to distributing the keys evenly over the address space.

A2.2.7 Treating Alphanumeric Key Values

In many cases, key values will be alphanumeric instead of numeric. For these situations, you will need to convert the alphanumeric data to numeric form. There are several ways to do this, so there is no need to panic. Figure A2-5 provides a summary of two commonly used techniques that have been proposed. Of course, you can come up with your own.

---

1. **Simple Character Sequencing**
   - Assign a unique number for each possible character that can be used as part of a key-value (a good place to start is characters on the keyboard). For example, A-Z could be assigned 1-26; a-z could be assigned 27-52; digits could remain 0-9; and so on.
   - For each alphanumeric key-value, convert each character to an integer, using the above-mentioned convention, and then add the individual numeric pieces to obtain a final numeric value for that key-value.
   - **Observe:** This approach would not guarantee that each key-value has a unique numeric value. For example, "care" and "race" would have the same numeric value.

2. **Use the ASCII/Unicode Character Sequencing**
   - Instead of developing your own sequencing, use the numeric value of each ASCII/Unicode character in the key-value. In Java, this can be easily achieved by invoking any of the following two static methods of the **Character** class (method signatures given):
     static int digit(char ch, int radix) /* Returns the numeric value of character **ch** in the specified radix. */
     static int getNumericValue(char ch) /* Returns the numeric value of the specified Unicode character. */
   - For each alphanumeric key-value, convert each character to an integer, and then add the individual numeric pieces to obtain a final numeric value for that key-value.
   - **Observe:** Again, this approach would not guarantee that each key-value has a unique numeric value.

Figure A2-5. *Converting Alphanumeric Keys to Numeric*

A2.3 Collision Resolution

As mentioned earlier, when hash functions are applied, collisions are likely to occur. Three collision resolution techniques are prevalent: *linear probing, synonym chaining,* and *rehashing.*

A2.3.1 Linear Probing

The linear probing strategy prescribes that whenever a collision occurs, the empty location that is closest to the hash address is found and used. If the end of the table is reached, wrap-around is allowed. Figure A2-6 illustrates this. In the figure, collision has been resolved for nodes D, E, and G.

Key Value	Hash Address	Storage Address
A	1	1
B	2	2
C	3	3
D	2	4
E	4	5
F	6	6
G	4	7

Figure A2-6. *Illustrating Linear Probing*

The *load factor* **f** is defined as the number of records (to be) stored in the table to the actual size of the table. Thus,

f = n/s where **n** is the number of records (to be) stored and s is the size of the table.

As items are added to the table, blocks of occupied cells start forming. This is referred to as *primary clustering*. The result is increased likelihood of collision and lengthened probes for subsequent items to be inserted. As the table fills up these searches become longer.

For insertions and unsuccessful searches, the expected number of probes is $\frac{1}{2}[1 + 1/(1 - f)^2]$. For successful searches, the expected number of probes is $\frac{1}{2}[1 + 1/(1 - f)]$. The derivation of these formulae is beyond the scope of this course.

Linear probing has the following advantages:

- The technique is conceptually simple and easy to implement.

- The amount of calculation done at each stage is very small.

Disadvantages of linear probing include the following:

- Primary clustering — the hash-table fills up in clusters, rather than in even distribution over the address space.

- Primary clustering leads to longer search and increased likelihood of collision, particularly as the file becomes full.

Linear probing sometimes described as an *open addressing* strategy. Another commonly discussed open addressing strategy is *quadratic probing*. Since its performance is not much different from linear probing, it will not be discussed any further. *Rehashing* is another open addressing strategy; it will be discussed shortly.

A2.3.2 Synonym Chaining

The synonym chaining technique uses the hash address, not as the actual storage location for the record, but as the index into a list (implemented as a linked list or array-list). This way, we can facilitate multiple records with the same hash address! Figure A2-7 provides a graphic representation of this approach.

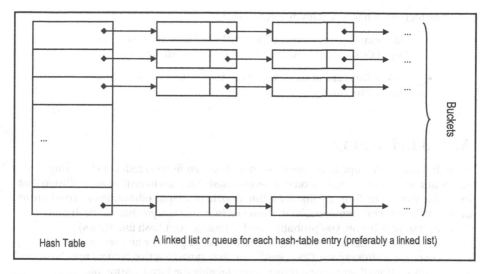

Hash Table   A linked list or queue for each hash-table entry (preferably a linked list)

Figure A2-7. *Graphic Representation of Synonym Chaining*

Programmatically, the hash table may be implemented via any of the following strategies (you are encouraged to try implementing this on your own):

- An array of linked lists or queues

- An array-list of linked lists or queues

- An array-list of array-lists

Observe:

- The table size **s** is the number of linked lists (chains), not the number of nodes.

- The average length of each chain is n/s where **n** is the number of records (nodes).

- The load factor **s** is therefore the average length of each chain.

- An unsuccessful search will involve the examination of **f** items; a successful search will require an average of 1 + f/2 examinations. So as expected, the performance is significantly better than linear probing.

Synonym chaining has the following advantages:

- The technique reduces access time for records with collision addresses.

- It is relatively easy to insert nodes in a given chain.

- There is even distribution of keys (nodes) over address space.

487

The technique has two main disadvantages:

- Additional space is required for the linked lists. However, since linked lists are dynamic structures, this is not significant.

- Linked lists cannot be accessed randomly; they are sequential access structures.

A2.3.3 Rehashing

Rehashing is another open addressing strategy that significantly reduces clustering. The technique involves the application of a second hash function to resolve any collision that might have occurred from the first hash function. In principle, rehashing can continue to other levels until collision is resolved. However, in practice, if you have to hash more than twice to resolve collision, you probably need to change your hash function(s).

The main advantage of rehashing is that it tends to produce an even spread of key values over the address space. One significant disadvantage is that records may be moved some distance from their home address, thus violating the locality principle.

A2.4 Hashing in Java

You can develop and implement hash functions in just about any programming language. However, as usual, Java provides you with some nice features that facilitate this. In particular, there are three Java classes that you should be familiar with — the **Hashtable,** **HashMap,** and the **TreeMap** classes. These classes reside in the **java.util** package.

The **Hashtable** class implements a hash-table that maps keys to values. A key can be any valid object. Each instance of **Hashtable** class has two properties that affect its performance: the *initial capacity* and *load factor*. The *capacity* is the number of *buckets* in the hash table, and the *initial capacity* is simply the capacity at the time the hash table is created. A bucket is simply a holding area for key values that have the same address (similar to a chain); the bucket is searched sequentially. The *load factor* is a measure of how full the hash table is allowed to get before its capacity is automatically increased. The conventional wisdom is 0.75. Figure A2-8 provides the UML diagrams for the class.

Hashtable <K, V> /* Implements a hash-table which maps keys to values as specified in the **Map** interface. Note: If K and V are not specified at instantiation, they revert to Object. */
int capacity, loadFactor

// Constructors
public Hashtable() /* Constructs an empty **Hashtable** instance with a default initial capacity of 11 and load factor of 0.75. */
public Hashtable(int initCap) /* Constructs an empty **Hashtable** instance with initial capacity of **initCap** and load factor of 0.75. */
public Hashtable(int initCap, float loadFactor) /* Constructs an empty **Hashtable** instance with initial capacity of **initCap** and load factor of **loadFactor**. */
 	
// Other methods of interest
public void clear() // Clears the hash-table
public boolean contains(Object value) /* Checks whether the specified value is contained in the hash-table. */
public boolean containsValue(Object value) // As for **contains**().
public boolean containsKey(Object key) /* Checks whether the specified key is contained in the hash-table. */
public boolean equals(Object obj) /* Checks whether the current hash-table (map) is equal to the specified object. */
public V get(Object key) // Returns the value that the specified key maps to, or null.
public int hashCode() // Returns the hash-code value of this hash-table (map).
public boolean isEmpty() // Checks of the hash-table is empty.
public V put(K key, V value) // Inserts a new key-value mapping into the hash-table
protected void rehash() /* Increases the capacity and internally reorganizes the hash-table. */
public V remove(Object key) /* Removes the specified key and corresponding value from the hash-table. */
protected int size() // returns the size (number of keys) of the hash-table.
protected String toString() // Returns a string representation of the hash-table.

Figure A2-8. *UML Diagram for the Hastable Class*

The **HashMap** class is roughly equivalent to **Hashtable**, except that it is unsynchronized and permits nulls. Additionally, there is no guarantee that the order of the hash-table will remain constant over time.

The **TreeMap** class implements a non-synchronized map (similar to a hash-table), in which keys are sorted. Figure A2-9 provides the UML diagrams for the class.

TreeMap <K, V> /* Implements a map which maps keys to values as specified in the **Map** interface. Note: If K and V are not specified at instantiation, they revert to Object. */

// Constructor
public TreeMap() /* Constructs an empty **TreeMap** instance, using the natural ordering of its keys. */

// Other methods of interest
public K ceilingKey(K thisKey) // Returns the least key that is >= **thisKey**, or null.
public void clear() // Clears the map.
public boolean containsKey(Object value) /* Checks whether the specified value is contained in the map. */
public boolean containsKey(Object key) /* Checks whether the specified key is contained in the map. */
public boolean equals(Object obj) /* Checks whether the current map is equal to the specified object. */
public K firstKey() // Returns the first (i.e. lowest) key-value in the map.
public K floorKey(K thisKey) // Returns the greatest key that is <= **thisKey**, or null.
public V get(Object key) // Returns the value that the specified key maps to, or null.
public int hashCode() // Returns the hash-code value of this hash-table (map).
public K higherKey(K thisKey) // Returns the least key that is > **thisKey**, or null.
public V put(K key, V value) // Inserts a new key-value mapping into the map.
protected void rehash() // Increases the capacity and internally reorganizes the map.
public boolean isEmpty() // Checks of the hash-table is empty.
public K lastKey() // Returns the last (i.e. greatest) key-value in the map.
public K lowerKey(K thisKey) // Returns the greatest key that is < **thisKey**, or null.

public V remove(Object key) /* Removes the specified key and corresponding value from the map. */
protected int size() // returns the size (number of keys) of the hash-table.
protected String toString() // Returns a string representation of the map.

Figure A2-9. *UML Diagram for the TreeMap Class*

A2.5 Summary and Concluding Remarks

Let us summarize what we have covered in this chapter:

- A hash function takes a key value, applies an algorithm to determine its location.

- The hash function maps key values from a relatively large domain to a relatively smaller range of address locations. Because of this, collision may occur and must be resolved.

- Among the commonly used hashing techniques are absolute addressing, direct table lookup, division-remainder, mid-square, folding, and truncation.

- Three commonly used collision resolution strategies are linear probing, synonym chaining, and rehashing.

- In linear probing, consecutive address locations are checked until a free location is found for insertion, or the sought item is found.

- In synonym chaining, each hash address is a reference to a linked list of items that have that hash address.

- In rehashing, successive hash functions are applied until the collision is resolved.

- Java facilitates management of hash tables via the **Hashtable, HashMap,** and **TreeMap** classes.

Hashing is widely used in the implementation of filing systems for compilers, operating systems and database management systems.

A2.6 References and/or Recommended Readings

[Carrano, 2006] Carrano, Frank and Janet Prichard. *Data Abstraction & Problem Solving with Java*. Boston, MA: Addison-Wesley, 2006. See Chapter 13.

[Carrano, 2007] Carrano, Frank. *Data Structures & Abstraction with Java* 2nd ed. Upper Saddle River, NJ: Prentice Hall, 2007. See Chapter 19 and 20.

[Drake, 2006] Drake, Peter. *Data Structures and Algorithms in Java*. Upper Saddle River, NJ: Prentice Hall, 2006. See Chapter 11.

[Ford, 2005] Ford, William H. and William R, Topp. *Data Structures with Java*. Upper Saddle River, NJ: Prentice Hall, 2005. See Chapter 19 and 21.

[Kruse, 1994] Kruse, Robert. *Data Structures and Program Design* 3rd ed. Eaglewood Cliffs, New Jersey: Prentice Hall, 1994. See Chapter 9.

[Langsam, 2003] Langsam, Yedidya, Moshe Augenstein, and Aaron M. Tanenbaum. *Data Structures Using Java*. Upper Saddle River, NJ: Prentice Hall, 2003. See Chapter 4.

[Lewis, 1982] Lewis, T.G. and M.Z. Smith. *Applying Data Structures* 2nd ed. Hopell, New Jersey: Houghton Miflin, 1982. See Chapter 8.

[Shaffer, 1997] Shaffer, Clifford A. *A Practical Introduction to Data Structures and Algorithm Analysis*. Upper Saddle River, New Jersey: Prentice Hall, 1997. See Chapter 10.

[Venugopal, 2007] Venugopal, Sesh. *Data Structures Outside In with Java*. Upper Saddle River, NJ: Prentice Hall, 2007. See Chapter 12.

[Weis, 2007] Weiss, Marl Allen. *Data Structures and Algorithm Analysis in Java* 2nd ed. Boston, MA: Addison-Wesley, 2007. See Chapter 5.

APPENDIX 3

■ ■ ■

Review of Information Gathering Techniques

This appendix provides a brief review of information gathering techniques. You would normally learn these techniques in a course in software engineering or systems analysis. Mastery of the techniques discussed will enable you to readily identify information entities, as you model and design a database system. Note, this appendix is not meant to replace a full course (and text) in software engineering or systems analysis. It should therefore be regarded as an overview, not a final authority on the subject matter.

In order to accurately and comprehensively specify the system, the software engineer gathers and analyzes information via various methodologies. This Chapter discusses these methodologies as outlined below:

- Rationale for Information Gathering
- Interviews
- Questionnaires and Surveys
- Sampling and Experimenting
- Observation and Document Review
- Prototyping
- Brainstorming and Mathematical Proof
- Object Identification
- Summary and Concluding Remarks

A3.1 Rationale for Information Gathering

What kind of information is the software engineer looking for? The answer is simple, but profound: You are looking for information that will help to accurately and comprehensively define the requirements of the software to be constructed. The process is referred to as *requirements analysis,* and involves a range of activities that eventually lead to the deliverable we call the *requirements specification* (RS). In particular, the software engineer must determine the following:

- **Synergistic interrelationships** of the system components: This relates to the components and how they (should) fit together.

- **System information entities** (*object types*) and their interrelatedness: An entity refers to an object or concept about data is to be stored and managed.

- **System operations** and their interrelatedness: Operations are programmed instructions that enable the requirements of the system to be met. Some operations are system-based and may be oblivious to the end user; others facilitate user interaction with the software; others are internal and often operate in a manner that is transparent to the end user.

- **System business rules:** Business rules are guidelines that specify how the system should operate. These relate to data access, data flow, relationships among entities, and the behavior of system operations.

- **System security mechanism(s)** that must be in place: It will be necessary to allow authorized users to access the system while denying access to unauthorized users. Additionally, the privileges of authorized users may be further constrained to ensure that they have access only to resources that they need. These measures protect the integrity and reliability of the system.

As the software engineer embarks on the path towards preparation of the requirements specification, these objectives must be constantly borne in mind. In the early stages of the research, the following questions should yield useful pointers:

- WHAT are the (major) categories of information handled? Further probing will be necessary, but you should continue your pursuit until this question is satisfactorily answered.

- WHERE does this information come from? Does it come from an internal department or from an external organization?

- WHERE does this information go after leaving this office? Does it go to an internal department or to an external organization?

- HOW and in WHAT way is this information used? Obtaining answers to these questions will help you to identify business rules and operations.

- WHAT are the main activities of this unit? A unit may be a division or department or section of the organization. Obtaining the answer to this question will also help you to gain further insights into the operations.

- WHAT information is needed to carry out this activity? Again here, you are trying to refine the requirements of each operation by identifying its input(s).

- WHAT does this activity involve? Obtaining the answer to this question will help you to further refine the operation in question.

- WHEN is it normally done? Obtaining the answer to this question will help you to further refine the operation in question by determining whether there is a time constraint on an operation.

- WHY is this important? WHY is this done? WHY...? Obtaining answers to these probes will help you to gain a better understanding of the requirements of the software system.

Of course, your approach to obtaining answers to these probing questions will be influenced by whether the software system being researched is to be used for in-house purposes, or marketed to the public. The next few sections will examine the commonly used information gathering strategies.

A3.2 Interviewing

Interviewing is the most frequent method of information gathering. It can be very effective if carefully planned and well conducted. It is useful when the information needed must be elaborate, or clarification on various issues is required. The interview also provides an opportunity for the software engineer to win the confidence and trust of clients. It should therefore not be squandered.

Steps in Planning the Interview

In panning to conduct an interview, please observe the following steps:

1. Read background information.
2. Establish objectives.
3. Decide whom to interview.
4. Prepare the interviewee(s).
5. Decide on structure and questions.

Basic Guidelines for Interviews

Figure A3-1 provides some guidelines for successfully planning and conducting an interview. These guidelines are listed in the form of a do-list, and a don't-list.

Do-List for Interviews:	Don't-List for Interviews:
1. Make an appointment.	1. Don't be late.
2. Plan. Consider topics to be covered.	2. " be too formal of too casual.
3. Make sure information requested is impersonal and objective.	3. " interrupt the speaker.
4. Prepare for the interview (theme & questions).	4. " use technical jargons.
5. Ask questions at the right level.	5. " jump to conclusions.
6. State the purpose clearly, up front.	6. " argue or criticize (constructive or destructive).
7. Communicate in the interviewee's language.	7. " make suggestions (not as yet; you will get your opportunity to do so later).
8. If compliments become necessary, be sincere.	
9. Be relaxed and help the respondent to be relaxed.	
10. Listen.	
11. Identify facts as opposed to opinions. Both are important.	
12. Accept ideas and hints.	
13. Check the facts.	
14. Collect source documents and forms.	
15. Make effective use of open-ended and closed questions.	
16. Part pleasantly.	

Figure A3-1. Basic Guidelines for Interview

A3.3 Questionnaires and Surveys

A questionnaire is applicable when any of the following situations hold:

- A small amount of information is required of a large population.

- The time frame is short but a vast area (and/or dispersed population) must be covered.

- Simple answers are required to a number of standard questions.

Guidelines for Questionnaires

Figure A3-2 provides a set of basic guidelines for preparing a questionnaire.

1. State purpose clearly }
2. Thank the participants } Usually in the form of a cover note or letter
3. Must have a topic or heading which reflects an apt summary of the information sought.
4. Should adhere to the principles of forms design.
5. Avoid ambiguity.
6. Decide when to use open-ended questions, closed questions or scalar questions.
7. Order questions appropriately.
8. State questions in a language the respondent will readily understand.
9. Be consistent in style.
10. Ask questions of importance to the respondents first.
11. Bring up less controversial questions first.
12. Cluster related questions.

Figure A3-2. *Guidelines for Questionnaires*

Using Scales in Questionnaires

Scales may be used to measure the attitudes and characteristics of respondents, or have respondents judge the subject matter in question. There are four forms of measurement as outlined below:

1. **Nominal Scale:** Used to classify things. A number represents a choice. One can obtain a total for each classification.

2. **Ordinal Scale:** Similar to nominal, but here the number implies ordering or ranking.

   Example 1:

1 = Extremely Rich 2 = Very Rich 3 = Rich 4 = Not Rich 5 = Pauper

3. **Interval Scale:** Ordinal with equal intervals.

   Example 2: Usage of a particular software product by number of modules used (10 means high):

1   2   3   10

4. **Ratio Scale:** Interval scale with absolute zero.

   Example 3: Distance traveled to obtain a system report:

0   1   2   3   . . . . 10 [Meters]

Example 4: Average response time of the system:

| 0   1   2   3   . . . . 10 [Minutes] |

Administering the Questionnaire

Options for administering the questionnaire include the following:

- Convening respondents together at one time.

- Personally handing out blank questionnaires and collecting completed ones.

- Allowing respondents to self-administer the questionnaire at work and leave it at a centrally located place.

- Mailing questionnaires with instructions, deadlines, and return postage.

- Using the facilities of the World Wide Web (WWW), for example e-mail, user forums and chat rooms.

A3.4 Sampling and Experimenting

Sampling is useful when the information required is of a quantitative nature or can be quantified, no precise detail is available, and it is not likely that such details will be obtained via other methods. Figure A3-3 provides an example of a situation in which sampling is relevant.

Shipping	Number of Orders	% of Total
As Promised	186	37.2
1 day late	71	14.2
2 days late	49	9.8
3 days late	35	7.0
4 days late	38	7.6
5 days late	28	5.6
6 days late	93	18.6
	500	**100.0**

Figure A3-3. *Examining the Delivery of Orders After Customer Complaints*

Sampling theory describes two broad categories of samples:

- *Probability sampling* involving random selection of elements.

- *Non-probability sampling* where judgment is applied in selection of elements.

A3.4.1 Probability Sampling Techniques

There are four types of probability sampling techniques:

- **Simple Random Sampling** uses a random method of selection of elements.

- **Systematic Random Sampling** involves selection of elements at constant intervals. Interval = N/n where N is the population size and n is the sample size.

- **Stratified Sampling** involves grouping of the data in strata. Random sampling is employed within each stratum.

- **Cluster Sampling:** The population is divided into (geographic) clusters. A random sample is taken from each cluster.

Note: Techniques (b), (c), (d) constitute *Quasi Random Sampling*. The reason for this is that they are not regarded as perfectly random sampling.

A3.4.2 Non-Probability sampling Techniques

There are four types of non-probability sampling techniques:

- **Convenience Sampling:** Items are selected in the most convenient manner available.

- **Judgment Sampling:** An experienced individual selects a sample (e.g. a market research).

- **Quota Sampling:** A subgroup is selected until a limit is reached (e.g. every other employee up to 500).

- **Snowball Sampling:** An initial set of respondents is selected. They in turn select other respondents; this continues until an acceptable sample size is reached.

A3.4.3 Sample Calculations

Figure A3-4 provides a summary of the formulas that are often used in performing calculations about samples:

Item	Clarification
Mean	$X' = \sum(X_i)/n$ OR $\sum(F_iX_i) / \sum(F_i)$ where n is the number of items (elements); F_i is the frequency of X_i; and X_i represents the data values.
Standard Deviation	$S = \sqrt{((\sum F_i (X_i - X')^2) / n)}$ where n is the sample size
Variance	Variance = S^2
Standard Unit	$Z = (X_i - X') / S$
Standard Error	$S_E = S / \sqrt{(n)}$
Unit Error	$r = ZS_E = ZS / \sqrt{(n)}$
Sample Size	From equation for unit error above, $n = (ZS / r)^2$

Figure A3-4. *Formulas for Sample Calculations*

These formulas are best explained by examining the normal distribution curve (Figure A3-5). From the curve, observe that:

- Prob ($-1 <= Z <= 1$) = 68.27%
- Prob ($-2 <= Z <= 2$) = 95.25%
- Prob ($-3 <= Z <= 3$) = 99.73%

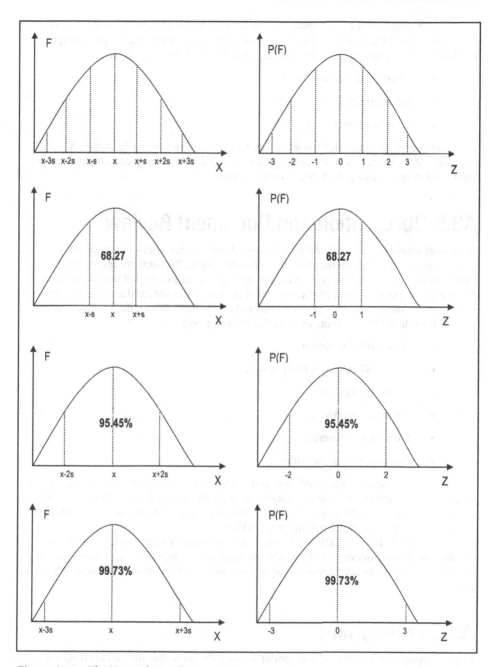

Figure A3-5. *The Normal Distribution Table*

The confidence limit of a population mean is normally given by $X' +/- ZS_E$ where Z is determined by the normal distribution of the curve, considering the percentage confidence limit required. The following Z values should be memorized:

- 68% confidence => Z = 1.64

- 95% confidence => Z = 1.96

- 99% confidence => Z = 2.58

The confidence limit defines where an occurrence X may lie in the range $(X' - ZS_E)$ < X < $(X' + ZS_E)$, given a certain confidence. As you practice solving sampling problems, your confidence in using the formulas will improve.

A3.5 Observation and Document Review

Review of source documents will provide useful information about the input, data storage, and output requirements of the software system. This activity could also provide useful information on the processing requirements of the software system. To illustrate, get a hold of an application form at your organization, and attempt to identify information entities (object types) represented on the form. With a little thought, you should be able to identify some or all of the following entities:

- Personal Information

- Family/Kin Contact Information

- Education History

- Employment History

- Professional References

- Extra Curricular Activities

Internal documents include forms, reports and other internal publications; external documents are mainly in the form of journals and other professional publications. These source documents are the raw materials for gaining insights into the requirements of the system, so you want to pay keen attention to them.

With respect to observation, it is always useful to check what you have been told against what you observe and obtain clarification where deviations exist. Through keen observation, the software engineer could gather useful information not obtained by other means.

A3.6 Prototyping

In prototyping, the user gets a "trial model" of the software and is allowed to critique it. User responses are used as feedback information to revise the system. This process continues until a software system meeting user satisfaction is obtained.

The following are some basic guidelines for developing a prototype:

- Work in manageable modules.

- Build prototype rapidly.

- Modify prototype in successive iterations.

- Emphasize the user interface—it should be friendly and meeting user requirements.

Kinds of Prototypes

There are various types of prototypes that you will find in software engineering. Among the various categories are the following:

Patched-up Prototype or Production Model: This prototype is functional the first time, albeit inefficiently constructed. Further enhancements can be made with time.

Non-operational or Interactive Prototype: This is a prototype that is intended to be tested, in order to obtain user feedback about the requirements of the system represented. A good example is where screens of the proposed system are designed; the user is allowed to pass through these screens, but no actual processing is done. This approach is particularly useful in user interface design (see Chapter 6).

First of Series Prototype: This is an operational prototype. Subsequent releases are intended to have identical features, but without glitches that the users may identify. This prototype is typically used as a marketing experiment: it is distributed free of charge, or for a nominal fee; users are encouraged to use it and submit their comments about the product. These comments are then used to refine the product before subsequent release.

Selected Features Prototype or Working Model: In this prototype, not all intended features of the (represented) software are included. Subsequent releases are intended to be enhancements with additional features. For this reason, it is sometimes referred to as *evolutionary prototype*. The initial prototype is progressively refined until an acceptable system is obtained.

Throw-away Prototype: An initial model is proposed for the sole purpose of eliciting criticism. The criticisms are then used to develop a more acceptable model, and the initial prototype is abandoned.

A3.7 Brainstorming and Mathematical Proof

The methodologies discussed so far all assume that there is readily available information which when analyzed, will lead to accurate capture of the requirements of the desired software. However, this is not always the case. There are many situations in which software systems are required, but there is no readily available information that would lead to the specification of the requirements of such systems. Examples include (but are not confined to) the following:

- Writing a new compiler

- Writing a new operating system

- Writing a new CASE tool, RAD tool, or DBMS

- Developing certain expert systems

- Developing a business in a problem domain for which there is no perfect frame of reference

For these kinds of scenarios, a non-standard approach to information gathering is required. Brainstorming is particularly useful here. A close to accurate coverage of the requirements of an original software product may be obtained through brainstorming: a group of software engineering experts and prospective users come together, and through several stages of discussion, hammer out the essential requirements of the proposed software. The requirements are then documented, and through various review processes, are further refined. A prototype of the system can then be developed and subjected to further scrutiny.

Even where more conventional approaches have been employed, brainstorming is still relevant, as it forces the software engineering team to really think about the requirements identified so far, and ask tough questions to ascertain whether the requirements have been comprehensively and accurately defined.

Mathematical proofs can also be used to provide useful revelations about the required computer software. This method is particularly useful in an environment where formal methods are used for software requirements specification. This approach is often used in the synthesis of integrated circuits and chips, where there is a high demand for precision and negligible room for error.

A3.8 Object Identification

We have discussed six different information-gathering strategies. As mentioned in section A3.1, these strategies are to be used to identify the core requirements of the software system. As mentioned then, one aspect that we are seeking to define is the set of information entities (object types). Notice that the term information entity is used as an alternative to object type. The two terms are not identical, but for most practical purposes, they are similar. An information entity is a concept, object or thing about which data is to be stored. An object type is a concept, object or thing about which data is to be stored, and upon which a set of operations is to be defined.

In object-oriented environments, the term object type is preferred to information entity. However, as you have seen, in most situations, the software system is likely to be implemented in a hybrid environment as an object-oriented (OO) user interface superimposed on a relational database.

Early identification of information entities is critical to successful software engineering in the OO paradigm. This is so because your software will be defined in terms of objects and their interactions. For each object type, you want to be able to describe the data that it will host, and related operations that will act on that data. Approaching the software planning in this way yields a number of significant advantages; moreover, even if it turns out that the software development environment is not object-oriented, the effort is not lost (in light of the previous paragraph).

Several object identification techniques have been proposed by the software engineering industry. Among the approaches that have been proposed are the following:

- Using Things to be Modeled

- Using Definitions of Objects, Categories and Types

- Using Decomposition

- Using Generalizations and Subclasses

- Using OO Domain Analysis or Application Framework

- Reusing Individual Hierarchies, Objects and Classes

- Using Personal Experience

- Using the Descriptive Narrative Approach

- Using Class-Responsibility-Collaboration Card

- Using the Rule-of-Thumb Method

These methodologies are discussed in the companion text on software engineering (see [Foster, 2010]). To get you adjusted to the idea of object identification, two of the approaches are summarized here.

A3.8.1 The Descriptive Narrative Approach

To use the *descriptive narrative approach*, start with a descriptive overview of the system (if it is small), or each component subsystem (in the case of a large or complex system). From each descriptive overview, identify nouns (objects) and verbs (operations). Repeatedly refine the process until all nouns and verbs are identified. Represent nouns as object types and verbs as operations, avoiding duplication of effort.

To illustrate, the Purchase Order and Receipt Subsystem of an Inventory Management System might have the following overview (Figure A3-6):

Purchase orders (PO) are sent to suppliers, requesting inventory items in specific quantities. If a PO is incorrectly generated, it is immediately removed and a new PO generated. The purchase invoice is the official document used to recognize receipt of goods from suppliers. All goods received are accompanied by invoices. Once received, the invoice is recorded. Items received are also recorded and appropriate inventory adjustments made to the inventory item master file. Receipt quantities can be adjusted, but if wrong items are recorded on receipt, or omissions are made, the whole invoice must be removed and re-recorded. When a receipt is correctly recorded, the associated PO status is adjusted.

Figure A3-6. *Descriptive Narrative of Purchase Order and Invoice Receipt Subsystem*

From this narrative, an initial list of object types and associated operations can be constructed, as shown below (Figure A3-7). Further refinement would be required; for instance, additional operations may be defined for each object type (left as an exercise); also, the data description can be further refined.

Object Type	Data Description	Operations
Purchase Order	Stores Order Number, Order Date, Supplier, Items Ordered and related Quantity Ordered, etc.	Generate, Remove, Adjust-Status
Supplier	Stores Supplier Code, Supplier Name, Supplier Address, Contact Person, Telephone, E-mail, etc.	Sent-Invoice
Purchase Invoice	Stores Invoice Number, Invoice Date, Related Supplier, Items Shipped and related Quantity Shipped, Invoice Amount, Discount, Tax, etc.	Record, Remove, Adjust-Quantity
Inventory Item	Stores Item Code, Item Name, Item Category, Quantity on Hand, Last Purchase Price, etc.	Adjust-Inventory

Figure A3-7. *Object Types and Operations for Purchase Order and Invoice Receipt Subsystem*

A3.8.2 The Rule-of-Thumb Approach

As an alternative to the descriptive narrative strategy, you may adopt an intuitive approach as follows: Using principles discussed earlier, identify the main information entities (object types) that will make up the system. Most information entities that make up a system will be subject to some combination of the following basic operations:

- **ADD:** Addition of data items

- **MODIFY:** Update of existing data items

- **DELETE:** Deletion of existing data items

- **INQUIRE/ANALYZE:** Inquiry and/or analysis on existing information

- **REPORT/ANALYZE:** Reporting and/or analysis of existing information

- **RETRIEVE:** Retrieval of existing data

- **FORECAST:** Predict future data based on analysis of existing data

Obviously, not all operations will apply for all object types (data entities); also, some object types (entities) may require additional operations. The software engineer makes intelligent decisions about these exceptions, depending on the situation. Additionally, the level of complexity of each operation will depend on the object type (data entity).

In a truly OO environment, the operations may be included as part of the object's services. In a hybrid environment, the information entities may be implemented as part of a relational database. The operations would be implemented as user interface objects (windows, forms, etc.).

A3.9 Summary and Concluding Remarks

Here is a summary of what we have covered in this Chapter:

- It is important to conduct a research on the requirements of a software system to be developed. By so doing, we determine the synergistic interrelationships, information entities, operations, business rules, and security mechanisms.

- In conducting the software requirements research, obtaining answers to questions commencing with the words WHAT, WHERE, HOW, WHEN and WHY is very important.

- Information gathering strategies include interviews, questionnaires and surveys, sampling and experimenting, observation and document review, prototyping, brainstorming and mathematical proofs.

- The interview is useful when the information needed must be elaborate, or clarification on various issues is required. The interview also provides an opportunity for the software engineer to win the confidence and trust of clients. In preparing to conduct an interview, the software engineer must be thoroughly prepared, and must follow well-known interviewing norms.

- A questionnaire is viable when any of the following situations hold: A small amount of information is required of a large population; the time frame is short but a vast area (and/or dispersed population) must be covered; simple answers are required to a number of standard questions. The software engineer must follow established norms in preparing and administering a questionnaire.

- Sampling is useful when the information required is of a quantitative nature or can be quantified, no precise detail is available, and it is not likely that such details will be obtained via other methods. The software engineer must be familiar with various sampling techniques, and know when to use a particular technique.

- Review of source documents will provide useful information about the input, data storage, and output requirements of the software system. This activity could also provide useful information on the processing requirements of the software system.

- Prototyping involves providing a trial model of the software for user critique. User responses are used as feedback information to revise the system. This process continues until a software system meeting user satisfaction is obtained. The software engineer should be familiar with the different types of prototypes.

- Brainstorming is useful in situations in which software systems are required, but there is no readily available information that would lead to the specification of the requirements of such systems. Brainstorming involves a number of software engineers coming together to discuss and hammer out the requirements of a software system.

- Mathematical proof is particularly useful in an environment where formal methods are used for software requirements specification.

- One primary objective of these techniques is the identification and accurate specification of the information entities (or object types) comprising the software system.

Accurate and comprehensive information gathering is critical to the success of a software engineering venture. In fact, the success of the venture depends to a large extent on this. Your information fathering skills will improve with practice and experience.

A3.10 References and/or Recommended Readings

[Daniel, 1989] Daniel, Wayne, and Terrel, James. *Business Statistics for Management and Economics* 5th ed. Boston, MA: Houghton Mifflin Co., 1989.

[DeGroot, 1986] DeGroot, Morris H. *Probability and Statistics* 2nd ed. Reading, MA: Addison-Wesley, 1986.

[Foster, 2010] Foster, Elvis. *Software Engineering — A Methodical Approach*. Bloomington, IN: Xlibris Publishing, 2010. See Chapter 5 and Appendix 4.

[Harris, 1995] Harris, David. *Systems Analysis and Design: A Project Approach*. Fort Worth, TX: Dryden Press, 1995. See Chapters 3, 4.

[Kendall, 1999] Kendall, Kenneth E. and Julia E. Kendall. *Systems Analysis and Design* 4th ed. Upper Saddle River, NJ: Prentice Hall, 1999. See Chapters 4 – 8.

[Long, 1989] Long, Larry. *Management Information Systems*. Eaglewood Cliffs, NJ: Prentice Hall, 1989. See Chapter 13.

[Pfleeger, 2006] Pfleeger, Shari Lawrence. *Software Engineering Theory and Practice* 3rd ed. Upper Saddle River, NJ: Prentice Hall, 2006. See Chapter 4.

[Sommerville, 2001] Sommerville, Ian. *Software Engineering* 6th ed. Reading, MA: Addison-Wesley, 2001. See Chapter 8.

[Sommerville, 2006] Sommerville, Ian. *Software Engineering* 8th ed. Reading, MA: Addison-Wesley, 2006. See Chapter 7.

[Van Vliet, 2000] Van Vliet, Hans. *Software Engineering* 2nd ed. New York, NY: John Wiley & Sons, 2000. See Chapter 9.

Index

■ N

■ O, P

Get the eBook for only $10!

> Now you can take the weightless companion with you anywhere, anytime. Your purchase of this book entitles you to 3 electronic versions for only $10.

This Apress title will prove so indispensible that you'll want to carry it with you everywhere, which is why we are offering the eBook in 3 formats for only $10 if you have already purchased the print book.

Convenient and fully searchable, the PDF version enables you to easily find and copy code—or perform examples by quickly toggling between instructions and   applications. The MOBI format is ideal for your Kindle, while the ePUB can be utilized on a variety of mobile devices.

Go to www.apress.com/promo/tendollars to purchase your companion eBook.